MANUFACTURING
INDEPENDENCE

MANUFACTURING INDEPENDENCE

INDUSTRIAL INNOVATION
IN THE
AMERICAN REVOLUTION

ROBERT F. SMITH

WESTHOLME
Yardley

Facing title page: the frontispiece for John Muller, *A Treatise of Artillery*, 1768.

Westholme Publishing, LLC
904 Edgewood Road
Yardley, Pennsylvania 19067
Visit our Web site at www.westholmepublishing.com

ISBN: 978-1-59416-373-9

Also available as an eBook.

Printed in the United States of America

CONTENTS

List of Illustrations   vii

Introduction   ix

1. "The people . . . cannot help themselves"   1
   THE FAILURE OF WAR MOBILIZATION AND
   THE CALL FOR A NATIONAL WEAPONS PROGRAM

2. "Laboratories . . . ordnance . . . artificers
   [and] Ammunition"   21
   THE DEPARTMENT OF THE COMMISSARY
   GENERAL OF MILITARY STORES

3. "On the same plan as . . . Woolwich"   51
   ADOPTING THE INDUSTRIAL REVOLUTION IN AMERICA

4. "Regiment of Artillery Artificers"
   and "hired men"   79
   PROMOTING A MANUFACTURING REVOLUTION IN PHILADELPHIA

5. "ARTIFICERS, WHO prefer LIBERTY to SLAVERY"   98
   MANUFACTURING INNOVATION AT CARLISLE AND SPRINGFIELD

6. "Devise ways and means for procuring [cannon]"   117
   DIRECTING PRIVATE MANUFACTURERS:
   INSPECTION AND INSTRUCTION

7. "We manufactured all the articles necessary
   for our defence"   142
   DIRECTING PRIVATE MANUFACTURERS:
   PROVIDING RESOURCES

8. "The American Foundery" 173
MILITARY STORES ACTIVITIES AFTER THE REVOLUTION

Conclusion 207

Notes 215

Bibliography 255

Acknowledgments 263

Index 265

List of Illustrations

1. Managed production system created by Congress.   *x*

2. Pennsylvania Committee of Safety musket.   *xix*

3. Field piece.   *xxi*

4. Types of artillery ammunition.   *xxii*

5. Gun carriages.   *xxiii*

6. The British North American colonies during the American Revolution.   *xxvi*

7. "Method of Refining Salt-Petre."   9

8. Samuel Hodgdon.   23

9. Benjamin Flower.   29

10. Structure of the Military Stores Management System, 1776.   34

11. Structure of the Military Stores Management System, 1779.   40

12. Structure of the Military Stores Management System, 1782.   47

13. Structure of the Military Stores Management System, 1784–1794.   48

14. The Royal Laboratory at Woolwich, c. 1777.   57

15. A colonial American blacksmith shop.   63

16. Carpenter's Hall, Philadelphia.   78

17. "Girls making cartridges, 1862."   83

18. Monthly output of cartridges from the Fifth Street Laboratory from August 1778 to March 1783.   85

19. Artillery accouterments.   92

20. "Carlisle Barracks, 1828."   IOI

21. Ammunition wagon. 103

22. Hopewell iron furnace. 120

23. Casting brass cannon at Woolwich. 123

24. "Profile of howitzer, 1781." 125

25. Cornwall iron furnace cannon. 127

26. Continental Army covered wagon and team. 167

27. Benjamin Lincoln. 177

28. "Continental Magazine at Springfield." 180

29. "Armory Hill About 1810." 203

30. Hessian magazine. 208

Introduction

*A*MPHITRITE WAS SURELY A SIGHT TO BEHOLD WHEN IT ARRIVED OFF Fort Point, New Hampshire, in March 1777. The vessel's low, sleek frame carried two large main sailing sheets, and it flew the bright white flag of the French monarchy. Displacing under five hundred tons and carrying few cannons, *Amphitrite* was a small ship built for the speed that had brought it successfully through the British blockade of North America. Rumors had circulated for months that France would send weapons to support the American Revolution, and *Amphitrite*'s arrival in New England had been eagerly anticipated. A sense of relief and excitement gripped the region when the ship finally appeared. Citizens of nearby Portsmouth were not disappointed when *Amphitrite* tied up at dock and discharged its cargo. The vessel delivered a prodigious bounty: twelve thousand muskets, accouterments for servicing the guns, kegs of gunpowder, and other items like clothing, fabric, and trade goods. The ship had been filled to the gunwales by secret agents of the French government to overcome America's "abysmal lack of guns, cartridge boxes, and every other accouterment of war."[1] And yet *Amphitrite*'s precious cargo was neither the windfall that Americans initially believed it to be nor the military deliverance that historians have recorded.

A congressional agent left Boston immediately for Portsmouth on hearing of the ship's arrival. He was charged with taking possession of the guns, testing them, and sending them to the army for use. After inspecting the French muskets, the agent found, to his chagrin, that the vast

Continental Congress

↓

Board of War

↓

Commissary General of Military Stores

↙   ↓   ↘

PUBLIC ARSENALS	PRIVATE OVERSIGHT	MATERIAL SUPPORT
at Philadelphia, Carlisle, and Springfield, contain management and facilities that coordinate the production of skilled craftsmen and unskilled workers hired by the DCGMS.	conducted by commissaries working for the Commissary General in Philadelphia, Carlisle, Springfield, and Boston, as well as a superintendent of arms and a superintendent of ordnance. Oversight included training, review of operations, and the testing of products for quality control.	given to private producers by commissaries working for the Commissary General as well as by the Commissary General himself. Support included cash, production resources, and transportation.

Managed production system created by Congress.

majority of the weapons were unfit for service. Over 50 percent of the musket locks failed testing when their firing springs broke; a portion of the barrels even burst during proof tests. In fact, the weapons were largely trade guns, cheaply made muskets used as gifts for African and Native American tribal customers; they had never been intended for military use. Major General William Heath, regional commander of the Eastern Department, ordered the agent to send the arms to the Continental arsenal in Springfield, Massachusetts, where they could be repaired and made serviceable for the army. The government agent secured horse teams and wagons, loaded the muskets, and sent them off through the maze of small farms and villages that was eighteenth-century Massachusetts. Traveling over muddy roads, the weapons took roughly a week to arrive at Springfield. The arsenal, a "magazine for the storage of weapons for the Americans" appeared in the rural landscape to receive the damaged arms. The complex had a "small, but very well built armory [and] various parks of artillery, with their trains. The store or magazine houses were filled from top to bottom; and workmen of all trades were seen in the houses engaged in the manufacture of ammunition, wagons, guns &c."[2] The guns shipped from *Amphitrite* were immediately distributed to armorers for repair. Other craftsmen in the government's employ made cartridge boxes, ammunition, and bayonets, all of which were necessary for a musket to be useful on the battlefield.

Within months, the Springfield Arsenal had produced and repaired enough military stores to supply four armies. American-repaired French guns and American-made accouterments were prepared in time for the battles at Saratoga, which forced the surrender of British general John Burgoyne's army. Additionally, three thousand arms were repaired and sent to Connecticut to arm the state's militia against invasion. Repaired arms were also sent to Maryland to reimburse the state for the loan of guns to the Continental Army. And newly manufactured wagons, cannons, and cartridge boxes were dispatched from Springfield to Valley Forge, Pennsylvania, to reequip George Washington's army, which had been badly beaten by the British in the battles for Philadelphia.[3]

When the American Revolution began, the British colonies in rebellion were not prepared for war and were slow to understand how to support themselves productively. As *Amphitrite*'s tale displays, it was also unlikely that Americans could rely on foreign supplies. So the US government embarked on a program to harness the resources of the nation's manufacturing sector and direct the production of equipment for the Continental Army. The pages that follow tell the story of how this was accomplished and the impact the program had on the war effort. The journey of *Amphitrite*'s cargo offers a glimpse of this narrative. Craftsmen and unskilled laborers were gathered together and coordinated at the Springfield Arsenal. There raw materials and broken items were manufactured into useable weapons, ammunition, and accouterments.

Using arsenals, government agents, and military discipline, the Continental Congress overcame the manufacturing limitations of the nation's wartime, craft-based economy to mobilize and manage the domestic production of military stores. The results were the successful equipping of the Continental Army and the demonstration of new forms of production to America's manufacturing community. The government initiated its program of domestic manufacturing in winter 1776–77 under a commissary general of military stores, whose department managed the program until 1794. The department comprised three divisions of oversight, the first of which gathered private craftsmen and hired workers into three national arsenals for the large-scale production of weapons, accouterments, ordnance, and other stores. The second oversight component, made up of government inspectors, directed private manufacturers in the production of military stores by instructing producers on their work and inspecting their finished products. Finally, the government provided private manufacturers with cash, raw materials, and transportation resources. Together, these three elements constituted a system not only to provide the army with military stores but also to maintain those stores once in use (see diagram on page x). While the system itself was important for the army's survival, the system also served to introduce new forms of production to the United States and demonstrate new technologies. The government then became a promoter of domestic manufacturing in the postwar period. Proponents of manufacturing used the Department of the Commissary General of Military Stores (DCGMS) as a model for how the nation could be secured against its enemies by producing its own goods. This was fitting, since the central government's oversight of manufacturing began as a result of the fact that the United States was unprepared for war and because the war had a destructive effect on the nation's infrastructure.

Military stores procurement efforts in the year after the Battle of Bunker Hill in 1775 demonstrated loudly that America was ill equipped for war. Congress and the colonies acquired weapons by confiscating those belonging to the British government and Loyalists, purchasing them on the open market, and contracting independent craftsmen to manufacture them. But weapons were slow to materialize. The colonies had never needed large supplies of military stores; they received most of what they needed for defense from Britain. After the French and Indian War, demobilized British troops took their stores home with them. Therefore, there were few significant stockpiles of weapons in the colonies with which to equip a large standing army.[4] The colonies' reliance on Britain for defense also meant that few domestic craftsmen were skilled in the production of military stores. Craftsmen did learn the skills of military store production, but that took time. A more pressing problem was that no matter how many military store craftsmen were trained, the nature of craftwork inhibited the large-scale production of such stores. American craftsmen were independent producers who made small batches of finished products. Colonial society had little experience with centralized coordination of labor or production. Without central-ized management, which the colonies failed to implement, craftsmen pro-duced as they always had, a few custom-made pieces at a time. Domestic manufacture in the early years of the war was a slow and precarious source of weapons for the American war effort. Therefore, in late 1775, Congress and all thirteen colonial governments turned to Europe to meet their needs for weapons. They began purchasing arms from the Netherlands via the West Indies while seeking aid from the French gov-ernment. As with the *Amphitrite* shipment, however, most European guns that arrived in America prior to 1781 were low quality items, orig-inally intended for sale in Africa and the West Indies.[5] By late 1776, America faced "an abysmal lack" of weapons and accouterments for the Continental Army.[6] The nation had embarked on a war for independence without the domestic availability of weapons, the productive design to make weapons, or the trade connections to import well-made weapons. These factors were exacerbated by the war itself.

The nature of craft production in America made military stores procurement difficult enough, but the war undermined the foundations of the craft sector of the nation's economy. To build a successful production operation, master craftsmen required investment capital, credit, raw materials, and transportation. Merchants, fellow craftsmen, and investors typically extended capital and credit to an entrepreneur. The war brought both dislocation and inflation. Merchants and craftsmen were put out of business by the destruction of their shops and markets. Investors put their money into privateers and blockade running rather than domestic producers. The collapse of congressional and state currencies undermined the value of personal savings and the basis of monetary exchange. These same circumstances made raw materials difficult to procure, as they became overly expensive or scarce. Troop movements and military occupation destroyed traditional economic networks. British control of waterways inhibited craftsmen who relied on waterborne trade.[7] It grew increasingly clear to Congress in the war's first two years that central coordination of, and participation in, military stores production was necessary. The battles of New York City, in which the majority of the Continental Army's military stores were captured, provided the final call to action.

Congress created a management hierarchy to oversee the private and the public production of military stores. The chief agent of Congress's oversight of domestic manufacturing was the commissary general of military stores. He was charged with coordinating all military stores production and procurement. One set of administrators reporting to the commissary general was charged with managing three public arsenals built at Springfield; Carlisle, Pennsylvania; and Philadelphia. Managers and overseers in the employ of the commissary general coordinated various types of craftsmen. Some craftsmen were enlisted as military personnel while others were hired contractors. In both circumstances, their productivity was managed and coordinated. Craftsmen producing for the government were no longer left in isolated operations. By mid-1777, damaged and poor quality foreign muskets could be sent to any of these posts for repair. When not repairing items, the craftsmen made a variety of new items such as muskets, cartridge boxes, and cannon carriages. A second set of government officers acted as inspectors and procurers of privately made items. Inspectors were commissioned to ensure that stores received by the government met patterns and specifications they had issued. What was unique about the government's inspectors, however, was that they also acted as manufacturing consultants for domestic producers. Private American manufacturers had little if any experience making the supplies needed by the Continental Army. Therefore, when a contract was signed, inspectors were dispatched to assist in the production of arms, ordnance, and ammunition.

Even as military stores administrators coordinated private and public production, they also worked to facilitate private production by providing the resources necessary for craftsmen to engage in their work. The DCGMS granted cash advances to manufacturers to cover some of the initial costs of converting their operations from consumer to military production. Such a shift often entailed hiring new employees or purchasing new tools. The department's arsenals also made available other assistance, including raw materials, fuels, and transportation. The department provided these resources at cost to contracted manufacturers to ensure the continued production of the stores needed for the Continental Army.

The range of fighting equipment the army needed was vast, a fact belied by use of the term *military* stores. A report compiled by the DCGMS in 1784 listed 838 distinct items of hardware being held in storage by the department. The inventory detailed various types of recognizable military items like cannons and cannonballs, muskets and ammunition, but it also listed items like forges, files, ladles, dowels, sheet metal, and carriages.[8] The report makes clear that American artificers produced not only weapons but the equipment that supported those weapons and the mechanisms and tools needed to manufacture the weapons as well. Files and drills were cast because they were needed to refine and complete the construction of weapons. Padlocks and buildings were constructed because weapons needed to be stored securely. Wagons, crates, and barrels were made because they were necessary to ship weapons. And then the weapons themselves needed various accouterments and ammunition to be useful on the battlefield.

The breadth of American military items produced and procured by the DCGMS serves to illuminate the innovations initiated in manufacturing by the department to support the war effort. It did not simply direct the production of military stores; the stores themselves were too complex for that alone to be useful. To produce and/or repair the 838 items that ended up in government warehouses, the department had to transform the production potential of the nation. It did this by turning craft operations into managed production sites, building factories to coordinate unskilled labor, and introducing domestic manufacturers to new technologies. Craftsmen at government arsenals were managed by officers and master craftsmen alike, not only within their crafts, but also across craft disciplines. Gunsmiths, for instance, were supported by blacksmiths and carpenters to make all the items necessary for a musket. Workspaces were made for laborers to assemble both musket and artillery ammunition. And the DCGMS introduced domestic metalworkers to the widespread use of anthracite coal in their operations. The department adopted these changes from the ideas of the Industrial Revolution in Europe. The American Revolution created the same opportunities for manufacturing development in the United States that had allowed industry to flourish in Europe. And so, Americans imported the Industrial Revolution to mobilize the resources they had available. The short-term result was the effective arming of the nation, but the long-term implications involved placing the government at the forefront of industrialization in the United States.

This book relies heavily on the papers of the DCGMS, a resource not extensively used by previous historians on the topic of manufacturing. The records of the department fall into two categories, those kept by Benjamin Flower, the first commissary general, and those kept by his successor, Samuel Hodgdon.[9] Flower's papers include inventories submitted to him by his subordinates and written reports of activities in the department. These records provide quantitative production data for government-supervised manufacturing from 1777 through 1780. They reveal the intricacies of management procedures and explain how the command hierarchies within the DCGMS operated. Flower's papers also illustrate how the department interacted with private contractors. Hodgdon's records include detailed production returns, inventory account books, contractor account journals, and correspondence from 1779 until 1794. Quantitative data Hodgdon recorded reveals the workings of the department's production operations, the interaction of private and public manufacturers, and departmental management procedures used later in the war. Hodgdon kept a thorough accounting of the department's budget, including how much was spent to support private manufacturing. Altogether, the papers of Flower and Hodgdon tell a story of proactive and productive operations during the revolution. Yet, despite the value of the records of the DCGMS, they also project a bias for which an accounting must be made.

Flower, Hodgdon, Congress, and military commanders all had different perspectives on what constituted a necessary level of supply for the Continental Army. Congress saw conserving money, rather than fully arming its troops, as its primary mission. It tended to order as few weapons as possible to meet the army's immediate needs and forced the DCGMS to pay less than the market price for each weapon. Congress never viewed market forces as a fair system in which to buy items for the war effort, but rather than understand and deal with it, Congress constantly tried to overrule the system, to its own, and the army's, detriment. The army, meanwhile, wanted the DCGMS to provide enough weapons for an army of thirty thousand to forty thousand men, which General George Washington hoped at some point to put in the field. The generals were continually incensed that Congress would not pay for more supplies and the DCGMS would not produce more than was needed for the troops enlisted at any one time. The department operated under the idea that it should procure as much as ordered by Congress and as much as was needed by the army in existence. It made no sense to Flower or Hodgdon to produce forty thousand muskets when there were only twenty thousand men in the field. Neither congressional nor army sources ever reveal a high opinion of the DCGMS, but departmental papers define the production that was achieved as a success because it met the needs of the army when the army needed those supplies. The story told here, then, is colored by the commissary general's rosy view of domestic manufacturing. While this may not be the whole story, it is a necessary perspective for the historical record. Returning to the *Amphitrite* will explain why.

Despite all the manufacturing activity that accompanied the dissemination of *Amphitrite*'s guns to America's armed forces, historians have generally ended the story on the Portsmouth docks and picked it up again at the army.[10] According to one author, "*Amphitrite* arrived in Portsmouth, New Hampshire, in time to provide supplies for the 1777 campaign, which for the Northern Army culminated in the victory at Saratoga."[11] Another reference was equally succinct. *Amphitrite* and another French ship "delivered 21,000 muskets, over 100,000 pounds of powder, and other incidentals [and] these supplies were quickly distributed among American regiments."[12] According to those stories, American craftsmen had no role in supplying the military at all, an omission that overlooks significant contributions of labor and materiel they made to their own victory. These historical examinations of *Amphitrite* are indicative of the larger historical coverage of American manufacturing during the revolution and the role of the Continental government in the mobilization of those productive efforts.

Using stories like those of *Amphitrite*, historians have claimed more broadly that the Continental Army was equipped primarily with foreign military stores and that Americans and their Continental government did very little to manufacture stores for their own army. In *Mechanical Metamorphosis*, Neil York held that Americans could do no more than limp through the war on the crutch of foreign military aid.[13] He argued that American society, and by extension its Continental Congress, was unable to comprehend the value of ideas and technologies developed by wartime innovators. York wrote that for Americans "[t]o experiment with new industrial processes, given their perilous situation, was almost unthinkable." And "even if patriot politicians had been inclined to promote [manufacturing], they lacked the resources to follow through" on those inclinations.[14] York's pattern of thought has come to dominate thinking among the handful of historians who have dealt with the subject. Besides York, historians Lucille Horgan and David Salay have examined revolutionary manufacturing. They paint a picture of American production that was inadequate at best and at worst descended into the hopelessly unorganized and useless. Horgan wrote that "policy makers

. . . were concerned with the management of R&D, and the fostering of necessary [military stores] expertise [among manufacturers]," but they were unable to effectively manage these efforts to a productive end.[15] Salay also gave some credit to government mobilization activities, noting that "the rapid development of wartime manufactures was due to government encouragement."[16] But this encouragement, according to Salay, was disorganized and ineffective on the national level. "After Congress assumed control of the war effort, it drew supplies from whatever source it could and the development of new industry was no longer a primary drive."[17] Such analyses have hidden the extent, complexity, and value of American wartime manufacturing, which was largely the result of the Continental government's mobilization of labor, money, and natural resources for the production of military stores. Available government and business records challenge the view prevalent among historians and reveal innovation and success in American manufacturing. This is not to say that American efforts were always sufficient for the nation's vast manufacturing needs during the revolution, but rather it is clear that the American government and American producers initiated a significant, innovative, and usually adequate program to provide for the army's materiel needs.

In 1776, the United States had the resources to manufacture a large portion of the weapons it needed to fight and win independence. Skilled craftsmen, natural resources, and innovative production ideas were available but needed to be mobilized. In the absence of other options, it was up to Congress and its agents to get America's productive forces moving. It would be no easy task, as many found out, and yet the very survival of the revolution depended on it. Benjamin Flower, the first commissary general of military stores, wrote in 1777 that "to Support . . . Our Independancy . . . nothing can tend to produce it more than our having all our wants Manufactured among ourselves, and those works to be Continental Property."[18] Flower expressed what the government he worked for had also come to believe: that to be free, the nation would have to manufacture its own independence.

MILITARY STORES AND EIGHTEENTH-CENTURY WARFARE

Armies in the eighteenth century attempted to achieve victory on the battlefield by massing enough firepower to overwhelm an adversary. Therefore, it took quite a number of military stores items to equip an army to fight. Those stores generally fell into four broad categories: muskets, accouterments, ammunition, and artillery. Each category had specific uses on the fields of war.

A *flintlock musket* (referred to as a firearm, a stand of arms, or a firelock) was composed primarily of three components: the iron barrel, the wooden stock on which the barrel was mounted, and the lock mechanism, which created a spark that lit gunpowder in the barrel that fired a bullet. Screws and brass straps, often referred to as furniture, held all these elements together. The lock mechanism comprised numerous intricate pieces, like the trigger and the main spring that reacted to the trigger to fire the hammer mechanism. A musket differed from a rifle in that a musket had a smooth bore inside the barrel and fired a larger bullet. A rifle had grooves inside the bore that imparted a spin to a smaller bullet, making a rifle more accurate than a musket. Muskets, however, were more widely used in battle because a rifle's grooved bore made it time consuming to load. The Continental Army used two basic types of muskets during the war: the .75-caliber British Long Land Pattern musket, known as the Brown Bess, and the .69-caliber French Charleville musket. Throughout the war, Americans also produced weapons of their own design, but even domestically produced muskets were modeled after the British and French examples. A musket was not, however, the only item a soldier carried with him on the battlefield.

A musket required a number of accouterments, including a ramrod, cartridge box, and bayonet. The ramrod was a thin steel rod used to push powder and ball all the way down the barrel. Cartridge boxes were made of a leather strap and a leather pouch that held a wooden block cut with tubes to hold musket cartridges. In the absence of leather, the Continentals often made tin boxes with leather straps to hold their ammunition. Boxes usually carried twenty-three cartridges, which an average soldier could fire in just over ten minutes. Therefore, troops were often supplied with extra ammunition before battle, and each battalion kept a reserve for quick distribution during battle. A bayonet was carried in a leather sheath, called a scabbard, that hung over the shoulder on a leather strap. When necessary, the bayonet was drawn and attached to the end of the musket. This only happened when soldiers were too close to fire their ammunition with effect. Then, with their bayonets, soldiers fought hand to hand.[19]

Professional armies at the end of the eighteenth century did not normally load loose ball and powder into their muskets for firing. Instead, soldiers used cartridges made of a paper or cloth tube filled with a musket ball and enough gunpowder for one shot. The whole was tied at both ends with string and inserted in a cartridge box for use in battle. A soldier used his teeth to rip open the cartridge, place a bit of powder in the lock mechanism, and dump the remaining powder and ball down the barrel. He then used the ramrod to ram the ball down the barrel. Muskets were not a precision weapon, so the size of ammunition varied. A larger ball that fit more snuggly in the barrel escaped with more force. Smaller bullets traveled more slowly, but more of them could be made per pound of lead. The smallest bullet that a standard musket could use

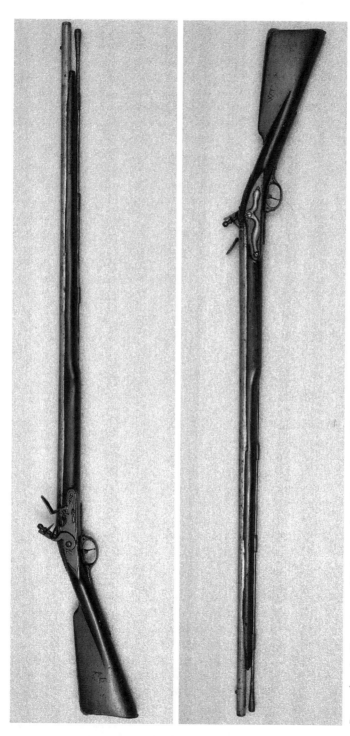

Pennsylvania Committee of Safety musket. Committee of Safety arms were usually copies of existing designs, such at the British "Brown Bess" musket. Weapons made during wartime rarely have a manufacture's mark since the production of these guns was an act of treason. (*The State Museum of Pennsylvania, Pennsylvania Historical and Museum Commission*)

was one-nineteenth of a pound, while the largest was one-thirteenth. Throughout the war, American commanders and producers of ammunition sought to split the difference between the sizes to produce significant firepower with an economy of lead.[20]

Artillery, also referred to as ordnance or cannons, supported soldiers armed with muskets on the battlefield and came in various types and sizes. The diameter of a cannon barrel depended on the size shot it was meant to fire, which ranged from a half-pound shot to a forty-two pound shot. Siege and fortification artillery fired twelve-, eighteen-, twenty-four-, thirty-two-, or forty-two-pound shot, though the Americans did not possess any of the largest size ordnance. Cannons throwing twelve-, nine-, six-, four-, or three-pound shot were used in the field against a mobile enemy. The length of a cannon dictated its range, so cannons that came in various diameters also came in various lengths. A longer cannon could receive more powder and send a shot farther with more accuracy than a shorter artillery piece. The metal used to cast cannons also varied in this period as generals and politicians debated the value of brass over iron artillery. Brass was more expensive than iron but weighed less and made cannons easier to move in the field. The varieties of cannon lengths and diameters made casting numerous types of them very expensive if done only in brass, therefore, the British decided to cast numerous sizes of brass and iron pieces so "the most particular artillery officer [could] choose just the right [one] for any given job."[21] This gave the British artillery service twenty-four sizes of iron artillery and fourteen types of brass artillery in 1764. The French had their own system, different from that of the British, which is important to note because Americans used whatever kind of cannon they could get during the war. When Americans seized artillery from British forts early in the war, they seized not only British weapons but also French ones the British had captured in the French and Indian War. Moreover, Americans imported French artillery during the war. While the French used the same diameter as the British, cannon lengths differed, which meant American artillerymen and artificers had to prepare ammunition for up to forty-three different types of artillery.[22] The casting of ordnance and ammunition was as much art as it was science and required both skill and judgment.

The American weapons situation was made more complex by the fact that artillery evolved in the decade prior to the American Revolution. New, shorter artillery, called howitzers, had been introduced that fired exploding shells rather than solid shot. Howitzers were joined by mortars, which were stubby, fat cannons that fired in a high arc up, over, and behind the enemy's front line. These two cannon types came in three sizes that fired five-and-a-half-inch, eight-inch, or ten-inch shells. The shells were filled with powder and were intended to explode over the enemy or

Model of a 3-pound brass cannon at Valley Forge National Historical Park. The DCGMS manufactured items like this for the Continental Army by coordinating the labor of multiple craftsmen including brassmongers, carpenters, and blacksmiths. (*Author*)

behind the enemy line among the soldiers. Making these shells involved not only casting them but also filling them with powder and preparing fuses that were inserted into the shells to make them explode when they reached the enemy. The process of manufacturing the artillery of the period required great skill as well as proper work organization.[23]

Besides solid shot and exploding shells, artillery used other types of projectiles. Patriots most often fired canister or grapeshot at the British. Canister was made up of small pellets in a tin case that disintegrated when fired, allowing the pellets to fan out across the field of battle. Grapeshot was essentially the same as canister except the pellets were larger and wrapped together by wire, making them look like a stem of grapes. Americans did produce fixed ammunition for their cannons, similar to musket cartridges, with a ball strapped to a bag of powder, but this approach did not dominate artillery loading. Because of the various sizes of artillery, it was easier for an artilleryman on the field to load a piece with powder and a loose ball than it was for an artificer at one of the arsenals to produce a cannon cartridge. Therefore, Americans fired fixed ammunition in close combat, while at longer ranges they used loose powder and ball in order to save their cartridges for emergencies.[24]

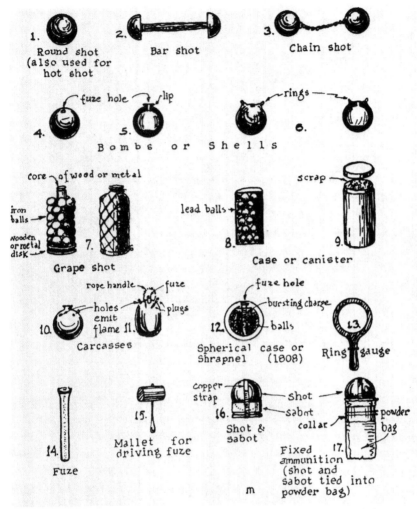

1. Round shot (also used for hot shot
2. Bar shot
3. Chain shot

4. 5. fuze hole — lip 6. rings

B o m b s   o r   S h e l l s

core of wood or metal
iron balls
wooden or metal disk
7. Grape shot
8. lead balls
9. scrap
Case or canister

rope handle — fuze
10. holes emit flame
11. plugs
Carcasses
12. fuze hole — bursting charge — balls
Spherical case or Shrapnel (1808)
13. Ring gauge

14. Fuze
15. Mallet for driving fuze
16. copper strap — Shot — sabot — collar
Shot & sabot
17. Shot — powder bag
Fixed ammunition (shot and sabot tied into powder bag)
m

Various types of artillery ammunition and projectiles. The DCGMS and its contractors produced the items shown here through the use of managed skilled and unskilled labor. Craftsmen produced shot and shells, which were filled and fixed into cartridges for use on the battlefield by proto-factory workers. (*Manucy, Artillery Through the Ages, 64*)

Artillery carriages, which held a cannon barrel for use, differed based on the potential use of the artillery piece they held and were made up of numerous components. Carriages used for siege guns were beds that planted the gun firmly in the ground and kept it from moving backward due to the force of firing the cannon. Fortification carriages were solid wooden cradles with four small wooden or iron wheels, similar to car-

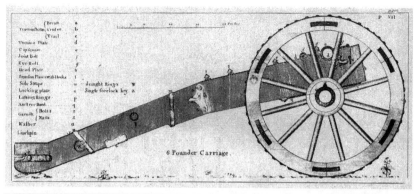

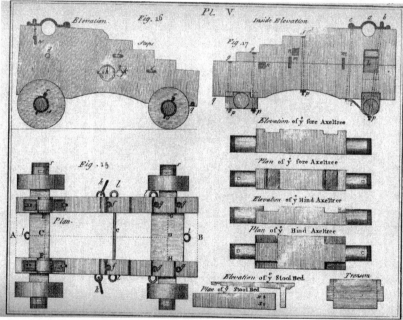

The top image is a diagram of a field carriage for a 6-pounder cannon, while the bottom image illustrates the pieces of a garrison carriage. These drawings from Muller's *Treatise of Artillery* accompanied dimensional charts and parts lists for accurately constructing various sizes of cannon carriages. Several of these charts were copied by Springfield Arsenal commander David Mason from Muller's book into his own daybook for use in guiding his craftsmen. Notice how the various perspectives presented could assist manufacturers in replicating these items. Comparing the images, one can also see how some stores like artillery could be made to operate in various military contexts by the proper application of other stores. The large wheels and high structure of the field carriage allowed cannons to be moved over rough terrain, while the small frame of the garrison carriage kept the weapon stable on ships and in fortifications, where movement was unnecessary. (*Muller,* Treatise of Artillery, *106, 95*)

riages used on ships. They did not have to be mobile, just capable of withstanding the cannon's recoil. The trajectory of a fortress cannon was expected to be flat, allowing the shot to fall on the enemy from a fortress wall high above. Field artillery carriages were much more complex, with two large wheels and a light frame suitable for mobility. The whole carriage was wooden but contained a great many iron fittings such as the iron tires bolted to the wheels, iron hubs holding the wheels in place, iron straps bracing the cannon to the frame, and an iron harness on the carriage leg for hitching it to a horse or wagon for moving.[25] With the many varieties of shot, shell, carriage, and bore surrounding the use of artillery, it was as complex a weapons system as a musket with its accouterments and ammunition.

Once an army was supplied with military stores, those stores were intended for specific uses on the battlefield. Battle in the eighteenth century was expected to play out like a very large game of chess in which the opposing sides moved to gain a better position on one another. Armies attempted to pursue one of two standard goals when they faced each other. Victory could be obtained by moving around the side, or flank, of an enemy, catching it off guard, and forcing it to retreat. The second option was to break the center of the enemy's line, also forcing the enemy to retreat. The reality of warfare was often far more complex than the theories applied to battlefield movement. Battles were often won or lost based on which side lost more troops in killed or wounded. Or the death toll caused by an opponent's artillery power could force an army into widespread panic and retreat. Nevertheless, commanders attempted to use the military stores in their possession to achieve goals they believed were predetermined by the effectiveness of the weapons being used.

Commanders initiated battlefield movements hoping to achieve the ideals of a turned flank or a broken enemy. As much as possible, commanders tried to keep their soldiers away from the enemy and allow firepower to do the fighting. At a distance of several hundred yards, opposing armies fired at each other using artillery with solid shot and while using their howitzers and mortars to fire exploding shells. Each army then moved closer to the other in a structured line of march. The soldiers were spread out across the battlefield in one, two, or three rows. When proper orders were given, the front row of men raised their muskets and fired. They were not instructed to aim. Muskets were inaccurate, and the belief was that thousands of soldiers firing at the same time would disable many of the opposing army's soldiers.[26] The volley of musket shot continued as the armies moved closer to one another. While the front line reloaded, the second and third lines of soldiers fired their weapons. Soldiers' fire was carefully managed to enhance the effect of collective shooting and conserve ammunition. If soldiers were allowed to shoot as they wished, some troops would run out of ammunition before others, limiting the effectiveness of the army as a whole.

As the armies converged, cannons, but not howitzers or mortars, were moved closer to the front loaded with grape or canister shot. This ammunition made the cannon into large shotguns. Up to this point, army commanders ordered the delivery of as much firepower as possible in order to force the enemy to break and run. Or if cannon and musket fire could turn a flank, troops could be sent into the rear of an enemy army and fire on it from two angles. As a last resort when faced with a stubborn enemy, a commander ordered hand-to-hand combat. Within about sixty yards of each other, the soldiers of each army were told to fix bayonets. They then charged at each other and fought face to face until one side gave way or an opponent got around a flank. Cavalry, when available, was used at the height of battle mainly for outflanking an enemy.[27]

Battles, however, rarely matched the idealized version for which commanders hoped. Fighting did not often occur on open fields. Units were separated by brush, forest, and artificial structures. Smoke from musket and artillery fire obscured movements and hid units from one another. Units drifted apart as the battle developed, order broke down, and commanders lost control of their forces. Artillery fire became disorganized and did not always switch to the most useful type of ammunition because artillerists could not see the battle or because orders did not reach them. Units did not fire their muskets in any organized way. And individual units, separated from the rest of an army, sometimes engaged the enemy before other units. Battlefield situations were much more complex than commanders wished them to be, but those commanders nevertheless used the military stores at their disposal to organize battles as best they could. Weapons and the items that made them useful on the battlefield were critical to getting the best of a foe on that battlefield.

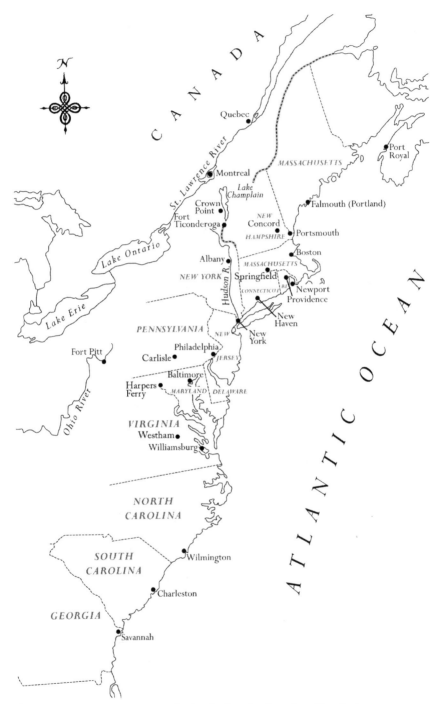

The British North American colonies during the American Revolution.

1

"The people . . .
cannot help themselves"

THE FAILURE OF WAR MOBILIZATION AND
THE CALL FOR A NATIONAL WEAPONS PROGRAM

I N MID-SEPTEMBER 1776, GEORGE WASHINGTON'S HEADQUARTERS SAT
on Harlem Heights, a ridge overlooking Manhattan that gave the
general a commanding view of the region. The landscape visible from
the heights, however, was a discouraging reminder of how far the British
had driven the Continental Army from New York City, Brooklyn, and
Staten Island. It was an opportune moment for a special Committee at
Camp to arrive from the Continental Congress and receive a report on
the conduct of the war. The general had been pleading with Congress for
months to create a military stores system to support the army. At Harlem
Heights, in the midst of defeat and retreat, Washington unloaded his
frustration and anger on the visiting congressmen. And he explained
what the army needed. The army could not engage the enemy effectively, he said, because it lacked a consistent source of accouterments and
stores for battle. The Battle of Long Island had been lost partly because
American troops had no bayonets with which to fend off a charge by the
British.[1]

The movement of the American army was limited by a lack of cartridge
boxes. Without this item, soldiers could carry no more than a pocketful
of ammunition. This limited number of cartridges was not enough to
fight a battle, and pockets could not protect the cartridges from dampness and damage. To fight a battle, the army would have to stay close to
supply depots and available supply wagons so suitable ammunition could

be distributed promptly. Washington was also worried because he did not possess enough field artillery with which to face the enemy's more numerous and well-supplied ordnance. The British, Washington feared, would simply blast his army apart when they next engaged in battle. But the general's deepest concern was for the muskets his troops carried, or refused to carry in some cases. During battle when muskets were damaged, men would simply throw them away because they did not know how to fix them and had nowhere to send them to be fixed. During retreats men often threw their weapons away because the weight slowed down their escape. Washington also found that troops took their muskets home with them when they deserted or were discharged from the army.

When he had finished explaining the situation, Washington offered a solution. The Continental government should create a central system to supply the army with the military stores it needed. The army needed public arsenals established at convenient locations with artificers employed to make and repair weapons and accouterments. Congress needed to employ ironmongers to cast and repair cannons. Washington concluded by offering a dire warning: without the proper support, his army would continue to be driven from the field of battle and the new nation's military situation would continue to deteriorate. The committee pondered Washington's words and issued a report to Congress on September 27 calling for the creation of a public military stores system. It offered specific details for how the system should be set up and the impact the system would have on the military's effectiveness. Congress tabled the matter.[2]

Washington's warnings regarding the military situation proved accurate, and the army's declining military fortunes mirrored the decline in the military stores situation. Following the congressional visit, Washington was forced to retreat north of the Harlem River to White Plains. At this strategic site, Washington hoped to stop the British advance, but his army was overpowered by British artillery and broken by a bayonet charge that it was ill equipped to receive. The general was forced to abandon the lower Hudson Valley to the enemy. The Americans continued to occupy Forts Washington and Lee on the Hudson River in the hopes that they could protect New Jersey from British invasion and keep a foothold in New York. But without freedom of movement, Washington could not adequately respond to British tactical movements. The result was the loss of both forts, including 146 cannons, 12,000 shot and shell, 2,800 muskets, and 400,000 musket cartridges.[3]

Washington again wrote to Congress pleading for action. The army fights "under infinite disadvantages, and without the smallest probability of success."[4] "Your exertions to secure the Arms[,] accouterments, ammunition &c., can't be too great. It must be done."[5] Congress called on the states to send Washington and his army whatever supplies they had available, and while adequate ammunition was procured, there were not enough cannons, accouterments, or muskets to recoup the materiel losses suffered by the army.[6] Washington was forced to abandon New Jersey. Even when Washington finally struck back at Trenton, he had only eighteen pieces of artillery left, and as much as a quarter of his army had to be left out of the assault for want of arms.[7] Reflecting on the impact of the campaign, a prominent Loyalist wrote that "one may venture to pronounce that it is wellnigh over with [the Americans]. All their cannon and mortars, and the greatest part of their stores, ammunition, etc. are gone. The people . . . cannot help themselves."[8]

From April 1775 to December 1776, Americans worked to mobilize their resources to support the Continental Army, but four months of brutal military campaigning had proven that work to be inadequate. Supplies could not be repaired, they could not be replaced, and they could not be provided in large enough numbers to deal with loss. Though Congress had not wanted to act on the Committee at Camp's recommendations regarding a public military stores system, it had hardly been inactive. Numerous attempts were made to meet the army's needs, but these had not been what Washington wanted. He wanted, and believed the army needed, exactly what he told the committee. Congress, however, did not believe the general and did not want the military to acquire too much independence from political oversight.[9] The committee had seen, and military failures had proven beyond a doubt, that the military stores system established to support the Continental Army had failed. Without dramatic action, Americans could, indeed, not help themselves.

Early weapons-procurement activities during the American Revolution fell into three broad categories: confiscation, foreign importation, and domestic purchase. Confiscation efforts before and after the Battle of Lexington in April 1775 revealed that Americans did not possess a domestic stock of military stores necessary to support a standing army. Congress and the colonial governments, therefore, attempted to purchase weapons overseas, but these efforts were stymied. Large supplies of stores were not readily available from foreign sources, and those that were imported were of poor quality. By the end of 1775, it was apparent to revolutionary leaders that they would have to rely a great deal on domestic production to support the army with military stores. However, American craft production methods were not up to the task of manufacturing large numbers of weapons. Congress relied on the state governments to promote and organize manufacturing, but the states could not mobilize craftsmen to meet the army's needs. While weapons procurement in 1775 and 1776 was a severe disappointment to Washington, Congress did not recognize how bad the situation was. The battles of New York City forced Congress to deal with the inadequacies of early procurement efforts and the limitations of the American economy. Painful experience taught Congress that without Continental oversight, the American economy would be unable to produce large quantities of military stores.

When the Continental Congress convened on May 10, 1775, the revolution was only three weeks old. A makeshift army of New Englanders surrounded Boston, confining British troops there. New England turned to Congress for leadership of the situation, and the legislators appointed Washington to create and command a Continental Army to fight the British. But even before creating a military structure, Congress began mobilizing military stores production and procurement. On May 27, two weeks before Washington's selection, Congress appointed a committee "to consider the ways and means to supply these colonies with . . . military stores."[10] The committee reported back that Congress should purchase weapons domestically and overseas. Congress, however, did not yet have the money available, or a consistent source of income necessary, to begin acquiring stores for the army. The colonies would not yet agree to give Congress taxing powers or the ability to borrow money. Eventually, Congress was given some funding options, but in the meantime, it was forced to ask the colonies to oversee army provisioning. Starting on June 10, Congress began requisitioning specific supplies from each colony. On July 16, when Congress asked the colonies to send troops to support Washington, it resolved that the colonies should arm those troops. Soldiers sent to Boston were to carry "a good musket, . . . with a bayonet, steel ramrod, worm, priming wire and brush fitted thereto, . . . a cartridge-box, . . . twelve flints and a knapsack."[11] To make this possible, Congress instructed the colonies to mobilize their gunsmiths and craftsmen to produce as many weapons as possible. The colonies were "to set and keep their gunsmiths at work, to manufacture good firelocks, with bayonets," and until such time as sufficient quantities could be made domestically, the colonies were to exert all effort to import them. For all supplies forwarded to the Continental Army, Congress promised to pay replacement costs for loss or damage.[12] Despite a committee recommendation that Congress direct the procurement of stores for the army, financial circumstances led it to rely on the colonies. This ensured that there would be no coordinated effort to produce military stores for the Continental Army during the first year of the war. The system, therefore, never met the army's daily needs and was not in a position to support the army's emergency and repair eventualities. The system's failure also proved the limitations of the American wartime economy without some type of centralized mobilization.

Arming for war and financing military operations were not new experiences for Americans. Most of the colonies had participated directly in the French and Indian War. Massachusetts and Virginia in particular had raised, armed, and paid for a significant number of their own troops to assist the British army against the French. Prior to that war, Americans

had fought in three imperial conflicts in the eighteenth century known as
Queen Anne's War, the War of Jenkins' Ear, and King George's War. The
colonies had learned how to raise militias, arm them, and send them off
to war. They had used those same militias to fight Native Americans on
the frontier. The New England colonies, New York, North Carolina, and
South Carolina had all fought major engagements with neighboring
Indian tribes. Virginia had just finished a brief conflict with the Shawnee
in 1775. Colonial governments had gained a knowledge base for wartime
organization and mobilization; the colonies had produced arms and built
powder magazines to store supplies for their militias. Colonists, however, had never had to gear up for large conflicts without the support of the
home country, which included access to the British market for the purchase of supplies and weapons. The revolution cut ties to British manufacturing, royal arsenals, and the imperial treasury, all of which stood
behind the colonies in their efforts to fight imperial and frontier enemies.[13] Without support, the colonies had to answer Congress's call for
arms with various, indiscriminate programs, of which confiscation and
purchase were the initial means of acquisition.

Even before Lexington, patriots seized military stores from domestic
sites and royal fortifications that were either lightly guarded or unguard-
ed completely. Late in 1774, Connecticut patriots took at least fifty-eight
cannons located in unmanned British fortifications at New Haven and
New London. Rhode Island's provincial government followed
Connecticut's lead and ordered the seizure of military stores at Newport's
lightly guarded Fort George. Forty-three cannons were taken, along with
two thousand five hundred pounds of powder and four thousand pounds
of lead. On December 14, 1774, the citizens of Portsmouth, New
Hampshire, seized Fort William and Mary, capturing sixteen cannons,
sixty muskets, and one hundred barrels of powder. British guards on
hand were unprepared for the patriot mob that rushed the fort. British
troops in Boston prohibited the seizure of royal supplies by patriots; but
Massachusetts patriots did direct local supporters to seize stores in their
community militia magazines and forward them to a patriot arsenal in
Concord for safe keeping. By April 1775, the province had amassed
"twenty thousand pounds of musket balls and cartridges, fifty reams of
cartridge paper" and nineteen pieces of ordnance.[14] Finally, just days
after the battles at Lexington and Concord, the patriot governments of
Connecticut and Massachusetts authorized the seizure of Forts
Ticonderoga and Crown Point on Lake Champlain. Together the two
forts provided the patriot cause with 181 pieces of artillery, eight small
kegs of powder, nine tons of lead, and more than five tons of shot and
shell.[15] Very quickly and with little trouble, New England revolutionaries had procured large amounts of stores by appropriating them from
supplies on hand.

Other significant captures were made as the war progressed. In August 1775, New York patriots decided to remove ordnance and other stores from the New York City battery and place them in a fort farther up the Hudson. They secured twenty-one pieces of artillery before troops from a royal vessel in the harbor stopped them. Patriots in South Carolina confiscated all the muskets, swords, and ammunition at the royal armory in Charleston and relocated the stores farther inland. This was followed by the seizure of a British ship carrying gunpowder off the Carolina coast. Washington, too, worked to seize stores by constructing a fleet of raiders for use near Boston. He had eight vessels fitted as warships and turned over to Colonel John Glover of Massachusetts and his regiment composed of professional seamen. During summer and autumn 1775, Glover's men captured fifty-five British cargo ships, including the royal ordnance ship *Nancy*, holding two thousand muskets, ammunition, and a mortar. Esek Hopkins of the newly formed Continental Navy led a successful raid early in 1776. His attack on the Bahamas, and subsequent ship captures, netted 119 pieces of artillery, 7,200 shot and shells, 24 barrels of powder, and other stores.[16] The British, however, were not the only sources of confiscated materiel.

Patriots often took weapons and stores from other Americans in their endeavors to secure enough supplies. Congress received information in December 1775 that a group of Loyalists in Tryon County, New York, was gathering weapons in the hopes of raising a force to serve the crown. The Northern Army commander, General Philip Schuyler, was ordered not only to subdue the Loyalists but also to seize their weapons for the patriot cause. The next month Congress encouraged patriots in Queens County, New York, to disarm Loyalists there.[17] In March 1776, Congress requested that patriot colonial governments search the property of nonpatriot citizens and confiscate their weapons. Congress recommended the same tactic to Philadelphia officials. "A diligent search [should] be made in the houses of all . . . who have not manifested their attachment to the American cause, for fire arms, swords, and bayonets."[18] City officials heeded the call and netted nearly five hundred weapons. The Pennsylvania Council of Safety, however, had to arm an additional one thousand men enlisted for Continental service. To meet the need for weapons, the council redirected its confiscation efforts toward patriotic and neutral Pennsylvanians as well. It ordered all patriots "who have . . . Arms in their Possession, to Deliver them to our Commissary, Robert Towers."[19] Pennsylvanians, however, were not prompt in relinquishing their weapons, which led the council to order Towers "to Collect as fast as possible, the Fire locks and spare Bayonets in the hands of" anyone loyal to the province.[20] By the end of 1775, Towers had collected "all the Arms belonging to the publick in every part of the Province," which totaled roughly one thousand four hundred weapons. [21]

It quickly became clear that confiscation alone would not meet the needs of the Continental Army. Washington took an inventory of all army stores in June 1775 when he arrived in Massachusetts to take command and found that he did not have enough muskets or ammunition to equip all his men. The colonial militias that became the foundation of the Continental Army had been supplied with gunpowder seized in 1774 and early 1775, but those supplies had almost all been used up by year's end. The Battle of Bunker Hill had exhausted in a day almost one-third of all the army's ammunition, and more was lost to waste and poor storage. Soldiers often held shooting contests and went hunting, which was an unnecessary use of ball and powder. Food was provided by the army, and as noted earlier, eighteenth-century battles were not known for their reliance on marksmanship, so target practice was not necessary. When not needed, ammunition was stored haphazardly among the ranks, who had neither cartridge boxes nor proper regimental magazines. By the end of August 1775, Washington reported to Congress that he had only thirty-three barrels of powder left for the entire army, enough to make just three cartridges for each man in camp. Moreover, the artillery on hand, which had been seized by Massachusetts, was not of the same caliber as the ammunition that had been sent from the surrounding colonies.[22] The cannonballs available would not fit his cannons.

The military stores situation continued to deteriorate, and there was little Washington could do about it. A congressional investigation in February 1776 found that though more than 442 pieces of artillery had been confiscated across the colonies, the military still needed at least 372 more cannons for field, garrison, and maritime duty. General Schuyler reinforced the findings when he reported to Congress that there were no cannons on hand with which to support the proposed invasion of Canada. Washington's own inventory in February 1776 found that only eight thousand of the ten thousand men in his army had weapons. Regimental commander Anthony Wayne, who was later a major general, noted at the same time that the entire Pennsylvania contingent in the northern theater in New York (one thousand two hundred men) had unserviceable arms in need of repair. Pennsylvania's provincial government had been able to confiscate nearly one thousand four hundred muskets. This was enough to arm the first and second battalions it raised. Unfortunately, when Pennsylvania recruited a third battalion, only 141 muskets were left in the state magazine. The men in this battalion were sent to Washington unarmed.[23] As early as August 1775, a Pennsylvania councilman lamented, "At this time . . . when the spirit of our People supplies more Men than we can furnish with Fire Arms, a Deficiency which all the Industry of our ingenious Gunsmiths cannot suddenly supply; . . . the use of [spears] is recommended."[24] Four months earlier, Washington wrote Congress, "I have repeatedly mention'd . . . the distressful situation we are in for want of Arms. With much pains and difficulty I got most of the Regiments from the Eastward tolerably well furnished, but find the [New] York Regiments very badly provided."[25] The general's problem stemmed from the fact that New York and New Jersey, like Pennsylvania, had sent whole regiments to camp without weapons. Those colonies did not have any more available. Congress and the colonies learned by late 1775 that confiscation was not a long-term solution to the army's needs. Confiscation provided myriad items, often of poor quality, that did not always work interchangeably or fit the army's needs. Plus, if confiscation could not keep up with current demands, it certainly would not support future requirements.

The government determined that measures were necessary to promote importation and domestic manufacture. Congress encouraged the import of weapons in two ways. First, it directed each colony to offer bounties to any importers willing to take the risk of trading overseas. Essentially subsidies, bounties paid for insurance and initial investments if shippers were willing to purchase trade goods, sail them to foreign markets, and bring home military stores. Second, Congress created several committees to facilitate trade by purchasing goods and trading them overseas. Congress's actions were facilitated by its decision to assume the power to borrow money and print money in its own name. None of the colonies objected to this development, but none allowed Congress the power to tax, a prohibition that was later written into the Articles of Confederation. Continental currency and bonds were given value by the fact that the colonies agreed to accept them in payment of colonial and local taxes. Once Congress began borrowing and printing money, it could offer bounties of its own, repay the colonies for their expenditures, and eventually purchase weapons outright. Only later did congressional monetary policy become a problem. In 1775 and 1776, Continental dollars still had value.

The Pennsylvania Council of Safety allocated $90,132 for the purchase of weapons overseas. When the average musket cost ten dollars, Pennsylvania's appropriation was a sizable amount of money that demonstrated the state's commitment to importation. The council did not, however, take the next step and appoint agents to administer the purchase and importation of weapons. In fact, each colonial government seemed to believe that merchants and importers would respond to the money being offered for military stores, but few did. Merchants were hindered by a British naval blockade, and independence later cut the states off from traditional British trade networks. Not until 1778 did Pennsylvania hire Robert Morris to act as the state's import agent. Other colonies did likewise. As provincial importation stalled, Congress assist-

"The Method of Refining Salt-Petre," an engraving attributed to Paul Revere for the *Royal American Magazine*, August 1774. Making salt-petre was a complex and multi-step process, which itself was only one part of producing gunpowder. Manure was boiled in several liquid solutions that raised the level of potash and removed impurities. The final process involved drying the mixture. The resulting salt-petre was then mixed with exact proportions of charcoal and sulphur to produce gunpowder. (*John Carter Brown Library, Brown University*)

ed the importation process by creating the Secret Committee to import five hundred tons of gunpowder, forty brass field pieces, twenty thousand gunlocks, and ten thousand muskets. The following week, the committee contracted with the firm of Willing and Morris to import six tons of powder. The committee also sent agents to the French government asking for assistance. After a great deal of effort by the provinces and Congress in 1776, only about two thousand muskets with powder and flints were imported. The problem was not so much that American actions did not stimulate the importation of weapons but that the process took too long and supplied items of poor quality. As it turned out, by 1783, over one hundred thousand muskets had been imported to the United States to support the war effort. But fewer than 50 percent of imported muskets arrived prior to October 1781, and half of those available before that time needed repair. By the end of 1776, barely enough guns for a single brigade had arrived from overseas.[26]

Without a significant domestic stock of weapons to confiscate or immediate access to foreign sources, America's revolutionaries had to rely on domestic manufacturing to provide the Continental Army with military stores. Colonial governments found, though, that while they were willing to invest large sums of money in domestic production,

American craft processes were not capable of large-scale output on their own. The Massachusetts provincial government initially authorized the expenditure of $7,259.40 in bounties to purchase stores as a supplement to importation and confiscation. When this was not enough, the colony authorized an additional $88,800 in bounties to purchase artillery, shot, shells, powder, and muskets domestically.[27]

Much of the money went unspent, however, because craft production could not match the colonial government's demand. Gunsmiths did not accept the government's bounties, because they could not promise to produce the amounts requested. At most, gunsmiths could be expected to produce two or three muskets a week, not including the bayonet, while colonial governments wanted fifteen to twenty a month. This amount of production was nearly impossible for craftsmen; they simply could not work that fast on their own or even with an apprentice or two assisting them. Production was further hindered by the fact that the war had destroyed trade networks and undermined the availability of raw materials. Despite the offer of bounties, gun production in Massachusetts was so poor that in early 1777, the government asked Congress for a loan of four thousand muskets. Maryland authorities estimated that 240 muskets could be purchased per month from gunsmiths in the colony, but this level of production was never reached. In early 1777, Maryland like Massachusetts sought a loan of one thousand five hundred muskets and related accouterments from Congress. In June 1775, the Pennsylvania Council budgeted $181,263, to purchase military stores in the province, a figure twice the amount allocated for importation. Yet craftsmen were only able to manufacture 363 muskets for sale to the Council by the end of the year. New York legislators offered interest-free loans for two years, and bounties of $444 to anyone attempting to build a powder mill or gunlock factory in the province.[28] The bounties went unclaimed, leading the New York Committee of Safety to report to Congress an "almost insurmountable difficulty of procuring Arms" for the Continental Army.[29] It was no wonder New York had to send its troops to Washington's camp unarmed. Finally, at the moment of independence, Virginia's new state government notified Congress that its purchasers could find no military stores for purchase in the whole southern half of the nation. State agents had been to North Carolina, South Carolina, and Georgia but had returned empty handed. Virginia's Council of State reported that those being manufactured by craftsmen on the frontier were being kept there for use against Native Americans.[30] Despite many and various efforts, money alone was not enough of an incentive, or an investment, to mobilize American gunsmiths to produce more than a handful of weapons.

On January 25, 1776, Congress assisted New Jersey by granting it $4,000 for the purchase of weapons. The following month, Congress took the further step of authorizing the Secret Committee to purchase weapons directly for Congress from any domestic source available. Other committees were subsequently set up to purchase specific military stores. Congress discovered what the states already knew: domestic sources of military stores were not available. Congress, therefore, approached Pennsylvania authorities for stores, and throughout 1776, it purchased items from the state magazine and several county magazines. Congress paid the state at least $30,000 for the items it purchased. None of these congressional activities, however, fixed the problem. New Jersey authorities used the money they received from Congress to purchase weapons from Pennsylvania, which limited the number of weapons available to Pennsylvania authorities. Congressional committees purchased stores that would have otherwise been purchased by the states, forcing manufacturers to choose between taking congressional or state contracts. This competition in turn forced up prices for military stores as various agencies bid for products all eventually bound for the Continental Army. Moreover, by purchasing stores from Pennsylvania, Congress inhibited the state's procurement of arms for its Continental troops. Rather than fix the situation, congressional assistance complicated already strained procurement circumstances.[31]

Only one state was able to effectively mobilize its domestic resources, but its success was short lived and further served to prove the case against decentralized mobilization efforts. The Connecticut General Assembly did as it was asked by the Continental Congress: It launched a campaign to confiscate weapons from Loyalists and then patriots. It appointed a committee in 1775 to oversee firearms production in the colony, and it offered a five-shilling bounty for each musket made according to specifications it issued. By mid-1776, Connecticut had secured over eight thousand two hundred weapons for its militia and Continental troops. Every one of the troops sent by the state to Washington's army was sent fully armed. Unfortunately, five thousand state muskets were lost in the battles for New York due to troop surrenders, retreats, and captured stores. Soon after the New York Campaign, the British raided the Connecticut coast and seized more guns. There was no money left in the budget to purchase more weapons, and even if there had been, there were no muskets left in the state to purchase. By early 1777, Connecticut was no longer in a position to support the Continental Army, and it even requested a loan of three thousand muskets from Congress.[32] State authorities, even when successful, found that the productive limits of American craft organization were difficult to overcome.

American manufacturing at the time of the revolution was not organized or equipped for large-scale production. The very nature of the craft-production process prevented Congress and the colonies from securing a large-scale yield of domestic weapons without making changes to the craft-production system itself. All the early efforts discussed so far were, therefore, doomed to failure. Only after Congress learned this lesson could it embark on a new direction of mobilization.

When the revolution began, the family was the production team, with wife and children assisting the artisan in a shop either in or attached to his house. A master craftsman took on an apprentice or two if finances allowed. Yet a craftsman and his workers could make no more than a handful of items per week, depending on the nature of the craft. It took a gunsmith three days to make one weapon from scratch with some of the more intricate parts premade. Building an entire musket could take up to a week and required the gunsmith to have the ironworking skills of a blacksmith, the woodworking skills of a carpenter, and the fine crafting skills of a clockmaker and engraver. There was little division of labor in gunsmithing in particular and craftsmanship in general in America. An artisan worked on all aspects of a single product. Because colonial markets were not large enough to call forth the development of large-scale production, general craftsmen were specialty producers. Thus, most gunsmiths were also blacksmiths and often produced rifles as well as muskets. With no requirement from the market to produce on a large scale, craftsmen never developed the means to do so. And, as will be seen in chapter 6, large-scale producers that did exist, like ironmongers, had no experience in making military stores. The American Revolution changed the nature of craft production, but in 1776, craftsmen were in no position to serve the military market on their own.[33] And the nation's need for craftsmen skilled in military stores production exacerbated the limits of craft production in that particular industry.

Americans embarked on the road to independence with the assistance of very few craftsmen trained in military stores production. There were roughly 350 craftsmen throughout the whole of the thirteen colonies that did gunsmithing work in the revolutionary period. About half of those workers appear to have learned the skill on the job during the war, thus there were only about 175 skilled gunsmiths in the United States at the time of independence.[34] Commissioners in Bedford County, Pennsylvania, reported that they had "but one Gunsmith in the County, who has engaged to make twenty-five Firelocks, and has been employed for these three months past, but has not got any of them completed."[35] He could not get the weapons done, the commissioners complained, because he could not find skilled journeymen to support him. Pennsylvania craftsmen, overall, were able to produce only 806 muskets for the state in all of 1776. Likewise, so few Pennsylvania craftsmen knew how to make the accouterments that went with a musket that the state Council of Safety had to educate them. The council issued a call for craftsmen to submit samples of military stores from which it could judge the best model to send to the state's other craftsmen to copy. Blacksmiths were hired to make bayonets and ramrods because they had the closest transferable skills, while for the same reason wire makers were hired to make priming wires and gun screws. Records indicate that over the course of the war, Congress hired only four craftsmen specifically skilled in bayonet making. No more artisans skilled in this craft were available to employ. Bayonets were not in high demand prior to the revolution. Ironmongers could also cast a cannon as easily as an iron pig and were employed by provincial governments to make ordnance. Like other craftsmen, however, ironmongers had no experience with military production, and many first-run artillery pieces were useless. Pennsylvania's Council of Safety contracted Berkshire and Warwick Furnaces to produce, between them, ninety-two twelve-pound and eighteen-pound cannons. Pennsylvania records suggest that only forty of those cannons withstood proof test and made it into service.[36] Congress and the states learned that the nature of craftwork did not allow large-scale production and that they were calling for production from a very small percentage of the craft population. Therefore, several state governments with available resources attempted to direct provincial craft production for greater output.

State governments realized by 1776 that to meet Congress's military stores requests, they needed to apply more effort than just offering money to make their craftsmen more productive. The provincial governments of Connecticut, Virginia, and Pennsylvania developed large-scale public manufacturing operations in response to meager private production. Connecticut's government focused its efforts on maximizing the potential of Salisbury Furnace, while Virginia and Pennsylvania built government gun shops. Yet these efforts toward state government manufacturing contributed little to the states themselves let alone the Continental Army, which most needed the weapons in 1776. The states' lack of success taught the Continental leaders very important lessons about military stores.

Salisbury Furnace was one of the largest manufacturing complexes in North America, yet it did little for the war effort until taken over by the Connecticut government. When the war began, Connecticut's government attempted to purchase cannons from Salisbury, but it belonged to Richard Smith, a Loyalist who refused to produce for the patriots. Provincial leaders believed that managed correctly, the furnace could provide iron for gunsmiths and cannons for defense of the coast. Faced with Smith's obstinacy, the Connecticut Council of Safety confiscated the site on February 2, 1776, and appointed militia colonel Jedediah Elderkin to establish a cannon foundry there. All provisioning and production orders were authorized directly from the state Council of Safety, and under state management, a furnace that had produced nothing for the war effort cast over one hundred pieces of artillery in 1776. Connecticut spent $78,792 on Salisbury from 1776 to 1779, but the cannons produced there were only for the use of the state. As Washington prepared for the defense of New York, he wrote Connecticut governor Jonathan Trumbull, asking for cannons. The governor responded that "it is not in my power to Comply with your requisition for Heavy Cannon, without leaving our Port and Harbour of New London in too defenceless a State."[37] Trumbull later in the year turned down General Schuyler's cannon request for the Northern Army. Not until Schuyler sent an inspector to Salisbury was it revealed that the site housed eighty-two cannons that Trumbull did not want to give up. The cannons were sitting idle in Connecticut while Washington's army faced off against the British in New York. Washington and Congress discovered painfully that the Continental Army could not rely on state production of military stores. Schuyler, however, was not going to let Connecticut's seeming selfishness cost him the northern frontier.[38] He sent horse teams to retrieve most of the cannons at Salisbury. Schuyler's actions helped support the American victory at Saratoga but cost Connecticut dearly. Ironically, in 1777, just after Schuyler took Salisbury's cannons, the British did exactly what Trumbull had feared and landed a raiding party on the Connecticut coast, which the state lacked the ordnance to oppose. In a subsequent irony, Salisbury ironmongers remained so focused on the production of ordnance that the casting of pig iron for gun skelps (iron rods for working into gun barrels) was completely ignored. This inhibited the production of Connecticut's gunsmiths, who were unable to replace all the weapons lost at New York, a situation mentioned above. By 1777, Connecticut's leaders discovered that though they were spending large amounts of money on a manufacturing project, they were still unable to provide for their wartime needs. Schuyler's actions also taught the state its own lesson. Salisbury could not provide enough iron for cannons and for guns, for itself and the Continental Army. There were too many demands for military stores. Moreover, by 1778, Salisbury Furnace had been in operation for two years with little maintenance. As raw materials, labor, and transport became scarce, production costs rose and output declined. Connecticut gave up on its Salisbury project.[39]

Virginia's government launched a manufacturing program that ended as ignominiously as that in Connecticut. The Virginia provincial government was disappointed in its efforts to support its Continental troops and militia with a public musket factory. As mentioned earlier, Virginia's western counties were not responsive to calls for the collection of weapons for the war effort. Westerners and their gunsmiths were more interested in arming themselves against Native Americans on the frontier. The result was that the state government had to rely on gunsmiths in the eastern half of the state. A committee was established shortly after independence to consider how to assist gunsmiths in their production activities. The committee decided that a centralized state gun manufactory should be built near Hunter Forge in Fredericksburg. In July 1775, a large armory and a grinding mill were built and put into operation. Yet, soon after production began at the site in early 1776, the state government sought permission from Pennsylvania authorities to purchase weapons there. Permission, apparently, was not granted, for a year later, state authorities confiscated five thousand muskets Congress had imported from France. Not only were Virginia's efforts inadequate for Washington's army in 1776 when the weapons were needed, but also for the state itself through the remaining years of war. No matter how much money the state of Virginia spent at Fredericksburg and how many weapons it produced, it was never able to produce enough to arm its own militia. From 1777 to 1781, Virginia's state quartermasters continually called on Congress for weapons for its militia. Congress generally declined, citing the five thousand weapons it had already "lent" the state.[40]

Pennsylvania likewise found its efforts at public manufacturing to be inadequate. Pennsylvania authorities believed, after individual gunsmiths were unable to meet state production expectations, that those same smiths could be managed and trained to improve their productivity. In February 1776, the Council of Safety hired gunsmiths Benjamin Rittenhouse and Peter DeHaven to construct and manage a state gun works. It instructed them to use their skills to make gun production more efficient and educate other craftsmen on the proper manufacture of muskets. The council spent $102,000 on its armory and sought craftsmen of any type to work there and learn the trade of gunsmithing. The state's operation manufactured about two thousand weapons over the course of two years, an average of about nineteen guns a week. Large-scale production was possible, but circumstances and legislative interference kept Rittenhouse and DeHaven from developing effective production over the long term. The first year of operation was occupied with purchasing tools, training craftsmen, and manufacturing gunlocks at a quickly rented building. Rittenhouse moved the factory out of Philadelphia late in 1776 and built a new facility near Phoenixville. For the next six months, the factory operated at its peak. Nineteen craftsmen who specialized in particular operations manufactured roughly one thousand complete muskets. The necessities of war then interrupted production. The campaigns of 1776 and 1777 left numerous state weapons in need of repair. The council directed those arms to the armory, where manufacturing work was displaced by repair work. All work was stopped in late 1777 by the British invasion of Pennsylvania, which forced the factory to relocate again. Production consequently declined, and the council grew weary of the factory's cost. The council tried to coax Congress into taking over control of the factory, but by 1778, Congress had its own arsenals in operation. The council shut down the factory and asked Congress for a loan to cover the state's accumulated manufacturing debts.[41] Pennsylvania, like Connecticut and Virginia, could not keep large-scale weapons production afloat, let alone support the Continental Army. It was around the time of independence in summer 1776 that the limitations of state procurement efforts and America's craft economy began to crystallize in Congress's view of the war.

Washington's preparations for the New York Campaign exposed to Congress how far short early procurement efforts had fallen from meeting the army's needs. The British army abandoned Boston in March 1776. Reasonable assumption and available information pointed to New York City as the army's likely point of return. Washington, therefore, began moving his army from Boston to the lower Hudson Valley to prepare for the British invasion. Forts Washington and Lee were constructed overlooking the Hudson, furnished with hundreds of artillery to defend the river, and stocked with enough supplies to make them self-sufficient against a prolonged enemy engagement. Entrenchments were built throughout the region, and provisions, arms, and ammunition were stockpiled. The process of taking supply inventories revealed to Washington how little military stores support he was receiving. He discovered while in Boston that militiamen with the army were departing for home with their weapons in order to return them to state magazines or keep them for later service. This problem was exacerbated as the army moved through Connecticut and New York, where militia joined the army, returned home, and later rejoined as the needs of the army dictated. Militia units did not often arrive in camp fully equipped, and when they left, they took with them the stores they had been issued.[42] Washington wrote to Schuyler that the militia "commit an intollerable Waste of Stores, which once put into their Hands, can scarcely be ever regained. . . . And for Want of Regularity in their Drafts of Ammunition & other necessaries, they consume much more than is convenient to spare from a Garrison."[43]

The drain on stores limited Washington's ability to arm all of his troops. Washington wrote Congress "that the Five (independent Boston) Regiments . . . are . . . deficient in arms, as are many other Regiments" because the Massachusetts and Connecticut men were returning home with the weapons they were issued.[44] Inventories revealed that only 90 percent of troops in the New England regiments were armed. One New York regiment reported in April 1776 that it had only ninety-seven muskets, less than one-fourth of the total number it needed. Washington found that only as many as 10 percent of the Continentals had bayonets, a dreadful situation if the army engaged in close-quarter combat.[45] Desperate for artillery ammunition, the patriots formed detachments to collect used British shot and unexploded shells. Washington reported to Congress that even as state governments claimed to be arming their Continental troops, they were actually sending those troops to camp without equipment.

The fact that Washington's army had been supplied by eleven entities caused chaos and confusion when it came to accounting and caring for materiel. Every province from Virginia north had, by mid-1776, supplied troops and stores to the Continental Army, and Congress had purchased weapons on its own for the army. Despite Congress's efforts to standardize items, the provinces sent their men to the Continental Army fitted out with whatever they could get. Some men, like those from Maryland and Delaware, came fully equipped with cartridge boxes, muskets, and bayonets. Others, like those from New Jersey, came without bayonets.[46] Those troops who came without cartridge boxes could not be issued musket cartridges because they had nothing to carry them in securely. Cartridges could not be carried in a simple knapsack because they fell apart. Thus, as noted earlier, just prior to battle, soldiers were issued as much ammunition as they could carry in their pockets or knapsacks. Those troops who brought rifles to service had to be separated from those with muskets because it took longer to reload a rifle and they were not made for use with bayonets. One historian has noted, "The great variety of firearms caused its own special nightmare for supply officers."[47] Troops arrived with arms of every type and size: muskets of British design, muskets of French design, American-made muskets that resembled either British or French designs, old large-bore hunting muskets, and rifles.[48] "The difference of bore made issuance of standardized ammunition impossible."[49] Washington, though, tried to work with what he had. He put troops to work producing musket cartridges, which had to be made in various sizes. Some units were just issued loose ball and powder. The benefit of the cartridge was that it increased the speed of loading a gun. Troops with premade cartridges could fire twice as fast as men with ball and powder. The benefits of cartridges were limited, though, if only 50 to 80 percent of the army had them. Washington did not lose an opportunity to make this point to Congress.

As Washington prepared his army for the showdown he expected in New York, he began pleading with Congress to address the military stores deficiencies in his army. Beginning in April 1776, Washington wrote about every two weeks to Congress with details about regiments without weapons or the limitations his army faced because of a lack of artillery or stores. Washington wanted to "build a centralized, 'national' army rather than a disparate conglomeration of state militias and provincial regiments."[50] To do that he needed "standard . . . weapons," like "King's Muskets, or Guns as near that quality as can be had."[51]

To accomplish this, the army needed a centralized production system for weapons and a national armory with trained gunsmiths and craftsmen to repair damaged stores. In July 1776, General Henry Knox, Washington's chief of artillery, presented an armory plan to the commander, who in turn passed it on to Congress. European armies, wrote Knox, had armories for the production of ammunition and the care of weapons. Since the chief artillery officer traditionally commanded such an establishment, Knox saw it as his duty to take charge of the military stores situation and wanted congressional approval to do so. Congress responded to Knox's ideas by sending a committee to camp in September 1776 to review the army's equipment situation. The committee was directed to inspect the army's materiel needs and make recommendations regarding what Congress could do to strengthen the army's military stores infrastructure.

The Committee at Camp arrived at Washington's headquarters just days after the Battle of Long Island and saw firsthand the state of the army before it suffered defeat at White Plains, Fort Washington, and Fort Lee. Washington and Knox explained the state of the army's military stores. There were not enough muskets for the army, and those that were in camp were of multiple types and sizes. Many of the muskets were old, grimy, or broken and needed repair or cleaning. Up to the end of 1776, hasty small arms and accouterment repairs were accomplished in camp; Washington put craftsmen in the ranks to work as repairmen and weapons cleaners, but this could not deal with the depth of work needed.

Washington continued his tale of woe. There was not enough field artillery, and many of the cannons on hand could not be used in the field, being either too heavy or too old. The army lacked enough artillery and musket ammunition, as well as the wagons and cartridge boxes necessary to carry each type. The army's military stores problems revolved around quantity and quality, neither of which, Washington explained to the committee, could be ensured without a centralized system. He had done as much as he could at the army level; a centralized ordnance department was needed to ensure a sufficient number of stores, well made according to Continental patterns. Washington presented the committee with another copy of Knox's plan.

The committee returned to Congress and made its recommendations. Congress took the committee's recommendation under advisement. In the meantime, reports from Washington arrived weekly explaining the losses the army was suffering and the deprivation it faced. The general explained that precipitous retreats had forced the army to abandon more stores and that scared soldiers were throwing away their guns. Congress's calls to the states for stores continually fell on deaf ears. In December 1776, Congress decided that the only way to ensure the continued armament of Continental forces was to centralize the administration of military stores under its own control. Congress created a department under a commissary general of military stores to oversee all procurement and the production of equipment at two arsenals—Carlisle, Pennsylvania, and Springfield, Massachusetts.[52]

THE PROCUREMENT OF MILITARY STORES FOR THE CONTINENTAL ARMY early in the revolution was a complex and cumbersome process. Congress relied on the provinces to provide weapons to the army, and the provinces in turn relied on confiscation, purchase, and in some cases government manufacturing to procure military stores. Confiscation had gathered thousands of weapons and other military stores across the colonies, but not nearly enough to support state militias and the Continental Army. Provincial governments attempted to rectify the situation by purchasing weapons domestically and overseas. Few weapons arrived in the country within the first year of war, and those that did were of poor quality and in need of repair, a fact that exacerbated the supply situation. American manufacturers were not in a position to produce weapons quickly. Traditional craft production was not equipped for large-scale output. So while American gunsmiths did provide weapons for the Continental Army early in the war, it was not enough. States tried to train craftsmen in the arts of gunsmithing to increase production, but such education took time and was not immediately reflected in increased production. Several states with the means available to develop government manufacturing did so, but these efforts reflected provincial willingness to spend money rather than any desire to reorganize American craft production. Connecticut, Virginia, and Pennsylvania spent considerable amounts of money on government manufacturing, yet none of those operations provided the level of production for which state authorities hoped. Virginia still had to request muskets from Congress, and Connecticut could not lend Congress cannons without compromising its defenses. By mid-1776, the Continental Army was either poorly equipped or not equipped at all.

The nation had started the war with limited resources, but no efforts early in the war had developed those resources to an extent necessary to put the army on a sound footing. Apart from the anecdotal evidence for this conclusion, the proof lies in the fact that 75 to 90 percent of the Continental Army was unarmed at any one time. The early military stores supply system could not keep the army in the field. The inadequacies of the army's military stores situation was driven home by the army's 1776 campaign in the Hudson Valley. Men went into battle without muskets, ammunition, bayonets, or cartridge boxes, and with insufficient artillery support. The resulting defeat was a wake-up call to Congress. Washington and Knox reported the problem as they saw it: There was no central control over the military stores being sent to the army. No steps were being taken to enhance craft production; no guidance was being offered to military stores producers; and Congress was exercising no quality control over production. Neither the state governments nor independent craftsmen were able to support the Continental Army. Congress was left the task of mobilizing the nation's resources so that Americans could "help themselves" secure independence.

2

"Laboratories . . . ordnance . . . artificers [and] Ammunition"

THE DEPARTMENT OF THE
COMMISSARY GENERAL OF MILITARY STORES

S AMUEL HODGDON, ASSISTANT COMMISSARY GENERAL OF MILITARY stores, had a great many issues on his mind in spring 1780, but they were all related to one thing: money. The Continental government Hodgdon worked for was bankrupt. "So general is the malady," he noted, "that not a dollar is to be found in any department."[1] Yet without money, Hodgdon was expected to continue providing weapons and supplies to the army. General Washington was planning an offensive against the British and continually sent orders for more artillery and ammunition. At the same time, Hodgdon was directed by the Board of War to supply a new Southern Army being mobilized under General Horatio Gates. Hodgdon issued orders to the arsenals under his command; the workers were to be kept on the job until the necessary supplies were produced. He expected his post commanders to see that muskets were finished, cartridges filled, cannons bored, and artillery shot fixed. But those commanders had begged off their assignments, pleading with Hodgdon for money. Without cash, the commanders warned Hodgdon in dire prose, they could neither purchase supplies to keep their men at work nor purchase food to keep the men motivated for work. "[T]he greatest difficulty at present seems to be how . . . any . . . persons employed in the public service are to be paid," he wrote in May 1780.[2] To make matters worse, all these departmental responsibilities fell to Hodgdon because the commissary general, Benjamin Flower, was terminally ill and incapable of command. It was in the midst of these troubling developments that Hodgdon sat down at his desk in Carpenter's Hall, Philadelphia, to write letters to his men about their circumstances.

Hodgdon engaged the situation with a single-minded determination. He wrote to the post commanders that the Board of War was "fully sensible" that it was "indispensable to procure materials and pay wages" to the workers. But even without money, he wrote, "the public interest calls for every possible exertion."[3] The work simply had to get done, and Hodgdon expected his post commanders to get it done. Money would become available, he told them. "[L]ight will spring forth speedily." Until then the commanders should work at such things as would allow "temporary relief."[4] He suggested that they encourage the men to work without pay, knowing that the Board of War would not ignore their plight. He encouraged them to sell any excess produce such as lumber, bricks, and spare parts to make money for paying the men. Hodgdon believed the workers' labor could also be hired out to earn money for the posts. He then followed his own advice and started selling stores to raise money. Within days Hodgdon was trading stores with manufacturers and other government departments, swapping bar iron for the use of wagons, or the use of wagons for clothing for the workers. Hodgdon faced down a seemingly impossible task: keeping his workers at their duties through a dire financial situation. And yet this was only one difficulty among hundreds that plagued the military stores department during the revolution. Hodgdon's comments and actions reveal much about the department over which he presided, and the man who, more than any other, made the department effective.

The Department of the Commissary General of Military Stores (DCGMS) did not exist in any singular form, but rather it evolved over time; it changed and adapted to America's fortunes in the revolution. Its survival and success were driven by the people and relationships that guided and surrounded it. Congress knew what it wanted, but since it made decisions by committee, it was often at pains to conceive of how it expected its goals to be achieved. Individual legislators could be remarkably prescient and insightful, but together they were often belligerent and shortsighted. Thus, rather than be conclusive on an issue, congressmen often left the details to their subordinates.

Circumstances also got in the way. Congress might be forced to deal with one issue and be interrupted in its deliberations by another. It was, therefore, the cast of characters involved in the DCGMS that drove the department, its story, and its innovations. There were four principle actors in the drama, each with his own vision and expectations for military stores operations. George Washington and Henry Knox were the primary drivers of developments in the military stores department early on. Once the department was up and running, Benjamin Flower and

Samuel Hodgdon played very adeptly at politics to see that their department operated as they believed it should. Throughout it all, Congress's insights were represented by the Board of War, a standing committee created to oversee the conduct of all military operations.

Efficiency, consistency, and military control of operations were the primary goals that Washington and Knox had for the military stores department. Washington's greatest anxiety with his army in the field was that he was receiving weapons, ammunition, and accouterments from multiple sources. He needed consistency in the form and in the amount of production of those supplies. Washington's earliest solution was staff officers, a group of logistical commanders answering to the general who organized procurement and provision for the army. He asked Congress to appoint such a group of assistants to manage the army's food, transport, supplies, and military stores. Congress responded to Washington's suggestion by creating the staff positions he requested: commissary general (food), quartermaster general (supplies), paymaster general (soldiers' pay), and wagonmaster general (transport). In the case of arms and ammunition, Congress created two positions: a chief of artillery, answerable to Washington, and a military stores commissary, who was not. The former was to oversee training of artillerists and the use of artillery in battle; the latter was to organize and store all weapons and ammunition in camp. This flew in the face of the British model of organization, in which the chief of artillery was also in command of all ammunition and weapons procurement.

Samuel Hodgdon (1745–1824) was appointed assistant commissary general of military stores in 1780 and commissary general the following year. He led the DCGMS until 1794.

Congress also took the time to initiate an additional administrative system to assist Washington. It created regional departmental offices to coordinate military activities in specific areas of the colonies and, after independence, the nation. The Northern Department was created to support the Northern Army in protecting the northern frontier against a British invasion from Canada. Eventually, four more permanent departments were created. When the war shifted south to New York, Washington's Main Army was assigned to the Middle Department, which stretched from New York to Virginia. New England was then organized into the Eastern Department. The Carolinas and Georgia eventually became the Southern Department, while the western frontier beyond the Appalachian Mountains was organized as the Western Department.

Though the systems of administrative regions and staff departments were supposed to relieve pressure from Washington, they actually made his work more difficult. Fearing that Washington and his army would act independently of Congress, the legislators made all staff officers and regional commanders answerable to Congress. Staff officers had no greater power than to request supplies from the colonies, and they had to ask Congress for permission to purchase supplies when they did not arrive from the colonies. Likewise, even though departmental commanders still answered to Washington as the commander in chief, all orders had to go from Washington through Congress to the regional commanders. Eventually, Congress loosened its control over regional commanders and staff officers, but until that point, Washington was stuck with the fact that no administrative officer's authority extended beyond the edge of the army's encampment without congressional involvement. As seen in chapter 1, Washington was able to consolidate and control the supplies used by the army in camp. He was also able to make it mandatory, with congressional approval, that all supplies sent to the departmental armies had to go through the Main Army supply system first. Nevertheless, after all of Congress's administrative reforming, Washington still had no way to influence the amount of military supplies he received or the quality of those stores.

Washington appointed Richard Gridley as chief of artillery and Ezekiel Cheever to military stores commissary because both men served in these capacities for Massachusetts. When the Continental Army left Boston in 1776, Washington replaced the men with Henry Knox, whom he appointed to both offices with congressional approval. Washington and Knox developed plans for a military stores program built on the British model. Knox had no end of ideas for the military stores department and took every opportunity presented to share those ideas with Congress. Knox, a born and raised Bostonian, was owner of the city's London Book Store. Through years of book sales, book collecting, and voracious reading, Knox had gained a fairly extensive amateur understanding of military affairs. As will be seen in chapter 3, he was well acquainted with John Muller, the English world's foremost artillerist and expert on ammunition. Knox expressed his expertise in such diverse avenues as designing drill exercises and drawing up plans for powder magazines. But Knox had no actual experience and was not able to easily attach himself to the Massachusetts militia or the Continental Army, though he did act as a consultant for both. It was only after convincing Washington and others that he had skills they could use that he was given his first assignment. Knox was given command of an expedition to move the cannons housed at Fort Ticonderoga, New York, to Boston for use against the British. He accomplished this nearly impossible task in the dead of winter 1775–76 and gained Washington's undying confidence and admiration. When the Continental Army left Boston, Gridley chose to stay with the local militia and Washington had his chance to appoint Knox to a command.[5]

Soon after conferring Knox with authority over artillery stores, Washington asked his chief to prepare a report on the condition of available stores. Knox not only prepared a numerical accounting but went on to propose how Congress should organize the procurement and distribution of future stores. He believed that all military stores should be obtained in one of two ways, either manufactured at government facilities or purchased and stored at government facilities. From those facilities the army could control the care, repair, and distribution of stores to the army's various encampments and fortifications. Knox believed that all procurement, care, and logistics should be directed by the chief of artillery. This was the way the system operated in the British army, and Knox was well versed in the operations of his enemy's ordnance system. Questionably from Congress's point of view, Knox ended his report by stating that it seemed logical that he be given responsibility of setting up the proposed system and assume direction over it because he was the artillery chief.

Washington forwarded Knox's report to Congress with his endorsement. Congress saw Knox's report as a grasp for power wrapped in a progressive package, and it took a political approach to military stores management. In June 1776, Congress created the Board of War, a permanent committee tasked with managing the procurement of stores as well as oversight of the various staff departments that had been created in 1775. The chief of artillery was legislated to be a purely military position, with direction of ordnance on the battlefield and the care of stores once they were in camp. The fact that Congress heeded Knox's advice at all was a sign that Congress respected their artillery chief and understood some of his goals. Unfortunately, despite congressional action, the efficient administration of military stores ran into two insurmountable problems. First, most congressmen had independence on their minds in summer 1776, and once the Board of War had been created, it was promptly forgotten. Second, as seen earlier, Congress had no willingness to invest money in the production of weapons. Thus, the Board of War had little encouragement to accomplish anything and no clear direction on how to accomplish what it was not told to accomplish in the first place. Knox was flabbergasted at what he saw as congressional ignorance, but he was not discouraged; he bided his time until the next opportunity came to convince Congress of the need to act.

Knox got his chance to again tell Congress what it should do when the Committee at Camp arrived at Harlem Heights in September 1776. He told the visiting congressmen that "the genius, industry, & care requisite in the preparation of all kinds of military stores, and the management of cannon render it necessary, that the best men should be employ'd in this service." There should be "one Commissary of military stores & as many deputy Commissaries & Conductors as the nature of the service may require & the Commander in chief thinks necessary." The commissary, Knox believed, should command a "Company of Artificers" and oversee "Magazines & laboratories for the reception & preparation of military stores of every species." He recommended that these facilities be built at "Hartford in Connecticut, and York in Pensylvania," very nearly where they were eventually built. Of course the whole establishment should answer to "the Commanding officer of Artillery [and] Commander in chief."[6] Knox believed that the responsibilities for procuring weapons should belong to the chief military officer using those weapons on the battlefield. Congress should not continue to divide those responsibilities as it had already done. Knox's final opportunity to offer his ideas to Congress came after the committee returned to Philadelphia to report its findings. Knox followed it in spirit by sending his report to Congress on his own, marking his third attempt to influence Congress's response to the growing need to change the military stores system. His recommendations matched the Committee at Camp's ideas for the military stores department almost exactly, except for one key, and ominous, difference.

The committee's report read as if it had been copied verbatim from Knox's report. However, the legislators displayed more knowledge of the topic than Knox may have expected. They explained in detail what work was to be accomplished at the public military stores sites. And they also realized that the workers and Knox's artillerists needed training. The committee suggested that

one or more capital Laboratories [be] erected at a distance from the seat of war in which shall be prepared large quantities of ordnance Stores of every species and denomination. That at the same place a sufficient number of able artificers be employ'd to make carriages for Cannon of all sorts and sizes, Ammunition Waggons, Tumbrils, harnesses, etc. etc. That [near] to the same place a foundry for Casting brass cannon Mortars Howitzers be established upon a large scale. [That] an Academy [be] established on a liberal plan . . . where the whole Theory of Fortification and Gunnery should be taught.[7]

Having elaborated on, but largely sanctioned Knox's ideas, the committee diverged from him in the area of command. It proposed that the military stores establishment be commanded not by the chief of artillery but by a Board of Ordnance. The congressmen knew something that Knox had failed to mention. Congress was well aware that though the British military stores system was nominally headed by the ranking general of the ordnance service, he was assisted by a committee styled the

Board of Ordnance. Since the cause of the war was dislike of central authority, the congressmen had no problem ditching Knox's leadership scheme and adopting a more democratic rule by committee.

Congress took the committee's and Knox's reports under advisement, and starting in November and December 1776, it enacted several bills that made policy of the recommendations. On November 27, Congress established an artillery yard in Philadelphia to store and repair broken gun carriages and artillery accouterments. The yard was also to serve as a practice field and school to teach artillery theory to young officers.[8] The Philadelphia artillery yard, combined with other operations, became the Philadelphia Arsenal. On December 27, Congress resolved to construct "at Carlisle, in Pennsylvania, [and Brookfield, Massachusetts] a magazine sufficient to contain ten thousand stand of arms and two hundred tons of gun powder, and also for erecting an elaboratory [for making ammunition] adjacent to such magazine."[9] A few days later, Congress followed up by contracting for arsenal construction with local bricklayers and stonemasons. President John Hancock wrote to the governments of Pennsylvania and Massachusetts to secure their assistance with the project. Congress also added a further resolution to build an ordnance foundry at the Philadelphia artillery yard.[10] Finally, Congress established the post of commissary general of military stores to manage the various operations it had established.

As with everything else in the history of the military stores department, developing the commissary general position was a process rather than a single act. Congress did not actually create the position of commissary general. Having set up the elements of the eventual DCGMS, Congress intended to turn these activities over to the Board of War, agreeing with the Committee at Camp that a board (or committee) should oversee military stores production. The Board of War created earlier in the year had tried working out contracts with manufacturers but had failed in the endeavor. Since that point, Congress had given the board no additional responsibilities or assignments. Now was the chance to give the board real power over military stores. At the same time, the board was given charge of the other staff departments and the regional departments, which had all heretofore answered directly to Congress. Circumstances, however, led Congress to ignore further details involved in implementing the military stores plan it enacted and leave them to Washington.

After defeating Washington at New York, the British chased his army into New Jersey. The Continentals then suffered defeat after defeat as they were forced to abandon more and more of the Garden State. Congress left Philadelphia in December 1776 out of fear the British would soon cross the Delaware River and capture the city. Congress gave Washington nearly dictatorial powers to manage the war. Because the board (made up of congressmen) had departed with Congress,

Washington was asked to appoint a commissary of military stores to get the department up and running for eventual management by the Board of War. On January 16, 1777, Washington appointed Benjamin Flower the first national commissary of military stores and drew up his instructions.[11] Flower was to go to Philadelphia and put men to work as quickly as possible at an artillery yard to deal with the emergency need for weapons in the army, and then he was to proceed to Carlisle and set up one of Congress's arsenals.

Flower was born in Maryland and raised in an artisan household. In 1777, he was only twenty-six and hardly a commanding presence for the role he was taking on. It was his business acumen and people skills that made him effective. Flower moved to Philadelphia in the early 1770s and worked as a hatter. Little is known of his early years as a journeyman, but by 1773 he had earned enough money to open his own store, which was the sign of a master craftsman. He purchased the site of the Black Alley Tavern and opened a store there. It is unclear if he kept the tavern, but from his later connections and activities, it is clear that Flower knew a lot of people and knew the right people. He was neighbor to merchants, cordwainers, lawyers, and wealthy Philadelphians, including Thomas Mifflin, the army's first quartermaster general. Flower joined the Continental Army in 1776. He was commissioned a major and appointed by Congress to serve as commissary of military stores for the flying camp serving Washington's Main Army.[12] This position became known as a brigade conductor. These individuals took supplies from the camp's main magazine, overseen by Knox, and delivered them to their units. They then cared for those stores and distributed them to the troops. When Washington was tasked with creating a military stores department, he raised Flower, the senior conductor, to the rank of lieutenant colonel and told him to get to work. Flower accomplished so much that when Congress returned to Philadelphia, it made Washington's appointment permanent rather than giving military stores responsibilities to the Board of War as originally planned. Flower simply answered to the Board of War as did other staff officers. The one change that the board made to the whole arrangement was to name Flower commissary "general" of military stores. Washington did not think Flower should hold this honorific title as a mere lieutenant colonel, but the board felt this was appropriate in order to give Flower standing with Washington's other staff officers, who were all "generals" in their departments (i.e., quartermaster general, paymaster general).

Knox was infuriated by the differences between his artillery plan and the one laid out by Congress. Knox felt that the creation of an artillery staff officer who did not answer to him diluted the command structure and made it more difficult than it already was for the army to procure supplies. Congress, however, in addition to its concerns over centralized

Colonel Benjamin Flower (1748–1781) by Charles Willson Peale, c. 1780. Flower is pictured standing in front of the Philadelphia ordnance yard guarded by a Continental solder. He is surrounded by the military stores his department procured. To the right is a mortar on a bed, while to the left is a barrel of gunpowder topped by artillery shell fuses. Behind him are five iron cannon, including one mounted on a field carriage. Flower seems to be pointing at the Pennsylvania State House (Independence Hall) in the distance expressing his belief that "to Support . . . Our Independency . . . nothing can tend to produce it more than our having all our wants Manufactured among ourselves, and those works to be Continental Property." (*The-Star-Spangled Banner Flag House and Museum*)

power, believed that as a field officer, Knox should not be bothered with staff work.[13] Knox wrote to Washington requesting that he raise the issue with Congress. Washington realized that Congress had made its move and was not likely to immediately reform a program it had just initiated. Events, however, allowed Washington to give his artillery chief a place in the military stores procurement system. Ever the pragmatist and being left with the ability to do largely as he wished without congressional interference, Washington followed the intent of Congress's wishes rather than the strict letter. With the power to appoint a director of military stores until the Board of War returned to Philadelphia, Washington split the department's responsibilities between the commissary of military stores (Flower) and his chief of artillery (Knox). This allowed him to quickly accomplish the creation of a procurement mechanism as well as assuage the frustration of his friend Knox. He also believed that two men answering to him on the issues of procurement could accomplish more than one. Washington assigned Knox responsibility for the arsenal at Brookfield. Throughout the following year, Congress's northern arsenal answered to Washington through Knox, while Carlisle answered to Washington through Flower. The Board of War, which was supposed to have meaningful oversight of all staff departments, was sidelined by Congress, which allowed Washington to run with the command structure he had put in place. Generally, until late 1777, the board served only as a court of last resort to settle disagreements among Congress, Washington, Flower, Knox, and contractors.[14]

Flower's instructions from Washington were to put repairmen to work in Philadelphia, establish a public works facility at Carlisle, raise an enlisted Continental Army Corps of Artillery Artificers, and procure a large supply of military stores. It was a daunting list, but necessity stressed that getting workers and procurement officials up and running was of utmost importance. Getting production and purchasing activities started in Philadelphia became Flower's first priority. The day after his appointment, Flower left the army's camp at Morristown, New Jersey, and traveled to the capital. There he secured $2,000 from Congress's Treasury Committee to carry out his orders. Flower's first act was to appoint two regional commissaries to organize procurement in the city and surrounding areas. Jonathan Gostelowe was named commissary of infantry stores with the rank of major and given direction over production and purchase of muskets, accouterments, ammunition, and other stores related to small arms. Gostelowe rented space and hired workers, so that by March he spoke to Flower of an armory in operation repairing damaged weapons sent to the city from the Main Army. Flower engaged Joseph Watkins as commissary of ordnance stores with the rank of major. Watkins rented a large courtyard with workshops and fitted them out as an artillery yard.[15]

Connected to either the armory or the artillery yard, Flower also established a laboratory to produce musket cartridges. While it is known to have existed in the city at this early date, it is unclear who managed it or where it operated. To support the armory and artillery yard with metal items, and to cast ordnance, Congress had mandated a furnace, and Flower's next mission was to put one in operation. Rather than build a new furnace, however, Flower rented the Pennsylvania state air furnace in the Southwark region of Philadelphia, which had "for some time past been neglected."[16] Pennsylvania's Council of Safety had given up on state operations as the costs rose and had left its furnace idle. Washington sent James Byers, a well-known New York brassmonger, to Philadelphia to work for Flower. Byers had operated a furnace in New York City until the British occupation, and he was brought to Washington's attention as someone with skills uniquely useful to the American cause. Byers put the furnace back in blast and began producing musket parts for the armory and bullets for the laboratory. He attempted to produce artillery pieces as well, but there is no indication he ever produced any in Philadelphia.[17] These operations were never given a coherent title but were often referred to as the public works in Philadelphia. Collectively, I will call these operations what, in effect, they were: the Philadelphia Arsenal. When not getting various production and purchase operations in motion, Flower spent his time recruiting workers and officers for his Regiment of Artillery Artificers. Then, having gotten the most critical support operations under way in Philadelphia, Flower set his sights on Carlisle.

Flower traveled to Carlisle in early spring 1777. He took with him Captain Isaac Coren of the Continental Artillery and Captain Nathaniel Irish, newly commissioned officer of the Artillery Artificers. Coren had directed the Main Army's temporary laboratory at Fishkill, New York, before being dispatched by Washington to support Flower. He and his artillery company would build and operate the post laboratory at Carlisle. Irish, a master carpenter in Philadelphia, joined the army for patriotic reasons when Flower recruited in the city. Once in Carlisle, Flower enrolled useful individuals to provide the overall management of operations at the post once it was completed. He met and took into service Charles Lukens, who had copious local connections. Born and raised in York County, Lukens was a well-known merchant as well as a craftsman and had been elected county sheriff. He gave this up to serve as a captain in the Pennsylvania Line of the Continental Army. Lukens applied to Flower for a position, was promoted to major, and was named regional commissary of military stores. His charge was to promote production at Carlisle and mobilize Pennsylvania and Maryland frontier enterprises to support the war effort. In the short term, however, Flower took on these responsibilities and sent Lukens to Philadelphia to recruit workers to serve as artillery artificers in Carlisle. Flower eventually hired a local merchant, Samuel Sargent, to serve as superintendent of overall operations at Carlisle. Sargent would manage Coren and Irish, and work with Lukens to turn his procurements into military stores. Sargent's command was never really given a name, but it came to be known as the Washingtonburg Public Works. This, however, was not a universally recognized name, and so I will refer to it as what is was, the Carlisle Arsenal. Having gotten things started there, Flower returned to Philadelphia to begin contracting with local craftsmen to produce stores for the army. He found a bustle of activity among his Philadelphia commissaries, so much so that he hired Cornelius Sweers, a Philadelphia merchant, as paymaster and bookkeeper for the department.[18]

In the weeks and months after Flower set his operations in motion, the procurement of stores became more efficient for the Main Army. The extent of communication among Flower's subordinates reflects the fact that they understood the supply system and worked well together within it. The military stores department set up a program of production, purchase, and storage of weapons, accouterments, ammunition, and ordnance. Flower's oversight of public production facilities assisted the process of procurement because Flower could direct production at the arsenals in anticipation of the requests he knew would be made through his commissaries. Flower traveled the country of the eastern mid-Atlantic working out production contracts and purchasing raw materials and some finished stores. These items were delivered to Gostelowe and Watkins, who supervised government workers manufacturing the military stores needed by the army. Lukens traveled the backcountry of Maryland and Pennsylvania (west to Pittsburgh, north to the Wyoming Valley, and south to the Shenandoah Valley) purchasing raw materials and finished goods for Carlisle. Sargent directed the production of goods by Coren and Irish's men, and stored goods purchased by Lukens. To access the items produced by Flower's department, Washington would send an order to Flower. Flower had two options: he could either direct the movement of supplies from Gostelowe's or Watkins's storehouses in Philadelphia, or he could pass the requisition on to Lukens in Carlisle. In either event, the commissaries would have workers pack up supplies and send them to the Main Army. Flower kept a detailed accounting of what stores were on hand, what was being produced at each arsenal site, and what was being purchased. When military stores arrived at the army's camp, they were turned over to a commissary of military stores. Eventually this was Samuel Hodgdon, whom Knox appointed to assist him and coordinate the brigade conductors. Hodgdon kept a camp magazine and distributed stores to brigade conductors who in turn distributed them to the troops. Rather than wait for the provinces or Congress to meet the needs of the troops sent to camp, by the middle of 1777, the army could request arms, ammunition, and artillery from Continental arsenals and storehouses.

While Flower was getting the DCGMS in order, Knox was mobilizing a separate arrangement of craft operations in the northern states. Knox knew immediately on reading his instructions that Brookfield was not suitable for an arsenal. He met with Washington and proposed instead that the second arsenal be built at Hartford, Connecticut. Brookfield, he said, was too far from major transportation routes and did not possess a watercourse powerful enough to support manufacturing.[19] Washington acceded to the recommendation and ordered Knox to Hartford to "contract for such buildings[,] materials[, and] Artificers as you think necessary for the Grand Continental Army and the northern army as well."[20] When Knox arrived in Hartford, however, he found labor rates and material prices too high to make construction there feasible. On his own initiative he traveled north up the Connecticut River to Springfield, Massachusetts, which he found "better suited for a laboratory and foundery than any other part of the New England States."[21] He wrote Washington that it was far enough up the river to be defensible, yet the river was wide enough for effective transportation. Copper, tin, and other materials, as well as labor, were also plentiful and less expensive than at Hartford. Rather than wait for congressional approval, Washington gave Knox orders to get construction under way in February 1777. Congress eventually gave its assent in April.[22] Oddly, Congress did not question Washington on the fact that he had ignored its directive that the northern arsenal answer to the commissary general of military stores. A situation therefore developed in which neither the commissary of military stores at Springfield nor the artificers at the post answered to Flower, though they were nominally part of his command. This came to haunt the post, as Knox became ever more focused on field command activities (as Congress believed he should have from the beginning).

As at Carlisle, responsibilities at Springfield Arsenal were divided between the work of the arsenal itself and the procurement of supplies and resources from the surrounding area. Command of the post was given to David Mason, a member of Knox's artillery regiment. A native of Massachusetts, Mason joined the Continental Artillery when it was first formed under Gridley. He stayed with the service when Knox took over and rose to the rank of major. He was promoted to lieutenant colonel in order to oversee Springfield. For direction of procurement, Knox and Washington turned to their former military stores commissary, Ezekiel Cheever. Washington directed Cheever to take command of operations at Springfield under Knox's direction as commissary of military stores at the post.[23] Recall that when the Main Army left Boston, Cheever had remained with the Massachusetts militia, but he later joined

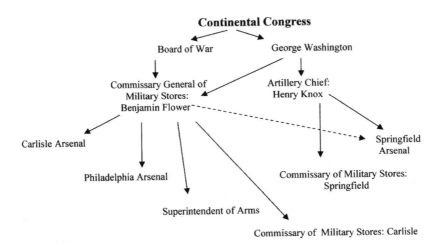

Structure of the Military Stores Management System, 1776.

the Continental Army as a staff member for the Eastern Department headquartered in Boston under General William Heath. Cheever coordinated the army's military stores purchasing, storage, and importation. By moving to Springfield, Cheever would specifically mobilize the Connecticut River valley region to support the war effort.

Cheever was given command at Springfield, but neither Washington nor Knox was clear in their orders on what that meant. This was a major problem. What happened at Springfield was that Cheever was never made aware that his position was equal to Gostelowe's and Lukens's positions. He assumed he commanded the Springfield Arsenal and was equal in stature to Flower. As we have seen, this was not the case. Theoretically at least, Cheever was to answer to Flower, but Washington had created two isolated supply systems by making Knox overseer of Springfield. Cheever was not dissuaded from his beliefs even when Knox appointed Mason as commander over the Springfield Arsenal and made the men partners in the procurement business. Until his resignation, Cheever operated under his command assumptions, and this led to a division of command at Springfield. Mason and Cheever seemed to have managed a working relationship; unfortunately, though, neither man fully understood what their command relationship was supposed to be. Both men hired their own set of artificers to work at the post. Both men purchased supplies and issued contracts. And ultimately, both men did the same job, though they were supposed to support each other in the manner that Lukens and Sargent did at Carlisle.[24] The result of the convoluted state of affairs at Springfield was that it took more effort than was necessary for the post to become half as productive as Carlisle or Philadelphia.

Despite the issues that eventually caused problems, the procurement of military stores and their shipment to the Main and Northern Armies proceeded apace at Springfield. As with Flower's operation, to get military stores for the army, Knox would contact Cheever or Mason with an order. Cheever, a military stores commissary, would either purchase the items needed, submit a request to the Springfield Arsenal for supplies, or have his workers manufacture the items. Mason would do likewise, though he did less regional purchasing than did Cheever. Cheever also purchased raw materials and finished components for the arsenal to use. Arsenal workers manufactured goods and stored them to fulfill requests made by Cheever. At camp, supplies would be distributed as has been discussed already.

Once the military stores system was in place, both Washington and the Board of War took opportunities to tweak and improve operations. The first major change was a personnel addition, the creation of a superintendent of arms to assist Flower with expert oversight of this area of operations. Before the position could benefit the DCGMS, however, it caused confusion as Congress, Washington, and Flower learned how to function together to make the military stores system work. Thomas Butler, a Baltimore gunsmith, was recommended to the Board of War as a master armorer. While Flower was in Carlisle setting up operations, the board appointed Butler superintendent of arms for the department "to prevent the abuses that have been so much practiced by Gunsmiths & others employ'd on the public Arms." What these abuses were is unclear, but when Flower returned to Philadelphia in mid-1777, he found orders waiting that all gun-making operations within the DCGMS were to be run through Butler. All weapons repaired or manufactured in Philadelphia and Carlisle had to either be done by Butler or inspected by him before they could be sent to the army.[25] This became a major headache.

Butler worked well with Flower for the first several months of their partnership. This changed in summer 1777, when the board told Washington to bypass Flower and send all repair orders to Butler, who was ordered to place himself at the general's disposal. This directive stemmed from Washington's wish to speed up the repair process. Butler took this to mean he was no longer answerable to Flower. The entire military stores system was then thrown into turmoil by the British attack on Philadelphia. Flower and Butler moved their operations first to Allentown and then to Lebanon, Pennsylvania. Butler then moved most of his work to Carlisle. Lukens began cooperating with Butler, giving him and his men a workshop at the arsenal and supplies for gun repair. Butler, however, failed to return any repaired muskets to Lukens, who reported to Flower that the armorer's men were rarely at work. Things then went from chaotic to bizarre as Butler began ignoring communications from Flower and the Board of War.[26]

The board attempted to explain Butler's behavior as extravagance, but in October 1777, Butler stopped answering Washington's messages. The board tried repeatedly to get information from Butler regarding his progress and the estimated repair capacity of his operations. Failing to hear anything, the board told Flower to settle accounts with Butler before doing any further work with him. Butler avoided Flower, who responded by traveling to York to get the board's approval to fire Butler.[27] The board, however, wrote to Flower, "We cannot think to discharge Butler until we have assurances of continued work by sufficient hands. He will continue until we can settle on a good footing."[28]

The board ordered Flower to help Butler do his work but also feel out the possibility of employing Butler's men directly. Butler's working relationship with the DCGMS, however, was at an end. Lukens refused to have anything further to do with Butler. He would not supply his men or send him more muskets to repair. Butler, on his end, would not return any muskets to the DCGMS unless Flower sent him an equal number to repair. Washington had had enough, and in March 1778 asked the board to fire Butler, which it did immediately. The board acted so quickly because it had found a more competent gunsmith in the person of William Henry of Lancaster. Henry was working for Pennsylvania by 1778 as the provincial superintendent of arms. His gun shop had been contracted to replace the provincial gunlock factory. The Board of War contracted Henry to be the Continental superintendent of arms as well but made it clear this time that Henry was answerable to Flower and part of his department. Henry was to inspect all arms repaired at the Carlisle and Philadelphia Arsenals prior to their return to camp. He accomplished this through a system of deputies at the arsenals.[29] Thus, despite a great deal of trouble, the board eventually augmented the military stores department with a competent superintendent of arms.

By summer 1777, Washington realized that though the DCGMS was an improvement, its operations were too distant from the army to supply daily needs. He wrote the Board of War explaining the situation: "If a small item in the [musket] lock breaks, we must return the gun to the Commissary of Military Stores and draw a new one." His solution was to reestablish a central commissary of military stories with the Main Army responsible for overseeing brigade armorers and conductors. Washington's plan seemed very similar to the framework Congress created for the army in 1775, except in this case, Knox had overall command of the military stores system in the army's camp. Flower was directed to supply the new army military stores commissary with traveling forges and proper stores with which to repair weapons and accouterments in the field. Washington appointed Samuel Hodgdon, a Philadelphia merchant, as commander of all commissaries in the field. This allowed brigade repair activities and the requisitions made of the arsenals to be channeled through one man. Hodgdon took direction of supplies with both the Main and the Northern Armies, overseeing their requisition from Flower's department and their distribution to the brigades.[30]

The board further supplemented the DCGMS by taking over several unproductive state and army operations and turning those activities over to Flower. It also authorized the employment of several assistants for Flower. Pennsylvania's brass furnace, where James Byers was working for the state at congressional expense, was destroyed by the British occupation of Philadelphia. The Board of War, therefore, took the opportunity to contract directly with Byers to rebuild the furnace and cast ordnance. The board then created a number of ancillary commissary positions to support Flower. A deputy commissary general position was created and assigned the task of managing the department from Philadelphia when Flower was away contracting or visiting his various command locations. A commissary was appointed at Boston to replace Cheever and purchase supplies that arrived at the port from France or on privateers. An arms repair facility built at Albany by General Schuyler was placed under Flower's command, and a commissary position was created to protect stores at Fort Pitt on the frontier. Another departmental agent was assigned to the Chesapeake region to purchase supplies there. Finally, the board instructed quartermasters at Carlisle and Philadelphia to take all measures possible to support the arsenals with wagons and horses for transport.[31] These many small modifications in 1777 and 1778, however, did not centralize the DCGMS command structure, which was still divided between Flower's operations, and Springfield's operations, and now had Hodgdon's command thrown into the mix.

Congress tried to centralize the DCGMS early in 1778, but it took a year of debate for the board and Washington to agree on the reforms Congress should implement. The DCGMS was a pawn in a political battle over control of the army fought by Washington and Congress. The primary sticking point among all parties was Knox. Washington was continually working to placate his friend and subordinate, whom he believed was invaluable to the army. But he also believed that Congress knew little about military policy and did not trust its judgment in military matters. In February 1778, Congress mandated that the commissary general of military stores control all aspects of weapons procurement and distribution, including Hodgdon's field commissary department.[32] This was difficult to implement because Knox refused to give up his oversight of Hodgdon's department. And Washington would not force him to hand over this responsibility. Knox wrote Washington missives similar to those written in 1776:

> I am, without any of the powers appertaining to the rank of commanding officer of artillery. . . . In all considerable armies in Europe a General officer has the command and direction of the artillery, and preparation of every thing appertaining to the ordnance department. . . . In the British service . . . the commander in chief of the artillery, has a Board of Ordnance over which he presides and regulates every thing relating to the artillery. [Yet] in the late regulations the commander of the artillery has no power to give . . . directions.[33]

Washington, too, was unhappy with the situation, telling Congress, "The armoury department is in as bad a situation as it can well be, and requires measures to . . . put it upon a proper footing."[34] Washington did not specify what the problems were in the department, but he complained to Congress again in August that there was great distress to the army from the commissary being independent of Knox's command. While Washington was willing to compromise with Congress in 1776, as the emergency situation of that period wore off, Washington again began promoting his artillery chief's plan. In his eyes, the military stores program was always just a half-step that did not fully live up to the ideal that he believed could be achieved if Congress would follow Knox's plan to the letter. Both Washington and Knox sought to extend the power of their commissary of military stores in the field as much as possible in order to force the DCGMS into subordination under the chief of artillery. As noted above, Washington appointed Hodgdon as principle commissary in the field. This was not only to assist the distribution process but also to challenge Flower's control of his own department. Despite Washington's cajoling, however, Congress and the Board of War adamantly refused to turn over command of military manufacturing to an officer who did not answer to them. Knox, similarly, would not turn over complete control of his operations to Flower, and Congress had no real interest in forcing him to do so. On his end, Flower had no ability to assume command of more than he already oversaw. As will be seen later in this chapter, he was in the midst of a protracted illness that eventually killed him.[35] But more impactful than all of these issues prohibiting change to the DCGMS was the command conflict that erupted between Washington and Congress in 1778.

During winter 1777–78, Washington and the board were at odds over the general's performance and his competence to command. This brought into question his judgment in the area of military manufacturing as well. Washington lost the battle at Brandywine in September 1777 and Germantown a month later. The British marched into Philadelphia in mid-October and secured control of most of southeastern Pennsylvania by November. All of Flower's operations in Philadelphia were thrown to the wind. The commissary general was forced to transfer men, materiel, and production operations to Pennsylvania's interior. If Washington believed he could control the DCGMS, Congress was doubtful he could even protect it. Meanwhile, General Gates had defeated the British at Saratoga and caused the British northern army to surrender. Washington's pride, image, and judgment were damaged.

Enter Thomas Conway, an arrogant Irishman in the French army who volunteered his services to the Continental Army in search of quick promotion. He used letters of introduction from the French government to mislead Congress into believing that by appointing him to a senior army post, the French government was likely to openly recognize American independence. Congress appointed Conway inspector general of the army in charge of developing drill and disciplinary parameters for the troops. Conway, however, only saw this position as a first step and believed he could secure a major generalship and field command for himself if he were able to replace Washington as head of the army with Gates. Gates, Conway believed, would be indebted to the Irishman and would reward him appropriately. Conway stirred up a hornet's nest of congressional intrigue in winter 1777–78, known as the Conway Cabal, in which Washington's reputation was undermined and his judgment questioned. Washington very nearly lost his command. Gates was made chairman of the Board of War and supervisor of military policy, a major challenge to Washington. Up to this point, the board had only been composed of and led by politicians. Washington, however, was too popular among certain elements of Congress and the army for Gates to wield real authority over military policy, and the power he was given was eventually quietly returned to Washington. Congress instructed Gates in mid-1778 that the board was only to advise Washington of congressional goals, while leaving military policy to the commander in chief. Washington and Gates built a working relationship that allowed Washington and the Board of War to coordinate their ideas and actions. Backbiting gave way to cooperation, and obstinacy gave way to compromise. By the end of 1778, Congress and Washington came to an agreement regarding how to effectively centralize and reform the DCGMS.

Congress passed a resolution on February 18, 1779, creating a system that reorganized and centralized the DCGMS. Flower's department continued to direct all arsenals and procurement. Springfield, including all artisans and military stores purchase operations, was officially placed under Flower's command. A new Field Commissary of Military Stores Department was created under Hodgdon. The commissaries of military stores with each army answered to him, as did all brigade conductors, who handled military stores distribution among individual army units.

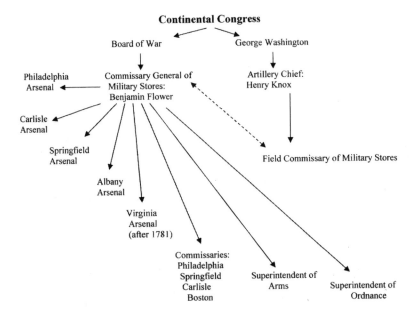

Structure of the Military Stores Management System, 1779.

Hodgdon received his funding and salary from Washington and was answerable to him through Knox. Flower became directly responsible to the Board of War with no secondary responsibilities to Washington as an army officer. Flower's department was now independent of the army, though he personally kept his rank. Knox was satisfied by regulations allowing military commanders to apply directly to Flower or the arsenals in case of emergency. Washington also placed Knox over the field commissary, and Knox was thus able to influence policy by determining the types, sizes, and quantities of stores that the field commissary requested from Flower. Since Flower responded to these requests when determining what the arsenals should make, Knox felt himself securely atop the chain of military stores command. Knox was also given influence over certain operations within Flower's department through the creation of a superintendent of artillery. This man, who was supposed to be appointed from the artillery service, was to inspect all ordnance, shot, and shells contracted for by Flower or his subordinates. As superintendent, this man would answer to Flower; as an artillery officer, he answered to Knox.[36] It was enough of a compromise to make Knox work within the system and not around it. In reality, however, Flower was the director of the department and overseer of all production.

The DCGMS had become a complex procurement agency by the end of 1779, built under the direction of Flower, Knox, Washington, and Congress. About four hundred men and women worked in the department as managers, laborers, craftsmen, and seamstresses.[37] There were two companies of artificers at Carlisle and a company of technicians in the laboratory making ammunition. Springfield had a company of artificers and a company of laboratory workers, while Albany also had a company of repairmen. Philadelphia had the most extensive production facilities. There was a company of artificers, an armory, two ammunition laboratories, a leather workshop, a drum workshop, an artillery yard, and an air furnace for brass work. Henry's operations in Lancaster amounted to another company of craftsmen in that city. In addition, Congress mandated the construction of a laboratory and repair facility in Westham, Virginia, to support the Southern Army. Artificers from Philadelphia and Carlisle were sent south under the command of Nathaniel Irish. That post operated through the end of the war, though it was interrupted by the British invasion of Virginia in 1781. At the same time that Flower directed public manufacturing operations, he also oversaw a cadre of six procurement commissaries in various locations as well as two inspectors. These men assisted private military stores producers by providing education on the proper construction of items as well as direction regarding what needed to be produced. Commissaries also purchased tools, raw materials, and components to assist the work of both public and private manufacturing operations. Thus, while departmental functionaries provided operational management of daily public and private manufacturing, the commissary general and regional commissaries provided strategic management over the whole system.[38]

Even as the DCGMS suffered through growing pains from 1777 to 1780, several unforeseen obstacles undermined the department's productive efforts until congressional bankruptcy in 1781 threatened the very continuation of government procurement efforts. Flower battled a protracted illness from 1778 until his death in 1781 that limited his ability to manage the DCGMS. Symptoms typical of tuberculosis struck Flower in January 1778, incapacitating him for the next six months. Cornelius Sweers, departmental bookkeeper, took over management of the department. At about the time Flower began to recover, Sweers was arrested for embezzlement and as a defense blamed Flower. Flower was consequently arrested by Congress in August 1778, and though only briefly imprisoned, it caused his sickness to return. Sweers was found guilty of misusing government funds and dismissed from service. He was eventually convicted of theft by Pennsylvania and imprisoned until after the war. Throughout this period, no effective accounting of the department's work was kept. James Pearson, who had been appointed a deputy commissary general of military stores, incompetently directed the department over the next six months. Pearson cared more about his title and impressing the Board of War than he did about managing the department. As a result, the various segments of the department operated independently with only loose oversight. Pearson did little actual work. He issued few orders and kept fewer records. He simply forwarded all orders for supplies from the field commissary to the various arsenal commanders and commissaries. Flower attempted to monitor departmental operations and tried to rectify Pearson's mistakes, but Pearson often ignored Flower's letters and refused to report in person to the commissary general. Flower, unfortunately, was too weak to travel to Pearson's office or in any other way impose his will on Pearson's activities. Flower did not return to active duty until well into 1779, when he was also promoted to full colonel. He managed the DCGMS through the balance of the year until he was again laid low by sickness. The Board of War stepped in at this point and on February 11, 1780, appointed Samuel Hodgdon assistant commissary general of military stores. Management of the department effectively passed to Hodgdon, though Flower remained the principal and occasionally exercised his authority. Flower took an extended leave of absence in summer 1780 to travel south to recover his health. He rebounded briefly but died on April 28, 1781. Flower's stubbornness was just as detrimental to the department as was his illness. Three men managed the department in Flower's name on three separate occasions because he refused to give up his position. As late as January 1781, he petitioned Congress for pay equal to his rank.[39] Thus, because Flower was too sick to do his job and too proud to resign, no one did his job effectively until Hodgdon was named his assistant. And even then, Flower did not give up complete control until he died, at which point Hodgdon became commissary general. Centralization of the department, and government manufacturing, was hindered as much as helped by Flower's participation. In at least one case, however, leadership further down the chain of command was no more stable than at the top.

Tensions resulting from the convoluted oversight of the post at Springfield undermined production at the site and nearly led to its closure. As mentioned earlier in this chapter, when Cheever was appointed commissary, Mason was appointed superintendent of the arsenal. Through 1777 and 1778, Cheever and Mason answered to Knox separately. Each hired his own set of artificers to work at the post. The men seem to have managed to work together, but neither understood what their command relationship was supposed to be. Since neither officer provided sufficient oversight to the post as a whole, discipline broke down. Their men began stealing small quantities of powder and other accouterments to sell in town. They also stole rations and hired their relatives to work at the post. Though the men involved were court-martialed and dismissed, the whole affair disrupted production at Springfield.[40]

The most serious problems at Springfield started when Flower took over direct command of the post at the end of 1778. Flower sent another company of artificers to work at Springfield, and they answered to Cheever, which threw off the balance of power. Mason attempted to exercise complete control over the post, and Cheever pulled rank as the local commissary of military stores answerable to Flower. The men and their company commanders took sides in the argument, and the two commanders forsook necessary production in order to secure advantages over one another. Cheever used his men to produce unnecessary quantities of accouterments to make himself look good, while Mason's men produced household items for his family. Flower, beset by illness, did nothing, and when Hodgdon became commissary, he was constrained by the fact that Cheever would not recognize his authority. The selectmen of Springfield were so upset at the state of affairs that they asked the state to investigate. The investigation found that Mason was abusing his position and had been derelict in his duty. The state government asked Congress to address the situation.[41]

In 1779, the Board of War sent an artillery officer to Springfield to determine what was going on and what should be done. John Lamb, the investigator, found that production at the post was almost at a standstill because, "The men that have superintendence here are not capable of that position."[42] He found that the militia serving as guards continually took stores, workers lived in private homes, and children were employed as craftsmen. There was no discipline, no productivity, and no benefit to the Continental Army from the site. The board reported to Congress that Springfield "has long been so very ill conducted that the benefits derived from it have been very inadequate to the expense of supporting it."[43] Lamb believed, however, that the circumstances could be turned around if useless officers were dismissed or reassigned and a proper number of public buildings were constructed.[44] These changes were integrated into Congress's reform of the whole DCGMS in 1780 as part of its cost-cutting measures. One year, though, had been wasted at the site because of a confused command structure and the failure of Washington or the Board of War to fix it.

Insufficient funds became the DCGMS's next major obstacle, and the one that hit it the hardest. Operations in the department—hindered by a sickly commander, a confused command structure, and command infighting—were just being put on a sound footing in early 1780 when financial disaster struck. Congress had funded the war largely by printing paper money, which had no intrinsic value save public faith that Congress would eventually exchange it for specie (gold). By 1779, Congress had printed $226 million, an amount far in excess of what the public believed Congress could ever convert to specie. Inflation followed each new printing of money. In January 1780, William Henry claimed that $1,000 in paper money could get him only $34 in specie. Congress's cash had lost 97 percent of its value. The situation was worse in other parts of the nation; $1 in specie traded for more than $100 in paper. Congress decided in March 1780 to repudiate its debt and offered to exchange all old paper currency for a new paper currency at a rate of forty old-emission dollars for one new-emission dollar. The new emission notes paid interest until their eventual conversion to specie, which helped them hold value somewhat better than their predecessors. Unfortunately for the staff departments, Congress also halted all currency printing and began relying on state contributions to the Treasury to pay its bills. As a consequence, the staff departments were ordered to cut spending and trim their rosters as much as possible to save money.[45]

The 1780 streamlining of the DCGMS had three main components, which were planned and executed by Hodgdon. First, unnecessary officers were relieved of duty. The entire command staff at Springfield was dismissed and replaced by one man. Lukens was dismissed as commissary at Carlisle, and Sargent took over his responsibilities in addition to those he already held. The artificer companies at Philadelphia were merged into one and the extra company commander relieved. The second step taken by the department was to return the Philadelphia air furnace to its owner, though this did not happen for three years. Hodgdon estimated it was cheaper to construct a government-owned brass furnace and rely on the government furnace already in operation in Carlisle. Finally, most operations at Philadelphia were transferred to Carlisle. Labor prices in the capital were judged to be too high, and the board saw no reason to continue renting buildings in Philadelphia when it already owned several in Carlisle. Hodgdon was ordered to pack up all military stores as tightly as possible, send all tools to Carlisle, and give up as many rented buildings as he could. Philadelphia would be no more than an issuing post for military stores; Carlisle was to be the nation's military manufacturing center. The DCGMS also saved money because it had no money to spend, a situation that forced cost-cutting measures. By 1780, about half of all artificer enlistments expired, and Hodgdon had no money to pay reenlistment bounties. As a result, about half the department's workers were not reenlisted, which saved money on salaries and provisions. By early 1781, the DCGMS was half the size it had been in 1779 and commanded by a third fewer officers.[46]

Hodgdon faced an overwhelming need for cash during his first year as manager of the department of military stores and an even more overwhelming lack of it. Just to keep the department running, Hodgdon estimated he needed $1.38 million in new paper. Knox called for an additional $5.1 million in spending for more ordnance and ammunition.

Moreover, the department entered the year nearly $4.2 million in debt to ironmasters who had already contracted for shot, shell, and artillery.[47] "We have money," wrote Hodgdon to his departmental paymaster, "but not a great deal."[48] Congress had provided for Hodgdon by issuing a $1 million warrant on the Continental loan office in Pennsylvania, but that office could not meet the request.[49] By mid-year, Hodgdon and his department were in dire straits. "I must renew my calls for your attention to my department's distress for want of money," he wrote to the board in early August.[50] The problem could not be ignored two weeks later when Washington ordered five hundred muskets, which could not be provided because there was no money to pay the men to fix them.[51]

The board transmitted Hodgdon's pleas for money to Congress, as well as an observation of the consequences. The report stated that "the whole [military stores] department for some time past . . . has not been productive of those advantages, which might have been expected, if it had been sufficiently supplied with money."[52] The men had been working patiently for more than a year as their pay fell into arrears and then depreciated beyond usefulness. Most simply wanted sufficient food, but this was unavailable because of the breakdown of the Quartermaster Department in 1780. "The men in my department are exceedingly upset," wrote Hodgdon to Congress, "some to the point of resignation."[53] Money was not available for the quartermaster and DCGMS because the states had not paid their budgetary quotas, according to Robert Morris, Congress's superintendent of finance. And Congress had no independent money-raising power. In such a situation, the national debt got worse rather than better. By October, the Board of War notified Congress that its debt to ironmasters had doubled to nearly $10.6 million.[54] Yet despite the distress, the department trudged along through Hodgdon's resourcefulness.

Hodgdon improvised a number of ways to pay his department's bills and support its creditability. Though his department had only a small amount of cash when 1781 began, Hodgdon paid out small sums to those owed money in proportion to how much they were owed. He also promised to make such payments whenever he received even the smallest amount of money from the Treasury. He then began paying ironmasters in iron. The department had broken ordnance and cast iron it had contracted for earlier in the war. These items Hodgdon traded to ironmasters in exchange for steel or shot and shell. In the case of the Durham Iron Works and Colebrookdale Furnace, Hodgdon traded up to ten tons of iron for one ton of steel. The Board of War assisted by providing interest on all debts not paid within six months. In this way, Hodgdon was able to provide his workers with materials for repairing muskets and accouterments, at the same time establishing a working relationship with the ironmasters. The ironmasters who were owed great amounts of money were consistently willing to work with Hodgdon because he provided something rather than nothing and proved his dedication to paying off debts as quickly as possible. To provision his men and secure transport, Hodgdon also traded commodities to the Quartermaster Department. The department had artificers of its own, and when those men needed supplies, quartermasters offered to trade wagons or horse teams to Hodgdon in exchange for supplies. Hodgdon was thus able to move necessary weapons to the army at a time when transportation was difficult to procure from the Quartermaster Department. Finally, Hodgdon pleaded with the Board of War and the superintendent of finance for even small amounts of cash to pay and provision his men.[55] This he was usually able to receive. With small payments of cash, commodities, or promises, Hodgdon kept a revolving system of debt operational until the department was demobilized.

Seventeen-eighty-one was a banner year for the DCGMS and exemplified how operations were continued despite challenging command situations. Beset by the looming death of its primary officer, haunted by the corruption of a secondary officer, and plagued by the government's bankruptcy, the DCGMS not only completed a total overhaul of the Main Army's weapons supply but provided materiel for Nathaneal Greene's Southern Army and the Yorktown Campaign as well. Through 1780 and 1781, the artificers of the DCGMS received weapons from the various divisions of the Main Army, cleaned and repaired them, and reissued them. Philadelphia Arsenal alone received 5,292 muskets for repair and issued 6,425 new and repaired muskets back to the Main Army. At the same time, armorers supplied the Southern Army with 4,079 muskets. A majority of those weapons were used to reequip the Southern Army after the surrender at Charleston, and the balance were used to reequip it again after the Battle of Guilford Courthouse. The DCGMS also supplied over four thousand weapons to Maryland and Virginia to face various British invasions. Perhaps the most important job done by the military department was its movement of equipment south for the attack on the British southern army of Lieutenant General Charles Cornwallis at Yorktown. Not only did the department equip troops as they marched through Philadelphia, but Hodgdon had every available accouterment and piece of artillery prepared for shipping. Thirty-one additional pieces of artillery and all related stores, along with all the necessary ammunition, were sent with the field commissary to join the army on its way to Yorktown.[56] The DCGMS provided each and every one of the 2,337 shot and shells fired by the Americans at the British during the siege there.

The Board of War continued to prune unnecessary men and operations from the DCGMS as 1781 ended. It was helped in this process by the arrival of a significant number of military supplies from France and the victory at Yorktown. Hodgdon was ordered to survey his department and make recommendations for limiting its operations. He recommend-

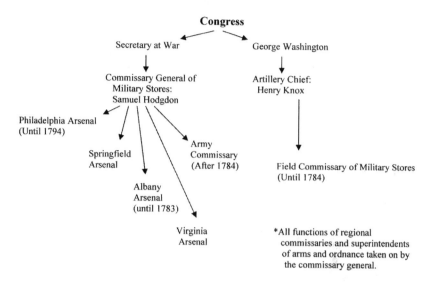

Structure of the Military Stores Management System, 1782.

ed eliminating the commissary position in Philadelphia, held by Gostelowe, because he felt the commissary general could fulfill that position himself. He believed that Springfield should continue, as it had been reformed the previous year, but entered into a debate with the board over the future of Carlisle. Since Philadelphia's operations had been moved to Carlisle, the labor and material cost benefits had been countered by transportation difficulties from such a remote post. The board, therefore, wanted to move all operations back to Philadelphia and close Carlisle. The Yorktown Campaign, however, breathed new life into the post in central Pennsylvania, and it remained in operation into 1782. Thereafter Springfield and Philadelphia served as the nation's military manufacturing centers. The board also initiated a budgetary process on the recommendation of the superintendent of finance. Beginning in 1780, all spending requisitions made to the board had to be made with cost estimates so the superintendent could better track expenses and refuse any he found frivolous. While this limited Hodgdon's options, it did cut spending and forced him to contract out musket repair work. Artificers were used primarily for construction projects at Springfield, ammunition production, and accouterment production. The vast stores taken from the British after their surrender, however, meant that further production by America's arsenals or private contractors would be unnecessary. The armament's situation improved even more when in November 1781,

Structure of the Military Stores Management System, 1784–1794.

great amounts of military supplies arrived from France. Hodgdon was ordered to store these supplies for future eventualities and sell the extra. The military supply situation had reversed itself. Knox and Washington hoped to launch an attack on New York City using the stores captured from the British and provided by the French, but further large-scale operations were postponed when word reached the nation in 1782 that the British were interested in negotiating peace. American artificers were no longer as necessary as they had been. Hodgdon released men from duty, retaining only one company of fifty men split between Philadelphia and Springfield to provide ammunition and fatigue duties. His staff included only himself, two deputies, and three laboratory directors.[57] The DCGMS was a shadow of its 1779 size.

Congress created the position of secretary at war with the intention that the man appointed to serve would streamline military operations. The Board of War was replaced in October 1781 with a war secretary, to whom Congress delegated many decisions because it did not know how best to structure the army for peace. Benjamin Lincoln, who was elected to the post of war secretary, proved a capable administrator. Lincoln is often remembered only ignominiously as the general who surrendered the American Southern Army at Charleston. Time has obscured the fact Lincoln was one of the finest administrative generals in the revolution and, by 1781, one of the most experienced. Lincoln had served with Washington in New York, Gates at Saratoga, and as southern commander in 1779 and 1780, before becoming Washington's second in command at Yorktown. He knew the American military better then perhaps anyone else among the senior officers. Lincoln's first task as secretary was to prepare a report to Congress that proved the need to support peacetime domestic manufacturing in the hands of the DCGMS. The nation,

Lincoln said, would be defenseless without a professional administration to care for and procure the army's weapons. This was a lesson learned by the nation in 1776, and it should not, he said, be forgotten. Lincoln presented a proposal to Congress for a redesigned DCGMS.[58] Congress accepted the plan, and it served the nation's military from 1784 until 1794.

Lincoln instituted four major changes to the DCGMS. First, he initiated a program of continual repair, cleaning, and repackaging of stored materiel in order to keep it prepared for action. This was organized around a system of contract labor centered on an arsenal at Springfield and magazines in Philadelphia and Virginia. Second, he ordered the construction of a national brass ordnance foundry so that the United States could provide its own artillery. Third, he eliminated the field commissary department and made the commissary of military stores with the army answerable to the commissary general of military stores. Finally, the superintendents of arms and ordnance positions, as well as all subordinate commissary positions, were eliminated and their functions devolved on Hodgdon and the superintendent of the Springfield Arsenal. Under this system, Hodgdon directly oversaw all stores contracting and procurement.[59]

THE DEPARTMENT OF THE COMMISSARY GENERAL OF MILITARY STORES evolved during the revolution as lessons were learned regarding the effectiveness of command structures. Initially, Congress's reliance on the provinces for supplies precluded the need for a centralized military stores system. Washington was only able to control military stores once they reached his camp. The inconsistency of provincial supplies, however, made it apparent that the government's commissary of military stores should have responsibility for operations away from camp as well. Thus, the DCGMS was created and given charge over all the government's weapons manufacturing and procurement operations. Congress, however, failed to delineate the chains of command in the new department, and Washington disbursed responsibilities for procurement to his artillery chief and the commissary general. In attempting to improve the situation, Washington then created a military stores care system at his camp that answered only to Knox. Military stores procurement had become a beast with two heads.

By 1779, procurement was centralized in the hands of the commissary general. Washington realized that he needed artificers at the front as much as he needed them at secure centralized posts removed from the fighting. He also found that the organization of these functions as they stood in 1778 was unacceptable. The result was the separation of military stores functions into the Commissary of Military Stores Department and the Field Commissary of Military Stores Department. The 1779 reform of the departmental system formally organized a clear channel for requisitioning, manufacturing, and supplying military stores that had developed over the previous year. Thereafter, the DCGMS managed all the government's procurement operations, overcoming corruption, leadership failures, and bankruptcy to do so.

The war's end brought further changes to the DCGMS. Congress was forced to streamline operations and eliminate personnel from the department as a result of budgetary constraints and the declining need for military stores. Benjamin Lincoln formulated a plan for military stores procurement that made the department critical in the postwar nation. He redesigned it and proved to Congress that it should be used to keep the nation prepared for future conflicts. Preparing for the war's end, Congress did what it usually did: legislate a solution after military stores personnel had worked out the problem themselves.

Congress legislated the centralization of procurement in 1776 but left the creation of procurement processes to men like Washington, Knox, Flower, Hodgdon, and Lincoln, as well as their subordinates. Thus, throughout the history of the military stores bureaucracy, it was individual initiative that drove the department. Nevertheless, the system managed government workers and private manufacturers, coordinating the integration of public and private operations to achieve the large-scale production of military stores. But how did these men, and Congress for that matter, know what steps to take to organize production and mobilize manufacturing? The Industrial Revolution had to be imported from the Old World.

3

"On the same plan as . . . Woolwich"

ADOPTING THE INDUSTRIAL REVOLUTION

IN AMERICA

L IEUTENANT COLONEL DAVID MASON KEPT A JOURNAL THROUGHOUT his service in the Revolutionary War. After being passed down through his family, the small book was given to the Massachusetts Historical Society, where it still resides. Mason's name appears nowhere on the book, and it is only through the family that it was identified. Made of cloth paper, it has a hand-sewn binding and a nondescript, unlettered cover. The corners of the book are upturned, and there are numerous cracks around the page edges making it difficult to leaf through. The journal is visibly fragile, but to the touch it is in remarkably good condition for its age and its usage. Moving from page to page, it becomes apparent that Mason kept this book with him at all times, but he did not use the journal to record events and thoughts; it was not a diary. Instead, it was Mason's memo book, notebook, and scratch tablet. Chronologically, the first notation came in 1775, when Mason joined the Massachusetts militia. He skipped several pages into the book and listed a receipt for some items and an outline of the structure of a battalion. More receipts are listed a few pages later, and a few pages after that there are some pay notations and artillery measurements. Over time the blank pages were filled in with more artillery measurements, details of equipment production, and the records of his soldiers' pay. He took time to list the names of those with whom he worked or those he commanded. He listed the back pay owed his men and purchase orders he had issued to suppliers. Mason occasionally listed random facts and figures, important information that he did not want to forget. Hidden among this randomness and the unobtrusiveness of the book itself is the fact that Mason's scribbling reveals one way Americans imported the ideas of the Industrial Revolution in order to design their own manufacturing processes.

Neither David Mason nor many of his artisan compatriots were knowledgeable enough to build the type of processes necessary to provide the tens of thousands of items needed by the Continental Army. The type of large-scale production that could produce the volume of stores required by the army did not exist in the United States, but the ideas of how to accomplish large-scale production were available. People who had achieved this type of production were also available. And examples of such production had come and gone in the colonies in the decade prior to the revolution. In Mason's case, to achieve successful production, he turned to the most innovative manufacturing theories available in print, those of John Muller. Muller was the English world's foremost theorist on military mathematics, weapons, and ammunition production and was a professor at Britain's Woolwich Arsenal Artillery Academy. Muller's treatises provided analysis of how military stores should be produced, focusing on how uniformity of production could achieve uniformity of results on the battlefield. Those treatises had become available in colonial America and were sold at, among other places, Henry Knox's bookstore and were part of the collection of lending libraries like the Library Company of Philadelphia. Mason's journal was riddled with production parameters and measurement tables copied directly from Muller's *Treatise on Artillery*. Mason used the ideas outlined by Muller to guide his artificers in the production of stores at Springfield. He coordinated the labor of his men in ways that made them more productive than they would have been separately. And he organized the arsenal in a way that facilitated how the men worked together.

Mason's activities were just one of the ways the American Revolution facilitated the transfer of the ideas of the Industrial Revolution from the Old World to the New. Continental officials also relied on immigrants, newspapers, personal military experience, and failed American experiments to learn how to best innovate manufacturing to make it more efficient and productive. More importantly, the revolution gave artisans and commanders an arena to experiment with new production ideas, labor organizations, technologies, and resources. The revolution pulled together different strands of cutting-edge technological knowledge into useable, adaptable American forms.[1]

The traditional understanding of the Industrial Revolution has been that it followed a specific course of mechanical adaptations that turned craft shops into factories. This traditional analysis came from Adam Smith and Karl Marx, who, writing in the midst of these developments, saw only a progressive pattern of specialization and mechanization that led ultimately to the factory: industrialization. Later historians traced the evolution of the factory, showing how the organization of labor around machines led to more and more automation and larger and larger automated systems, until the assembly line was born. In this version of the story, large workshops were built and owned by wealthy entrepreneurs who organized their workers based on a fixed daily wage. Wage labor was born. Those entrepreneurs, be they merchants, bankers, or some type of early venture capitalists, were known as factors. They invested in the centralization of work location and labor system as a way of lowering input costs and increasing output. Slowly, centralized sites that were still segregated by specific production task were organized under a single roof; the factory was born. Factories could make more products more cheaply than previously were assembled in craft shops. The advent of industrial machinery made the shift to factories more desirable because machinery could be centralized around a power source (water or steam), and workers could be centralized around the machinery. This has been the story of industrialization, despite the fact that the assembly line was far removed from the inauguration of the Industrial Revolution. Changes in labor, wages, and organization all happened because of the rise of machines.

Recent historians, however, have questioned this and shown that during the period of the Industrial Revolution from the late 1600s to the mid-1800s, mechanization was not always the motivation behind industrial development, and not all industrial development led to the factory. The transition from craft shops to factory production was a long and complicated process that included various developments that did not survive competition with the factory paradigm. There were other options available to factors wishing to develop production efficiency without factory production or mechanization. To understand the impact of the American Revolution on the nation's economy, it is necessary to divorce the concepts of manufacturing and mechanization. Manufacturing was the large-scale fabrication of goods by hand or with simple machines that enhanced human labor. Mechanization was the use of machines to replace human labor. Both types of production existed within the industrialization process, and both types took on numerous forms.

The eighteenth century was a period of manufacturing transitions that saw various production methods. "Putting out systems coexisted with artisan and cooperative forms of production," historian Maxine Berg wrote in 1994, "and all these systems frequently interacted with some type of manufacture or proto-industry."[2] Putting-out was a process and organizational form that led directly to factories within the textile industry. Factors bought materials from various sources and distributed the materials to various women in their employ. These women did the work in their houses and produced (or put-out) finished goods. Factors created systems of working women who turned cotton into thread, thread into cloth, and cloth into clothing. Eventually, these operations were all brought together under one roof and mechanized. Craft specialization, also known as centralized manufacturing, emerged as the most serious competitor to the use of the putting-out system and machine technology in the production of finished products in Europe. Installing skilled management over laborers and their work systems increased the output of craft production. Private manufacturers appointed managers over their operations and implemented production control systems to improve efficiency. European governments also adopted craft specialization and instituted systems to coordinate various elements of military manufacturing operations. The result in both cases was a limited division of labor and increased reliance on managerial oversight of production.[3]

Centralized manufacturing developed in Europe because of rising prices for labor, raw materials, and power sources. Craftsmen needed to find ways of economizing in order to survive among the growing power of factors. They discovered that "larger scale workshops and small factories yielded economies of scale at even such low threshold levels as 6 to 15 employees due to a division of hand performed tasks . . . and a more disciplined work force."[4] Master craftsmen and entrepreneurs realized that by gathering workers together in one place they saved on raw material costs, rents, and transportation. Such savings were relative to having craftsmen work in isolated shops in separate locations. Larger numbers of employees led to greater output, which in turn led to a greater volume of sales, all at lower costs. Blacksmith shops gave way to furnace plantations employing various craftsmen to finish cast iron products and use iron in their items. In Britain's most famous example, Josiah Wedgwood gathered skilled and unskilled labor around his pottery kilns. By doing this, Wedgwood could provide materials and kiln space to various artisans to produce various types of pottery for multiple markets.

Ken Alder identified how efficiency could develop by centralizing craftsmen at a single location. Alder's work *Engineering the Revolution* explored how gunsmiths working in proximity to the French Royal Armory at Saint-Etienne developed, over time, a limited division of labor. This city of blacksmiths, gunsmiths, carpenters, and ironmongers made its livelihood from contracts with the French government. The whole city was an industrial center that employed craft specialization of musket manufacturing in order to take advantage of contracts that arrived from the royal government. Craftsmen bid with the government to contract for the manufacture of items they believed they could produce at a particular time. Gunsmiths might shift from making locks to barrels and purchase the locks from another smith in town in order to secure a specific contract. This taught craftsmen how to be flexible and innovative in production. The government used contracts to coordinate production for a better end result, learning over time how to efficiently contract out the production of musket components and have their armorers assemble the muskets in the armory. A gunsmith, rather than making a single weapon, was contracted by the government to focus on one component, for instance a trigger or a main spring. Another gunsmith was contracted to make musket stocks, and so on. In the end, government workers assembled the various pieces.[5] From 1765 to 1773, the craftsmen at Saint-Etienne produced an average of twenty thousand muskets per year. But developments in France went further than unorganized and semiorganized cooperation among craftsmen.

Jean-Baptiste Gribeauval was a French artillery officer and champion of innovation within his country's royal army. He and adherents of his ideas attempted to introduce interchangeable parts manufacture to the production of artillery and muskets for the army. Alder saw in this process an engineering revolution that rivaled technological developments in the British Industrial Revolution. Rather than use machines to produce more efficiently, Gribeauval envisioned a series of gauges and universal production specifications that craftsmen throughout France could use to produce items for the army. Working from the same patterns, craftsmen created items that could be fit together without regard to who had produced them. Such an interchangeable system allowed the army to repair arms and artillery more quickly and put weapons into service more quickly from a store of random components. Gribeauval had no intention of replacing traditional craft production. He wanted the government to coordinate that production more fully for a better end result. Such coordination, however, was unwelcome among France's independent-minded craftsmen and did not take hold. Alder's description of centralized arms production is the best example available of how armory and artillery operations were carried on at the American arsenals during the revolution, despite the fact that France had only a slight influence on American manufacturing organization during the war. Instead, it was British protoindustrialization activities that influenced Americans.

Maxine Berg found alternatives to factory industrialization in Britain similar to those found by Alder in France. In Birmingham, for instance, artisans cooperated to build a centralized processing center for brass and copper, which in turn supplied the city's artisans with the specialized pieces they needed to complete their products. Berg found this system comparable to what watchmakers did elsewhere in Britain, contracting out to other artisans for specialized parts and pieces, which they then fit together into a whole product. It was in British gun making that she saw "an extensive division of labor elaborated within a structure of small scale units of production."[6] In these cases, what can be called a managing gun maker purchased a central shop and either subcontracted finishers or hired them outright. He then supplied the finishers with purchased parts like barrels, locks, triggers, ramrods, and bayonets from other independent manufacturers. This flexible system allowed production to increase during periods of high demand and kept large groups of skilled craftsmen employed during periods of low demand. Artisans used market forces to specialize their own work within a region with other craftsmen for greater efficiency in producing final products. Flexible specialization also developed in Britain because, "Small producers offered economic advantages of creativity, nimbleness and easy entry; they could . . . easily change across products and activities, as well as skill-intensive processes and a range of product choices for localized and regional tastes."[7] British artisanal production developed into centralized cooperatives. This was exactly the kind of production occurring in Saint-Etienne.

The British military, like its French counterpart, adopted the ideas of centralized craft production in the latter half of the eighteenth century. The Woolwich Arsenal eventually became Britain's premier manufactory for artillery and ammunition, but early in the eighteenth century it was simply "a collection of garden workshops . . . each self-contained within its walls."[8] Blacksmiths made parts for carriages made by carpenters for cannons being made by brass founders. All the items were deposited at the arsenals' storehouses and assembled when needed. Meanwhile, laborers assembled artillery ammunition in the post laboratory. There was no coordination of activity among arsenal craftsmen whose shops were located randomly around the arsenal compound. A building plan was instituted in 1717 to make Woolwich a "convenient place near the metropolis, where production, proof, inspection, and storage could be grouped in one spot." The building process took roughly four years and coincided with the creation of the Royal Regiment of Artillery; the goal being for the military to coordinate production to provide "a steady flow of [military] equipment" from a "national factory." The "Great Pile of Buildings" constructed at Woolwich was extensive in its scope. Smith shops, an engraving house, and a new brass foundry surrounded an Artificers' Court. At a distance from the foundry were a "collection of toolsmiths' shops with their crude machines, [forming] the mechanical engineering nucleus of [Woolwich's] technical activities." Despite all the developments in production infrastructure, several factors limited productive growth at Woolwich. First, the men hired to run the site reverted to their craft roots and failed to encourage cooperative production. Second, the artillery service made little investment in understanding the activities involved in producing their weapons. Together, those led to the third factor, which was that most arsenal work was actually contracted out to local craftsmen.[9] Since neither the producers nor the managers wanted innovation, it failed to develop.

The Royal Laboratory at Woolwich, c. 1777. First constructed in 1696, the laboratory was used for the invention and development of weapons. By 1777, the facility and surrounding land covered 104 acres and employed more than 400 persons. (*National Maritime Museum, London*)

Just over twenty years after construction of the Artificers Court and the mechanical shops, the artillery regiment finally took an interest in applying scientific principles to its own activities and the production taking place at Woolwich. In 1741, the regiment received permission to create a Royal Academy at Woolwich to train artillery officers in the science of ballistics as well as the proper use of artillery. As officers began to graduate from the artillery program, their greater numbers and the presence on campus of such men as John Muller led the service to reexamine the production processes at Woolwich. In 1749, the British ordnance department began another building program that transformed military stores production at the arsenal. The department built two central craft shops. One was a large compound that contained blacksmith, carpenter, and armory shops so they could assist each other in the completion of carriages and weapons for the ordnance department. The arsenal's chief storekeeper was assigned to oversee these operations and coordinated their work. Next to the storekeeper's shops was a laboratory that manufactured artillery ammunition by coordinating the work of carpenters, smiths, and unskilled labor.[10] Military stores manufacturing evolved from a collection of individual craft shops into two organized craft production facilities. And it was these facilities that were referenced by Muller in his books on artillery and mathematics. Woolwich became a production powerhouse for the British military despite the fact that it did not introduce mechanization until well into the nineteenth century.

When challenged to build a national manufacturing infrastructure and mobilize private craft industries, the Continental Congress and military stores administrators had to decide which production systems could best increase the output of a nation of farmers, craftsmen, and unskilled laborers. The Industrial Revolution that Americans saw as they looked to Europe for innovative ideas was not one of static production concepts. Industrialization in the eighteenth century was an open field of competing ideas regarding labor organization and machine use. Factories gathered unskilled workers under one roof to operate machinery for the production of goods. Protofactories brought skilled workers and semiskilled workers together in a single location to produce items, either with or without machines. In the case of both factories and protofactories, managers were used to oversee and direct production. Centralized manufacturing or craft specialization were very similar to protofactories, but they made use of more levels of management, and operations could be spread out over a larger physical area than could be done in a protofactory. Craft specialization stayed truer to traditional craft operations than did protofactories, and this made sense in many industries. There were also putting-out operations in this mix of labor activities. Putting-out labor was organized like a factory, but the workers were physically spread out, often working in their own homes to produce goods for finishing at a factory or protofactory. Each of these production methods had their advantages and disadvantages when applied to the production of various goods, and investors often experimented with several methods.[11]

The Committee at Camp and the congressmen who drew on Henry Knox's ideas for designing the commissary of military stores were well versed in the dynamics of the Industrial Revolution when they set their minds to putting the nation's economy on a war footing. The committee consisted of three men: Elbridge Gerry of Massachusetts, Francis Lewis of New York, and Roger Sherman of Connecticut. All were experienced merchants who had at one time owned and managed mercantile houses. Gerry came from a wealthy family, was well educated, and had engaged in his family's trade business only briefly before entering politics. Lewis had the most commercial acumen, having run stores in New York City and Philadelphia, as well as securing a contract to clothe the British army in America during the French and Indian War. Moreover, Lewis was a Welsh immigrant who had worked in a London counting house. Sherman brought a craftsman's eye to understanding the army's needs. He apprenticed as a cobbler before becoming a storeowner and surveyor. Together, these men knew how to interpret Knox's plans and understood the impact they could have on supplying the Continental Army. Others in Congress late in 1776 also understood the military supply issues under discussion. Nine congressmen in addition to Sherman had artisanal backgrounds, including George Taylor, a Pennsylvania ironmaster whose furnace eventually supplied the DCGMS. Four congressmen had led troops in battle prior to the revolution, and John Alsop, like Francis Lewis, had contracted to supply the British army with clothing during the French and Indian War. Some congressmen were manufacturing promoters, including Benjamin Rush and Stephen Hopkins. Rush led the effort to charter the United Company of Philadelphia, the city's first textile proto-factory, and Hopkins was part owner of Rhode Island's Hope Furnace, which also supplied the DCGMS.[12] Aside from these men with direct manufacturing connections, the members of the Continental Congress were some of the most educated men of their generation and partook in the exchange of ideas across the Atlantic.

Information for educating Continental leaders about the innovations available for increasing the productivity of craft industries abounded in America. Americans knew about European industrial developments through the expertise brought by immigrants to the colonies, and colonial print media were awash in information about manufacturing. Moreover, American and European entrepreneurs had attempted to produce textiles, ironwork, glass, and pottery using European industrial examples. Nine of the men who signed the Declaration of Independence were immigrants to what became the United States. Thirteen congressmen had either studied in Europe or traveled extensively there. Colonial leaders had seen the Industrial Revolution and brought back stories of how America could benefit from European industrial ideas. Moreover, when the revolution began, Europeans arrived with ideas for how to transform American manufacturing. French army officers Louis Lebègue dePresle Duportail and Philippe Charles Tronson du Coudray brought extensive military manufacturing knowledge with them when they arrived to fight for American independence. Information about manufacturing was also widespread through written resources. Bookstores and lending libraries contained vivid accounts of innovation, and newspapers reported on European manufacturing. Benjamin Franklin's *Pennsylvania Gazette*, for example, reported routinely about the activities taking place at Woolwich. Examples of manufacturing innovations also abounded in America for congressmen to glean knowledge from when creating the military stores department, and they put those influences to good use. Examples of protofactory and coordinated production existed in the colonies when the war broke out, though none had reached the complexity of European models. The United Company was the most extensive operational manufacturing example available in 1776, but ironworks were also prevalent across the colonies, and they displayed the potential of large-scale craft operations.

The United Company of Philadelphia was the enterprise that came closest to importing British ideas of factory development to America. The primary impetus behind the United Company enterprise came from Americans, and European immigrants, interested in importing European manufacturing. The company's director, Christopher Marshall, wrote that the "Almighty . . . seems to have cast among us a great number of persons who are acquainted with manufacturing. [T]he public state of affairs now speaks with the voice of a trumpet, 'Americans, manufacture for yourselves.'"[13] Marshall, like most of his native-born colleagues on the board of directors, was a merchant who understood the value of producing in America the goods formerly imported from Europe. Four of the first thirteen directors of the company's board were from Europe, however; two from Britain and two from Germany. These men clearly had an influence on the company's operations, as the two British directors were constant companions of director Marshall. The company's advertisement for stock sales expressed to all what Marshall had spoken in private. "As the establishing of Manufactories among ourselves must be of great advantage to the Public, it is hoped that every friend of his country will endeavour to promote [this] plan."[14] But the loudest voice of support behind this manufacturing venture was a founder who spoke eloquently about the need to bring European ideas of production to North America. Addressing the first shareholders meeting on March 16, 1775, Benjamin Rush said, "Manufacturers, next to agriculture, are the basis of the riches of every country. By establishing manufactories [of our own] we . . . invite timid manufacturers to come in. It might afford us . . . new sources of happiness . . . to . . . their settlement in our country."[15] If Americans used European ideas of large-scale factory production, Rush believed, Europeans would bring their expertise to make America an even greater manufacturing power. The United Company was for Rush and others a means by which the Industrial Revolution could be brought to America.

The directors believed that by importing ideas of the Industrial Revolution, they could have an immediate economic impact, and this hindered the enterprise from fully implementing European factory production. United Company directors wanted to build a hybrid textile mill that took advantage of the putting-out process that existed in America by combining it with British ideas of factory labor. American women were already highly engaged in putting-out excess cloth and clothing they made in their homes. The company planned to buy these domestically made "Cloths, Linnens, Blankits & various other articles . . . daily brought to this City."[16] Besides purchasing cloth and thread, the company planned to hire unskilled workers from "the poor people in [the] city" in order to weave or spin on company-owned machines in a company-owned factory.[17] It was hoped that all company activities, both factory and putting-out, would excite "a general and laudable spirit of industry among the poor."[18] To raise money for its operations, the company sold shares at £10 per share, using the funds to purchase a building and a jenny, and to recruit managers and workers. Just five months after beginning operations in September 1775, the company employed over four hundred factory workers, and independent weavers and spinners. Tasks of dressing, spinning, and weaving were specialized to increase productivity and make use of unskilled laborers who could be taught simple operations.

The company, however, was unable to overcome its reliance on domestic putting-out methods. The majority of company employees were actually working at home at their own looms and spinning wheels. It was difficult to recruit workers to stay in the factory and produce finished items for sale. Neither female artisans nor unskilled workers were interested in factory jobs; they wanted to work from home. Workers at the factory did not like the factory environment, and many began to drift away, looking for other work opportunities. The factory workforce declined to fewer than fifty. The managers turned fully to the putting-out system to make up the difference in production and advertised for women to sell their wares to the company. It supplied some women with thread but more often relied on women to produce their own thread. It then accepted completed cloth but did not have enough workers to sew the cloth into clothing. In the meantime, putting-out women were continuing to bring finished clothing to the company for sale. The company got caught in a vicious circle. It could not afford to turn away any of its domestic workers, but neither could it afford to keep stockpiling cloth in the hopes of employing weavers and sewers at the factory. The company remained in operation through 1776, but even in wartime, domestic textiles were still more expensive than those purchased overseas.[19] The war added complications to the business environment by making it more difficult to sell and transport goods outside the Delaware Valley. After its initial level of activity, the company was never able to sustain a profitable level of production, and it closed permanently in 1777 when the British occupied Philadelphia. Despite its failure, the company's activities were a clear example of factory organization and the scales that could be reached if an effective factory could be organized.

Europeans brought ideas for other large-scale operations with them from the Old World. Caspar Wistar arrived in America from Germany and sought a natural supply of high-quality silica that he could use for a glassworks. He built a small glass manufactory in southern New Jersey that by the 1770s contained two furnaces and many finishing shops. The whole operation supplied raw glass for individual craftsmen at the site to finish into panes, bottles, and jars.[20] Henry Stiegel borrowed Wistar's idea and built a glassworks in Lancaster County to reach the markets of Philadelphia and its hinterland. Stiegel recruited German glassblowers to work at his furnace in the same individual capacity as those at Wistar's glassworks.[21] His operation lasted less than a decade, from 1765 until 1773, when it closed because of financial overextension and an inadequate market.[22] These were isolated examples of crudely organized centralized manufacturing. The most widespread examples of centralization in North America and the best developed by the time of the revolution were iron plantations.

European adventurers had tried to introduce the large-scale smelting of iron ore to the colonies at least as far back as the 1630s. These ventures failed because American iron was less desirable and more costly in the British market than European alternatives. This changed in 1717 when Parliament restrained the import of European iron to Britain. British investors leapt at opportunities to invest in American iron production and "inaugurated a new era in American ironmaking."[23] The output of cast iron steadily rose in North America as entrepreneurs built blast furnaces to supply the British market with raw materials for its manufacturing sector. The iron industry in America began to change in the mid-eighteenth century as the population of the colonies rapidly grew. Iron smelting was supplemented by the manufacture of finished iron products for the domestic consumer market. Iron making was a complex enterprise that was subdivided into numerous specialties by the late seventeenth century. Furnaces were two-story, stone structures that contained a hollow center where iron ore, charcoal, and limestone were set on fire and allowed to burn into molten iron. Roughly every twelve hours, a small hole at the base of the furnace was opened, and the molten iron was run out into molds, making cast iron. A forge was an iron-processing facility in which cast iron was worked into wrought iron. Forges used large hearth fires and water-driven hammers to make iron plates and strap iron for craftsmen, and other smaller retail products. Forges were also used to convert iron to steel, and over time forges specialized into the manufacture of exclusive products, becoming slitting (cutting) mills, steel furnaces, plating mills, and naileries. Blacksmiths then used the wrought iron in their smaller forges to make products for local markets.

By the eighteenth century, furnaces were no longer built in isolation; they were constructed with carpenters shops and forges so that craftsmen could produce barrels, wheels, wagons, and iron utensils from cast-iron pigs. Specialization within the iron business gave way to more cooperative production activities. Maryland's Principio Furnace started as a smelting operation in 1722, but by 1736, "the company had . . . a furnace, forge with two fineries and one chafery, store, gristmill, and blacksmith shop."[24] Baltimore Furnace records for 1736 show that though it relied on cast iron for most of its income, the furnace employed two blacksmiths, one wheelwright, two sawyers, and two carpenters to produce finished goods.[25] By the 1770s, Berkshire Furnace, near Reading, Pennsylvania, was employing dozens of craftsmen to finish products.[26] In 1775, eighty-two blast furnaces and 175 forges were producing thirty thousand tons of cast and wrought iron annually.[27] More important than raw iron production, however, was the fact that "the larger part of all iron produced at the furnaces and forges was manufactured into tools, imple-

This image from the mid-1700s shows a large blacksmith shop organized for managed craft work. There are two furnace fires, two anvils, and a carpentry station allowing multiple craftsmen to work simultaneously and coordinate their production. Here blacksmiths can be seen working on separate components of a project while to the left a carpenter finishes wooden elements. (*The Book of Trades and Library of Useful Arts*)

ments, and wares, used chiefly by the colonists themselves."[28] European examples of centralized manufacturing laid the foundation for such operations to occasionally grow out of other American craft operations.

As villages grew into towns and cities, entrepreneurs gathered craftsmen together to work collectively in larger establishments or in close proximity. Agricultural refining operations, leather factories, and forges were built in Bethlehem, Pennsylvania, and Salem, North Carolina, to serve frontier markets.[29] In each case, skilled craftsmen gathered around water power and took advantage of their proximity to each other to expand their operations. Similarly, gunsmiths in Lancaster, Pennsylvania, increased their productive capacity to meet the demand for rifles from families and adventurers moving to the frontier in the aftermath of the French and Indian War.[30] Many gunsmiths built their own shops in Lancaster to take advantage of iron deposits in the vicinity. They then took advantage of their proximity to one another to subcontract work and integrate their operations. In Philadelphia, the Southwark China Works emerged to produce fine pottery goods, while in Trenton, New Jersey, a large pottery works was established to meet the needs of more proletarian tastes. Both cities also developed large-scale paper-production facilities. Markets for finished products developed sufficiently in Virginia for John Blaney and Company to open a leather manufactory for men's and women's boots and shoes.[31] Blaney hired craftsmen to transform the leather he made into finished items. Large-scale manufacturing operations were able to grow because of their access to large markets like Richmond, Trenton, Philadelphia, and Lancaster, and the availability of labor. Such development, however, was the exception rather than the rule in America. Several attempts to manage labor on a large scale failed abruptly, and only a handful survived over the long term. Those operations that did succeed were smaller-scale, coordinated craft operations that shared resources. Nevertheless, by the time of the revolution, Americans had gained knowledge of innovative management systems through the operational examples Europeans brought with them to the New World.

Europeans and Americans with European experience worked with the military stores department during the American Revolution and shared production ideas with Continental administrators. Daniel Joy was an ordnance inspector for Congress before becoming superintendent of ordnance for the DCGMS. He gained his qualifications as an ordnance inspector through service as a ship's captain and study as an amateur scientist. Prior to the war, Joy was master of the trading brig *Mulberry*. Between 1754 and 1766, he captained it on voyages from Philadelphia to Jamaica, London, and South Carolina. As captain, Joy would have gained experience with his ship's weapons and ammunition. He probably learned even more about naval ordnance in 1760, when the Royal Navy commandeered his ship. Joy took *Mulberry* to Quebec as a supply ship in support of Britain's final assault on Montreal. Joy settled in Philadelphia after his maritime career ended and joined the city's scientific community. When the revolution came, he volunteered as a member of the Southwark neighborhood committee of safety. He served with other craftsmen who became involved in mobilizing Pennsylvania for war.[32] Joy's career provided many opportunities for him to learn artillery science. He shared this knowledge as an administrator in the DCGMS in two ways. He assisted private manufacturers in the production of stores, and he assisted with government production in the artillery yard at the Philadelphia Arsenal. Joseph Perkins, director of the Philadelphia armory, was trained by Scottish immigrant James Hunter. Hunter arrived in Virginia just prior to the Revolution and set about building a forge near Fredericksburg. By the time the war began, the forge had grown into a complex that included a nailery, tanyard, carpenter shop, and wheelwright shop.[33] Perkins, who was raised as a gunsmith, went to work in this environment and learned the importance of centralized production from someone who had brought the idea with him from Europe.

Several French officers came to the United States seeking fame and fortune from the war. Two of the most famous were Louis Duportail and Philippe du Coudray. Duportail shared knowledge of French war making with his American associates as the army's chief engineer, which may have influenced how the military organized itself. But there was no direct connection between Duportail and the DCGMS. Coudray, however, was a different story. He was more experienced in artillery and ballistic operations than Duportail and provided greater insight into the production of stores. Unfortunately, Coudray was a bombastic elitist who valued his own knowledge above all else. This haughty attitude made him seem highly valuable to congressional leaders, but it alienated him from America's military commanders. He had little influence on either before his death in 1778. One of Coudray's assistants, though, lived longer than his commander and had a more welcoming personality. He went on to present Congress with a full recommendation of military manufacturing. Lewis Garanger, captain of artillery to the French king, believed that the United States had the resources to mobilize its own manufacturing and that what it lacked it could import from Europe. He believed that the knowledge of warlike activities was widespread in the Atlantic world, writing that the "Sciences [of war] are now so Generally known [that they] flourish and abound."[34] Americans had a great deal of resources, he said, they had only "to superintend, improve, and perfect these manufactories, [to render] their Practice as Easy and vulgarly Known as might be." In areas where Americans could not match the knowledge or organizational skills of Europeans, "it would be . . . advantageous . . . to borrow and transplant it from Europe." It was, wrote Garanger, Congress's duty to mobilize Americans to produce for the war effort. The chief way "of Encouraging and Emulating the Manufactories of warlike stores now existing in this Continent, and of exciting the formation of new ones, would be the assurance given to manufacturers by the Government to their Proprietors."[35] He encouraged this idea by providing detailed instructions on cannon casting and gunpowder preparation for Congress to use in directing private manufacturers. Garanger's extensive writings were presented as a way to secure the author employment with Congress. In this he was disappointed, and he returned to France in the early 1780s. Nevertheless, his words reveal that a reasonable amount of knowledge about French manufacturing went into organizing the military stores department and its operations.

Pierre Penet was another Frenchman who arrived in the United States with a desire for personal gain and a willingness to share valuable knowledge with the DCGMS. Penet first came to North America in late 1776 ahead of a shipment of weapons and ammunition he had helped arrange for the revolutionaries. Prior to leaving France, Penet had extensive dealings with Gribeauval and the French artillery leadership to determine how best to supply the Americans and assist them in their war effort. Once in the United States, Penet spoke often to Congress and George Washington about the need to mobilize American manufacturing and how he could help in this process. Writing to Congress years later, Penet said, "I have . . . supply'd several States of America with [gunpowder, weapons and] accouterments for your Troop: it is therefore my duty & my own advantage to give you . . . Intelligenc[e]" about European innovations.[36] In 1779, Penet approached the Board of War to "contract to make and deliver 100,000 muskets with bayonets of the best kind, completely finished."[37] The board and Congress were enthusiastic about the potential for this contract. After presenting his offer to the board, Penet requested a cash advance and special favors for his friends who would come from France to direct the production process. Congress agreed to the terms, and Penet returned to France to recruit gunsmiths to help him set up a manufactory. The French government, however, would not allow anyone contracted with the government to leave the country. This killed Penet's contract, but he returned to the United States with a private gunsmith and a determination to set up a small manufactory. This he did, contracting with the DCGMS in 1781 to repair several thousand muskets. His company continued to repair muskets for the United States well into the 1780s. Despite all of his activities, though, his most important contribution to the revolution was transmitting manufacturing knowledge from France to the United States. He knew the major innovative players in France and how French government arsenals were able to achieve the production scale mentioned previously. This knowledge he shared with American government manufacturers, like Samuel Hodgdon and Joseph Perkins, during the war.

Despite all of the ideas and examples of innovative production available to Americans before and during the war, it was the printed word more than any other influence that directed military stores production techniques. Americans received "information from a variety of sources such as newspapers, magazines, letters, . . . and books."[38] There existed in pre-revolutionary America subscription libraries in various colonies. There were bookstores whose owners, alongside general import merchants, secured the newest works from Europe and ordered books by special request. Henry Knox was only one of several booksellers in Boston in the 1770s. American publishers were also keen on republishing European works, with or without permission. William Aikman of Annapolis, Maryland, not only owned a bookstore but regularly reprinted European titles for sale in America.[39] Newspapers, however, were the most widespread form of written communication. Fifteen newspapers circulated weekly or semiweekly in colonial America in the early 1770s. Isaiah Thomas, publisher of the *Massachusetts Spy*, claimed a prewar circulation of three thousand six hundred issues of his newspaper.[40] Information was therefore available broadly in the colonies among the people who eventually served in Congress and the military stores department and wanted to be knowledgeable. Moreover, the various written means of idea exchange provided Congress, the DCGMS, and the army with information about the chief example of how to organize military stores production: the Woolwich Arsenal and the British Royal Artillery that managed it.

Congress was explicit in its military stores instructions that it wanted a system of labor managed on what it knew of British operations. The plan for government manufacturing called for "one or more capital Laboratories . . . , [shops where] artificers be employ'd, . . . [and] a foundry for Casting brass cannon . . . to be nearly on the same plan as that at Woolwich."[41] Americans knew about the arsenal at Woolwich from the written sources available, including colonial newspapers and the writings of John Muller, who wrote a half dozen books on artillery, fortification, and mathematics.

The *Pennsylvania Gazette* regularly carried stories about Woolwich and the role it played in Britain's military manufacturing establishment. Most of the stories, reprinted from London newspapers, examined preparations for war, but a significant few analyzed arsenal operations: "Last Saturday there was a great Number of new Greate Guns prov'd," and "there was a Proof of Gunpowder . . . which answer'd to Satisfaction."[42] The newspaper also noted work schedules at Woolwich: "All the artificers in the musquetry and ordnance branches, . . . work such extra hours, as to be allowed for nine days per week, and some even more."[43] Clearly, operations at Woolwich were flexible, and laborers could be organized and worked as needed by the government. This was an important lesson to American leaders. One brief story in 1766 illuminated the government's role in manufacturing, noting that "a large number of iron cannon are now casting at the new cannon water-manufactory near [Edinburgh] to be shipped for Woolwich."[44] The government contracted out to support operations at Woolwich. A story the next year revealed how the government's manufacturing works could support innovation: "We are told, that a young man from Ireland, lately invented a machine for destroying enemies . . . , which was used at Woolwich . . . and found to answer; but has been since condemned."[45] Several years later, "his Majesty . . . went . . . to Woolwich, to see the experiment of firing a cannon, of a new invention, which was discharged 24 times in a minute."[46] Taken together, these simple stories told the tale of a manufacturing center that could be used to flexibly manufacture weapons, store and test weapons, and innovate new weapons.

Newspapers provided a superb overview of Woolwich, but those interested in the details turned to Muller's books to get a full picture of how the arsenal operated. The most influential of Muller's books among Continental commanders were *A Treatise Containing the Practical Part of Fortification*, also known as *A Treatise of Practical Fortification*, and *A Treatise of Artillery. A Treatise of Practical Fortification* circulated widely in America before the American Revolution in its imported editions, while *A Treatise of Artillery* was disseminated in an American reprint to the Continental Army. Each of Muller's books was meant to be an instruction manual for artillerists, but the author took pains to make them readable and relevant to a broader audience. Taken together, the books became a guide for the manufacture and care of military stores in America. Anyone paying attention to war-making activities in the empire like Knox or members of library companies could combine the knowledge offered in circulated newspapers and Muller's books to learn how the British government was organizing the production of its military stores.

Published in 1755, *A Treatise of Practical Fortification* predated *A Treatise of Artillery* by two years. *A Treatise of Practical Fortification* was part of a pair of books on the theory and application of the principles of fortresses in war and national defense. The first book, *A Treatise Containing the Elementary Part of Fortification*, dealt exclusively with the mathematics and design of fortifications in a perfect situation, assuming the designers and builders had unlimited resources and complete geographical and mechanical freedom to build the perfect fortress. *A Treatise of Practical Fortification* applied the concepts from the first book to the real world and examined the mathematics and necessities for designing and building fortresses in the field. The subtext of Muller's undertaking this project was to provide English audiences an understanding of the concepts of the great French fortress designer Sebastian de Vauban. In this he surely succeeded, as the pair of Muller's books on fortification offered an impressive amount of detail in mathematics and topical coverage. However, there was one element of Muller's book on practical fortification that made it especially useful to America's arsenal builders.

It was, as the title states, focused on fortifications, but Muller consistently used examples from the Woolwich Arsenal to discuss the best way to construct buildings useful for military stores work. Unwittingly, Muller's *Treatise* gave Americans the written blueprints for physically constructing its public arsenals. *A Treatise on Practical Fortification* was divided into four sections that progressed through the planning and construction of fortresses and then examined special defensive circumstances. Muller began his work with a look at theory and then expanded from there to the application of concepts. He first examined the mathematics and science of wall construction, arches, foundation piers, and timbers. The second section of the book discussed the properties of building materials. Muller demonstrated, as he did later with artillery, that the military could accomplish a great deal if it understood the mathematics and science behind minerals. He examined stones, sand, and lime and how they could best be made into bricks, mortar, and plaster. Part 3 of the *Treatise* was the most extensive, offering instructions on fortress layout and written blueprints for constructing the most effective fortifications. But Muller went beyond the fortress itself and discussed the various buildings needed within any fort's walls: casemates, sally ports, necessary houses, hospitals, barracks, storehouses, and powder magazines. The final section of the book considered what Muller called "aquatic buildings"—like bridges, harbors, wharfs, and aqueducts—exploring the mathematics involved in their design and construction.

Part 3 of the book was the most influential for the DCGMS. In it, Muller not only provided specific guidelines for building useful military stores structures but used Woolwich as his example. "Barracks," he wrote, "are built different ways, according to their situations. When there is sufficient room to make a large square, surrounded with buildings they are very convenient."[47] Muller was describing exactly how the Woolwich Arsenal was laid out, and how the Springfield Arsenal would be laid out. Pages 215 through 222 describe meticulously how to design and construct small and large powder magazines. Muller examined how to prevent degradation of the buildings. "To keep the floor from dampness, beams are laid longways, and to prevent these beams from being soon rotten, large stones are laid under them." He went on to say that "a window is made in each wing . . . very high, for fear of accidents . . . to give air to the magazine." Such vivid descriptions were invaluable to Americans building the magazines at Carlisle and Springfield and those organizing the Fifth Street Laboratory in Philadelphia. Muller elaborated on how usage and production influenced the design and construction of buildings. He explained, almost offhandedly, how production activities were organized within buildings at Woolwich to make the best use of space and work flow. "The ground floor of a store-house ought to consist in a shed to place guns and their carriages, tumbrels, ammunition, waggons, mortars, and their beds; . . . there must likewise be forges for smiths, places for carpenters to work in, . . . and wheelwrights shops, and every thing of this sort. The first floor ought to contain an armoury." Best of all for the Americans, Muller provided diagrams of the buildings he discussed. "To give an idea of these kind of works, we have represented the plan . . . with the elevation of one of the insides, executed at Woolwich."[48] While all the buildings Muller discussed were presented as structures to be housed within any substantial fortification, they did not necessarily have to be. The value of Muller's writing, for the public in general and specifically the Continental government and army, was that the book was "a plain and easy [treatise of] the construction and executive part of the works belonging to a fortress and *add whatever might contribute to the improvement of this useful art.*"[49] Muller's goal was to make the knowledge in the book easily transferable to multiple military situations and not solely applicable to fortifications. By using Woolwich as his example for certain structures, Muller drifted back and forth between discussing the layout of fortresses and military posts in general. Thus the information was easily useable for the Americans reading it.

Despite the fact that *A Treatise of Artillery* was nearly twenty years old by the time of the American Revolution, it was still a cutting-edge work that documented the efficiency of standardizing the mathematics behind artillery. Muller believed that with his work, "a nation [can] have its artillery carried to such perfection, as to make use of as little metal and workmanship as possible."[50] In other words, Muller was saying that his work would help any nation carry out the most efficient production of artillery. He held that the effective execution of artillery activities began with a thorough understanding of the arithmetic involved in the manufacture of stores and their use on the battlefield. Therefore, he began his book with a long and thorough examination of the mathematics necessary for artillery service. He listed several experiments that had been undertaken to determine the amount of gunpowder to use when discharging a cannon and the relationships between the length of the gun and its range of fire. From these he illustrated through mathematical formulae and functions how to determine the most effective manner to load and aim artillery. He also examined the explosive properties of powder and the physical properties of cannons. This included detailed analytical mention of the mathematics and properties of artillery shells, solid shot, and leaden bullets.

Muller then took all this information and determined the most effective proportions that brass and iron ordnance should possess. He diagrammed the guns and explained the diagrams in conjunction with an analysis of their proper proportions. This was followed by a thorough analysis of the proper size and proportions of various types of artillery carriages. Muller took time to discuss all types of ordnance, including field guns, mortars, and howitzers. But he did not stop there. Parts 4 and 6 of his book presented details and diagrams regarding the proper construction of various artillery vehicles and tools, such as a tumbrel, a powder cart, an ammunition wagon, a traveling forge, a pontoon carriage, petards, fuses, limbers, rammers, and sponges. Muller also included a host of organizational information that was invaluable to the Continental Army: how to organize an artillery regiment, how to build a powder laboratory, how to determine the amount of stores needed for an army, how to determine firing ranges, and how to properly pack powder. While Muller was not exhaustive in every detail of his various topics, taken together with his other works, the author explained how production could be organized and coordinated by a cadre of managers, as was done at Woolwich.

Muller's concepts for standardizing military stores usage were similar to but distinct from those of his contemporary Gribeauval in France. As noted earlier in this chapter, Gribeauval engineered tools, gauges, and designs that allowed craftsmen to create weapons to answer to specific purposes and could be used interchangeably with other weapons of the same type. This was handy for repair; if one part of a cannon carriage broke, it could easily be replaced; if one part of a musket broke, it could easily be fixed with a spare part. But this manufacturing system was really all about control and organization. If all weapons were produced using Gribeauval's specifications, then all officers and soldiers could be expected to know how to use each weapon, and the whole army would be more effective, able to operate more efficiently. From a technological perspective, Gribeauval's system was an exciting step on the way to industrial mass production. But Gribeauval's goals were not new. European military commanders were universally searching for ways to more efficiently control their armies.

Muller took a different view of the solution to this problem from Gribeauval. While the latter attacked the problem mechanically, the former approached it mathematically. "To put the artillery upon a better footing than it has hitherto been," wrote Muller, "geometry . . . is sufficient." For Muller, it was not the weapons and their use that would make an army more efficient but rather how well that army understood the mathematics behind their actions. With this knowledge, an army could use any type of weapon for any of the specific functions for which it was made. There was no need to standardize the weapons. Muller's work was, therefore, a pioneering application of science to artillery, which had theretofore been seen as a craft skill. "Artillery," wrote Muller, "has hitherto been considered merely as practical, without conceiving that for want of . . . mathematics, no improvements can possibly be made."[51] The DCGMS learned from Muller that with proper organization, military stores production could be made more productive and efficient.

Muller's ideas for military manufacturing and his explanation of Woolwich were circulated in North America in three direct ways: colonial booksellers, subscription libraries, and engraver John Norman. Henry Knox was widely known to be fond of ordering and reading military texts for pleasure. *A Treatise of Practical Fortification* was on his London Bookstore shelves. He may well have purchased *A Treatise of Artillery* for his own use, but there is no record that his bookstore ever carried it. Garret Noel's bookstore in New York City did carry both books as early at 1759, getting them while they were newly in print. Noel eventually moved his business and took on a partner, but he continued to sell the *Treatise of Practical Fortification* in 1771. The new store stood next to the Merchants Coffee House, which became a popular meeting place for patriots and those generally opposed to British policies. The year 1771 was also when the Library Company of Philadelphia first listed Muller's fortification book in its catalog, but Redwood Library in

Newport, Rhode Island, had the book since at least 1765. Muller's books were available in four of the major cities in colonial America, and the designer of the military stores program, Knox, owned and distributed it. It was engraver Norman, however, who put A Treatise of Artillery and its ideas into the hands of military stores leaders.[52]

At some point just prior to the American Revolution, John Norman stepped ashore in Philadelphia after crossing the Atlantic from Great Britain. Norman had trained as an engraver in London and seems to have grown up in the world of publishing between Drury Lane and Whitehall. There is no record of why he came to America, but he brought many ideas with him and immediately got to work engraving and publishing in the New World. In late 1774, he launched a subscription to secure publication of an American edition of Abraham Swan's British Architect, for which he prepared sixty copperplate prints. Publishers at this time often sought money up front in the form of subscriptions in order to fund the printing of a book and to ensure a profit from the enterprise. Norman's next major works made him a household name among the reading public early in the war. In 1775, he engraved a plate for Thomas Hanson's book The Prussian Evolutions in Actual Engagements. In 1776, he produced a plate titled "The Death of Warren" for Hugh Henry Brackenridge's The Battle of Bunker Hill.[53] Norman's success in engraving and working with publishers led him to take advantage of the wartime market. In 1777, he advertised a subscription in Philadelphia to produce an American version of Muller's Treatise of Artillery. During the first round of sales, twelve military commanders made deposits for the book, with some ordering multiple copies. Washington and Knox each purchased the book, as did Benjamin Flower and Jonathan Gostelowe.[54] In fact, Flower and Knox both ordered multiple copies in order to use the book as a resource among their respective subordinate officers. The book was published in 1779 and disseminated around the military stores department in particular and the army in general. Inventories taken in later years reveal the book was on hand as a resource and reference to military stores commanders.

David Mason's journal, which was discussed at the beginning of this chapter, is a clear example of how far Muller's ideas disseminated among military stores administrators. Mason transcribed seven specific pieces of information from the Treatise of Artillery, but interestingly, he occasionally made changes that better fit the needs of his work. "Diameter of Shot" was the first chart the arsenal director included in his journal, copying it precisely from page 6 of Muller's book. When it came to the dimensions of artillery carriage wheels, however, Mason adjusted the number that Muller provided on page 108 of his book. Mason designed his artillery wheels several inches shorter and smaller than Muller prescribed, though the proportions were the same. One can surmise that this was to be economical with wood usage. Mason went on to copy charts for howitzer construction, mortar bed construction, traveling forge construction, and the manufacture of fire barrels. In the latter case, once again, Mason adjusted the numbers to fit his usage. This time, however, he prepared larger barrels for production, possibly to provide for a larger burning potential. The remainder of Mason's journal had smaller morsels of Muller's *Treatise* spread throughout; a formula here and a piece of information there. This information showed not only how military manufacturing information was transmitted from Woolwich to Springfield but also how that information was exploited. Mason used Muller's knowledge as blueprints for what his arsenal was producing: cannon carriages, traveling forges, shot, and ammunition. Muller's scientific understanding of military production and usage was a direct ingredient into the production activities within the DCGMS as well as a guide for the overall organization of that department. Acknowledging the valuable impact Muller had, it is still necessary to return to the overall view that he was just one element of a plethora of ideas and examples available to revolutionary Americans about manufacturing.

Congress and military stores administrators applied the numerous illustrations and lessons they possessed to the organization of manufacturing both in the government's arsenals and in private operations with which they contracted. The government made use of all the sources available to it, from examples of production through firsthand observers of those methods to extensive writings about manufacturing in Europe. As has already been seen, Congress used the British ordnance department as a model to guide it in creating the position of the commissary general of military stores and the department answering to him. The department was not identical to the British model, which was part of the value of this process of idea transfer from Europe. Congress and its administrators manipulated and used ideas in ways that made the outcomes valuable to the specifics of American needs. The first Continental manufacturing enterprise examined in the next chapter is the Fifth Street Laboratory. The DCGMS established several iterations of ammunition-production facilities labeled laboratories before establishing Fifth Street. The earlier laboratories seem to have been typical musket-cartridge-forming facilities in which gunpowder and musket ball were wrapped for use on the battlefield. Workers rolled cartridges on their own, without oversight or coordination, rather than cooperating for larger production. Fifth Street was organized in the manner of a protofactory, making use of what Continental administrators knew about factory organization. The laboratory was to be a munitions factory in which unskilled workers were divided in function and managed to properly measure gunpowder, cut and fill cartridge paper, and attach cartridges to projectiles. The factory was useful for large-scale production of a single item, but administrators used centralized manufacturing to mobilize craftsmen working in government arsenals.

Congress and military stores administrators did their best to organize arsenal production according to what they knew about military manufacturing at Woolwich and at large craft operations like iron furnaces. Military stores artificers were organized by Congress into a Regiment of Artillery Artificers. Though this regiment was part of the Continental Army, it answered directly to the Board of War rather than to General Washington. Four companies of craftsmen were authorized by 1779 to serve under Flower's command: Nathaniel Irish's and Thomas Wylie's at Carlisle, John Jordan's at Philadelphia, and Nathan Chapman's at Springfield.[55] Companies were generally to consist of sixty artificers— "24 blacksmiths, 16 carpenters, 14 wheelwrights, 4 drummakers, [and] 2 coopers"—but recruiters like Charles Lukens took anyone in the character of "Carpenters, Blacksmiths, Gunsmiths, Locksmiths, Wheelwrights, &c."[56] The genius behind this organization was that as soldiers, the artificers were subject to military discipline and oversight, but as craftsmen they were subject to the direction of the master in their craft. Such a workforce was conceived to eliminate the individualized nature of craft operations and promote the management of craftsmen for the production of finished products. Operations at all the government arsenals were structured so that the company commander oversaw operations as a whole and was a master of one of the specialties. Subordinate officers also managed each of the specialties, and the commander could then cross coordinate activities. There were subcompanies (or what we might call platoons) within each company, but seldom were these organized by craft specialty. They were organized randomly or by production unit, so that craftsmen coordinated their production based on the fact that they were members of the same subcompany. Craftsmen, therefore, answered to numerous overseers, their officers first and their craft master second. Officers oversaw two groups, their subcompany first, then their craft operations. America's Regiment of Artillery Artificers was organized to foster cooperative production as much as possible and manage that production through central leadership.

In addition to command organization, the DCGMS paid attention to physical organization. At Woolwich, each craft specialty had its own shop, but the shops were located adjacent to each other so arsenal managers could coordinate their operations. Likewise at the larger ironworks in America, the furnaces were surrounded by blacksmith and carpentry shops. Congress intended a similar system for its craftsmen. One of the areas of innovation that will be examined in more detail in chapter 5 was how the physical spaces of production were designed. Continental arsenals and their systems were constructed to foster cooperation among craftsmen of various specialties. Craft shops were either placed in the same building or their buildings were organized around a central commons. Workflow was intended to be streamlined through the physical structure of the arsenals.

Congress intended that all production in the military stores department be carried on by enlisted craftsmen, but many craftsmen had to be hired because of the government's materiel needs and its desperate financial situation. It was difficult to recruit men to Flower's Regiment of Artillery Artificers. Skilled craftsmen did not want to exchange their knowledge for Congress's meager pay, or their freedom for a soldier's life.[57] Gunsmiths, and blacksmiths with any type of gunsmithing experience, were almost impossible to recruit. The necessity of repairing and manufacturing military stores thus forced Congress to allow Flower to hire men for more money than was being paid to enlisted recruits. While this may have caused some problems within the overall centralized management system, it would not have undermined it. The hired craftsmen and laborers reported to a manager, who reported to or worked with a Continental officer. Whether blacksmiths at the Philadelphia ordnance yard were enlisted or hired, they answered to the master blacksmith. The gunsmiths at Philadelphia all answered to a manager, who reported to the commissary general. It was not exactly the system Congress wanted, but it worked. Hiring men also made sense after 1780, when Congress went bankrupt. Enlisted artificers could not simply be dismissed. They signed contracts of military service in which their work was exchanged for pay, room, and board for a legally binding length of time, usually three years or the duration of the war. Such an arrangement was extremely expensive for the Continental Army. Nonmilitary hired workers, on the other hand, were only hired day to day, week to week, or for the completion of a specific project. And they could be hired and fired at will, on a daily basis if need be, in order to save money. Hired men were a much more economical tool for manufacturing than soldiers. Therefore, Congress retained both types of workers throughout the war. The majority of hired men were employed in Philadelphia, though there were about a dozen at both Carlisle and Springfield working as either short-term laborers or in highly specialized production. By early 1779, Flower oversaw a multifaceted operation that managed military production using various forms of organization. Continental administrators did not, however, limit their organizational focus to government manufacturing activities.

In addition to organizing government workers, Continental administrators took an active role in promoting large-scale manufacturing techniques among private manufacturers. As has been seen, and will be seen in more detail in chapter 6, the DCGMS utilized inspectors to guide contractors in their operations. These inspectors taught manufacturers how to organize their production and often encouraged them to use centralized craftsmanship. William Henry, for instance, was hired by the DCGMS as superintendent of arms. He had created an extensive arms-manufacturing operation in Lancaster through the use of centralization. Henry subcontracted some of his operations so that his gunsmiths could produce finished goods from parts manufactured by others. Through his position overseeing private production for the government, Henry was able to influence private manufacturers to use this technique. The DCGMS also provided resources to producers who were willing to use innovative techniques. Hodgdon provided cash advances to John Jacob Faesch to update his iron-making operations in order to produce the items needed by the government. He also provided coal, transport, and other resources to manufacturers that allowed them to centralize and specialize their operations around production and turn away from some of the ancillary activities of craft production. In these ways, the government promoted the use of innovative manufacturing techniques during the war.

After the revolution, the government continued to encourage the development of the ideas of the Industrial Revolution within the United States. The DCGMS invested its meager budget heavily in creating a national brass foundry for the continued production of artillery for the army. This site, located at Springfield, attempted throughout the 1780s to re-create in America the type of large-scale brass operation seen at Woolwich. The DCGMS also subsidized several experiments in manufacturing operations, including new steelmaking enterprises and production organizations. The secretary at war, Benjamin Lincoln, led the charge for government involvement in developing America's manufacturing sector by reporting to Congress on how the DCGMS had operated during the war and how those operations could continue to benefit the nation. Lincoln's words influenced Alexander Hamilton's "Report on Manufactures" and the building of military manufacturing sites at Springfield and Harpers Ferry, Virginia. These armories were some of the most innovative manufacturing operations in the nation during their existence.

THE AMERICAN REVOLUTION WAS A TURNING POINT IN THE HISTORY OF American manufacturing and a key factor in the development of the Industrial Revolution in America. The need for increased production capacity resulting from the war led America's leaders to plant the seeds of knowledge they found from Europe. America's leaders understood the value of the Industrial Revolution taking place in Europe during the eighteenth century. They had either read about developments or they had experienced them. Others had been part of attempts to start manufacturing operations in the British colonies before the war. Manufacturing ideas were brought to the United States from France and Britain by men who had seen these sites and knew how they operated. Books and newspapers brought knowledge about manufacturing to the colonies. During the war, men with military manufacturing experience shared their knowledge with Continental administrators and congressmen. The Revolutionary War stimulated germination of these ideas and examples into manufacturing operations that supported the Continental Army. Government arsenals at Philadelphia, Carlisle, and Springfield utilized methods of production that allowed the manufacture of military stores far beyond what could have been accomplished by individual craftsmen. Production by a Regiment of Artillery Artificers was managed by craft experts and commissioned officers. Even hired individuals had to subsume their craft skills beneath the direction of an overall superior. Craftwork gave way to large-scale manufacturing. These operations were supplemented by government assistance to manufacturers in adopting the ideas of the Industrial Revolution in order to support the war effort. Continental dollars were invested in upgrading craft operations to large-scale parameters. Administrators also taught craftsmen how they could function on a large scale. The ideas and values of the Industrial Revolution were implemented and encouraged during the American Revolution. Examining these undertakings in action will illuminate how the United States was able to manufacture its independence.

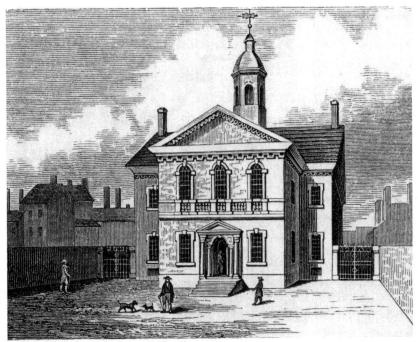

Built between 1770 and 1774, Carpenter's Hall was the meeting place for the Carpenter's Company of the City and County of Philadelphia. It hosted the First Continental Congress in 1774, and from 1778 to 1784 served as the headquarters of the DCGMS, housing Flower and Hodgdon's offices, and a warehouse for military stores. (*New York Public Library*)

4

"Regiment of Artillery Artificers" and "hired men"

PROMOTING A MANUFACTURING
REVOLUTION IN PHILADELPHIA

ARPENTER'S HALL WAS ONLY THREE YEARS OLD WHEN THE FIRST
Continental Congress met there in 1774. The bricks still held
their deep red color, and the wood trim was all freshly painted.
The cobblestone patios surrounding the building were relatively clean
and unworn. It had been built by the Carpenters' Company of the City
and County of Philadelphia to house its regular meetings and any special
events held among its artisan brethren. Set back from Chestnut Street
down a private alley, the two-story Georgian structure was more myste-
rious than imposing. The interior of Carpenter's Hall was nearly as splen-
did as the exterior. A large gallery dominated the first floor, with large
windows encased in finely crafted wooden trim. The second floor held
offices, a library, and more meeting space. The hall was an ideal location
to house colonial representatives who arrived in Philadelphia to discuss
united colonial action against Great Britain. The first meeting of the
Continental Congress was supposed to happen in the State House
(Independence Hall), but that building was occupied by the Provincial
Assembly and was unavailable. The carpenter's craft guild stepped up
and offered its convenient facilities so the congressmen had somewhere
to meet on September 5. The next three months were a singular moment
in the building's history, a moment when America's colonial leaders
agreed to work together and continue their cooperation until the British
government backed down. But this was not the end of the building's service to the revolution.

In summer 1778, Carpenter's Hall became the headquarters of the DCGMS. The first floor and basement of the building became a warehouse for muskets, accouterments, and ammunition. The second floor housed the offices from which Benjamin Flower, Samuel Hodgdon, and their assistants worked. And the patios surrounding the building became storage areas for artillery, ordnance supplies, departmental tools, wagons, and other large items. Carpenter's Hall was the depot through which most of the stores sent from the DCGMS traveled to George Washington's army. It did not take long for the paint to chip and wear down or the handsome brick and woodwork to be ravaged. Supplies were constantly moving in and out of the hall, and the necessities of war transformed the stylish new building into an overused warehouse.

The transformation that occurred to Carpenter's Hall was indicative of the economic transformations that took place throughout Philadelphia during the war. Buildings found new uses, and people found new sources of employment. There were also structural changes to the nature of production and the work environment. Philadelphia became the military stores department's largest manufacturing center, where a system of arsenal-wide coordination existed alongside managed production within the arsenal's component parts. Skilled workers were organized to complement each other's activities in ways that increased their production, and unskilled workers were organized in protofactory settings. Each section of the arsenal had its own superintendent, with the commissary general of military stores the overall director of operations. The commissary issued production orders to the separate managers and informed those managers where their work should be delivered for final completion. Though located in separate parts of the city, the arsenal's various components were managed to become an interdependent whole.

The Philadelphia Arsenal contained eight components spread out around the city that were remarkably interconnected. The armory and ordnance yard were most likely near the State House or Carpenter's Hall. The department rented several buildings on Chestnut Street, and any one of these could have been a workshop, as could the area around the State House, which is known to have housed ordnance during the war. The leather shop was probably in Henry Lisle's tanyards along Dock Creek, which was the dye and tanning center in the city. This site could have also housed the drum factory owing to the need for leather, though Chestnut Street was also a likely candidate. The Continental Air Furnace was first rented from Pennsylvania in Southwark but seems to have moved to the grounds of Carpenter's Hall in 1781. The Fifth Street Laboratory was in a building at Fifth and Sassafras (now Race) streets, while the Knight's Wharf Laboratory was at Peter Knight's Wharf in Northern Liberties, but the exact location of that wharf is unknown.[1]

From these various locations, workers supported each other's production. Ordnance yard workers delivered raw materials and tools to the furnace, leather shop, armory, laboratories, and drum factory. The leather shop dressed leather and forwarded it to the ordnance yard and drum factory. The furnace cast components for the armory and musket balls for the laboratories. The laboratories returned artillery ammunition to the ordnance yard for shipment to the army alongside artillery. Any items not needed by the army were stored in the department's warehouse at Carpenter's Hall under the direction of the commissary general. At its height, the "Regiment of Artillery Artificers" and "hired men" at the Philadelphia Arsenal totaled 308 individuals.[2] These government operations were supported by local private facilities such as paper mills, iron furnaces, powder mills, gunsmith shops, and sawmills, whose work the regional commissary coordinated to match the arsenal's needs.[3] Despite the overall organization of the Philadelphia Arsenal, three components of the site stand out as examples of managed production: the Fifth Street Laboratory, the ordnance yard, and the armory. At these locations, specialization and coordination of labor achieved a high level of sophistication, creating production efficiencies greater than could be achieved with traditional craftwork.

The various laboratories established by Congress operated like factories to a certain extent, but none rose to the level of production and division of labor achieved by Philadelphia's Fifth Street Laboratory. Workers there only made musket cartridges, while workers at Carlisle, Springfield, Philadelphia's Knight's Wharf Laboratory, and the other regional laboratories made musket cartridges and artillery ammunition as needed. Production at other laboratories was coordinated by managers, but it was difficult to impose labor specialization consistently because workers were called on to make different items at different times.[4] The Fifth Street Laboratory was an improvement on British models of ammunition production. At the Woolwich laboratory, workers were specialized in the various segments of artillery ammunition production, but their production was not coordinated for large-scale output. This was also true of the musket armories at Woolwich and Greenwich that turned out cartridges. As late as the revolution, the British army manufactured the bulk of its musket ammunition in the field. Between battles, soldiers were issued lead, powder, and paper and ordered to make enough ammunition for an upcoming campaign. Such production practices remained in place in wartime because it was cheaper and easier for the British to transport the component parts of ammunition than to move the constructed whole.[5]

The Fifth Street Laboratory did not materialize instantly in summer 1778 but rather was the result of earlier efforts by Congress to supply the army. Flower rented buildings and put men to work producing munitions in Philadelphia sometime in 1777. Munitions production was moved from the capital to Lebanon, Pennsylvania, during the occupation. The latest evidence of the Lebanon site in operation was dated July 31, 1778, and the Fifth Street Laboratory was in operation by the end of the preceding August.[6] Thus it appears that Flower made the decision to move cartridge-production operations back to the capital when the campaign season was winding down. At this point, Flower rented a building at Fifth and Arch Streets for the cartridge makers.

Operations at the laboratory were organized to keep the production of cartridges constant and to ensure that quality cartridges were prepared for shipment to the front. Flower and Hodgdon kept all necessary production inputs for the laboratory in the departmental magazine at Carpenter's Hall. They sent lead to the furnace for conversion to ball and acquired powder, paper, and thread from domestic and foreign suppliers, sending each item to the factory when requested by Joseph Boehm, the laboratory superintendent, who received and signed for all supplies. Once delivered, all input materials were organized for production. Paper was delivered to cutters, who sized it for the cartridge formers, while powder was measured out in pint-sized batches for each former. Cut cartridge paper looked like a triangle with one corner cut off to make a trapezoid that measured six inches, by five and a half inches, by two inches, by seven and a half inches. Also, lengths of thread were cut for each worker.[7]

A well-ventilated forming room was a separate section of the laboratory that contained forming tables for the cartridge makers. The room had to provide a free flow of air to reduce the risk of static discharge and to keep the powder from absorbing moisture. Most likely, workers wore as little loose clothing as possible to reduce the risk of static. Once in the room, formers sat at twelve-foot-long tables made to allow for workspace while also holding materials with which the formers worked. Formers were issued batches of musket balls at a single time, usually five hundred balls, though more-productive workers received up to one thousand at a time while less-productive workers received as few as two hundred at a time. Each worker received cartridge paper, a length of thread, and perhaps a pint of gunpowder.[8]

Though they seem to be a simple item, musket cartridges followed a complex construction process. It began with the worker placing a single piece of cut paper on the table in front of her. To form the paper into a cartridge, a worker used a six-inch wooden dowel that was concave at one end to hold a musket ball. The dowel was placed one inch from one edge of the paper, a ball was placed in the concave end of the dowel, and the paper was then rolled around the whole to form a tube. The end nearest the ball was tied off, and the thread was trimmed with a knife.

O. F. G. Hogg, "Girls making cartridges, 1862." This picture, though dated later than the period under discussion, provides a general idea of what cartridge making looked like at the Fifth Street Laboratory. (*The Royal Armory, vol. 2*)

The dowel was removed, and using a small tin measure, the worker took about an ounce of powder from his supply and poured it into the open end of the cartridge. The second open end was then folded over to seal the cartridge. The cartridges were then stacked near each person's workstation until all inputs had been used. When a worker had finished wrapping all the balls he had been issued, he returned completed cartridges to Boehm, who counted them, judged their fitness for use, and delivered them to packers. On average, each worker produced 131 cartridges per day.[9]

Proper packing and shipment were as critical to the production process as was forming each individual cartridge. Once Boehm had received completed cartridges, he turned them over to packers, who placed them carefully in ammunition crates made by artificers in the ordnance yard. They then waterproofed the crates with grease and sent them to Hodgdon for storage at Carpenter's Hall.[10] Hodgdon issued cartridges to the Main Army. General Nathanael Greene revealed how important each part of the process was to the successful supply of the army when he complained in 1782 that "the Cartridges that came last from the Northern Laboratories are too small, and badly made. Stores on the road suffers such damage, delays, and embezzlements that a great part of them are frequently lost, and rendered useless."[11] Cartridges not only had to be properly made but properly packed and shipped to prevent damage.

By far the greatest complaint made against Continental cartridges was the inappropriate size of the musket balls produced. At least five cartridge sizes emanated from the Fifth Street Laboratory referred to simply by a number: 17, 19, 24, 28, and 36. Each number referred to how many balls could be made from a pound of lead. A 17 was thus a large ball, while a 36 was very small. The variety of sizes was due to the variety of weapons being used in the Continental Army. Some troops were armed with British muskets, which had a larger bore barrel, while other troops were armed with American-made muskets of various sizes relative to the

British. By 1779, however, a large number of American troops were carrying French muskets, which were smaller bore than British ones. To make greater use of the available lead, the factory produced a great number of 19s, while Washington and his subordinates would have preferred 17s.[12] This problem, however, was not a significant one, and while Washington and others complained about ammunition size, it was never more than an annoyance to them.

Workers at the laboratory produced approximately 4.2 million musket cartridges of various sizes during the factory's five-and-a-half-year existence from August 1778 to February 1784. About one quarter of the factory's total output came in its first six months of operation at a point when lead and money were readily available. Between August 1778 and January 1779, approximately 1.2 million cartridges were made. February, however, brought a precipitous decline in production. After reaching a production high of 274,992 cartridges in January, workers in February turned out only 159,480.[13] Output then declined over the next five months until June 1779, when monthly production bottomed out at 70,286 cartridges. By summer 1779, lead supplies had been used up, and new stocks had not arrived. Moreover, Congress had decided early in 1779 to stop printing its Continental currency because it had driven inflation so high that it was not nearly worth the paper on which it was printed. Workers were laid off from the laboratory, and production slumped, increasing during periods when money and resources were available (see chart 1).

The arrival of several supplies of lead and rebounded currency values helped Hodgdon establish a level of consistency in cartridge production beginning in fall 1780. Just under one hundred thousand pounds of lead became available in summer 1780, half from domestic sources and half from the French government. Production until the spring remained meager but steady at an average of twenty-nine thousand per month between September 1780 and March 1781. That, however, was not enough to support a planned assault on New York City being considered by Knox and Washington. They pressured Congress to authorize the production of as many cartridges as possible. Hodgdon provided Congress with an estimate of expenses and identified the location of lead available for purchase by his department because he did not have sufficient amounts in store. Washington's endorsement of the project forced Congress to authorize Hodgdon's proposal. Production jumped to an average of one hundred twenty-seven thousand cartridges per month in April and May 1781 but was scaled back when the assault on New York City was scrapped. The possibility of capturing Cornwallis's army, however, led Congress to once again pour money into the laboratory, which produced roughly one hundred seventy-five thousand cartridges for the Yorktown Campaign.

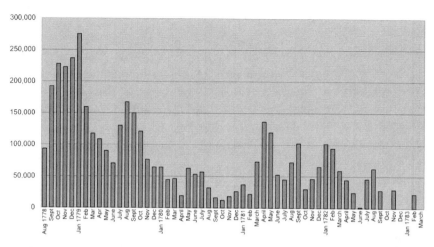

Chart 1. Monthly output of cartridges from the Fifth Street Laboratory from August 1778 to March 1783.

Supplies of lead and money were at this point plentiful, at least as far as the Fifth Street Laboratory was concerned. Production remained steady and even increased over winter 1781–82, when Washington again considered an attack on New York City. That operation, like its predecessor, was canceled, but this time it was put off because a peace treaty was in the offing. Without a specific need for more cartridges, production at Fifth Street dwindled, despite an ample supply of lead and modest supplies of money thanks to Hodgdon's budgetary finesse.[14] When discussing the needs of the Southern Army and the frontier in 1782, Hodgdon could tell the secretary at war that he expected "to be able to furnish the whole [of their needs] from our own laboratories from the materials now returned [accounted] for and those we have on hand."[15] Production was not extraordinary at the Fifth Street cartridge factory from autumn 1780 until February 1783, when production ceased, but it was able to react consistently to the needs of the army. Production increased to meet the expected demands of the northern and southern campaigns and declined to meet the daily needs of an army encamped in the Hudson Valley.

Supplies needed to complete a musket cartridge, other than lead, seem to have been more readily available to the laboratory according to military stores account books. Throughout its existence, workers cut and folded 613 reams of paper into cartridges, filled them with 963.25 barrels of gunpowder, and tied those cartridges off with 435 pounds of thread. These components seem only once to have been in short supply.

Delivery records show that rather than dictate production, as did supplies of money and lead, the amount of powder, paper, and thread expended reacted to ups and downs in the production cycle. When the laboratory needed powder, paper, or thread, Hodgdon sent it, and he never complained to Congress that he did not have any of those supplies. This situation seems to reflect the large number of paper and powder mills in the Philadelphia region and the greater availability of powder, rather than lead, from overseas sources. Continental, French, and private ships usually delivered arms and powder, and only rarely raw lead, which was what the factory needed most. Therefore, the stores of powder Hodgdon kept were significant. In July 1778, the military stores department had 2,921 barrels of gunpowder on hand. By March 1780, that figure was down to 368.75 barrels, but by July 1781, Hodgdon had over 1,067 barrels of gunpowder. Paper and thread, likewise, were used up rapidly but replenished sufficiently to keep the department well stocked for supporting its manufacturing activities. The department had 982 reams of cartridge paper available in July 1778 and 319 reams in March 1780. Reserve stores of paper ran out in July 1781 because Hodgdon did not have the cash on hand to prepare for future production. Laboratory records reveal, however, that it was not lacking necessary supplies. Hodgdon, it appears, was able to purchase paper, because supplies at the factory rebounded rapidly after this point. The availability of thread actually increased from 1780 through 1781.[16]

At least 184 identifiable individuals were employed at the laboratory during its operation from August 1778 to February 1783. Based on turnover rates, an additional forty-six unrecorded individuals may have joined the employee roles at Fifth Street on an interim basis. The greatest number of workers in any one-month period came in January 1779, when eighty-six men and women were employed in the forming room making cartridges. As many as fourteen more individuals may have been employed in preparation and shipping functions, but this is unclear from the records. The average number of workers on hand through the first two years of production was thirty-seven per month. This average most certainly dropped below twenty during the last two years of the factory's operations, but there is not enough information to be sure of an exact number. Of the total number of workers specifically identified, 106, or nearly 60 percent were female. Workers, on average, remained at the lab for only 129 days, or just over four months, but fully half of all identifiable workers worked sixty days or less. Unfortunately, it is impossible to determine why they stayed this relatively short amount of time. Tellingly, however, the median number of workdays was 227, or seven and a half months, revealing that some workers were employed for a rather extended period. There was, apparently, a cadre of employees who made up the core of producers at Fifth Street.

Generally, workers at the factory fell into three categories based on their length of service. The first category was made up of short-term employees, most of whom made cartridges during the first few months of production when lead and money were in large supply. These workers were relatively unproductive, each making about 109 cartridges per day. About 35 percent of workers took jobs at the factory several months after it began operations and remained for perhaps eight months. These workers were more productive than the short-term workers but appear to have been seasonal, or budgetary. They returned to the factory when needed as money became available or left the factory for other employment. These workers averaged 116 cartridges per day. The third category included the twenty-one recorded workers who spent more than one year employed at the factory. This group made an average of 145 cartridges per day. The three longest serving recorded workers were Catherine Bryan, Sarah Cribs, and Catherine Friend, who each worked 570 days at the factory, from just after it began operations until employee records end in July 1780. Catherine Friend also stands out as the single largest producer of cartridges, fabricating 211,300 during her tenure at Fifth Street. In fact, of those who worked longest, over half (eleven) were women. It might be expected that the most productive workers were the ones who were retained in employment longest, but the records do not reflect this. Several very productive workers who could form five hundred cartridges per day worked for only a few days or weeks, while at least one woman, Susanna Querrill, is recorded working for just over a year, having produced only six thousand cartridges.[17]

There is significant evidence to suggest that a piece-rate pay scale operated at Fifth Street during its first two years, until workers were converted to a day-wage system. Flower was under significant pressure in 1778 to spare no expense producing ammunition for the Continental Army. Washington was convinced that the army was destitute of munitions and consequently unable to face the enemy. Such pressures, combined with the great deal of latitude Flower was given to hire workers on whatever terms possible meant there was impetus to institute a piece-rate system of production. The Board of War wrote Flower, "we agree with your plan and encourage you to enact it, whereby the several officers are directed to pay the workers based on their ability and industry."[18] Flower's laboratory records substantiate this system's existence. Flower's employee account book listed the numbers of musket cartridges made rather than the days of a worker's employment. The account book suggests that formers were paid per each hundred cartridges they formed. The account book also omitted several laborers listed on departmental returns. Men listed on these returns were apparently paid a daily wage. Thus, Flower and his subordinates differentiated between types of workers at the factory.

A change occurred in 1780 that altered the pay system at the lab. The government's money supply dried up as the year progressed, forcing Hodgdon to dismiss workers. The total number of workers at the factory dropped below twenty. From this point on, laboratory workers were paid a daily wage. Such a system served two purposes. Workers could be hired and fired on a daily basis, which saved money for the department. Further, people had little faith in Congress's money. A high daily wage made working for the government more appealing than a long-term commitment. Such a commitment combined with spiraling inflation meant that when a worker finally got paid, the money was worthless. Workers in the department as a whole were paid ten dollars per day in 1779. In summer 1780, Hodgdon secured a raise for the workers to twelve dollars per day. The following year, inflation and need forced Hodgdon to pay cartridge makers thirty dollars per day.[19]

The Fifth Street Laboratory was a protofactory managed in order to efficiently regulate the use of the government's laborers, raw materials, and money. Using "capital, the congregation of workpeople, the division of labour and the exercise of supervision," the military stores administrators clearly built a recognizable eighteenth-century protofactory.[20] The only feature missing that would have made this operation a factory in the modern sense is the use of machinery. To start with, operations at Fifth Street were a significant investment for the military stores department, which spent over $3,370,400, or about 80 cents per cartridge, to operate the laboratory for four years.[21] Production at Fifth Street relied on the centralization of labor. On average there were twenty workers congregated at the laboratory, and for at least a year that number was significantly higher, averaging closer to forty workers. And unlike earlier American operations such as those at the United Company, Fifth Street relied in no way on putting-out methods. All production was done under one roof by unskilled and semiskilled workers. Putting-out could not be used; the production inputs were too valuable and too volatile to send home with workers to assemble, so everything had to be done in-house. Once munitions production had been centralized at Fifth Street, labor was divided between preparation, shipping, and forming. Workers were specialized in their activities, and there was no crossover or exchange of activities. An interesting element to this dynamic was that female workers were only employed as cartridge formers. They were hired for their lack of skill and their cost-effectiveness just as later generations of women would be hired in factories for the same reasons. Again, unlike the United Company, which relied on typical female methods of production to stay operational, Fifth Street brought women into factory-labor organization. And Fifth Street had similar turnover statistics to later factories, which were notoriously unable to retain workers for long periods of time. The final element of efficiency of this operation was that Joseph Boehm had superintendence over the whole operation, judged the quality of the cartridges, oversaw the workers, and paid them for their work. While Fifth Street was not as sophisticated in its production methods as nineteenth-century factories would become, it was one of the earliest and arguably most successful factories America had yet seen. Moreover, Fifth Street was a clear link between the semifactory organizations of the colonial period and the full-factory organizations of the nineteenth century.

The military stores department did not limit its management activities to unskilled workers but also used master craftsmen and military officers to coordinate the production of skilled craftsmen. Philadelphia's ordnance yard and its armory used centralized manufacturing to increase the level of production of the semiskilled and skilled workers operating there. The ordnance yard possessed various craft-specific workshops employing a roughly equal number of hired and enlisted men. The yard was originally established to contain a magazine for housing artillery stores, a smith's shop for repairing artillery stores, and an open space for storing and proving artillery. As operations in the city grew, other types of artificers were located at the yard, and workshops were constructed for them to use. By early 1779, the yard possessed not only the blacksmith shop but also workshops for carpenters, wheelwrights, file cutters, tinsmiths, and finishers (whitesmiths). A December 1779 report listed thirty-two enlisted artificers working at the yard from both John Jordan's, and Nathan Chapman's companies. Forty-eight hired men were employed at the yard as well. From 1779 through 1780, when operations were moved to Carlisle, the number of artificers in the yard seems to have declined only slightly as it became more expensive to hire workers and the government had less money with which to pay them. Nevertheless, there were likely never fewer than fifty craftsmen at the yard before the move to Carlisle.[22] In 1779, blacksmiths were by far the largest craft specialty at the yard, making up 36 percent of the workforce with a total of twenty-nine men. There were eighteen carpenters, seven wheelwrights, five finishers, three turners, three file cutters, a cooper, and several laborers and colliers.

Management of the ordnance yard was convoluted but coordinated with several levels of management as was indicative of centralized manufacture. Three men shared oversight of the yard: John Jordan, commander of the enlisted artificers; Daniel Joy, superintendent of ordnance; and Valentine Hoffman, superintendent of the hired blacksmiths. Each workshop in turn also had its own foreman. Hoffman was the senior man and therefore coordinated most activities at the yard. Technically, though, he managed only the hired workers, and only the hired foremen answered to him. Jordan commanded all the enlisted artificers and could issue production orders separate from Hoffman, though he could not force the hired men to heed his orders. Joy was chief inspector of all

Continental ordnance and ordnance stores and had authority through that inspectorate, though no one at the yard answered directly to him. What confused matters is that foremen sometimes approached Hodgdon directly for material and orders, and he in turn often bypassed his own superintendents and ordered work directly from the workshops. Nevertheless, Hoffman, Jordan, and Joy seem to have shared leadership of the post effectively, as there exist copious communications among the men that illuminate their cooperation. There is no record of conflict over command, and when Joy went on inspection tours in 1780 and 1781, Jordan and Hoffman took up his responsibilities as inspector at the yard. Hodgdon's communications addressed each man as equally responsible for activities at the yard, and he relied on each to produce what was needed when it was needed, regardless of whom it was requested.[23] Ultimately, the commissary general imposed order on the yard by acting as the central manager of all Philadelphia operations. The commissary general's direction was a critical factor in balancing the distribution of power at the yard. As will be seen with the Springfield Arsenal in chapter 5, without a stable command infrastructure, centralized manufacturing could easily fall apart.

The ordnance yard was founded primarily for the storage and repair of ordnance and ordnance accouterments. Ordnance artificers never cast or recast cannons but left that to private manufacturers. Instead, artificers at the ordnance yard focused their efforts on the carriages and accouterments necessary to operate artillery. From March 1780 through November 1783, artificers at the ordnance yard constructed or repaired 212 cannon carriages. Of the total carriages worked on, 187 were traveling carriages sent to the Main Army or the state militias, either with cannons or to replace damaged carriages in the field. Five garrison carriages were provided to Washington's army on its march south to Yorktown, and an additional thirteen garrison carriages were supplied to the Continental Navy. Only seven mortar beds were constructed by the ordnance yard after March 1780.[24] There were, however, not that many mortars in operation with the army, which may explain the small number produced.

Gun carriages were not made in colonial America; the nearest similar product was a chaise or personal carriage. Traditionally, a wainwright made the whole carriage, or perhaps farmed out some of the items and assembled the whole himself. At the yard, carpenters, blacksmiths, wheelwrights, and turners combined their efforts to manufacture a cannon carriage. The spine of a traveling carriage was made up of two cheeks and tails held together by two platforms, one between the tails and one between the cheeks. This was then fastened to an axle to which two wheels were attached. Each wheel consisted of a hub, axletree, spokes, fellies, and tires. Carpenters made the cheeks, tails, and platforms out of boards cut at a local sawmill. They then fastened them together using iron clamps and sockets made by the blacksmiths. Meanwhile, the wheelwrights made the wheels, and once they had fastened the wood pieces to one another, they strengthened the whole with iron screws, again made by the blacksmiths. The blacksmiths then took the wheel and fastened an iron tire to it. They also attached iron rests for the firing apparatus as well as clamps for holding the cannon trunnions to the carriage, and handles for attaching ropes or harnesses for moving the cannon. It was up to Jordan or Hoffman to see that all the pieces were put together properly. It is not clear which artificers did the final assembly, but construction procedures could have been as convoluted as the management structure: whoever was available put the final product together. A garrison carriage and mortar bed could be constructed by the carpenters with only outside assistance from the blacksmiths. A garrison carriage had truncated cheeks and tails bolted together with a wood platform underneath. Four small wheels were attached to the four corners of the carriage. Iron clamps held the wheel axles in place as well as the cannon's trunnions. A mortar bed was a simple, heavily constructed, wooden platform with iron clamps for the trunnions and iron handles on each side for attaching ropes or poles to move the mortar.[25] A cannon was not considered complete, however, until it was accompanied by the many tools necessary to fire it. The ordnance yard artificers produced these tools as well.

Artillerymen required four or five tools to prepare and fire a cannon. A worm was necessary to clear the bore of any material left from the previous firing. A sponge was then soaked in water and rammed into the bore to extinguish any embers from the previous firing. If fixed or previously prepared ammunition was available, a ladle was not needed. If not, a ladle was used to scoop powder and place it in the cannon. A rammer was then used to push the powder to the back of the bore before a cannonball or canister was loaded. A linstock, with a slow match burning on the end, was then used to fire the cannon. Carpenters made each of these tools, which all started out as wooden poles. In the case of the rammer and sponge, a block was placed at the end and wrapped, the rammer in cloth and the sponge in sheepskin. At least five hundred artillery sponges and rammers were produced at the yard.[26] The finishing of these items was probably done by hired laborers working for Jordan or Hoffman. The linstock and worm were tipped with iron components by the blacksmiths. The linstock had an iron branch, like a fancy "T," at the end, around which the slow match was wrapped. The worm was finished with a coil of iron fastened to the end. Brass founders made the ladle, which was probably attached to the pole by the blacksmiths. Brass was used instead of iron so as not to accidentally spark when used with an iron cannon.[27] What made these processes beneficial to the Continental

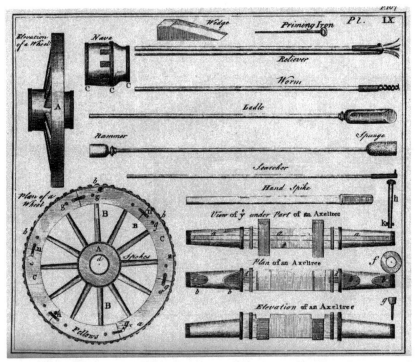

This image of cannon carriage elements and artillery accouterments accompanied the field carriage diagram in Muller's *Treatise of Artillery* that was shown on page xxiii of this volume. Here are displayed various perspectives of carriage wheels and axels that could be compared to measurement tables in the book for scale. This picture also illustrates accessories used with a cannon, though dimensions are not provided. From top to bottom, and not in the order of usage: A wedge was used to hold the wheels in place for firing. A priming iron cleaned out the touch hole and punctured the ammunition bag of a fixed shot for firing. The reliever and worm removed large cartridge remnants from the cannon's previous firing. The ladle was used to scoop an appropriate measure of gunpowder into the cannon for firing if fixed ammunition was not being used. A sponge and rammer were sometimes, but not always on the same staff, because the wet sponge was used to clean out the cannon barrel after firing, while the rammer tamped down the powder and cannonball for the next firing. A searcher was used to occasionally check the inside of a cannon for cracks in order to avoid a cannon bursting during firing. Finally, a handspike was used to rotate and aim a field artillery piece. (*Muller,* Treatise of Artillery, *107*)

Army was that the craftsmen could continue making their specific components and laborers or other craftsmen could assemble the whole when it was required. This was not interchangeability, because finishing work still had to be done for all the components to fit together properly.

Moreover, if a cannon carriage arrived in need of repair, the craftsmen could interrupt their work and repair it because they had enough component parts on hand to allow production elsewhere in the yard to continue. When the army was in desperate need and work at the yard backed up, the yard could send the parts of a carriage necessary for the artillerymen to repair it themselves. Correspondence suggests, however, that artificers moved from one project to the next. When carriages had to be fixed, they were fixed; when accouterments had to be made, they were made.

The second most important function of the artificers at the ordnance yard was the manufacture of tools and parts for the rest of the arsenal and the field commissary. The blacksmiths forged files that were sent to the file cutters to be etched for use by the carpenters, the Knight's Wharf Laboratory, and the armory. They also made gouges, vices, hammers, drill bits, saws, and chisels for the carpenters, turners, and armorers. For the leather makers they created shoemaker's tools, stretching pins, knives, and punches. The most extensive blacksmith work was the preparation of over a dozen traveling forges, including their attendant tools for the field commissaries. These were miniforges, each one set on a wood platform and raised on two wheels, so it looked like an oversized cannon carriage. It comprised six sections: a bellows, a box to store tools, an iron plate for the fireplace, a wooden trough for water, an iron plate to lay the tools on while working, and iron side plates that enclosed the work area. At one end of the wooden superstructure were the limbers for attaching to a horse harness. At the opposite end was the iron work area. In between the ends was the bellows surmounted by a wooden cage that held a handle for working the bellows pulley mechanism. On either side of the bellows, between the bellows and the wheels, were the tool boxes. Frontline artificers used traveling forges to make minor repairs to weapons and accouterments. Carpenters, using leather provided by the leather works, made smith's bellows. Using hardware made by the blacksmiths, they also created ammunition boxes and arms chests for storing and shipping munitions. In addition, they made hammer, axe, and handsaw handles. Coopers worked with blacksmith products to make powder casks. Finishers polished blacksmith products like linstocks and foundry products like buckles and musket parts. Buckles were used to make shoes as well as cartridge boxes, while musket parts were sent to the armory. Turners at the yard formed some of the stocks used at the armory according to patterns made by the armory. Blacksmiths occasionally forged musket barrels and iron bands for connecting musket barrels to stocks. The completion of work throughout the arsenal relied on the coordination of tool production at the ordnance yard, which was an overall example of coordinated production within the department. Tools were sent to Carlisle and Springfield for workers at those posts to use. Workers at the ordnance yard were required to coordinate their own work, as well as to make and repair tools for themselves.[28] The ordnance yard, however, was not the only element of the Philadelphia Arsenal where craftsmen were managed to increase overall output.

Managers at the armory specialized and coordinated the work of skilled gunsmiths to produce finished muskets. The armorers' main product was the gunlock, though workers were segmented at the armory to produce other major musket components. Those components included tin cartridge boxes, musket stocks, musket barrels, bayonets, ramrods, and the furniture necessary for completing the muskets like screws and bands. Forty-four men worked at the Philadelphia armory in December 1779, but their jobs were not delineated in departmental returns. Inventories, however, reveal that there were three turner's wheels in Philadelphia, and at least one of these was at the armory, accompanied by at least one set of turner's tools and three sets of planes. There were three bayonet borers and thirty-four ramrod borers in the department, though it is not stated how many were at any one location. The largest set of tools were those for lock making, including 405 "Punches, Stamps, Drills, Reamers, Taps, etc." and 158 various files. There were also twenty-two smith's tongs, twenty-six vices, eleven hammers, one large drill, one lock piece grinder, and at least one barrel grindstone.[29] Each of these items could be used for either lock or barrel finishing. The composition of tools at the armory suggests that a majority of the armorers were lock makers and finishers. A second significant segment of men were barrel makers. Three smaller groups of men, perhaps of three men each, made bayonets, ramrods, and stocks. Joseph Perkins, the superintendent, oversaw production by a final group of armorers.[30] There are no indications how these operations were physically organized in the armory building or buildings, but a glimpse of the Continental armory is available based on the description of a large-scale gun shop by gunsmith John Nicholson.

Nicholson presented the Pennsylvania Council of Safety with an armory plan hoping it would hire him to organize its gun works. Pennsylvania's armory was never built on the scale of Nicholson's example, but production figures suggest that the Continental armory was built on that scale. According to Nicholson, a gun factory would first have three or four forges for making gun barrels, complemented by a water-powered boring and grinding mill for the barrels. Though the Philadelphia armory did not have a boring or grinding mill, it did have hand-powered machinery for the purpose, and it likely had several forges for gun barrels based on the number of people employed. Moreover, the armorers had access to the blacksmith's shop in the ordnance yard to assist them in making gun barrels. Nicholson then recommended a second shop that would contain three forges to support lock making, where lock filers could harden and temper the springs and case harden the locks. The large number of lock maker's tools relative to other gunsmith tools make it likely this function was segregated from the others at the Philadelphia armory as Nicholson recommended. A third shop was to include the gun-stocking operation, and a fourth shop would house the brass founder, who would make the mountings. Again, tool records suggest gunstocks were made at the ordnance yard and at a separate site in the armory. The brass founder, on the other hand, was in another part of the city, where the Continental armory had a dedicated brass smith. The bayonets and steel ramrods necessary to fully outfit a musket would be contained in a fifth shop, according to Nicholson. A final assembly shop would be next to the brass and stocking shops. All this was to be kept together through the efforts of a knowledgeable superintendent and responsible clerk.[31] Perkins was just such a manager for the Continental armory. The example Nicholson provided fits the other historical records available, making it a useful diagram for understanding how operations were organized at the armory. The numbers and types of tools relative to the number of people employed at the armory make it more than likely that functions were separated. The fact that brass and turning operations were done off-site further reinforces that the gunsmiths at the armory shared their work in an adaptable craft fashion for more-efficient production because they were receiving their inputs from segregated operations. This organization was important because it allowed Perkins to peer in on every operation and certify that each musket was finished to Continental standards.

If the analysis of the Philadelphia Arsenal's component parts is assembled into a view of the production system as a whole, a major efficiency is revealed that demonstrates just how innovative Hodgdon and his team were. The production, types and locations of tools, and types and locations of workers within the Philadelphia Arsenal reveal that managers developed labor divisions to some extent. This was an organizational development that had not been fully imported from Europe, though there were examples of it at the Fifth Street Laboratory, the Knight's Wharf Laboratory, and the United Company protofactory prior to the war. It seems likely from the sources that managers in the arsenal created divisions of labor organically because workers could then more easily be managed and could be coordinated more effectively. The tools present at the Philadelphia armory suggest that though gunsmiths there engaged in numerous production functions, their primary role was gunlock production and musket finishing. Components for musket locks as well as the weapons' brass construction hardware were forged at the air furnace by blacksmiths and brass founders. Blacksmiths at the ordnance yard produced iron skelps for the armorers, which would be worked into gun barrels. Those same blacksmiths manufactured screws, butt plates, and other iron furniture for the muskets. Carpenters at the ordnance yard, where most of the turners' wheels were located, manufactured most of the gun stocks. All of these component parts were then sent to the armory, where gunsmiths assembled the pieces. There is strong, though not conclusive, evidence that there was a division of labor at the armory. There were not enough forge tools available to employ each individual gunsmith in making barrels and then completing the musket. Instead, based on the tools available, there were probably four separate jobs completed at the armory. Some gunsmiths made barrels, some made ramrods, some made gunlocks, and some assembled everything into a complete musket. The organization of labor and the layout of the production system at Philadelphia was not a perfect model of the division of labor that industrialists achieved in later generations, but it was a start.

Disbursements identified in Hodgdon's account book illustrate the productivity of the armorers for the second half of their three-year term of production. From March 1780 through August 1781, the Philadelphia armorers repaired 5,577 muskets and manufactured an additional 9,659. These figures suggest that on average, the workers of the armory repaired 310 damaged muskets and produced 536 new muskets each month. Much of the production can be attributed to the six-month period prior to March 1780 when forty-two men were employed at the armory and over eighty at the ordnance yard. Nevertheless, distribution records support the conclusion that the production of at least fifteen thousand muskets and the repair of ten thousand more was not out of the question during the armory's existence from 1778 until 1781. By March 1780, with 1,124 new and repaired muskets fit for service in store, there were enough pieces to make only a dozen new muskets. Yet within three months, the arsenal supplied the main and southern armies with 4,526 muskets. In the course of four months, arsenal workers had manufactured and assembled the parts for just over two thousand five hundred new muskets and repaired seven hundred more.[32] Hodgdon told the Board of War in June 1780 that he had two thousand eight hundred repairable muskets in store and that he could have one thousand "of the best . . . ready in one week provided I am furnished with money to pay workmen and they are supplied with the usual rations."[33] If Hodgdon could foresee a one-week repair time for one thousand muskets, there was no reason why arsenal workers could not repair and manufacture at the levels indicated above. By way of comparison, if the gunsmiths had been organized as was typical of craft operations (i.e., one gunsmith with two assistants), they would have been able to produce only two thousand two hundred weapons a year, just over one-third of average annual production at the armory. The arsenal, and the armory within it, was organized for rapid production through the management of crafts skills.

FROM HIS OFFICE AT CARPENTER'S HALL, THE COMMISSARY GENERAL OF military stores oversaw a complex interplay of manufacturing activities. Each operation relied on the work done at the others, and none of the operations could have been as effective as it was without the others. Workers at the furnace and tannery provided components to the ordnance yard and the armory for the production of weapons, artillery, and accouterments. Ordnance yard workers produced tools for their own use as well as the use of smiths, tanners, armorers, and ammunition formers. The weapons manufactured at the armory were irrelevant without the cartridges made at Fifth Street, and the artillery produced at the ordnance yard was useless without the work done at Knight's Wharf Laboratory. In a sense, the entire operation of the arsenal was a proto-factory, which used labor-enhancing machinery to support human productive efforts. The component parts then used various types of cutting-edge organization to ensure that military stores could be produced at levels far beyond typical craftwork. The Philadelphia Arsenal in its separate operations and its structural whole revealed how the ideas of the Industrial Revolution were imported to mobilize the American economy for wartime production needs. But Philadelphia was not the only military manufacturing center in the United States, and it is to those facilities in Carlisle and Springfield that we now turn.

5

"ARTIFICERS, WHO prefer LIBERTY to SLAVERY"

MANUFACTURING INNOVATION AT CARLISLE AND SPRINGFIELD

ONGRESS CHOSE CARLISLE, PENNSYLVANIA, AS ITS MAIN MILITARY manufacturing center because the British had built several buildings near the town in 1757 during the French and Indian War. Nathaniel Irish believed he was marching his men west in mid-1777 to take possession of these buildings, which were said to include some storehouses, a blockhouse, and perhaps some outbuildings. The site had been an army post and was supposed to look like one; at least that's what everyone from Congress to George Washington to Benjamin Flower to Irish believed. At most, the commanders believed, the army's new artificers would have to complete repairs and construct a few outbuildings. Imagine Irish's surprise when he arrived in Carlisle to find instead several crumbled and rotten buildings surrounded by overgrown meadows bisected by a swift and flood-prone creek. Worse yet, the property and buildings Irish expected to use were not even vacant property left free to occupy. They had been purchased from Pennsylvania several years previously by a Carlisle farmer. Irish, however, was not a man to be intimidated easily and he knew "Great things were expected of Carlisle."[1]

Despite lacking the anticipated foundation on which to build, Carlisle remained an ideal choice for an arsenal. It was central to the numerous large towns and furnaces in western Pennsylvania and close to roads and rivers, and operations could be built to suit the governments manufacturing goals. Over the next few months, Irish transformed the landscape. He rented the land from owner Thomas Wilson, a thorough patriot, and put his men to work clearing it. The men then constructed eleven buildings before winter snows brought their work to a halt. By then the artificers and townsfolk were calling the site Washingtonburg, a manufacturing "city" that had grown from nothing to supply the general's army.

Carlisle, unlike Philadelphia, was designed and built as a manufacturing arsenal. Flower had begun operations in Philadelphia as a temporary extension of the ordnance yard until Carlisle was operational. The capital's military stores activities were kept in place to support the 1777 campaign and then disrupted by the British occupation. Congress, Washington, and Flower all recognized the advantages of Philadelphia as a manufacturing center during the months they had to do without it. It had a large labor supply and proximity to transportation and raw materials, and it was closer to the army than was Carlisle. Flower was therefore more interested in getting manufacturing activities operational after the occupation and less interested in designing the facilities for those activities. He rented whatever buildings he could and put both hired and enlisted men to work. But Flower had to build Carlisle from scratch. It gave him the opportunity to construct a site conducive to productivity. It took almost half a year to construct the post, but during that time and into 1778, men were also at work making accouterments and repairing items for the Continental Army.

Flower left Irish with detailed instructions of what he wanted out of the arsenal.[2] Irish was to take possession of any buildings he needed while he constructed buildings "sufficient for forty carpenters, forty black smiths, twenty wheelwrights, four tin men, and four turners, twelve harnessmakers and four coopers."[3] Flower wanted a "wooden building 100 feet long by 36 upon the south end of the lot . . . for the use of the armourers" and other "wooden buildings where the artificers etc are to be employed."[4] In addition, Irish was to build a boring mill and furnace at suitable locations. Within seven months, Irish mobilized enough men to build over thirty thousand square feet of work and living space, including seven workshops, a hospital, a prison, a powder magazine, and a warehouse. The largest building was a two-story, thirteen-thousand–square-foot brick armorers' shop. This building followed the dimensions provided for such a structure by John Muller in *A Treatise on Practical Fortification*. A boring mill was begun in the mountains south of Carlisle near a sawmill that was commandeered and repaired. A large air furnace was built on the LeTort Creek, just beyond the workshops. But this was only part of Irish's accomplishments. Before construction could commence, Irish's men had to use the few tools sent from Philadelphia to craft all the tools they would need to build the arsenal. As the carpenters set to the construction work, other craftsmen made armorer's and smith's tools for all the artificers to use once the post was built. Then, once all the workshops and tools had been crafted, Irish's artificers still managed to repair 591 muskets, 380 cartridge boxes, 200 bayonets, and 30 wagons by November 1777. They were also able to craft five new carts for use at the post and weld together four wrought iron artillery pieces. Irish and his men had built a manufacturing site for the Continental Congress from virtually nothing, but that made all the difference in terms of allowing efficient process.[5]

Congress used the loss of Philadelphia as a reason to force the growth of inland manufacturing for the war effort. Flower was instructed in January 1778 to raise a second company of artificers for Carlisle under the command of a local craftsman, Thomas Wylie. Flower then placed Wylie and Irish under the command of a civil officer, Samuel Sargent, who operated as superintendent of the arsenal from 1778 to 1782. Washington augmented Sargent's command by moving Isaac Coren's company of artillery ammunition makers to the post. The three company commanders were then ordered to launch a recruiting drive to raise their units to their allowed strength of sixty men each. Flower assisted enlistments by advertising in Philadelphia newspapers that "ARTIFICERS, WHO prefer LIBERTY to SLAVERY has now an opportunity of shewing their abilities . . . by inlisting into the corps of artificers."[6] Recruitment was a difficult process that seems to have come close to meeting its goal, but it is unlikely that the overall number of artificers at Carlisle was much above 150 by spring 1778. Flower, however, was directed to expand operations at Carlisle beyond the work of enlisted artificers. Congress desired that the post operate as a hub for coordinating local private manufacturing with government activities. With the loss of Philadelphia, the Board of War sought to mobilize craftsmen in Lebanon, Lancaster, and York, Pennsylvania, and in Frederick and Hagerstown, Maryland. Flower ordered Charles Lukens to Carlisle to coordinate the purchase and production of military stores at regional iron furnaces and craft shops for the use of the arsenal and the army. Flower intended that Lukens and Sargent should work as a team, integrating private and government manufacturing for greater overall productivity.[7]

Flower's goal was that Sargent's companies would work physically close enough to one another to coordinate their activities. Descriptions of the post, written to satisfy Flower that his orders had been followed, bear out what his goal was as well as the fact that it was achieved. At the center of the arsenal were four brick and stone buildings laid out parallel to one another. These buildings were the armorers' shop, the warehouse, and two brick workshops. Surrounding the masonry buildings were four wooden workshops: the carpenter's workshop and shed, and two smith shops. Beyond these buildings were the large foundry furnace and the stone powder magazine, on opposite ends of the compound from

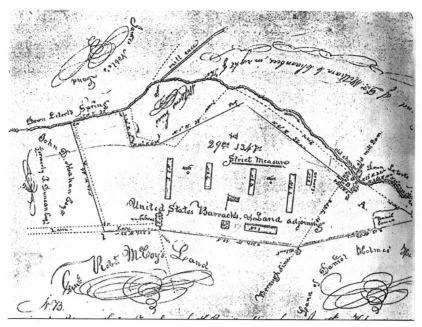

"Carlisle Barracks, 1828, Drawn at request of Colonel Wm. Linnard, August 1828," Though this diagram was drawn forty years after the Carlisle Arsenal was built, it fits the description given by Flower of buildings at the site. (*Military History Institute, Carlisle, Pennsylvania*)

one another. Within the stone buildings were twenty-one smith forges and three small furnaces. There was also a separate, larger furnace to melt lead into ball. The two smiths' shops were 25 by 38 feet, large enough for four forges each. A forge shop was built in town as well, accounting for a ninth forge used at the post.[8] Assuming a forge and small furnace were built with the foundry, there were at least ten forges in the massive armorers' workshop in the center of the post. It is thus extremely likely that Carlisle's armory operation matched the design made by John Nicholson, except that the entire process was gathered under one roof. What is also apparent from this layout is that while the smiths, armorers, and carpenters were segregated into their own shops, all other artificers were gathered into the two larger brick workshops in the center of the compound. The location of the smiths and carpenters shops on the outer edge of the post make it clear that their work passed through the brick workshops on the way to the warehouse for storage. The relatively smaller size of the wooden workshops compared to the armorers shop and the brick workshops also make it apparent that while items were hammered, cut, or formed elsewhere, they were assembled at a different location into a complete military store. The types of workers gathered in each of the shops further illuminates the organization of production.

An idea of the production process at Carlisle can be gleaned from an analysis of the post layout as well as the number and type of craftsmen at the post. There were 122 craftsmen at Carlisle in spring 1780, representing twelve crafts. There were only five armorers at Carlisle in early 1780, but seventy-seven workers were classified as artillerymen. It is also known that at this point the three largest outputs of the post were ammunition wagons, cannonballs, and artillery carriages. The artillerymen were likely divided among the production of those stores. Thus, a large number of artillerymen worked in the armory casting shot next to the five armorers who repaired damaged muskets sent to the post. Likewise, artillerymen also worked in the foundry where they welded iron into cannons. Finally, some artillerymen were in one of the brick workshops making cannon carriages. They were joined by two wheelwrights. The construction of cannon carriages, however, probably began in the carpenter shop, where eleven of those skilled craftsmen worked wood that had been cut into boards at the post's sawmill south of the post. There were twelve blacksmiths in the blacksmith shop. The second large brick workshop housed the post's harness maker, stonecutter, tailor, five shoemakers, and laborers. The arsenal's two brass workers probably labored at the furnace, though they could have made pieces for muskets at any of the smaller furnaces, so their location is unclear. Most of these men were recruited from Philadelphia and transported inland, though there were several enlistments of men from the Carlisle area. Even semiskilled and unskilled workers could be hired in a specific area because they could be trained, and according to Lukens, any men not engaged on a specific project were engaged in making musket cartridges.[9]

The command structure at Carlisle revealed much about how production was carried out at the arsenal. As post superintendent, Sargent commanded the work of the men in Irish's, Wylie's, and Jordan's companies. These men were in turn masters of the various trades going on at the arsenal. Irish was the post's master carpenter. Jordan was the arsenal's master wheelwright, and his second-in-command was in the carpenter's shop. Wiley was the master blacksmith, and his second was the post's master armorer.[10] As company commanders, Irish, Jordan, and Wylie directed the production of their men based on what Sargent ordered. They directed the production of stores in their own shops as well as overseeing the work done by their seconds in the shops they commanded. As master craftsmen, the company commanders and their assistants made sure to coordinate production to match the work of the other crafts within their companies. Craft cooperation is further revealed by a letter from Cornelius Sweers, Flower's assistant, to Irish in January 1778. Acting on

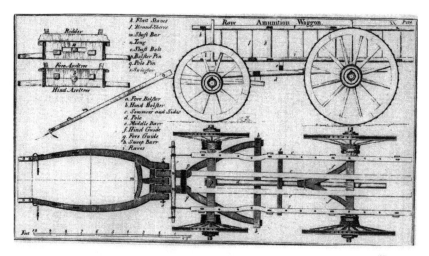

Diagram of an ammunition wagon. The DCGMS constructed over 200 of these, and similar, wagons during the course of the war to move military stores between manufacturing sites and to the Continental Army. Muller's drawings with scale would have been invaluable to the construction process. (*Muller,* Treatise of Artillery, *128*)

Flower's behalf because of his illness, Sweers wanted Irish to raise his company to sixty men, to consist of twenty-two smiths "including nailers, gunmakers, [and] filemakers."[11] There were two important points here. First, Irish was a carpenter and commanded the woodworkers at the arsenal. His orders, however, also show that he was to have command over metalworkers that on-post would be directed by Wylie, the master blacksmith. Second, Sweers's instructions to Irish make clear that skilled men were desired, but any metalworkers were useful. Sweers understood that the arsenal's work was being coordinated for adaptable production. Irish was also to enlist twenty carpenters "including gun stockers," again revealing that these men would be working with the smiths to produce a completed product.[12]

Artillery stores were the main product of the Carlisle Arsenal. From 1778 through 1781, craftsmen at the post built at least seventy cannon carriages and repaired an unknown quantity of damaged ones. At the same time, the Board of War requested that the artificers build one hundred covered ammunition wagons and twelve traveling forges. The production of carriages, wagons, and traveling forges relative to the Philadelphia ordnance yard was discussed in chapter 3. Smiths made the iron elements of the wheel hubs, and they made nails and bolts for the carriages and wagons. Carpenters made rough boards into finished pieces. All of these items were sent to the artillery shop, where wheelwrights and artillerymen fastened them together and worked them into carriages and wagons. Prior to their attachment, each of the wheels was, of course, returned to the smith for tires. It is unclear if Carlisle's artificers finished the wagons originally requested of them, but Lukens's correspondence reveals that the arsenal never lacked wagons with which to send stores to the front. Instead, horse teams were usually in short supply. Few wagons, the correspondence also reveals, ever returned. And more wagons were requested from the post. Similar to work at the Philadelphia ordnance yard, carpenters and smiths combined their efforts to make gun screws, and tools not only for the post but for the traveling forges as well. Leather workers and carpenters coordinated their work to make smith's bellows for the post's forges, as well as for Fort Pitt and Philadelphia. Smiths, artillerymen, and leathermen also cooperated to make tin cartridge boxes, bayonets, and bayonet belts.[13]

Another item produced in great quantity was cannonballs. Artillerymen made some twenty-five thousand cannonballs in one of two ways. They could cast them whole in a sand mold or cast two halves of a shot in the floor of a furnace room and weld them together. Roughly 50 percent of these shot ended up at Knight's Wharf, where workers welded iron hoops to them and attached cannon cartridges, thus fixing the ammunition for quick use on the battlefield. Prior to Coren's move to Philadelphia, ball produced at Carlisle would have been fixed on the spot at the artillery workshop. Carlisle's artificers also made roughly one hundred thousand single-pound grapeshot that was also sent to Knights Wharf for fixing into a grape "vine."[14] This example reveals that adaptability existed on a departmental scale as well as within each arsenal. Carlisle produced what Knights Wharf needed based on directions from Flower and eventually Hodgdon. More importantly, however, this example reinforces an important point: the artillerymen, smiths, and carpenters at Carlisle were focused on the production of artillery stores, but when the army was in need, orders could arrive that transformed the post in an instant.

On numerous occasions during its existence, production at Carlisle was redirected to meet the priorities of the Continental Army. The Butler fiasco, discussed in chapter 2, deprived the army of needed weapons through winter 1777–78. The Board of War addressed the situation by ordering Lukens to see that "all hands at Carlisle who are capable of repairing small arms be forthwith employed in that service and the others in making bayonets and the iron work for gun carriages and ammunition wagons." Smiths around the post were pulled off their assignments and put to work forging and casting parts for muskets and wagons. The board did allow that "the iron cannon already forged and welded may be completed but the others [were to be] left for a time of more leisure."[15] Lukens put all the men skilled at gun repair to work, yet he made clear to the board that progress was slow because some of the men doing the work were not gunsmiths. He followed up by asking permission to recruit more gunsmiths for Sargent's team. But this was only the first time that production was shifted. Each subsequent year, Congress asked for continued production of wagons, carriages, and smith's items like traveling forges, while Sargent's men were also called on for special production. In 1779, they were set to work making musket cartridges, while in 1780 it was two thousand gun screws and more cartridge boxes; in 1781, it was bayonets and spare wagon and carriage parts. The craftsmen at Carlisle were expected to move from job to job based on the needs of the army, and this was exactly what they did. Despite large numbers of specific items like carriages, wagons, tools, and artillery supplies, the artificers also produced muskets, bayonets, and cartridges, which were not their forte. From 1777 through 1781, Carlisle's artificers repaired approximately four thousand five hundred muskets and made three hundred thousand musket cartridges. In that same period they made or repaired over three thousand bayonets and made over ten thousand gun screws for cleaning muskets. This was a respectable production of nonprimary materiel when it is realized that the workers also made over seventy cannon carriages, probably more than one hundred wagons, at least two dozen traveling forges and tools, and countless wrought iron cannons that were supplied mostly to frontier posts in the Wyoming Valley, the Juniata River valley, and Fort Pitt.[16] The post was able to restock and repair thousands of muskets, though there were only five armorers at the arsenal in 1780. In order to accomplish this repair operation, men had to be taken from other assignments. This is corroborated by the fact that there were three thousand repairable muskets at Carlisle at any one time, yet they were not a priority until the Board of War issued special orders for their repair. Carlisle's managers adapted operations at the arsenal to produce what either the board or Flower directed them to produce.

The success of managed craft production at Carlisle rested on workplace design, lines of authority, and direct communication. The Carlisle Arsenal was built in such a way that craftsmen could assist one another, easily moving from one workshop to another. By facilitating interactions, the physical design of the post expanded the production potential of the individual craftsmen and craft shops. Craft interactions were also aided by the command structure of the post. Carlisle had one overall commander and several company commanders. But this structure was facilitated by the fact that commanders also doubled as master craftsmen who managed their subordinates in production. Carlisle, therefore, actually contained two overlapping chains of command that gave managers the opportunity to share information in numerous ways. It was easy within this system to direct production projects to specific craftsmen, who were in turn ordered to work with other craftsmen on a certain project. Finally, a major factor in Carlisle's success was the communication between post commanders and departmental commanders. Flower and then Hodgdon carried on regular communication with Sargent and Lukens and guided them both on their individual jobs and on how they were to work together. Centralized manufacturing relied on critical factors of workplace design, worker interaction, and managerial communication. Reflecting on how these were done well at Carlisle will allow an analysis of how operations at Springfield went sideways.

The Springfield Arsenal had numerous characteristics that should have made it a successful centralized manufacturing center, but its activities were undermined by poor communication systems. In fact, Springfield's limitations reveal the general limitations of managed craftwork and provide insight into why this type of labor organization did not develop as extensively as factory production. From conception through maturity, Springfield was hampered by a lack of communication and the absence of clear lines of authority. Two men, Ezekiel Cheever and David Mason, divided management of the Springfield Arsenal, but their responsibilities were never defined by the men who commanded them. This was because four men commanded the two commanders at Springfield and none of them ever took the time to develop a management structure at the post. Cheever and Mason built their own management partnership, and this worked for a time until the men grew annoyed at each other's pretentions and their relationship broke down. In this dysfunctional environment, no amount of physical organization and regimental command organization could overcome the lack of effective management. Production commands arrived at Springfield from four general officers addressed to each of the two post commanders and even in some cases to the various master craftsmen. Production, therefore, was severely hampered at Springfield during the time when the post's work was needed most. Communication problems were not fixed until 1781. The post did play a useful role in the revolution, but not as large as it could have.

Operations at the Springfield Arsenal began almost as soon as Knox had chosen the site for the post. The general sent to camp for men to run the post: Ezekiel Cheever was sent to the region to procure both buildings for workers and to house supplies for the army. David Mason was commissioned to recruit craftsmen and laborers and set them to work producing military stores. Neither man was ever given further instructions regarding how to do his work at the post. They carried on based on their original goals, and over time those goals continually overlapped. Cheever "secured a schoolhouse, a small home, and nearby farmhouses to secure the powder and guard for such stores."[17] Almost immediately, large numbers of stores were sent to Springfield for storage and repair. William Heath forwarded all the government's powder from Boston, and by the end of the month, twenty-five cases of arms that arrived from overseas were forwarded to Springfield. These were quickly followed by the twelve thousand muskets from France that had arrived in Portsmouth. The muskets were accompanied by several cannons, barrels of flints, powder, tents, and lead ball, all of which were sent to Springfield. Just as quickly as Cheever obtained buildings, Mason enlisted thirty-six carpenters, thirty-seven blacksmiths, fifteen wheelwrights, two tinsmiths, fifteen saddlers, two painters, three turners, six nailers, thirteen armorers, one sailmaker, and twenty-three artillerymen.[18] These men included several artisans from France who had arrived aboard *Amphitrite*.

Despite all of the proactive work being done, there was a problem underlying the whole operation. Cheever, Mason, and Knox had never examined the production processes they wished to create when they began Springfield. The buildings Cheever rented were inadequate for large-scale production. The small size and dispersed placement of the buildings forced Mason to segregate his men according to craft. This limited the ability of workers to coordinate their activities and strengthened the influence of shop superintendents. Rather than look to Mason as a manager, the men looked to their master craftsmen.[19] The simple convenience of having the various craftsmen in close proximity did make repair and production simpler than normal craftwork, but this was not as efficient as organized elsewhere. And though Knox developed a useful plan for managed production, he did not spend enough time in Massachusetts to execute it.

Knox, being an amateur expert in the military field, had developed plans for an ideal arsenal. It would have a two-story laboratory of four rooms in the center with wings sufficient for storerooms. It would also contain shops for carpenters, smiths, wheelwrights, harness makers, tinmen, and armorers. Finally, there would be a magazine for powder and one for arms.[20] Knox, however, visited the arsenal only once after sending Cheever to Springfield, and there is no mention by any of his subordinates that he discussed his arsenal layouts with them. Thus, despite all the ideas that Knox continually bandied about, it seems that when it came to Springfield, he simply assumed things would go as he believed they should. Despite this failure, Springfield benefited from people who made use of the knowledge they had of Woolwich and modern English military manufacturing.

The Springfield Arsenal was designed and built based on what Americans knew about the Woolwich Arsenal. Oddly, neither Knox nor Cheever nor Mason had anything to do with constructing the permanent arsenal that replaced Cheever's rented space. It was the people of

Springfield who pushed for an arsenal complex. They complained about the operation's disordered arrangement to the town fathers and then to the Massachusetts Council of Safety, the state's executive committee, which advised the governor. Citizen's reported that the public buildings being used in the city held live ammunition and explosive stores and were, therefore, a hazard to safety. Cheever and Mason readily agreed with this assessment. Cheever needed more secure magazines, and Mason needed more useful workshops. In July 1777, without guidance from Knox or Congress, the Massachusetts Council of Safety decided to take the lead in building suitable structures for government manufacturing operations. On July 17, the council appointed a committee to purchase land from the town of Springfield on which to construct the arsenal. It also commissioned militia colonel Thomas Dawes to draw up plans and hire appropriate persons to construct workshops and magazines.[21] The council forwarded him the money necessary to proceed with construction as he saw fit. Heath reported several days later to Washington, "Dawes has informed me that in a few days he shall begin the building of a large magazine, lab, stores, etc. at Springfield, agreeable to a resolve of Congress."[22] By August 9, Dawes had secured a lease of land from the town and begun seeking out contracts for construction.[23]

The arsenal as laid out by Dawes resembled the Woolwich Arsenal after its redesign in 1749, when a number of buildings were constructed around an open storage yard. It was situated on the western end of Springfield, close to, but not on, the Connecticut River. The several buildings that made up the arsenal were organized on the northern, eastern, and southern edges of a central square, which became an ordnance and training yard that held "various parks of artillery, with their trains, and . . . twelve entirely new 4 pounders of French make." There were two large, long structures: one that served as an armory and one that served as the post magazine. There were also several smaller workshops and barracks where "workmen of all trades were . . . engaged in the manufacture of ammunition wagons, guns, &c."[24]

The organization of the site, combined with Mason's journal, reveal how work was conducted at Springfield. Components of various craft shops could be deposited in the storehouse, ordnance yard, or armory, and workers from the other craft shops could use those components to complete an overall project. Carpenters could send wheels to the blacksmiths for tires; and tanners could send leather to the harness makers for leather goods. Springfield did not make harnesses, so it was likely the harness makers recorded at the post were used as general leather workers. Blacksmiths could make parts for the gunsmiths to make into muskets. Laborers could use any components made by their colleagues to repair items brought to the ordnance yard or storehouse. Mason was able to use what he had learned from Muller to efficiently organize the craftwork at Springfield. Unfortunately, inadequate oversight of the post inhibited development of the arsenal and its use of centralized manufacturing.

The Springfield Arsenal fell under the jurisdiction of four officers who oversaw the post commanders or in some way influenced activity at the post: George Washington, the commander in chief; William Heath, commander of the army's eastern district; Henry Knox, Washington's appointed manager of the arsenal; and Benjamin Flower, commissary general of military stores. Springfield was part of Flower's department; therefore, technically, Mason and his men were members of the Regiment of Artillery Artificers and answered to Flower. Cheever, as a commissary of military stores, worked for Flower, the commissary general. It will be remembered, though, that Washington ordered Knox to oversee the post, so despite any oversight that Flower might offer, Knox was supposed to be overseeing Springfield. Moreover, Mason was an artillery officer and he had never been formally transferred from the artillery regiment to Flower's command; so as long as he served in the military, he answered to Knox. Despite his interest in being chief in all aspects of the artillery service, Knox was too busy with frontline issues to dispense any orders to either Cheever or Mason, but only occasionally issued orders for certain stores. None of his directives were production orders regarding what the post should be preparing for the army. Instead, they were requests for stores the army needed at a particular point. Mason and Cheever often sought Knox's direction about how to prepare for the army's coming needs, but Knox rarely gave any input. Heath was Cheever's direct superior, as well as commander of all army activity east of the Hudson Valley. And he, more than anyone, attempted to assist Mason and Cheever in understanding their jobs and their goals. Unfortunately for Heath, he was hamstrung by direct orders from Washington that told him he had no authority over what was to be produced at Springfield but could only direct the military activities there. Heath was also not allowed to order supplies from Springfield but had to order all his stores from the field commissary with the Main Army, who ordered them from Springfield. It was a convoluted structure meant to ensure Washington's control over the whole system.

Nevertheless, Heath often gave Mason and Cheever advice about what they should produce. He provided the arsenal with money and secured supplies as he was supposed to but gave no oversight to how those resources were used, which turned out to be a major problem. Above the three overseers of Springfield was their commander, Washington, who often circumvented his subordinates and issued several conflicting orders. Washington, who knew Cheever and had worked with him, often took it upon himself to bypass Knox, issuing orders directly to Cheever. Washington often made requests from the arsenal magazines but never worked with the post commanders to plan out production. Planning production to meet the needs of the army was why Springfield had been built in the first place, and yet neither Washington nor Knox used it for that purpose. Oddly, with so many officers given some level of supervision over the post, none of those officers did manage the post until Flower finally took charge at the end of 1778. But when Flower was clearly given responsibility for Springfield, his illness prevented him from taking that responsibility. Thus, until they were finally removed from command, Mason and Cheever were effectively without oversight.[25]

Another command issue that confused matters at Springfield was Knox's creation of his own corps of artillery artificers. Knox allowed Cheever to recruit his own repairmen to care for items that he deposited in the magazine at Springfield. This development was part of Knox's plan to have a component of the military stores department with him at the army's camps. Recall, it took until 1779 for Congress to create the Field Commissary of Military Stores, which handled repairs and supply operations with the army. In the meantime, Knox authorized Cheever to do this work for him. Unfortunately, Knox never transferred these men to Mason's command when the department was reorganized in 1778. Nor were they transferred to the field commissary when that department was created in 1779. So the artisans Cheever recruited for Knox essentially remained Cheever's artisans until 1780. Therefore, Springfield had six separate master craftsmen directing the three main branches of craft production. There were two foremen over the carpentry shop, one Mason's, the other Cheever's. There were two foremen over the blacksmith's shop, one Mason's, the other Cheever's, and there were two foremen over the wheelwrights, one Mason's, the other Cheever's. The laboratory and tin-men answered to Mason, while the leather workers and armorers answered to Cheever. Mason and Cheever had agreed to segregate their functions because Cheever was unwilling to give up the men under his command. He allowed them to answer to Mason for a brief time in 1777 and 1778, but ultimately, he made himself and his artificers independent of Mason.[26]

All the command and organizational problems over Springfield were exacerbated by the fact that there were two commanders at the post, and this prohibited a clear chain of command at Springfield and led to a breakdown of operations there. Mason and Cheever had each been dispatched there with specific directives from Knox, but over time the execution of these directives brought the two men more and more into conflict. And neither Knox nor anyone else took the time to clarify the situation. Mason was told to hire workers and produce supplies, while Cheever was to purchase and prepare supplies. Neither man was really directed to work with the other, though that was how others in their respective positions operated elsewhere. Over time, their relationship became strained as they had no effective oversight, with the result that neither supported the other as they had when the post was established. Mason had to start purchasing supplies from the area in order to keep his men employed at their crafts. Cheever had to start hiring workers to manufacture goods because Mason did not allow his men to work for Cheever. Resentment grew between Cheever and Mason because Cheever believed that all stores deposited in the magazine at Springfield were under his control. Mason, however, deposited items made by his artisans in the same magazine and believed that he maintained control over anything made by his men. Mason was also under the impression that he had to authorize the transmission of all the stores his men made. Cheever thought he alone oversaw the transmission of stores. He wrote Heath in August, "Col. Mason sayes he has the order and Direction of all affairs relative to the Army at this Place, . . . [but] I did not think it at all necessary for me to Apply to Him for his Sanction to any orders sent to me by a Genl Officer, unless it concerned the Field Artillery." He went on to say that he had large demands for supplies that he could not fill without cooperation from Mason. Cheever asked Heath to ask Mason if, "He would take . . . pains to cultivate Harmony" at the post. Before Heath could intervene, however, Mason wrote to him, saying, "I Seen Col. Cheevers Letter & Every thing is Settled in the most Amicable Manner you Can Desire or wish for."[27]

They seem to have agreed that Mason would direct the arsenal while Cheever would operate the distribution network, issuing stores from the magazine whether they were made at the arsenal or procured by Cheever. The situation was not as settled as Mason, Cheever, or Heath might have thought. Mason and Cheever were only willing to work together because each believed that by doing so, he would gain greater favor with Heath. Heath became the one force that held the officers from conflict. Mason and Cheever's correspondence with Heath in 1778 suggests that they jockeyed for their commander's favor in order to secure dominance over the arsenal. Both men hoped that Heath would at some point choose one of them to be overall post commander. Neither man seemed to realize that Heath was not allowed to make that decision. Heath, however, was transferred to another command in 1779, and that left Mason and Cheever with nothing to fight over but the arsenal itself. Heath's command was taken over by Ezekiel Cornell, but he seems not to have factored into the drama occurring at the post. Things at the post broke down before Cornell could even get a handle on what his role was regarding Springfield.

The conflict that was allowed to simmer exploded in 1779. Cheever wrote to the Board of War for guidance: "The grate difficulties attending this Department for want of proper Authority & regulations constrain me."[28] Mason began making reports to the board separate from

Cheever's returns. Cheever began recruiting more men for his command so he could oversee repair and production without cooperating with Mason. Cheever's personal staff ballooned to six men, about which a member of Springfield's town council observed, "there is more business done by . . . three persons [in the Commissary office] than in Col Cheevers's with his five or six. He [Cheever] thinks it the duty of his office to be always employed as if about his own private business."[29]

Mason and Cheever both forsook their responsibilities at the post to be about their own business. They left their subordinates in charge and without oversight. The men, in turn, began making goods for sale in local markets rather than military stores. There was a complete breakdown in the arsenal's activities. Craft captains began taking sides, regardless of who was their designated commanding officer. They gave their allegiance to whichever commander could secure rations and clothing for them. Mason and Cheever began using their artisans for the manufacture of personal goods for themselves and their families. The people of Springfield noticed the change, and they complained to their town council. The town council complained to the Massachusetts Council of Safety, which investigated the site in order to bring the information to Congress.[30]

The state committee sent to Springfield found that not only had Mason and Cheever abused their power but their subordinates had taken advantage of their commanders' ignorance in order to do the same. The captain of Mason's harness makers reported to the committee that "Mason gave orders to make a harness in lieu of one that he knew Knox had of Mason's." For such a job the master harness maker was able to attend to his duties at the arsenal shop only "two or three hours on average" a day. To work for both the government and Mason, the superintending harness maker hired a foreman for the arsenal harness shop, but that foreman was "absent about two months" in late 1778. A carpenter under Mason reported to the committee that he had "made a bedstead at his shop for Mason which took him four or five days." Likewise several leather workers reported that Mason had requisitioned leather and had them make it into shoes for his family. A worker at the laboratory that served Cheever testified that Mason often took cartridge paper to make his own hunting cartridges. Cheever, though, had his own problems. His major crime was not embezzlement but nepotism. He hired his son as a clerk and appointed many of his friends to posts. Cheever also allowed his commanders to hire their own sons, even children. One of the boys, age thirteen, was found to be drawing rations and pay as an artilleryman even though he spent the whole day at school. Having found serious causes for concern with operations at Springfield, the state committee forwarded its report to Congress.[31] Congress had already realized there was a problem at Springfield; it had just failed to comprehend the extent of it.

Congress began the process of centralizing Springfield under Flower's command because it was clear that Knox was not taking responsibility for the post. What Congress failed to see was just how convoluted operations were at Springfield. Neither Congress nor the Board of War recognized in 1778 that Cheever's men were independent of Mason's command. Nor did they fully realize that Mason was independent of Flower. Congress's responsive actions only served to make matters worse. Congress authorized the creation of a new company of artificers under Nathaniel Chapman.[32] It was modeled on Irish's company and sent to Springfield to increase production there. Chapman was answerable directly to Flower. The company that Mason commanded was under the immediate supervision of Major James Eayers. Congress directed Eayers to make reports to Flower and look to him for supplies and pay.[33] Eayers and Chapman now answered to Flower, which undermined Mason's authority, though he was still commander of the arsenal. Mason's command now answered to Flower, but Mason was not discharged from the service. Without clear authority, he stopped managing altogether, but that was a problem because Mason's men were loyal to him and would not continue to work under either Eayers or Chapman. As mentioned, Flower was too ill to enforce his authority or make changes to the situation. Cheever became the primary officer at the post, but that actually undermined his position with his subordinates. They did not want him to wield too much power, and they began flouting his orders. Production at the arsenal collapsed shortly after the state's 1779 investigation. General Gates wrote Washington that he "was disappointed in every . . . Application" he had sent to Springfield for stores.[34]

Finally, in 1779, the extent of the problems at Springfield began to come to light. They were summarized exquisitely in a letter from Gates, now president of the Board of War, to Washington. He started by saying that several letters had come to his attention from Cheever, Mason, and Eayers reporting the mutiny of several men at the post because of a lack of provisions. Gates thought Washington and Knox were overseeing Springfield, as he explained to Washington: "Since my being Commanded to This Department, I have not given any Orders with regards to the post at Springfield, lest my directions should Clash with Those given by Your Excellency, or General Knox." Gates realized there was a command problem at Springfield because he was informed of a mutiny by correspondence other than from Washington. Gates continued, "I wish I could acquaint Your Excellency, that proper and Regularity of the Care, and Distribution of the Ordnance Stores in this Department had being Observed: I am sorry to say the Contrary is too Apparent." If Washington or Knox had true oversight of the post, they would have known about the mutiny before Gates did. Gates was also concerned because he noticed that production at Springfield had been slacking. The refusal of certain men to work was not an isolated problem; it was indicative of a breakdown of the post's integrity. Gates, therefore, asked Washington to send an artillery officer, Colonel John Lamb, to Springfield to "make a thorough inspection into the Posts & present management thereof."[35] Lamb was dispatched the following month and returned to camp in September 1779 with a report.

Lamb discovered why an efficient production system was unable to develop at Springfield. The commanders had no control over their men. There were more companies and commanders at the post than were necessary. Consequently, no one had complete responsibility for any parts of the production process. He wrote that "[W]hat works can be done . . . cannot be precisely determined with respect to the Carpenters, Smiths, and Wheelwrights unless the kind of work is specified as they have not kept steadily at any particular kind." No one, according to Lamb, was coordinating the work being done by the men. In fact, he found that Chapman's men were actually employed under other officers, making Chapman superfluous. Lamb was horrified to find a teenager employed at the works. He even found that the buildings were unsuitable for activities at Springfield. The magazine was wooden and not secure, and there were not enough barracks for the men. Vanity and greed, according to Lamb, had led the post commanders astray.[36]

Congress directed Samuel Hodgdon to reorganize operations at Springfield Arsenal. Hodgdon recommended to the Board of War in July 1780 that all the commanders at Springfield be fired and their functions centralized under one or two men. In September 1780, after receiving approval from the board, Hodgdon cashiered Mason, Cheever, Eayers, and Chapman along with their staffs. John Bryant, assistant director of the laboratory, was given command of Springfield Arsenal and served in that capacity until 1794. Under Hodgdon's direction, Bryant transformed Springfield into a model of efficiency for the department. Bryant not only oversaw production at the arsenal but also coordinated regional contracts for Hodgdon. From 1780 to 1783, Bryant was assisted by Luke Bliss, an artisan at Springfield whom Hodgdon made regional commissary of military stores. Hodgdon made clear to both men that Bliss was in charge of the magazine and the distribution of stores, while Bryant was director of production at the arsenal. Production at Springfield increased dramatically after the reform. Hodgdon took an active role in overseeing operations there and was in constant communication with Bryant. Hodgdon managed the budget and issued production quotas. The post finally had an internal and external command structure that allowed for efficient production. However, the end of the war and the shrinking of the military stores department meant fewer workers were needed at Springfield. After 1782, the arsenal complement remained relatively small, averaging ten workers in the armory, ten in the craft shops, and ten in the laboratory.[37]

Production at the Springfield Arsenal revealed the limitations of craft production without coordination. Though the arsenal was in operation from 1777 until the end of the war, the output of Springfield's artisans did not match the output of workers at the nation's other arsenals. Armorers repaired eighteen thousand nine hundred muskets during the arsenal's existence, which was six thousand fewer than Philadelphia's armorers were able to manufacture and repair over the course of just three years. Moreover, there is no evidence that Springfield's armorers ever manufactured weapons. Springfield artillerymen fixed six thousand shot, made four thousand cannon cartridges, and rolled 1.2 million musket cartridges. By contrast, craftsmen at Philadelphia fixed five thousand shot and made 4.2 million musket cartridges, while Carlisle's craftsmen fixed about twelve thousand shot. Finally, Springfield craftsmen made roughly forty wagons, one hundred ammunition carts, and forty cannon carriages.[38] Nearly two hundred wagons and seventy cannon carriages were made at Carlisle. Revealingly, the majority of Springfield's output came in 1777 and 1778, before command and communication began to significantly break down at the post. The simple fact of centralizing various craftsmen in one location did increase overall productivity. Nevertheless, without consistent oversight, workers could not continue nor improve on their increased level of output. Not until after the revolution did Springfield reach its potential and become the backbone of the military stores system.

The command and communication flaws that haunted the Springfield Arsenal inhibited, but did not prevent, the rise of coordinated craftwork there. Though workers at the post labored together, their activities were not well managed. Senior commanders took little interest in implementing a cooperative system there, and though the post was built to make cooperation among craftsmen convenient, it was not fully taken advantage of. There was no clear chain of command, and the commanders refused to work together. Springfield's limitations, however, illuminate how Philadelphia and Carlisle could be so productive. Workers were under the direction of both their master craftsmen and their company commanders. Blacksmiths in the ordnance yard answered to master blacksmith Valentine Hoffman as well as company commander John Jordan. Together, these officers coordinated their workers based on the orders of their commander, Samuel Hodgdon, or his assistant in Philadelphia, Jonathan Gostelowe. This system existed at the Philadelphia Arsenal's other production segments and the arsenal as a whole. Similarly at Carlisle, Nathaniel Irish commanded his carpenters as well as his company, coordinating work with his commander, Samuel Sargent, who was also the master blacksmith. Production was not done in isolated workrooms but in coordinated manufacturing centers.

MILITARY STORES COMMANDERS AND ARSENAL SUPERINTENDENTS INSTI-tuted a command system of production at the Continental arsenals to overcome the limitations of American craftwork. The arsenals, however, could not and did not provide for the army in isolation of other sources. Private manufacturers were needed to supplement the production of the arsenals and to provide raw materials for government craftsmen to work into military stores. Congressmen had learned that craftsmen had failed to meet the early needs of the Continental Army because they had not been properly mobilized by government authorities. Therefore, the second procurement objective initiated by Congress, after the arsenals, was to encourage private manufacturers with the guidance and resources they needed to produce quality stores according to pattern. With these forms of support, private manufacturers could supplement the work of the government's arsenals.

6

"Devise ways and means for procuring [cannon]"

DIRECTING PRIVATE MANUFACTURERS:
INSPECTION AND INSTRUCTION

S AMUEL AND DANIEL HUGHES DID NOT HAVE A LENGTHY BACKGROUND
in iron production when the American Revolution began in 1775.
Along with their father, Barnabas, the Hughes brothers had secured
land near Hagerstown, Maryland, and built fairly extensive ironworking
facilities before the war, so that when their father died, the brothers came
to possess three iron furnaces and the manufacturing operations that
went with them. But the family as a whole had been in the iron business
for only about a decade when the war began. It was not surprising, therefore, that the brothers' first attempt at supplying the Continental Army
with artillery came to naught. In 1776, the Hughes brothers bid on a contract to cast iron ordnance, won the contract, and cast an artillery piece.
The piece turned out so badly that they did not even bother to melt down
the metal and reuse it—they had the piece buried. It was hidden so well,
in fact, that it was not found again until 1984.[1]

Clearly, the brothers needed assistance to manufacture artillery for the
war effort. They communicated their needs to Congress and kept
attempting to cast cannons in the interim. Congress had heard of similar
concerns from other iron producers and came up with a solution. It contracted with Daniel Joy, a Philadelphia ship captain and respected merchant, to work with its contracted ironmongers. Joy wrote out instructions, drew up patterns, and explained the metallurgy of artillery in a letter and then sent that off to the various iron furnace owners. He followed

this up with visits and other personal communications. The Hughes' iron production improved, but not enough. The significant capacity of the brothers' iron facilities made it critical that they produce effectively for the army. So Joy returned to the Hughes' furnaces and spent months on end with the brothers. He observed their castings, proved their cannons, instructed their workers, and detailed the results. Joy went from working directly for Congress to working for the commissary general of military stores and was eventually appointed superintendent of ordnance. In this capacity, Joy traveled to every iron furnace contracted with the Continental government and offered the same oversight and instructional services he offered to the Hughes brothers. By the end of the war, the Hughes ironworks were producing not just ordnance but cannon shot and shells as well. With government help, the Hughes operations became a critical element of material support for the war effort.

Congress learned early on of the need to provide instruction to, and inspection of, its contractors when those manufacturers could not fulfill their contracts. As early as 1775, Congress initiated two programs to mobilize domestic manufacturers for wartime production and to help craftsmen overcome the challenges they faced. Congress began by establishing a system of inspection and instruction to train craftsmen with whom contracts were made. To mobilize domestic producers to support the arsenal system that had been established, Congress hired craftsmen skilled in military stores production to inspect government-contracted manufacturing operations and provide direction to those operations when necessary. These efforts developed into a comprehensive system of inspection and review under the commissary general of military stores. Government inspection representatives became consultants working to ensure not only that items were produced to government specifications but also that private manufacturers gained knowledge for the continued production of stores for the war effort. In this way, the Department of the Commissary General of Military Stores (DCGMS) disseminated manufacturing knowledge that would otherwise have been overlooked.

The government's inspection administration evolved over the course of the war. Starting in 1775, Congress hired individuals to review individual contracts; there was no overarching system of inspection. With the creation of the DCGMS in 1777, Benjamin Flower hired numerous individuals to assist him in the inspection of purchased stores. Congress also added several inspection officials to the department. The result was a three-tiered system of production oversight: regional commissaries, the superintendent of arms, and the superintendent of ordnance. The commissaries reviewed all products they procured from foreign and domestic sources before depositing them in the magazines at Springfield, Philadelphia, or Carlisle. Flower's officials, however, were not the government's only military stores contracting agency. Henry Knox and the field commissary department under Samuel Hodgdon, which operated in 1778 and 1779, also worked to supervise production facilities. When Hodgdon took command of the DCGMS in 1780, all inspection functions became centralized under his authority until the end of the war. Yet he was forced to cut staff and spending because of Congress's budgetary crisis, and this brought on the final chapter of government activity, when Hodgdon made use of artillery officers as inspectors and placed greater responsibility on himself and officials at the Philadelphia armory. Throughout the story, inspection activities reveal the extent to which government officials took an active role in the private manufacture of military stores. The inspection processes were not simple review activities but rather direct involvement in the mobilization of American production.

Congress began contracting for weapons and supplies within the first year of the war and at the same time took the first steps toward a systematic review process. On January 15, 1776, Congress "Resolved, That a committee of 5 be appointed . . . to devise ways and means for procuring [cannon], and that it be an instruction to the said committee to enquire how large cannon can be cast in this country."[2] The following month, the committee was empowered to contract for the production and purchase of necessary artillery. Because of his reputation in Pennsylvania, Mark Bird of Hopewell Furnace in Berks County was contracted first to cast 150 iron cannons worth $8,880.[3] At the same time, the committee hired Daniel Joy of Philadelphia to "make alterations and improvements as was needed for making [Bird's] cannon good."[4] The committee then contracted with Cornwall Furnace in Lebanon County, Pennsylvania, for forty-four iron cannons and directed Joy to review those guns as well. Within the month, another five-man committee was established to contract for the making of muskets and bayonets for the army. This contract, however, went unsupervised.[5] Though Congress did not create a comprehensive review system for military stores early on, it did take steps to ensure the proper production and delivery of the ordnance for which it contracted.

The Continental government did not issue contracts without providing specifications in the form of a pattern for the product in question. These were wood or iron models of the finished product that the government expected from its contractor. Cannon shot and shell patterns were generally cast iron, while cannon patterns were made of wood. When the government issued a bayonet, ramrod, or cartridge box pattern, it used actual accouterments. Likewise when pattern muskets were issued to contracted gunsmiths, the patterns were the best constructed muskets then in service so that new muskets made to that pattern would be of similar quality. Patterns after 1777 were made by government artificers from either verbal or written specifications provided by the Board of War.

Hopewell Iron Furnace, Elverson, Pennsylvania. Hopewell has been rebuilt by the National Park Service to look as it did when it and other furnaces like it were producing cannons and artillery ammunition for the DCGMS. The stone furnace stack can be seen in the rear of the wooden casting house surrounding it. The casting house contained work facilities for casting iron and working the iron into wrought iron and steel. Carpentry space and other workspaces were located in buildings nearby. The large shed above and to the right of the stack housed charcoal, lime, and iron ore for charging the furnace, which was done from the top. (*Author*)

Prior to 1777, the government hired skilled craftsmen to make individual patterns for every new contract. When Daniel Joy was hired by Congress to prove cannons being made by Hopewell Furnace, he was also directed to provide them with a proper pattern from which to cast the cannons. In later years, Hodgdon provided contractors with patterns cast at the air furnace or crafted at the ordnance yard and armory by government artificers under his orders.

Patterns, however, were not the only way to issue contract specifications. Another method was the preparation of design schematics that could be sent to manufacturers. Joy, for instance, reviewed several plans for brass cannons possessed by the Board of War in early 1777 and redrew them. He provided the board with several detailed drafts that could be sent to iron furnaces as blueprints for what was to be cast. Likewise, Knox provided a detailed cross-section drawing of what he wanted shells to look like. His drawing provided exterior and interior measurements as well as instructions for properly casting the mouth of the shell that received the fuse.[6] Diagrams and patterns were often followed up by visits from government representatives. Joy took several tours of iron furnaces to see how production was progressing and to correct flaws in the application of patterns. After several individual assignments from the cannon committee and the Board of War, Joy was appointed superintendent of ordnance for the DCGMS. He served in that position, performing various functions, including inspections, until his death in 1784.

Joy was charged not only with reviewing government contracted artillery but also with taking an active role in production to ensure that government desires for efficiency were translated into private action. He traveled to Hopewell and Cornwall Furnaces to inspect the molds being used to cast the cannons. He improved the designs and molds being used.[7] Based on the fact that he charged Congress for simultaneous work at both furnaces, Joy probably traveled back and forth between the two furnaces during alternating casts to review the work as it was being done. Using a government representative to oversee production saved the furnace owners money, and it increased the possibility of more immediate delivery of the ordnance being cast. Though Joy was sent to assist the furnace owners, ultimately he worked for the Continental government and had to ensure that its contract needs were being met. Joy was also empowered to prove the cannons once they had been cast.

Casting a cannon out of iron or brass in the eighteenth century was a laborious process. A mold of the cannon first had to be prepared. Joy, for instance, would have made or overseen the making of a wood pattern for the cannon. A large wooden box, outlining the dimensions of the cannon, would have been built and then cut in half lengthwise. Half was then filled with wet sand or clay, upon which the cannon pattern was placed. The second half of the mold was then placed on top of the pattern and filled with sand or clay. The top of the mold was removed; then the pattern was removed and the top of the mold replaced on its lower half. Bands of iron were then used to clamp the whole mold together into a single unit. While the mold was being made, the furnace was being completely charged because casting just one iron cannon used up all the molten iron in a single eighteenth-century iron furnace. A brass furnace could cast up to four cannons at a time because less brass was used per cannon than iron. Americans, however, cast few expensive brass cannons during the war. In the meantime, the area in front of the furnace was being prepared for casting. A large pit was dug, into which the cannon mold was placed with the mouth of the cannon pointed up. The rest of the pit was then backfilled to keep the mold stable. A clay core was suspended into the mold to ensure that the cannon was cast with a bore for firing. Finally, iron was poured into the mold. The cannon was allowed to cool, and then it had to be dug out of the ground. A new mold had to be made for each subsequent cannon. A large furnace like Hopewell or Cornwall was generally tapped twice a day for normal production and so could be expected to cast at most two cannons a day. Casting, however, was not the end of the process.[8]

Several finishing procedures were needed to complete a cannon. The cannon mold had been made with extra space on the mouth end to allow the iron to expand as it cooled. When the piece was dug up, the excess iron at the mouth had to be cut off to make the cannon its proper length. Then the core had to be bored out with a large drill. Boring was done at a separate boring mill, which used a vertical drill that worked out the core and then reamed out the iron to the desired size. Once the bore had been drilled, the cannon face needed to be ground down in a process called facing. Here a grindstone was used to scour away the rough outside left from casting. The cannon was now ready for testing, and if proved, for mounting on a carriage.[9]

The proving process required great caution. One small flaw in a cannon, be it an air pocket or impure iron in the mix, could cause it to burst on firing. The ultimate test of a cannon was to charge it with twice the normal powder and discharge it. Cannons were inspected for casting flaws, however, before they were fired for proof. Joy would have searched for air holes and air pockets in the cannon both by sight inspection and by tapping it with a hammer. Iron casting was still an art rather than a science in the eighteenth century. If the furnace was tapped too early, or not charged with the proper mixture of iron ore, charcoal, and limestone, the quality of the iron could vary dramatically.[10] In that case, good cast iron could cool beside very brittle, not-fully-smelted iron, creating a weakness in the cannon. By hammering around the cannon, Joy could detect these flaws; if the face of the cannon buckled or chipped, the metal was revealed to be defective. The only way to test the bore was to blank fire the cannon with a powder charge. Congress provided powder to Hopewell and Cornwall Furnaces for their cannons to be tested.[11] The records do not indicate how many of the cannons Joy tested withstood proof, but by the end of 1776, he was procuring wagons and arranging the transport of the cannons to Philadelphia.

Congressional and ironwork records suggest that the 194 cannons made by the Hopewell and Cornwall Furnaces were sent to Philadelphia without being bored or faced. The ironmasters may have built their own boring mills. However, in March 1777, Joy reported to Congress that he had made the tools for a boring and facing mill. He then went on to bore out, face, and prove thirty-two cannons. Joy does not say where he did this, but his comments lead to the conclusion that early in 1777, he built a boring mill in or near Philadelphia. Saving ironmongers the expense of building their own mills made it much more appealing for them to cast cannons for the government. Moreover, by boring and facing the can-

This picture shows the moment just after the Woolwich brass furnace has been opened. Molten brass has run out into the cannon molds, which are buried securely in the dirt floor of the foundry. If this were an iron furnace, there would typically be only one cannon mold in the floor, as it took more iron than brass to cast a cannon. At Woolwich, cannons were cast solid and their bores were drilled out after they cooled. American iron furnaces during the war would have had a clay core suspended over the mold to make room for a bore in the cannon as it was cast. (*Jackson and de Beer*, Eighteenth Century Gunfounding, *126*)

nons himself, Joy imposed the government's manufacturing standards directly on the product of American manufacturers. Joy worked as an inspector for the Continental Congress until April 1778. He redrafted diagrams used for casting cannons and making patterns, calculating the dimensions used for wrought iron cannons in sizes from three to twelve pounds. The Board of War sent him to view and assist the work being done at Mount Etna Furnace near Lebanon, Pennsylvania. There he redesigned the cannon patterns they were using, oversaw production, and proved the resulting cannons. Early in 1778, Joy took his last assignment, traveling to Berkshire Furnace, where he proved 759 cannon shells.[12]

Field cannons traditionally fired two types of projectiles: round solid shot and hollow shells, each of which had specific inspection requirements. As identified earlier, shot were simple iron balls, but a shell was a hollow ball with a mouth for receiving a fuse. Several problems could arise in the casting of shot and shells. Just as with casting a cannon, if the furnace had not been heated or charged properly, a casting could set good metal next to poor quality metal, leading a projectile to fragment when fired. Occasionally, air became trapped in a casting making pockets, like those in Swiss cheese. This was not always a problem with solid shot, but it could weaken the wall of a shell, causing it to fragment on firing. An air pocket could also cause a hole in the shell, which would either lead it to fragment when fired or leak powder. If powder leaked into a cannon before it was fired, the shell could explode in the cannon. Air pockets could also deform the mouth of a shell and make it unable to receive a fuse. The final problem to arise from casting was that a shot or shell could be made too big or too small for the cannon for which it was intended. If a ball or shell was too small, the energy of the firing would go around the projectile and it would not go as far as desired. If a shot or shell was too big, it would not fit into a cannon. A shell additionally required that the mouth be exactly the size for the fuse. Too big or too small and the fuse would not fit and the shell would be useless.[13]

There were three ways to test the soundness of shot and shell. First, the projectiles were visually examined for obvious imperfections. Second, the inspector hammered the projectiles to check for brittle metal, similar to the process already described for cannon testing. Shot was then weighed because size was relative to weight; if a shot weighed nine pounds, it would fit a nine-pound cannon. If a ball weighed nine-and-a-half pounds, it was too big; if it was eight-and-a-half pounds, it was too small. Not all shot were inspected, because they were produced in such large quantities. A random sample of them was taken out, hammered, and weighed. If they met proof, they were all certified. If more than a handful failed, another sampling would be taken to review the extent of any problems discovered. Shells were all individually examined because the slightest problem on any one could spell disaster. Once hammered, shells were measured externally and internally. The external size determined if it would fit in the cannon, while the internal size determined if it would carry a proper amount of powder. The mouth was then measured. Finally, a shell was placed mouth down in a bucket of water. Bubbles of air emanating from the shell revealed structural flaws. A shell that passed each of these tests was proved. Those that were too small or big might be accepted if they were within certain parameters, usually a quarter of an inch. Those with structural flaws were rejected.[14]

One of Congress's goals when creating the DCGMS was to centralize the purchase of war materiel to see that both private and public production was directed through a single source to the army in the field. Flower originally considered himself to be the central purchaser of supplies, but the size of the department quickly made this an impossible situation. The DCGMS purchased a host of items: muskets, gunlocks, tools, cannonballs, nails, cannons, leather hides, cut wood, and iron ore. Flower appointed men to purchase supplies for him in various areas. Charles Lukens was the first to be appointed, empowered to purchase goods

from private manufacturers throughout the Susquehanna River valley to
supplement government production at
Carlisle Arsenal. When the Philadelphia Arsenal was reestablished after
the British occupation, Jonathon
Gostelowe was given powers similar to
Lukens for the Delaware River valley.
Flower was at this time also given
oversight of an independent government agent in Boston, Nathaniel
Barber. Barber secured whatever supplies arrived in New England from privateers, blockade runners, and the
French government. These he forwarded to Springfield. Ezekiel Cheever
should have been procuring domestic
manufactures in the Connecticut and
Hudson river valleys, but his command conflict at Springfield undermined this. A final commissary,
Samuel French, was appointed in the
Chesapeake watershed, but his activities had little impact on the depart-

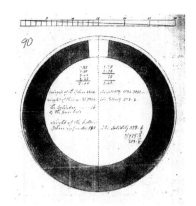

"Profile of howitzer, 1781,"
Papers of Henry Knox, LV:162.
This diagram, presumably drawn
by Knox, shows the blueprints
made by the DCGMS from
sources like Muller's *Treatise of
Artillery* for distribution to private contractors who would then
produce items to government patterns.

ment as a whole.[15] Each of these men had a departmental magazine used
to store supplies and inspect them before sending them on to the arsenal
magazines or the front. Though each assistant answered to Flower, their
disparate locations made them effectively independent of his authority.
This was reinforced by Flower's recurrent illness. Rather than being a
coherent system as it was intended, what developed under Flower's command were four separate contract systems, which varied according to the
personal temperament of each contract overseer. It took Samuel
Hodgdon's assumption of departmental leadership in 1780 to unify the
system.

MISCELLANEOUS STORES INSPECTION PROCESS

Records indicate that Flower oversaw only two contracts before his illness removed him from many of his activities. He made a contract with
John Patton of Berkshire Furnace early in 1778, and it was this contract
that Joy was sent to review in March of that year. Nevertheless, Flower
visited the furnace and inspected the work being done there during the
first months of the contract, though he did not prove or test the shot,
shell, and ordnance made by the furnace workers. Instead, he had all the
furnace products sent to the ordnance yard, where his artificers tested

them. By contract, from mid-1778 through the end of 1779, Berkshire Furnace produced 12,525 variously sized solid shot, 4,321 shells of various sizes, and over 5,000 individual grape balls. The furnace also cast six iron mortars for the army.[16]

Flower mobilized production at Andover Furnace in northeastern New Jersey because its Loyalist owners refused to put it in blast. Though a formal contract was never written between Andover and Flower, it was the commissary's second major production project. Andover was well known as an excellent source of high-grade pig iron and steel due to the purity of the ore used and to the skill of furnace master Whitehead Humphreys.[17] However, William Allen and Joseph Turner, the furnace owners, were Loyalists and refused to make iron for New Jersey. In January 1778, Congress directed Flower to bypass the owners and contract with Humphreys for the making of steel for the use of the artificers at Carlisle. To make this possible, Flower was also to request that New Jersey's state government confiscate the property and sell it to a patriot. Flower did as he was ordered and found that Humphreys was willing to do the work, but the project went awry after the state confiscated the furnace.[18] No one came forward to purchase it, leaving Flower with no one with whom to contract. On his own authority, Flower ordered Humphreys to put the furnace in blast. Once it was in blast, New Jersey's state government was able to secure people to lease the furnace and produce pig iron for the DCGMS. Thomas Mayberry and James Morgan took up management of Andover Furnace and under "Contract with your Commissary General of Military Stores and under his direction have in the years 1778 & 1779 carried on the Andover Ironworks in the said State [New Jersey] and from time to time delivered to the said Commissary General at his orders large Quantities of Pig Iron on account whereof they have received of him several Sums of Money and sundry Provisions."[19] A simple contracting procedure led Flower to take direct involvement in the private production of iron for the war effort. Flower's efforts were, however, supplemented by those of his subordinate commissaries.

Charles Lukens built an extensive network of government contracts to support the post at Carlisle. He began in 1777 to purchase bar iron for artificers at the arsenal, which they were using at the time to melt into cannonball and work into wrought iron cannon. In November of that year, he received twenty tons of pig iron from Cornwall Furnace. He went on to make supply arrangements with Carlisle Furnace, Mary Ann Furnace, Pine Grove Furnace, and Elizabeth Furnace in Pennsylvania, and the Hughes Iron Works in Maryland. Such a network ensured that iron was constantly prepared for the arsenal and would not disappear if one or two of the furnaces went out of blast. Elizabeth Furnace also provided Carlisle with steel for making musket parts. It was Lukens's

Twelve-pounder cast iron cannon located in the Cornwall Iron Furnace State Historic Site visitor center in Cornwall, Pennsylvania. This cannon was cast at Cornwall, but did not pass proof. Not enough metal was poured into the mold and it cooled improperly. It was discarded. (*Author*)

responsibility to inspect the iron and steel when it arrived at the arsenal before transferring it to Sargent's control for use by the artificers.[20] As the work done by the furnaces and the arsenal expanded, Lukens took the opportunity to transfer some of the work into private hands.

In 1779, Lukens began supplementing arsenal production by purchasing cannons and ammunition from his network of furnaces. Maryann and Carlisle Furnace cast shot that was delivered to the arsenal for inspection and storage before being sent to Philadelphia. Maryann provided 893 ten-inch shells, 714 eight-inch shells, 843 twenty-four-pound shot, 2,137 eighteen-pound shot, and 289 twelve-pound shot. Shot and shells were also cast at Cornwall Furnace under Lukens's direction. Lukens used Elizabeth and Cornwall Furnaces to cast several shot and shell patterns that were then sent to forges in the vicinity of Carlisle. Elizabeth Furnace was contracted for forty tons of shells that were ready for delivery in April 1780. By 1781, a contract made under Lukens with Pine Grove Furnace had yielded twenty-three tons of eight-inch shells, ten-inch shells, eighteen-pound shot, and twenty-four-pound shot.[21] These bypassed inspection because the Quartermaster Department wanted to move them as quickly as possible to the south for the Yorktown Campaign. Unfortunately, Lukens's records are incomplete, making it impossible to say how much shot and shells he inspected and deposited at the arsenal during his tenure as commissary of military stores. By making Carlisle a central government contracting location, however, Lukens had set the stage for significant government involvement in private manufacturing in central Pennsylvania.

Lukens made Carlisle a focal point for generating private iron production by using the site as a center for the delivery and inspection for privately made goods. Flower's original plan for Carlisle included the construction of a boring mill for the completion of either brass cannons cast at the arsenal or wrought iron ordnance produced there. It took more than two years, however, to get the mill constructed because the emergency needs of the army continually pulled artificers away from its construction. Finally, near the end of 1779, the boring mill was complete. There is no direct evidence that government contractors used the mill, but a great deal of circumstantial evidence suggests that it became a hub for finishing government produced and privately produced cannons before they were mounted at the arsenal and sent to Philadelphia. After mid-1780, the mill was in constant operation for a year and a half. The arsenal could never have produced enough cannons to require that much boring and finishing work. At the arsenal's height in 1778, artificers had only managed to work four wrought iron cannons. The first recorded cannon castings by Cornwall Furnace since 1777 were done in 1780, which suggests that the Grubb brothers who owned the furnace were awaiting the building of another boring mill to finish their products.[22] The Hughes Iron Works, too, was making cannons for the government at this time. The most likely scenario was that Daniel Joy was inspecting the weapons cast at these various firms before sending them to Carlisle for finishing. Hodgdon's correspondence makes it clear that Carlisle's boring mill was the only one available for government service. And private production of ordnance for the government rose in 1780, meaning that manufacturers took advantage of government machinery to finish their own goods destined for the military. Lukens' activities made him much more than a government contractor. He coordinated and assisted private manufacturers by providing oversight and guidance in the production of stores.

Activities performed by Lukens at Carlisle were similar to those taken on by Jonathan Gostelowe to mobilize domestic manufacturing in Philadelphia. From August 1778 until August 1781, Gostelowe inspected leather products and cartridge paper, as well as specific infantry stores: cartridge boxes, bayonets, and ramrods. Until he was relieved from service, Gostelowe also managed all the departmental storage magazines in Philadelphia. He purchased hides from farms surrounding the city and saw to it that local tanners properly dressed the hides for use by the leather shop. Gostelowe contracted urban craftsmen to repair damaged infantry stores. The most important purchases he made were of bayonets and ramrods. While government armorers often repaired these items, Gostelowe delivered bayonets to private craftsmen to have steel tips welded on for a longer lasting sharp edge. He also purchased 8,925 ramrods because it was easier to convert steel to wire at a private furnace than to buy steel plates and have them worked by government smiths.[23] Every item purchased by Gostelowe or repaired by arsenal workers was then deposited into the magazines he rented for the department. He was required to keep account books of the stores on hand and their condition, which were then used by Flower or Hodgdon when determining what was available for the army. When stores were needed for the front, Hodgdon left it to Gostelowe to gather and package them for transport.[24] Such a circumstance made Gostelowe the final inspector of goods before their use by the army. Unfortunately for Gostelowe, Hodgdon was much more active than his predecessor. Within a year of becoming head of the department, Hodgdon was bypassing Gostelowe for convenience rather than any failing on Gostelowe's part. Gostelowe became redundant.[25] Hodgdon could do his own job and that of his subordinate, which, when combined with budgetary constraints, led to the release of Gostelowe from duty.

While the focus of the military stores department was domestic manufacturers, assuring the quality of foreign made items was equally important. Inspections of imported goods were necessary because if any damaged or deficient supplies arrived at the front, they wasted time and money in transportation and threatened the army with defeat. Congress lost no time in hiring men to purchase stores that arrived from overseas, but it also commissioned them to inspect the stores as well. Nathaniel Barber was hired as an agent at Boston for Congress in 1776, and he alternately served the quartermaster and DCGMS. Barber purchased items such as tents, canvas, rope, glue, powder, and balls that arrived on privateers or blockade runners from Europe and the West Indies. He also received items sent to Congress from the French government. Once he had reviewed stores, Barber would comment on their condition to Congress or the commander of the Eastern Military District and ask for instructions as to where they should be sent. If items needed repair, they were sent either to Springfield Arsenal or he was ordered to have workers at the Massachusetts state magazine at Cambridge repair them. Items not needed at the front were usually sent to storage magazines at Springfield or Brookfield.[26] After 1778, Philadelphia was also a major entrepôt of donated and purchased goods for the war effort. When a ship arrived with military stores, Gostelowe, Joy, or Joseph Perkins, superintendent of the armory, was sent to inspect them and determine their disposition. The stores would be placed into a magazine directly, marked for repair at the armory or ordnance yard, or placed on the open market for sale. Hodgdon took over these inspection activities in summer 1781 and relied on his staff of clerks and conductors to view the items. Though Congress gratefully received a large amount of war materiel from the French, it did not receive those stores blindly.

In conjunction with the regional commissaries, Flower's command came to include two hired inspectors: a superintendent of arms and a superintendent of ordnance. Congress created the superintendent of arms position in 1777, shortly after appointing Flower. A superintendent of ordnance was not appointed for another two years. Washington and several congressmen were of the opinion that a skilled gunsmith was needed to inspect all privately and publicly made muskets. Such an inspectorate would allow the commissary general to focus on the work of the arsenals. Instead, once Flower had set men to work at the arsenals, he took great interest in promoting the private production of artillery stores. Flower's illness, however, made his artillery oversight sporadic at best. Therefore, when Congress reformed the department in 1779, it created the superintendent of ordnance position to inspect all privately produced ordnance stores purchased by the DCGMS. The superintendent's main function was to judge the quality of stores purchased and manufactured by the DCGMS.

The inspection of arms carried out by government officials was, by necessity, a fairly simple operation. Guns were normally first tested visually. An inspector viewed the barrel for imperfections and the stock for any splits that might lead it to break. The weapon would then be dry fired to test the lock mechanism. The final standard musket test was to fire them once or twice with double the usual amount of powder. This would prove the strength of the barrel and the ability of the stock to take the shock of the discharge. Unfortunately, Congress did not possess enough powder to allow for the widespread test firing of the repaired weapons. It did provide powder for test firing on occasion, but more often the superintendent of arms and his assistants relied on visual inspections of arms to prove them. Such a system actually placed a great deal of inspection responsibility in the hands of the private gunsmiths and government artificers who repaired the weapons. They had to ensure that the barrels they made were straight and the locks they made were strong. When it came to accouterments, visual inspection was the only useful means of inspecting the leather straps and wood block of a cartridge box and the strength of a steel bayonet.[27] Thus, inspection procedures created by Congress for its arms, accouterments, and artillery were truly meant to prevent widespread abuses and neglect on the part of the craftsmen. The processes were not meant to catch every imperfection in every item produced.

MUSKET INSPECTION PROCESS

Congress instituted a musket inspection process as part of its 1776 military stores program, but the extent of work done by the DCGMS led to an evolution of that process. Desperation rather than conviction led Congress to choose Thomas Butler as its first superintendent of arms.

Congress faced a complex military stores situation at the end of 1776. Washington was continually calling for arms and accouterments. Tons of military stores had been lost to the British, and the threat of a British attack on Philadelphia made Congress abandon the capital for Baltimore.

Even as Congress began debating the military stores situation, it contracted with many gunsmiths, blacksmiths, and carpenters to repair and manufacture weapons as quickly as possible. The arsenals Congress then authorized partially resulted from the contractors' failure to respond quickly enough and in large enough numbers to meet the army's need. What Congress found more curious was that as the British conquered more and more of New Jersey and inched closer and closer to Philadelphia, none of the arms contractors were completing their work.[28] While this was largely a result of militia musters and the dislocation caused by the British, Congress blamed the disruption on "abuses [and embezzlements] so much practiced by Gunsmiths & others employ'd on the public Arms."[29] At this point, the Baltimore gunsmith Thomas Butler arrived. Butler, learning of Congress's need for trained military stores craftsmen, offered his services. After Congress got references from Butler's Baltimore neighbors and friends, he was hired as superintendent of arms.[30] He was commissioned "not only to superintend the repairing and proving of all the public Arms, but likewise to see that no more than a just value is paid the [private] workmen repair[ing] such of the public Arms at Philad. as are defective."[31]

Once Congress had appointed Butler, the Board of War integrated him into the larger DCGMS being developed under Flower. Flower had already set his own men to work repairing arms in Philadelphia by the time Congress directed Butler to put his own men to work. The Board of War therefore made Butler answerable to Flower. Flower could direct arms to either his own arsenal men or to Butler's gunsmiths for repair. Butler, however, had to inspect all the arms being repaired at the arsenal before they could be sent back to the front. Thus, no matter who repaired the guns, they all had to pass through Butler's shop. To deal with the arsenal being constructed at Carlisle, Butler hired an assistant who was to be stationed there once the post was in operation.[32]

Unfortunately for Congress, Butler was not a committed public servant, and an efficient inspection system failed to materialize. Butler traveled to Philadelphia, hired men, and put a gunsmith shop into operation within a few months after his appointment. In February, he hired Philadelphia gunsmith John Hall as his assistant. Butler made grand pronouncements regarding his value to the patriot cause, but Flower's correspondence makes it clear that by mid-year, neither Butler nor his staff were doing much work for the government. Flower forwarded thousands of muskets to Butler for repair, none of which were repaired and forwarded to Washington. Flower had to rely on the men employed by commissary Jonathan Gostelowe to complete most of the department's arms repair work. By October 1777, Butler had still failed to return to Flower or Washington any of the arms sent to him either for repair or inspection. When Philadelphia fell to the British, Butler moved his operations to Allentown and then to Carlisle, taking with him all the government weapons in his possession. As noted in chapter 2, Butler's intransigence over his place in the command structure led to his dismissal. By the time he was fired in March 1778, Flower had already hired John Hall to replace him and had begun sending all weapons to Hall for inspection.[33]

The British conquest of Philadelphia, oddly, led to the creation of an efficient arms inspection system for Congress in Pennsylvania. Carlisle was the DCGMS's main arsenal from October 1777 until July 1778, while Philadelphia was occupied. For half of those months, Butler failed to do any work. Flower, therefore, hired Hall directly. He was put to work inspecting the arms being repaired by Samuel Sargent's men at Carlisle. In April 1778, the Board of War hired William Henry, the Lancaster gunsmith, to replace Butler. Henry had already done a great deal of work for the Pennsylvania government, and he was a well-respected patriot. Flower directed Henry to inspect all weapons being repaired at the department's temporary depot in Lebanon, where Gostelowe's men were living out their exile from Philadelphia. In the meantime, Hall was made answerable to Henry as his representative at Carlisle. The system that developed operated in this fashion: Washington had weapons packed at the army's camp in Valley Forge and sent to Lebanon, where Flower rented temporary repair facilities for the Philadelphia armorers and workers. About a third of the weapons were then sent to Carlisle and another third to Henry in Lancaster. Sargent's men repaired the weapons at Carlisle. Hall inspected the repaired weapons and made a report to Henry on the outcome. Those weapons sent to Henry were either repaired in his workshop or subcontracted to other gunsmiths.[34] Gostelowe was still in charge of inspecting the production of Philadelphia workers in Lebanon. Despite the fact that Henry was not involved in Lebanon's arms operations, once he took over the superintendence of arms, backcountry Pennsylvania gunsmiths were mobilized for the war effort.

Henry's inspection system was an integral part of the military stores program from August 1778 until Carlisle was effectively closed in December 1781. The number of weapons sent to Carlisle was too great for the small number of armorers recruited to work at the site. Hall and Lukens, therefore, began subcontracting the repair of weapons to gunsmiths in Cumberland County and York, Pennsylvania, as well as western Maryland. If the weapons were returned to Carlisle, Hall inspected them. Most often, however, the weapons were sent to Lancaster for storage in a military stores depot in that city. Henry then took on the responsibility of inspecting them. Henry also continued to subcontract the repair of weapons to his neighbors and inspect the results. Henry's commission carried a responsibility that Butler's had not: he was given charge over the repair of accouterments as well. This stemmed from Henry's secondary position as superintendent of hides in the Quartermaster Department. Henry used his access to leather and timber to assist Carlisle workers in the construction of cartridge boxes. He also used his commission to subcontract with Lancaster craftsmen in the manufacture of bayonets. He delivered these supplies to either Carlisle or Philadelphia.[35] Through a number of manufacturing and inspection avenues, Henry and his assistant Hall ensured that the products made by private and public craftsmen in the Pennsylvania interior met the quality needs of the Continental Army.

The size of the Philadelphia armory and its distance from Henry's location required that it operate independently of the superintendent of arms. This did not mean, however, that the DCGMS did not institute an inspection process at the site. Philadelphia was closer to the front line than Lancaster, making it unfeasible to send weapons 120 miles west for inspection before sending them 160 miles east from Carlisle to the army. The Philadelphia armory repaired and manufactured some twenty-five thousand muskets, more than records indicate came from Carlisle and Henry. All of the arms repair work done in Philadelphia came under the direction of Joseph Perkins.[36] Once those weapons were certified, they were passed on to Gostelowe's magazine for storage until called on by Flower or Hodgdon. The major inspection activity in Philadelphia, though, was done by Gostelowe until his dismissal, which was discussed in chapter 2. Much of the accouterment manufacturing and repair accomplished by the department was contracted out to local craftsmen. Gostelowe inspected each of these items before storing them and issuing a receipt for payment on the contract.[37] These processes continued when the department began contracting out most of its arms and accouterment repair work.

Several factors led to the government's reliance on private contractors, making the superintendent of arms critical to activities in Philadelphia. The DCGMS, low on cash in 1781, was seeking ways to cut expenses. Many of its hired men were laid off, and much of the enlisted workforce in Philadelphia had been sent to Carlisle. Still, Congress wanted Hodgdon to cut spending even more. In response, he shut down the armory and began contracting out the production and repair of weapons and accouterments. The first contractor was the French firm of Penet and Couloux, which built a private armory in Philadelphia for the repair of guns.[38] Hodgdon then began contracting former gunsmiths from the government's armory to repair weapons. Perkins, once armory superintendent, became a private contractor. In the midst of this, Gostelowe was released from service to save money. To deal with the need for inspections, Hodgdon called Hall from Carlisle and developed a new inspection process.[39] All arms repaired at Carlisle or Lancaster were, from early 1781, to pass through Hodgdon's departmental magazine at Philadelphia and be inspected by Hall. Hall was also sent on inspection tours of contractor operations to oversee their activities.

In June 1781, Hall was sent to James Pearson's grinding mill, where bayonets were being manufactured for the government. Hall approved 483 bayonets, provided by Pearson over the next two months.[40] Hall also inspected the work of nine other contractors who produced everything from cartridge boxes and bayonets, to fully finished arms. Though the government no longer controlled the production of weapons by employing the gunsmiths, it nominally controlled their production through inspections by the superintendent of arms. Thus, the quality of weapons sent to the army could be maintained and the expense of repair kept low.[41]

The superintendent of arms position did not survive the war. When Hall arrived in Philadelphia in 1781, he was made primary inspector of arms in the department, superseding Henry. But Hall only held the position for a year. In May 1782, two large shipments of newly manufactured muskets arrived from France, and Hodgdon informed Hall that his services were no longer necessary. Repair and manufacturing work declined to such an extent that Hodgdon could do the inspection work himself. The position of superintendent of arms was done away with, and the responsibility was taken over by Hodgdon.[42] From 1778 until 1782, however, the actions of the men who held the position contributed greatly to the efficiency of the DCGMS by certifying the quality of all weapons emanating from it for use by the army. During the same time, the superintendent of ordnance provided the same service for artillery stores.

Daniel Joy, who earlier in the war had shown great skill in the execution of such responsibility, was named superintendent of ordnance. Though he was directed to contract with various furnaces for shot, shells, and ordnance, his chief responsibility was to act as the government's chief inspector of privately produced ordnance stores.[43] His contracting powers in any case only lasted for about a year until Samuel Hodgdon took charge of the department. From that point on, Hodgdon oversaw the negotiations and signing of all government military stores contracts to ensure his control of the department. From 1779 to his death in 1784, Joy inspected production at furnaces in Maryland and Pennsylvania, proved ordnance and ammunition, and saw to the finishing and care of all these items at the Philadelphia ordnance yard. His actions mobilized a dozen iron furnaces for the war effort.

Joy's first assignment under the DCGMS was to the Hughes Iron Works in Maryland. In April 1779, the Board of War entered into a cannon contract with the Hughes brothers and directed Joy to oversee it. Joy traveled to Maryland and proved the cannons with powder provided by Carlisle Arsenal. Joy then secured transport from the Quartermaster Department to move the cannon from the Hughes works to the Main Army in the Hudson Valley. While he was working with Hughes on the completion of the artillery pieces, Joy signed a contract for the production of shot and shells. Hodgdon later renewed this contract, using Joy as an intermediary. Joy made numerous trips to the Hughes furnace over the next two years, consulting on the design and production of ammunition. At Joy's request, four new twelve-pound shot patterns were sent to Hughes by Hodgdon in October 1780, and Joy returned later that winter to inspect the shells made thus far.[44]

Between inspections of the Hughes works, Joy took time to review work at several eastern Pennsylvania furnaces. In the first months of 1780, Joy made contracts with Oley and Berkshire Furnaces and later returned to prove and transport their castings. Oley produced 245 usable shells, while Berkshire cast 1,936 shells of various sizes.[45] After visiting the furnaces to prove and secure the ammunition, he traveled to Durham Furnace in Bucks County, Pennsylvania, to secure a contract. By that point he was working under Hodgdon, and after making the contract asked Hodgdon to send patterns for proper casting. Joy was also sent to examine 2,912 shells cast by Rutter and Potts in Chester County.[46] He was then sent by Hodgdon to examine the potential of contracting ammunition at furnaces in Maryland and Virginia.

Joy's visit to the Hughes furnace in summer 1780 coincided with a tour he took to the south in search of ironworks with which he could contract, but he "met no success to the southwards."[47] He found that iron facilities south of the Mason-Dixon Line had been ravaged by the war. In mid-1777, when the British had sailed up the Chesapeake Bay toward Philadelphia, they took time to destroy the Principio Furnace at Head of Elk, Maryland. This was the largest ironworks in the state and one of the largest in the country. In 1780, just before Joy's tour, the British had raided Virginia's James River valley and destroyed iron furnaces in that region. Only on his return through Baltimore toward Hughes in northern Maryland did Joy find hope. James Johnson's iron company was willing and able to cast shot and shell, and they were duly contracted. Unfortunately, Johnson did not meet the expectations placed on him. The first batch of shot and shells proved defective, but were sent north to Philadelphia by the firm without being inspected.[48] As Joy later reported, "If I had stayed with them a few days all would have been well and their shells good, but the late governor who was there repeatedly declared to me that he had not a doubt but that his brother James would get them executed in the best manner and agreeable to my directions. If they had expressed the least desire of my staying I should not have hesitated to stay."[49] Joy had assisted iron firms in the casting of ordnance stores in the past, but his services were declined in this case. Most of the ammunition provided by Johnson's first casting ended up being faulty. Hodgdon scolded him, saying he would not pay for defective products. Before Johnson sent his second supply of shot and shells to Philadelphia, he waited for Joy to inspect them in Baltimore. When Joy made that inspection in summer 1781, he found that 482 of the shells cast were flawed, not being airtight. This was "Chiefly owing to a defect in the ears of the said shells they not being made any ways similar to the plan and directions I left."[50] Johnson never did honor his contract, and in 1784 still owed the government for money forwarded him to put the furnace in blast.

Joy was ordered on a second tour at the beginning of 1781. His instructions reveal the government's commitment not only to receiving quality stores but also to assisting private manufacturers in achieving that quality. Joy was directed to the furnaces he and Hodgdon had contracted with in late 1780, to "have the shot and shells by them cast, proved, properly piled to prevent damage or embezzlement and an accurate return made of such as stand proof."[51] Taking such an active role in manufacturing made quite a difference in the quality of stores, as is evident by comparing the failure of activities at Johnson's Furnace with the results of Joy's work in 1781. From January through June, Joy visited six furnaces: Elizabeth, Cornwall, Berkshire, Oley, and Durham in eastern Pennsylvania and Batsto in southern New Jersey. Working with each site's furnace master, he oversaw the production of 36,251 shot and shells. Of the six furnaces, Joy found that Elizabeth, Cornwall, Berkshire, and Oley produced consistently useful shells. Joy was also pleased with forty-seven tons of shot and shells he inspected at Batsto Furnace. He made an inspection of that site on the Great Egg Harbor Bay in mid-May before returning to Pennsylvania to finish his tour.[52] Joy spent his time not only proving ammunition but also assisting furnace operations as the ammunition was being made. Joy's participation was critical to the production of stores at these sites in 1781.

In 1781, when Joy returned to Philadelphia, he was given greater responsibility at the ordnance yard, and inspection activities were turned over to others. Hodgdon had Joy supervise the repair and finishing of ordnance stores. As the likelihood of Washington's move to the south grew, Joy was ordered by Hodgdon to prepare the heaviest ordnance in the yard for shipment. Once the army had moved south, he was ordered to oversee the repair of ordnance delivered from the Pennsylvania magazine. These, Hodgdon hoped, could quickly be made ready for shipment south to Yorktown. It was at this point, too, that Hodgdon began relying on artillery officers to inspect contracted shot and shells. Hodgdon apparently shifted assignments to take advantage of the skills available to him. While artificers could be used to repair artillery, they needed the guidance of a trained individual. Joy had made his talents apparent through his inspection activities. At the same time, numerous artillery officers were available, individuals who had been trained either on the field, at the government's laboratories, or by both.

Hodgdon came to the job of commissary general with experience in government contracting. While the Board of War was trying to centralize contracting and inspection processes in the DCGMS, Knox decided that the board was wasting the army's time. Hodgdon would eventually centralize government inspection as desired by the board, but until he became commissary general, a separate and distinct contract and inspection system existed under the commander of artillery. Knox, assisted by field commissary Hodgdon, began making contracts with Hudson Valley ironmongers in summer 1778. Knox had not been happy with the disposition of the DCGMS since it had been created. Under the British model, he, as commander of artillery, should have had control over Flower's department. Congress, however, had deemed it wiser to separate the two functions. In his own opinion, Knox had struggled to no avail throughout winter 1777 and 1778 to secure a proper supply of ordnance, arms, and ammunition for the army's 1778 campaign. He blamed the lack of activity by Flower's department on the fact that Flower did not answer to him. In summer 1778, Knox decided to take matters into his own hands, investigating the possibility of putting furnaces in the region into the employ of the army. He appointed Hodgdon to the task.

Hodgdon was first sent to Hibernia Furnace to explore contract possibilities, and the initial success he had led Knox to expand his activities. Hodgdon met John Faesch, owner of Hibernia Furnace, in early September 1778, with instructions from Knox to contract for one thousand six-pound shot, one hundred twelve-pound shot, and one hundred nine-pound shot.[53] These Faesch made by the end of the year, and the Board of War approved payment for them. Within a year, Hodgdon had made several more orders from Faesch's furnace. By August 1779, Faesch had cast more than two thousand six hundred twelve-pound shot, one thousand three-pound shot, five hundred four-pound shot, and five tons of grapeshot. Hodgdon and his conductors acted as inspectors for Faesch's work. Faesch's original contract work was reviewed by Hodgdon when he went with wagons to the furnace to bring the shot and shells back to the army. In later months, Hodgdon sent one of his assistants, James Boyer, to review Faesch's castings. Hodgdon's correspondence, however, makes it clear that he spent a great deal of time at Hibernia Furnace working with Faesch. The two spent so much time together coordinating production for the artillery corps that they became friends, exchanging informal letters and dining together.[54]

Congress wanted military stores; it wanted as many as it could get, as fast as it could get them, which is why it allowed Knox to contravene its authority. Despite Congress's desire to centralize military stores procurement, if Knox were able to secure more supplies, why should congressional policy get in his way? As long as Knox did not interfere with Flower's department, he could operate his own contracting operations. Congress's views on the subject can be seen in its 1779 reform of the DCGMS. Not only did Congress make the field commissary separate from Flower's command, but it allowed that in extraordinary circumstances, the commander of artillery could requisition supplies from the arsenals without the approval of the Board of War. Knox took this to mean that the field commissary he commanded could also make contracts independent of Flower's department. Moreover, any circumstance could be declared extraordinary in wartime, allowing him to requisition supplies. If Congress were going to allow him to use the arsenals in such cases, why could he not employ private contractors as well? Neither Congress nor the Board of War interpreted the 1779 commissary reform differently from Knox. Congress clarified its position in summer 1780 when it recognized that Knox's contracts were necessary for carrying on that year's campaign. It then authorized $4 million to purchase shot and shells from all available furnaces.[55] Congress gave Knox its approval for his contracting program while at the same time centralizing its original program. For the time being, necessity dictated production not consistency.

Hodgdon left for Philadelphia early in 1780 to assume responsibility for Flower's department. Knox continued making contracts with Faesch, contracts that again led to the involvement of the government in mobilizing American manufacturing. Knox believed that the DCGMS had not prepared sufficiently for the 1780 campaign, which was to involve a siege and attack on New York City. Knox therefore approached Faesch with a new contract. Faesch had, however, let his furnace go out of blast after the end of the last contract in January, and it had fallen into disrepair. He could, he told Knox, put the furnace back in blast by the beginning of August and make twelve to sixteen tons of ammunition per week, but this would require some assistance from the army and government. To get the furnace operational he would need his men released from militia duty, food to feed them, and £20,000 up front to pay for salaries, supplies, and a new hearth for the furnace. In addition, Faesch requested the use of troops to install a new hearth, army carpenters to build a new mold house, and an inspector to review the shells.[56]

Knox saw that Faesch got all that he asked for. Faesch got his furnace into blast, but he did not deliver on his contract with Knox until December. Lieutenant James Hall of the 3rd Artillery Battalion was sent to examine the castings. Hall found that out of 3,823 shells inspected,

3,269 passed, 270 failed, and 284 required further review. Faesch also produced 6,900 one-pound shot that met army standards. Despite the expansion of his contract with Faesch, Knox felt the need to contract elsewhere as well. To that end he contracted for an indeterminate number of shells with Pompton Furnace in northern New Jersey. To prove the ammunition, Knox dispatched an artillery officer to the furnace. Lieutenant John Callender of the 3rd Artillery Battalion was sent there in July 1780, and he proved 136 thirteen-inch shells.[57] Knox, however, did not play a significant role in contracting and inspection after 1780. By the end of that year, Hodgdon had taken singular control of the DCGMS, and he worked with Knox to get the contracts that he wanted. In that way he assumed leadership not only of Flower's functionaries but of Knox's as well.

Hodgdon was better equipped in 1780 to manage Flower's department than was Flower himself. He suffered from no illnesses that took him away from his duties. Hodgdon had served as field commissary and thus had a working relationship with Knox that Flower had never developed. Service with Knox had involved Hodgdon with activities at Springfield, a post Flower had never visited or seemed to have taken a direct hand in managing. Hodgdon also benefited from the experience that Gostelowe, Joy, Perkins, and several artillery officers had gained while working under Flower and Knox as contractors and inspectors. By the time Hodgdon assumed leadership of the department, job responsibilities, lines of communication, and departmental conflicts had largely been settled. Hodgdon also brought an important asset with him from the field commissary department in the person of James Boyer, who assisted him in the review of production at Hibernia Furnace. When he arrived in Philadelphia, Boyer served the DCGMS as a clerk to transact business in the city. Hodgdon's first two years in charge of the DCGMS, therefore, marked the point at which the various inspectorates discussed in the preceding pages became effectively coordinated and their operations centralized under one manager. Neither Joy nor the regional commissaries acted independently after Hodgdon arrived in Philadelphia in 1780. All contracts entered into by the DCGMS, the Board of War, and Knox became Hodgdon's responsibility. Hodgdon coordinated all contract inspection and delivery through the activity of the inspectors of arms and ordnance, all the regional commissaries, and Knox's artillery inspection staff, all of whom answered to him.

From 1780 until the end of the war, Hodgdon's personal staff and artillery personnel were used to supplement the work of the DCGMS. In October 1780, Hodgdon sent Boyer on a mission to the north. Boyer first visited Faesch in New Jersey to secure "an Accurate Return of Shot and Shells cast by him in Consequence of his last contract." He then went to

Massachusetts, where Hodgdon had just entered into five contracts for the production of over eleven thousand shells. Hodgdon wanted all the contracts canceled because the campaign season was at an end. If any of the furnaces had already begun production, Boyer was to "forward accurate Returns of the Number & weight of each sort cast."[58] When Boyer got to Stafford Furnace in Connecticut, he found that it had already begun casting ammunition. He therefore halted the contract and inspected what had been produced. After reviewing the work of the furnaces, Boyer went to Springfield, where he inspected the post and took an inventory of all the stores available there.[59] Upon finishing all of his inspections by the beginning of 1781, Boyer returned to Philadelphia to make his report.

ORDNANCE INSPECTION PROCESS

John Faesch became the nation's leading supplier of artillery ammunition in 1782, despite the fact that four other contracts were issued. A number of reasons explain this. At the end of the preceding year, Benjamin Lincoln was named secretary at war, and he assumed responsibility for all military stores contracts. Those he sought out for advice on the topic were all intimately connected with Faesch. Lincoln relied heavily on the counsel of Henry Knox, who had worked extensively with Faesch. Faesch, in turn, had befriended Hodgdon, who became a de facto assistant to Lincoln over the course of the year. Faesch was also a logical choice. He owned two furnaces, with significant production capacity within two day's travel of the army. Lincoln therefore contracted with Faesch in late spring for over eighteen thousand shot and shells for the 1782 campaign.[60] Hodgdon replaced Boyer and Joy as inspectors with officers from the artillery service. He dispatched Captain William Stevens of Colonel Lamb's battalion to inspect Faesch's production operations and prove the shot and shells he produced. As with Joy, Stevens was directed to remain at the furnace as long as necessary and "give such directions as are necessary to enable [Faesch] to proceed without loss of time."[61] By November, Stevens certified to Lincoln that he had inspected 11,422 five-and-a-half-inch and eight-inch shells, of which 10,653 stood proof. At the same time, he inspected 6,306 eighteen- and twenty-four-pound shot, of which only 5,571 stood proof.[62] This was Faesch's last contract for the government, and, in fact, the shells he cast in 1782 never arrived at camp for use against the British. Peace came before they could be delivered.

While Faesch was the largest supplier of artillery ammunition to the army in the waning days of the war, he was not the only one. Lincoln also contracted in 1782 with Salisbury Furnace in Connecticut and Pompton Furnace in Massachusetts to supplement Faesch's production. Salisbury produced only 1,814 five-and-a-half and eight-inch shells, and 2,000 eighteen- and twenty-four-pound shot, just under one-third of Faesch's production total. But Salisbury had been an inconsistent producer of iron since the state government gave up management of its operation in 1780. Inspection of the shot and shells cast by the renting founder, William Whiting, proved that production standards had not improved. Of the shells cast, just 801 passed proof tests by Lieutenant Hall of the artillery corps. The others were either too large, too small, or not airtight. Hall also found that all the shot cast were smaller than the patterns forwarded to the furnace by Lincoln. By contrast, all of the 1,504 cast by Pompton passed proof, and they were delivered to camp by the end of 1782.[63]

As the war came to a close, Hodgdon did most inspection work himself because budgetary constraints forced him to reduce his staff. No ordnance contracts were made after 1782, and therefore no artillery officers were dispatched for inspections. From 1781 until 1784, however, the department did contract out over five thousand muskets for repair and eleven thousand for cleaning. These Hodgdon only visually inspected, relying on the skills of the gunsmiths involved for quality control. The majority of men contracted for the repair work had once served at the Philadelphia armory. Postwar inspection and contracting work done by Hodgdon and his department are subjects of the final chapter.

GOVERNMENT INSPECTION PLAYED TWO IMPORTANT ROLES IN THE patriot war effort. First, inspectors provided guidance to manufacturers in the production of military stores. Many craftsmen and ironmongers had never made weapons and ordnance. They needed and wanted oversight. Several ironmongers such as the Hughes brothers and John Patton asked for government assistance in the form of an inspector stationed at their works. Inspectors also provided patterns, written instructions, and verbal instructions to contractors regarding government specifications. Once inspectors had instructed contractors, they then took on the role of examining stores to ensure their proper manufacture. Then, inspectors judged the quality of items made for the government. Inspectors physically and visually examined items before placing them in government magazines. Inspection and instruction were not, however, the limits of government efforts to mobilize and direct private manufacturing. The government's desire to ensure that the army was sufficiently supplied led it to involve itself even further in the productive processes of contracted craftsmen.

"We manufactured all the articles necessary for our defence"

DIRECTING PRIVATE MANUFACTURERS: PROVIDING RESOURCES

D
ANIEL ROBERDEAU CAME TO UNDERSTAND THE NATION'S MILITARY stores limitations intimately by spring 1778, and he was not shy about his belief that he could personally do something about it. Born in Saint Kitts, Roberdeau had immigrated with his widowed mother to Philadelphia in the 1730s. He grew up among the merchant houses of the port city while completing a private education, and he turned his knowledge and experience into a successful mercantile career. His wealth, in turn, allowed Roberdeau to serve in the Pennsylvania Assembly for fifteen years. He was an early advocate of independence, and on July 4, 1776, the state rewarded him with the rank of brigadier general and gave him command of the militia.

Roberdeau spent the next several months preparing raw troops to defend Philadelphia from British invasion and leading troops to support George Washington's army. He discovered quickly how limited the supply of military stores was in the United States and how precarious the weapons situation was. Roberdeau was elected to the Continental Congress in 1777; serving there, he learned that even with a military stores department and public arsenals, the nation was struggling to produce enough items to keep an army in the field. As a merchant, his attention was consistently drawn to the nation's need for lead, which had to be imported from France or captured from the British. The military stores department was almost always in need of lead. Roberdeau had seen enough of the situation by spring 1778 and decided to attempt a solution to the lead-shortage problem.

The general took leave of Congress and, at his own expense, outfitted an expedition to the Pennsylvania frontier to search for lead deposits. After a few months of recruiting workers, purchasing supplies, and investigating, Roberdeau took his expedition to Sinking Valley, just east of modern-day Altoona. There the enterprise began mining and smelting lead ore into pigs for transport east to Carlisle Arsenal. Unfortunately, Roberdeau discovered, shortly after beginning, that his mission was financially unsustainable, and he turned to Congress and the military stores department for assistance.[1]

Roberdeau's mining initiative encountered difficulties that most American craft and manufacturing operations were experiencing as a result of the war. The general had little choice but to turn to the government for help. Reflecting on his lead-mining activities in mid-1779, Roberdeau told Congress the problems he faced. "My feeble Efforts have been opposed [by the] great System of war devised by a potent Enemy. I cannot procure hands to labour in so exposed a Situation. I have applied to the board of war for . . . supplies and [for] the labour of some Continental workmen in carrying on the Works." Native Americans and frontiersmen loyal to the British had been attacking Roberdeau's works since its inception. This violence not only ran off the general's initial laborers but made it difficult to recruit new ones at any reasonable cost. Moreover, despite his own investments, Roberdeau did not have enough cash to purchase everything the operation required. Without help, he said, "the works . . . will in all probability . . . be lost to the public."[2]

The Board of War responded by directing Charles Lukens to supply Roberdeau with the items and laborers he needed from Carlisle Arsenal.[3] The board also dispatched troops from Carlisle along with weapons and artillery to defend the post while the laborers worked. With government support, Roberdeau's venture continued to supply lead to the Continental Army until late 1780, when the site became unaffordable because of high labor costs and inflation. The military stores department had embraced an opportunity to assist in the mobilization of this lead-mining enterprise, and it went on to mobilize many more endeavors like it.

The American Revolution had a profound impact on the established economic patterns that existed in the United States. While it is common to think of craftsmen as small, simple, independent producers relying on their own sweat and tears, the reality of eighteenth-century artisanal work was much more complex. Colonial artisans were more akin to small business entrepreneurs than artists. American craftsmen with their own shops performed many more tasks than the skilled manufacturing in which they had been trained. A master craftsman had to secure all his own supplies, provide his own financing, and market his own products. Such activities, which took time under normal circumstances, were made extremely difficult by the destructiveness of the war. As historian Thomas Doerflinger noted, "[T]he United States was occupied by a hostile power [that caused] not only widespread destruction of property but [also] a derangement of basic mechanisms of transport and commercial exchange."[4]

Congress discovered the extent of the dislocations faced by producers in the execution of its early purchasing efforts as well as through the purchasing efforts of the DCGMS. Craftsmen could not meet production contracts, because they could not secure raw materials or transportation. Many craftsmen also lacked the cash to prepare their operations for military production. As the war progressed, congressional administrators realized they had to take a material role in American manufacturing in order to secure military stores. To make production possible for many of its contractors, therefore, the DCGMS took over several of the management roles performed by those craftsmen. It mobilized private manufacturers for the war effort by providing cash investments, raw materials, and transportation for their production operations. The support provided to its contract manufacturers was not universally free. Cash and materials were subtracted from manufacturer accounts and treated as payment for work accomplished. However, by being provided support at different points in the production timeline, craftsmen were freed from engaging in certain elements of operations management and allowed to focus their efforts on production. Moreover, many manufacturers, as seen already, were unskilled in the production of military stores, and government support allowed them to invest in new tools and test production methods. Finally, by acting as a central supplier of raw materials and transportation, the government released manufacturers from some of the constraints of the wartime economy. To fully understand the importance of government efforts, a brief examination of wartime dislocations is necessary. It will then be apparent how cash, raw materials, and transportation could be used to mobilize American manufacturing.

Colonial master craftsmen took on many responsibilities in addition to production when they opened their own shops. They had to purchase raw materials and fuels. They marketed and sold their products, often relying on their wives to monitor a store attached to the craft shop. Craftsmen extended credit to their buyers. Credit not only made products more attractive but was a necessity in the cash-strapped colonial economy. Finally, larger operations like forges, furnaces, tanneries, gristmills, and sawmills had to transport their goods to the market for sale. The war made many of these business functions difficult.

The acquisition of raw materials for manufacture was inhibited by two factors. First, traditional transport networks were destroyed. Before the war, most bulk items like wood, hides, ores, and grains were moved by boat in coastal and river trade. The British, however, instituted a blockade of the American coast, and the various movements of the British army and navy made water transport precarious and unreliable. The Chesapeake Bay was a major highway of trade for Americans prior to the war, and occasionally during the war, but it could never be completely trusted that the British navy was not on patrol. Rivers were risky, too, because they offered avenues of potential enemy attack. In response, Americans had to use land transportation: wagons along post roads and cart paths that were made for local trade, not national transportation. Doerflinger wrote, "Nothing was more damaging to the economy than the wrenching shift of the interstate transport system from coastwise maritime trade to inland carriage."[5] Carting goods was much more expensive than floating them, making the price of raw materials higher. This was especially true of wood, ores, and hides, all of which were acquired primarily on the frontier. A second factor that made raw materials difficult to obtain was inflation. Congress printed $226 million by 1779 to pay for the war, and the states each printed their own money, which added to the enormous amount of paper money in circulation. By 1780, this financing system had destroyed the value of Continental money. Hard currency (specie) was rare. Wartime disruptions raised the prices of goods around the country, but the capital at Philadelphia suffered dramatically. In 1776, £100 paper money could buy 143.3 hundredweight of flour, but just five years later, it could buy only half that amount.[6] Inflation also destroyed the credit system on which craftsmen relied. Creditors could legally pay off their old debts with depreciated paper money. This ruined many men who had extended credit before the war. Such a circumstance made it prudent for craftsmen to withhold credit to customers, which in turn made it impossible to do business. As business slowed down, craftsmen and larger manufacturers stopped investing in their own, as well as other, enterprises.

The final problem producers faced was the destructiveness of the war itself. Property damage was widespread around the United States. For instance, Batsto Furnace, New Jersey, was raided by the British; Valley Forge, Pennsylvania, was destroyed prior to the British occupation of Philadelphia; and the Southwark Air Furnace was pulled down when the British occupied Philadelphia. Native American, Loyalist, and British raids on the frontier threatened iron ore and coal deposits in Pennsylvania's Lancaster and Northumberland counties. Native raids also inhibited the production of charcoal because the chief sources of wood were also on the frontier. The DCGMS went to great lengths to mitigate the effects of these disruptions on its private contractors.

Samuel Hodgdon's account book revealed that the DCGMS purchased items from craftsmen representing at least thirty-one craft specialties.

The department made use of numerous men skilled in military stores production like bayonet makers, gunsmiths, cartridge makers, sword makers, and powder makers.[7] In addition, government work provided generally skilled craftsmen with the opportunity to develop their skills with military products. Carpenters were hired to make cartridge box blocks, ammunition boxes, and cannon carriages. Blacksmiths made bullet molds, cannon carriages, and files. Leather workers made cartridge box sacks, cartridge box straps, and gun belts. The department also relied on many manufacturers who provided the raw materials of arsenal production. Ironmongers provided cast iron, bar iron, nail rod iron, and steel. Sawyers cut planking, scantling, and charcoal. Tanners provided hides and dressed leather. Papermakers made reams of cannon and musket cartridge paper as well as writing paper for the numerous reports made by departmental administrators.[8] All these many specialties fell into two broad categories: craftsmen processing raw materials like spirits, lumber, iron, or hides; and others producing finished products like muskets, bayonets, cartridge boxes, or barrels.

Private craftsmen were employed to support the activities of each of the nation's arsenals during the war, but the majority of contracts were issued in the vicinity of Philadelphia. By 1782, only about fourteen craftsmen were contracted in the Springfield area to support the arsenal. Ezekiel Cheever, Springfield's regional commissary of military stores, allowed these operations to stagnate. Private production of military stores in Springfield did not really develop under government oversight until 1781, when Luke Bliss replaced Cheever. Roughly half of the men that Bliss hired provided finished military stores, including cartridges and fuses. The other half of Bliss's private contractors processed raw materials like charcoal and planking for use by arsenal workers. The private craftsmen employed by Charles Lukens at Carlisle likewise provided processed materials for arsenal workers. Most of Lukens's private contracts were for lumber, lubrication oils, lime, and bar iron. The extensive public operations at Carlisle that included a sawmill, furnace, and forges meant that the arsenal processed most of the raw materials it purchased. Lukens did contract with York and Carlisle gunsmiths and blacksmiths, but there are no arsenal records that reveal how extensive these operations were. In contrast to the limited private contracting at Carlisle and Springfield, commissaries in Philadelphia hired at least 139 local craftsmen. Sixty-eight, or just under half, of contracted craftsmen produced finished goods; the remainder processed raw materials.[9] The larger number of private craftsmen contracted in Philadelphia reflected the relatively larger size of the Philadelphia Arsenal compared to other arsenals. As the center of government manufacturing operations, as well as the departmental headquarters, Philadelphia was the hub of government actions to materially assist government contractors.

The DCGMS provided support to Philadelphia manufacturers with whom it had long-term contracts for the specific production of military stores. Fifty of the 139 private craftsmen who worked for the government in this region were provided with either cash advances or raw materials for the execution of their contracts.[10] Those fifty provided finished military stores or finished components of larger military stores. They were gunsmiths, blacksmiths specializing in sword or bayonet making, and carpenters skilled in carriage repair and cartridge box production. All four private bayonet makers working for the government received support, as did both sword makers. Eight of twelve ironmongers contracted for shot, shells, or cannons were provided with either cash advances or raw materials. Fourteen of twenty-one gunsmiths contracted received incentives, and seven of thirteen carpenters were also supported. Therefore, while the government subsidized only 36 percent of all contracted craftsmen from Philadelphia, it supported 65 percent of those producing finished military stores. Forty-three of those craftsmen receiving support worked for the department for longer than three years, from 1780 until 1783, and all but one of those forty-three were still working for Hodgdon two years after the war was over. Of the remaining eighty-nine private craftsmen who worked for the department at some time between 1780 and 1785, all but twelve provided only incidental services such as repairing a single musket or selling several gallons of glue or paint to the department. In other words, only twelve craftsmen developed long-term working relationships with the government without receiving government support as part of their contract.[11] Material support was thus clearly used as a means of developing productive relationships between government and private manufacturers.

Congress did not spend a great deal of money in the form of cash advances. The department spent a total of $832,000 from 1780 through 1783, the years for which records of cash advances are available. Only $25,000 of the total DCGMS budget was in the form of cash advances to manufacturers. By far the majority of government cash advances went to ironmongers who used the money to refit their furnaces for the production of cannon, shot, and shell. Eight ironmongers were advanced $22,099 in the final three years of the war, while forty-two other craftsmen shared roughly $3,000 in cash advances for the production of military stores.[12]

Though not a large amount compared to overall spending, the DCGMS's cash advances assisted craftsmen in developing their activities. When Philadelphia weaver Nathan Clifton was approached in March 1780 to manufacture blankets, he had neither the tools nor the wool to complete such a contract. Flower advanced him $798 in cash to purchase the wool and gave him $133 worth of wool carding tools out of the government's stores. By May, Clifton had produced 155 yards of blanketing and 145 yards of wool cloth for the department worth $4,484.[13] Later that year, blacksmith George Heighberger agreed to work for the department for an advance of $512 with which to purchase tools to manufacture horsemen's swords.[14] William Perkins, a saddler, was engaged by the department in 1781 to make cartridge boxes. With an advance of $500 he purchased leather and worked it into pouches for five hundred cartridge box blocks he received from the government. Hodgdon was so pleased with the work that an additional $350 was advanced to Perkins for one thousand more cartridge boxes. His success led to his retention by the department for continued work. Perkins worked under contract, making cartridge boxes for two more years and performing $3,888 worth of work, all of which began because the government advanced him the money with which to purchase his original supply of leather.[15] Tanner Martin Gouil, who had built a government relationship by providing hides to the DCGMS, was contracted to make cartridge boxes. To entice him, the department advanced him $622 in spring 1782 to purchase the necessary equipment and hire additional workers. Gouil manufactured 1,001 cartridge boxes valued at $1,868.[16] Henry Stroop built a significant relationship with the DCGMS. His entry in Hodgdon's account book reveals that Stroop contracted with the department prior to summer 1781, when he delivered sundry arms chests, ammunition boxes, and tables. He was then forwarded $133.75 to purchase additional materials for the performance of more carpentry work, which he delivered in December. Stroop reappears throughout Hodgdon's ledger well into the 1780s as a government supplier.[17] Although cash was not advanced in the beginning of Stroop's service, it was useful to keep him in service to the government. Finally, in June 1782, turner William Keats was advanced $38 with which to purchase turning tools to use in repairing gunstocks. From that point his name reappears throughout the 1780s in Hodgdon's cash ledger. For at least three years, Keats provided carpentry services for the department.[18]

Perhaps the most important business relationships built by the government with cash advances were those with America's ironmongers. Two reasons explain why ironmongers required the lion's share of cash advanced by the government. First, producing cast iron was expensive. Huge amounts of fuel, ore, and lime had to be stored up to keep a furnace in blast, and the furnace itself was a large capital investment. Furnace owners did not put their furnaces into blast without the foreknowledge they could sell their iron.[19] Second, Congress was desperately short of funds by 1780, and virtually everyone in the nation knew it. Large manufacturers were unwilling to enter into government contracts without some down payment for the work to be accomplished. As noted earlier, any gunsmiths or ironmongers who developed a long-term production contract with the DCGMS received either cash or raw materials as an advance on the contract to begin production. This assistance was given because the bankrupted Congress could not be trusted to pay its bills on time. Nevertheless, Congress was, despite its financial problems, the only organization with the borrowing power and purchasing power to finance large-scale operations. And those powers were brought to the aid of American iron manufacturers.

Congressional monetary support helped keep numerous iron furnaces in blast through the economic turbulence of the war years. Mark Bird had owned Hopewell Furnace for only four years when the war began, but he quickly offered his services to the Pennsylvania and Continental governments. Bird spent hundreds of dollars to equip his own company of militia as well as to supply the province with stores. Eventually Congress named him a deputy quartermaster for Berks, Northampton, and Northumberland counties. The result of his many activities was that he had few funds on hand to put his furnace in blast for the production of artillery and artillery ammunition when Congress requested these items. Congress, therefore, advanced Bird $2,000 in August 1776 to prepare the materials necessary for casting. Bird, however, was not very adept at financial planning and seems to have confused his records as a furnace master, contractor, and quartermaster. Moreover, some of his original castings cost far more than he budgeted. In 1778, Congress amended Bird's original cannon contract to allow $106 per ton of cast iron when the going rate was roughly $93 per ton. Another year passed before Bird finished his contract, the delivery of which he withheld until Congress paid the balance of his account: $125,691. This sum included not only the artillery casting but also his expenses as quartermaster. Bird was calling for the payments of debts despite the fact that the government had advanced him cash and agreed to bail him out of his financial difficulties. Neither Flower nor Hodgdon ever made another contract with Bird, and the Board of War challenged his accounts because of their inaccuracies. There are no records that Bird's accounts were ever settled, so it seems unlikely he was paid.[20] Other ironmongers ran into financial conflicts with Congress but ultimately found themselves in positions to request government assistance.

As early as 1778, Congress had begun working with three other Delaware Valley ironmongers to secure artillery stores. When named military stores commissary, Benjamin Flower took over the Board of War's contract with Bird and signed three new contracts: with John Patton of Berkshire Furnace, Daniel Udree of Oley Furnace, and Robert Coleman of Elizabeth Furnace. Patton's are the only complete furnace records available with matching DCGMS documentation. Later records made by Hodgdon, however, indicate that all three ironmongers shared Patton's experience. Patton's records indicate that he contracted with Flower sometime in early 1778. Those same records note that just under ten thousand shot and shells were delivered to Flower on that contract by the end of the year. Flower's complete payment of the contract, totaling $68,200, was recorded six months later. Patton renewed his contract with Flower for 1779, but Congress soon after ran out of money, and Flower was not immediately able to pay the full balance of the contract. Udree and Coleman also contracted with Flower in 1778, though the extent of the contracts is unclear. Nevertheless, they, too, required payment on their contracts when Congress's finances collapsed. Patton, Udree, and Coleman joined Bird in requesting payment on their contracts in early 1780. They pleaded with Congress for money, claiming that without payment their furnaces would be forced to go out of blast. This seems an unlikely prospect considering that government contracts accounted for only 20 percent of Patton's total output in 1778 and 1779. Patton's contract (and most likely Udree and Coleman's as well) was paid off in December 1780. The payment of Udree and Coleman's contracts is suggested by the fact that they renewed their contracts with Hodgdon in 1781.

Patton, Udree, and Coleman's furnaces were out of blast by the end of 1780 and needed repair to be put into blast in 1781, when Hodgdon approached them with new contracts for shot and shells. Most of the cash the ironmongers had received from Hodgdon had been used to pay off debts and salaries, but the maintenance of a furnace and the materials for smelting were expensive. To renew their contracts, each ironmonger requested a cash advance. This money would cover not only the costs of preparing the furnaces but the risks in contracting with a government that might take years to pay off its debts. There is no record of what Patton received, but Udree got $892 for a contract ultimately worth $5,471 and Coleman $5,757 on a contract that amounted to $12,118. Patton was paid a total of $9,176 for his 1781 shot-and-shells contract.[21] The government's desire to assist ironmongers convinced others to contract with Hodgdon for shot and shells in 1781.

Six ironmongers contracted with Hodgdon in 1781 after receiving cash advances to put their furnaces in blast. Richard Backhouse of Durham Furnace signed his first contract with Hodgdon and received $302 for the production of fifteen tons of shot and shells worth $1,750. It is clear that other ironmongers needed the money because of work they had done earlier in the war. A furnace could not stay in blast for more than three years without a thorough relining. Nor could a furnace go into blast without a stockpile of smelting ingredients. Batsto Furnace's owner, Charles Pettit, was engaged in a contract for $974, though it is unclear how much he ultimately produced. Batsto's previous owner had cast stores for Pennsylvania's government in the early years of the war, but the furnace had fallen into disrepair. Pettit, an assistant quartermaster for Congress, purchased a share in the furnace in 1779 hoping to get a contract for artillery stores. Hodgdon's cash advance to Pettit allowed him to repair the furnace and put it back into blast for government work. Curtis and Peter Grubb, owners of Cornwall Furnace, were advanced $3,300 to repair their stack and gather supplies. Congress had engaged them early in the war for cannons and ammunition. They had also cast pig iron for Carlisle Arsenal in 1777 and 1778. By the end of the war, the Grubb brothers' contract had produced $9,700 worth of ammunition. James Johnson was paid $747 to put his Baltimore furnace into blast for the government. Of all the government's contracts, his was the only one that failed to provide beneficial results. As noted in chapter 6, Daniel Joy had found Johnson's shells to be of inferior quality, and his contract was canceled. The final contractor was John Faesch, lessee of Mount Hope Furnace, New York, and owner of Hibernia Furnace, New Jersey. Faesch had provided shot and shells for Hodgdon as field commissary in 1779, but with the conclusion of that contract he had allowed his furnace to go out of blast. It was in need of repair, but rather than repair it, Faesch used his government income to purchase a significant stake in Hibernia Furnace from its debtors. When Hodgdon contracted Faesch again in 1780 for more ammunition, he was advanced $5,388 to purchase food, replace the hearth lining, and build a new mold house. By 1782, he was Hodgdon's chief supplier, providing $58,228 worth of services to the government over the next two years.[22]

In each of the cases just discussed, cash advances built relationships that developed into important sources of artillery ammunition for the Continental Army. Congress provided support for private manufacturers to develop wartime production with cash investments as much as it did with inspection and instruction procedures. But of the ironmongers examined, no one built a stronger financial relationship with the government than Faesch. That relationship makes him an important crossover figure from the examination of Congress's cash support to the examination of its material support of private manufacturers. Faesch's story also reveals the extent of the government's involvement in private manufacturing.

John Faesch began his business affairs with the Continental government as a simple contractor, but he quickly made use of congressional resources to further develop his own operations. Field Commissary Hodgdon engaged Faesch in 1779 for shot and shells. A year later, as assistant commissary general of military stores, he approached Faesch for more ammunition. Faesch took advantage of this to request funds for reconstructing his operational infrastructure. Mount Hope Furnace was quickly back in operation, and Hibernia Furnace followed about a year later. By the end of 1780, just after putting the furnace back into operation, Faesch realized he could use his account with Hodgdon as a bank. He requested that part of the funds owed him be paid to the representatives of William Alexander, the self-styled Lord Stirling, the man from whom he purchased Hibernia. Then, early in 1781, he directed payment of part of the money owed him by the government to two men to whom he owed money. Faesch paid off his debts by transferring them to Congress, which needed ammunition to such an extent that Hodgdon was willing to accept the debts in Congress's name. Hodgdon also knew Faesch and trusted him to provide ammunition. After financing his debt, however, Faesch moved toward financing both his operations and his lifestyle. In late March and early April, he purchased a watch chain and several yards of calico cloth and charged both items to his government account. Later in the year, he charged rum, steel, and writing paper to the account, apparently for furnace operations.[23] It is not clear whether these items were provided to Faesch from Hodgdon's magazine or Faesch wrote receipts drawn on the account. In either event, Faesch's expenditures were credited to the amount owed him by the government for shot and shells. Several later account entries show clearly that Faesch wrote receipts against his account. Hodgdon was providing him with banking services, and Faesch's receipts were valued because Hodgdon had already provided the ironmonger with small amounts of specie. People doing business with Faesch trusted that their debts would be paid by Hodgdon. And Hodgdon's account book shows that he did pay Faesch's debts, either with specie or a mixture of specie, paper cash, and loan certificates.

Faesch continued to make use of his government account well into 1784. He paid off more debts in 1782 by transferring them to the government. These debts appear to be for work done by hired labor at the furnace. In April 1783, he paid Jonathan Gostelowe with a government receipt for a stove pattern he probably intended to use for developing new products. In late 1783, however, Faesch used the account for a virtual shopping spree. Using receipts he purchased sugar, coffee, tea, cloth, brandy, shot, salt, and steel. These items were purchased in amounts too large for personal use and were probably intended for the iron plantation store. Despite all this spending, though, Faesch was not a major government debtor. The original payment on his account in loan certificates was deposited with Hodgdon. Faesch's ammunition production regularly debited his account and either reduced his debt or increased his equity depending on the status of the account. The account was so regularly used that unlike other accounts that follow a strict chronological order, Faesch's account moves between years, showing that so many receipts were issued on the account that they did not flow into the department in regular order from the account holder alone. Faesch paid his account several times in both cash and interest certificates. And Faesch also provided Hodgdon with bar and cast iron in excess of the ammunition contracts he made. By the time Hodgdon settled the account early in 1784, the government had provided Faesch with credit, cash, and raw materials to sustain and expand his business.[24]

Faesch used his government relationship to secure his business in the postwar period. During the war, Faesch was able to purchase the controlling share of Hibernia Furnace, which he apparently sold after the war.[25] He purchased more lands for charcoal production and expanded the output of his Mount Hope mine. He purchased Middle Forge and added the production of bar iron to his operations. Faesch was able to keep his workers paid and his store supplied. Finally, Faesch was able to purchase Mount Hope Furnace from the owner he had been renting it from since before the war. As Faesch's story reveals most distinctly of all, government cash advances assisted manufacturers in developing the production of military stores. The contracts that then developed became productive relationships that supplied the army. Those relationships allowed the government to monitor production and retain manufacturers who could be trusted. Cash advances were a means by which the DCGMS could ensure that manufacturers produced quality stores by securing the service of skilled craftsmen. As seen from the example of John Faesch, however, the government provided more than just financial assistance. Several manufacturers received payment or advances on their contracts in the form of raw materials.

Cash paid to contractors, as well as credit extended to them, played an important role in mobilizing the activities of those manufacturers. But where did Hodgdon get the cash when the government was bankrupt? And how could the man who said "the bills I have has ended our credit among the public" find any means of extending credit?[26] He got cash three ways: he issued credit and supplies to producers who paid him back in specie and paper money; he sold stores in the private market to raise cash; and he constantly begged the Board of War, Treasury Committee, and superintendent of finance for cash. All these sources provided Hodgdon with a limited supply of money at a time when the government had very little of it. Hodgdon then used his monetary and material resources to build the department's credit among manufacturers. He gave contractors faith that the department would pay its bills. Hodgdon did this by rotating the department's credit in the following fashion. Hodgdon's account book reveals that he paid bills in small increments as he had cash available, using a mixture of paper and specie money. He would then pay larger amounts of departmental debts with government loan certificates. Hodgdon also paid interest on all departmental debts if they were still outstanding after six months. As will be seen in chapter 8, Hodgdon also paid debts in kind as a means of building credit. Manufacturers often received payment in the materials they needed to produce military stores.[27] In this way, Hodgdon not only assisted in the production of stores but also built credit with the firm doing the producing. Hodgdon kept the DCGMS solvent even as the government it worked for struggled for financial survival.

The DCGMS spent a significant part of its budget on the purchase of raw materials for its contracted manufacturers. Sixty-three percent of the department's total expenditure for 1780 through 1783 was directed toward the purchase of just four raw materials: iron, steel, anthracite coal, and charcoal. Of the over $525,000 spent on the purchase of those four, $493,000 was used to buy steel, a commodity necessary to produce bayonets, gunlocks, and ramrods. To procure steel from contracted blacksmiths, however, the department had to purchase two hundred twenty-one thousand pounds of pig iron for them to convert. This cost $9,165. To power smelting operations, the department purchased or supplied its own coal and charcoal, at a cost of $23,000 for 1,100 bushels of coal and 152 bushels of charcoal.[28] These were not the only raw materials purchased for contractors. The department bought hides, lumber, and lubricants as well.

The DCGMS provided raw materials to craftsmen with the skills most necessary to the war effort. In 1780, Hodgdon engaged the services of four bayonet makers in Philadelphia. He supplied them each with the resources they needed to begin operations. Adam Myrletus was forwarded a half ton of iron between March and May. He returned two batches of bayonets to Hodgdon before receiving payment. In April, 119 bayonets were delivered and in June ninety-five.[29] Samuel Homes was given one thousand six hundred pounds of iron periodically from March through June, which he returned periodically to Hodgdon in the form of 327 bayonets.[30] Myrletus and Homes received only partial support from the department and seem not to have developed extensive operations. By contrast, William Rose and Jacob Eckfeldt received raw materials and fuel from Hodgdon and developed their government relationship into the basis for commercial sales. Rose was advanced 980 pounds of iron, 12 pounds of steel, and 4 bushels of coal. But after completing two hundred bayonets, he was only an occasional supplier of materiels to the government. He produced bar iron for Hodgdon intermittently until the end of the war.[31] Eckfeldt was given iron, steel, and anthracite with which to make 226 steel-tipped iron bayonets. By war's end, he had received from Hodgdon 8,600 pounds of iron, 375 pounds of steel, and 147 bushels of coal, and produced 776 bayonets.[32] The bayonets produced by Eckfeldt, however, do not reflect the amount of materials he received. It appears from the numbers that about 60 percent of the materials credited to Eckfeldt's account were used in his private operations.[33] He used his productive relationship with the government to access materials available in government stores. Eckfeldt was able to build this relationship because bayonets were the one item the Philadelphia Arsenal workers could not produce enough of to meet the needs of the army. Likewise, Eckfeldt's fellow bayonet makers could request an advance of materials as a condition of employment because their skills were in demand. Hodgdon built mutually beneficial relationships with manufacturers as their supplier of raw materials in order to secure the production of necessary stores from the few men with the skills to make them.

Hodgdon, however, also took advantage of his situation relative to manufacturers. While he could not always pay craftsmen in cash, he could pay them in material that he had, and this helped him develop several very important production contracts. When Hodgdon needed a single item like a trumpet or a drum, for example, he gave craftsmen an excess of components from which to make the product. Craftsmen like Andrew Isenhoot kept the excess of copper given him to make a trumpet to use in his own business.[34] George Heighberger was given 1,509 pounds of iron, 762 pounds of steel, and 49 bushels of coal with which to make swords. About half of this was in partial payment for the fifty-seven swords Heighberger produced. The other half the sword maker later purchased from Hodgdon using the cash he had received for the balance of his contract.[35] Despite the convoluted way Heighberger got the materials, he got them from the government and used them to develop his private business. In these cases of small production, Hodgdon secured the manufacture of needed specialized items by supplying the materials for their fabrication. But he did not limit the exchange of raw materials to the completion of only small contracts. On taking command of the DCGMS, Hodgdon used the cast iron he had on hand to secure the bar iron and steel he needed.

Hodgdon found when he went to Philadelphia that he inherited a department oversupplied with cast iron. Flower had taken extreme measures to put New Jersey's Andover Furnace into blast. No private entrepreneurs came forward to rent the furnace from New Jersey, which had confiscated it from its Loyalist owner. The DCGMS needed the furnace's iron.[36] Drawing on exceptionally pure local ores, Andover had made a high-quality cast iron that was in great demand by bar iron and steelmakers in the Delaware Valley. Flower wanted the iron not only for his arsenals but also to provide to his contractors. Unable to attract renters, Flower appropriated the furnace and put it into blast himself. Shortly thereafter, Thomas Mayberry rented it and continued the production of military stores for the government. Mayberry assumed that Flower had been renting the furnace on his own with a government contract. Unfortunately, he also believed that he inherited that contract from Flower. Thus, Mayberry continued operating, believing he had a contract without ever actually signing one. Flower was unable to deal with the situation because he fell ill. Mayberry continued to cast iron for the department but refused to deliver it until he got paid. Without a valid contract, however, the treasury department would not pay for the iron. Mayberry pleaded with Congress in 1780 for payment. He said he was close to defaulting on his lease and unable to sell much of the iron privately. Congress saw no reason to pay Mayberry, and Andover's temporary ironmonger went bankrupt. Hodgdon arrived in the aftermath of the confusion and found that no one was claiming the iron that Mayberry had cast and no one had paid for. So Hodgdon claimed it, and the department was suddenly awash in good cast iron.[37]

Hodgdon used the iron from Andover Furnace not only to strengthen the government's manufacturing operations but also to develop private manufacturing in America. The DCGMS had little need for extensive supplies of cast iron unless it came in the form of artillery or artillery ammunition. However, the department did need steel for armory workers to make gunlocks, bayonets, and ramrods. Steel was a difficult product to make in the eighteenth century. The most common way of making it was to bake a sheet of wrought iron between layers of charcoal to allow the iron to absorb enough carbon to transform the pure iron into steel.[38] In May 1780, Hodgdon wrote Thomas Wylie at Carlisle that he had sent Samuel Sargent "some steel [yet] the steel is but poor but it was all we had on hand, and I suppose it possibly might answer the present purpose."[39] The purity of Andover's iron made it easy to convert to steel and, in consequence, a useful tool for negotiating a contract for its conversion. Hodgdon retained refinery forge owner John Thompson under an agreement that the ironmonger would receive seventeen-and-a-half tons of Andover iron, convert one-third of it into steel, and keep two-thirds of it in payment for his services. By May 1780, Hodgdon had shipped thirteen tons of iron to Thompson. Teamsters delivering the iron reported to Hodgdon that Thompson was in the process of converting the iron to steel. Nevertheless, Thompson delivered no steel to the department. Instead he sold the first steel he made on the open market. As late as February 1781, Hodgdon had sent twenty-one tons of iron to Thompson, and the ironmonger had returned only three tons of steel. At that point Hodgdon canceled Thompson's contract. He then negotiated with forge master George Ross for the conversion of the Andover iron to steel. Ross, however, did not have the capacity to convert so much iron as quickly as Hodgdon needed it, and that contract was soon abrogated.[40] Hodgdon was forced to seek a new steel contractor.

Despite Thompson's failure to honor his contract, Hodgdon had no qualms about supporting the ironmonger's private business. He could purchase Thompson's steel in the market, and any means of getting steel was better than getting no steel at all. When Hodgdon ended the conversion contract with Thompson, he asked the Quartermaster Department to remove all US-owned iron from Thompson's forge and deliver it to Ross. This threatened Thompson's business. He gladly gave up the iron, but he then approached Hodgdon in order to purchase the materials necessary to run his forge. Hodgdon took the opportunity to raise cash that his department needed in exchange for raw materials the department was not using. During the years 1781 and 1782, Hodgdon sold Thompson 3 tons of iron, 162 bushels of coal, and 87 bushels of charcoal. When arsenal operations began slowing down in late 1782, Hodgdon even sold Thompson one thousand three hundred pounds of the precious steel he went through so much trouble to get.[41] Even though Thompson's contract did not come to fruition, Hodgdon had helped develop private business in order to secure his department's needs.

Thompson's failure led Hodgdon into another contractual relationship in which the government again took an active role in the development of private enterprise for the sake of the nation's defense. The iron firm of Rutter and Potts was one of the oldest in the nation. Thomas Potts had settled in southern Berks County, Pennsylvania, in the first decade of the eighteenth century. In 1724, he built Colebrookdale, the colony's first iron furnace. The family went on to expand its land holdings, build a new furnace at nearby Warwick, and build forges to refine cast iron into bar iron and steel.[42] It was logical that the firm be approached for the casting of ordnance and ammunition when the revolution began. Unfortunately, there are no clear records of when contracts were signed and under what circumstances they were signed. However, it is recorded that by 1779, Rutter and Potts furnished artillery shells for the army. Flower wrote Congress at the end of that year that "large Sums are due [Thomas Potts] for Bom Shells."[43] Three months later, Congress issued a warrant on the Pennsylvania loan office for $260,205 payable to Rutter and Potts. The company went on to provide an additional 1,553 shells over the following two years.[44]

The failure of Thompson and Ross to provide steel became the opportunity for the Potts family to engage in new contracts with the DCGMS. The government needed steel, and Potts had been looking for a way to transform his iron operations into a well-known steel operation. Potts, therefore, approached the department with a proposition: he would exchange one ton of steel for six tons of pig iron. If the DCGMS found the steel agreeable, proposed Potts, the government could purchase two more tons for $47,250 each. If Flower and Hodgdon were not satisfied with Potts's product, they could refuse the steel and Potts would pay all the costs and charges the department had incurred. Potts wanted Flower and the government to try his product, hoping they would buy more. The contract also served Potts's purposes by stipulating that he receive cast iron from Andover Furnace. Potts signed an agreement with the department at the same time as Thompson. When it became clear to Hodgdon that Thompson was not going to honor the contract, Hodgdon began shipping more and more iron to Potts instead of Thompson. Almost immediately upon signing the original contract, Flower and Hodgdon began shipping iron to Potts's furnace. From April through December 1780, the department delivered sixty-two tons of Andover pig iron to Potts, expecting to receive just under ten-and-a-half tons of steel in return according to their agreement. He received only one-and-three-quarters tons.[45] While this return had apparently bothered Flower, he chose not to confront Potts because his furnace was also providing the department with artillery shells. But the headache that developed was not Flower's to bear. Flower had only recovered long enough from his illness to sign the contract with Potts.

In September 1780, the Potts contract passed from Flower to Hodgdon, and Potts pushed for new terms, which were granted. He agreed "to contract with Hodgdon for . . . any steel to be made at the following exchange. For any seven pigs of Andover iron I will produce 1 ton of good blistered steel."[46] But the contract does not seem to have been enforced, because Potts's furnace was in the process of making shells. Eight months later, in July 1781, Hodgdon once again renewed his contract with Potts. By this time, however, Potts had partnered with Trenton steelmaker Samuel Downing. Hodgdon seems to have believed that if he provided Potts and Downing with greater opportunities for production, they would be able to set up larger scale operations for the production of steel. Hodgdon, however, was sorely disappointed in these hopes. By early 1782, he had not received much steel in return for the iron he and Flower had sent. Hodgdon wrote Potts and Downing in March that it had been some time since he had heard from him and wanted to know the status of the contract.[47] On April 9, he wrote Potts and Downing again, "I expect to see . . . you at my store and to hear further on the subject. I have not a bar of steel on hand and have not heard from you."[48] This was Hodgdon's final letter. When again the steelmakers refused to respond, Hodgdon acted. He wrote to the quartermaster office "the contract made with them being shamefully visited on their part in justice to the public[;] I must suspend any further advance of metal or bar iron until they shall have accounted for what they have already received."[49] Hodgdon drew up his accounts of delivered metal so he could settle Potts's accounts and bill Potts and Downing for the money he owed the government. Within a month, the partners had delivered another ton of steel to Hodgdon, but that was the last Hodgdon would see for six years. He continued to press for delivery, but Potts's death in 1783 seems to have ended the partnership and put the situation off for some time. Not until 1788 did the Potts family make another delivery of steel on the 1781 contract. Hodgdon's account of the contract drawn up at that time calculated that the Potts family still owed the government just over seven tons of steel, worth $2,000 including interest and depreciation.[50]

The government's investment of iron in Potts's operations seems to have borne fruit for this domestic manufacturer. Hodgdon wrote Potts in

1782 that "I hear you are selling in all parts of the country."[51] That was one of the reasons Hodgdon was so annoyed with Potts. The ironmaster could apparently sell goods far and wide yet not fulfill his government contract nor bother to respond to Hodgdon's letters. The amount of iron sent to Potts and Downing supports the idea that they used the iron to make shot and shells and that they made steel, selling it in the private market without delivering any to Hodgdon. The expansion of the business was revealed in 1783, when Stacy Potts, who took over the company at the death of his brother, sought congressional approbation for his steel that would "recommend his Manufacture to Persons of Note and Business in the several States."[52] Potts's statements shed light on the relationship he and his brother had been building with the Continental government. "Hoping," Stacy Potts wrote, "that Congress may take such measures to spread the demand for this Steel through the United States and wherever it may be vended to Advantage . . . shall be glad of their advice from time to time that a sufficient quantity may be always in readiness to answer the demand that may arise in consequence thereof."[53] Potts wanted to sell steel not only to the US government but to whoever else might want it. He believed a large contract with the government would enable him to build a market for steel in the nation. And even as the family was using the Continental government to make that happen, they were requesting the approbation of that government. The only problem was that they had not fulfilled their contract with that government. The largest contract they could possibly have received at that time the Potts family had let go unfulfilled, and that more than anything else was their undoing.

To prove the value of his steel to Congress, Stacy Potts proposed a test of his product by the government. He asked Congress "to say no more in it's (the steel's) favour than may be necessary to recommend it to tryal and Proof, confident that on due examination, it will be found to answer well wherever it may be used, having truely obtained the best Character in general for Edge Tools of any ever before made in America, some of which has been pronounced by good Judges (from experience) to be eaqual in fininess, and superior in strength to either English or German Steel."[54]

Congress, still waiting for steel from Potts, appointed a committee to review the situation. It reported to Congress that it had "examined many Certificates from Mechanics who have made a thorough Tryal of Mr. Potts's Steel in edged Tools and other Instruments and declare that it is at least equal to the best British Steel."[55] Nevertheless, the committee said that the nation had no money to invest in such enterprises and that Congress should not involve itself in the support of one state's industry over another. The unspoken problem was that the Potts family had never completed the deliveries of steel that it owed the government. Potts would have to discharge his family's government debts before Congress would continue to help him develop their steel process.

Hodgdon waited seven years to settle his accounts with the Potts family, but when he did, he renewed his efforts to benefit the government from the development of innovative steelmaking. From May 6 to October 31, 1788, Hodgdon forwarded eleven-and-a-half tons of iron to Potts so the original contract could be fulfilled, all the original iron having been used up. The iron was converted by November 3 into just under ten tons of steel. Once Potts had settled his accounts, Hodgdon approached the treasury department and asked if it would review the steel and determine if it was worth the involvement of the DCGMS.[56] The ability to convert iron into steel with such little loss of scrap and in so quick a time would have been quite a coup for an American iron manufacturer, but the Potts process had failed. The commissioners called on by Hodgdon wrote that they "attended that service and after repeated trials find that by reason of a faulty conversion arising from a partial immersion in the furnace or duration there, the greater part [of the resulting metal] can only be considered as bar iron, and that injured by the attempt made to convert it[,] a very small part[,] perhaps not more than an eighth of what we examined[,] can be used for any purpose that requires good blistered steel."[57] After eight years, Hodgdon was only able to force the completion of a contract for steel by securing a great deal of bar iron.

Yet the failure of the Potts family to develop a useful steelmaking process should not overshadow the fact that the Continental government was intimately involved in developing the potential of private manufacturing. The DCGMS wanted to get steel for the war effort as well as develop a domestic supply of steel for the nation's future armaments needs. To accomplish this, Hodgdon and the Board of War were first willing to extend lucrative contracts to Thomas Potts, allowing him to expand his operations and experiment with the large-scale steel production. The government was also willing to trade large amounts of iron for lesser amounts of steel. Unfortunately, government aid was not enough for Potts to create a successful steel process. But the disappointments Hodgdon encountered in trying to develop America's steel industry did not keep him from encouraging other manufacturing sectors. Hodgdon's diligence bore fruit in his successful efforts to promote domestic gunsmithing in the later years of the war.

Several factors led to the demise of the Philadelphia armory and the concomitant rise of government reliance on private gun manufacturers. The government's bankruptcy in 1780 put a great deal of pressure on Hodgdon to save money. After most Philadelphia Arsenal operations were moved to Carlisle in late 1780, Hodgdon cut costs further by paying armorers on a daily basis and allowing them to take on private work when not employed by the government. This only lasted for a short time, because in mid-1781, nearly seven thousand new muskets arrived from the French government's armories. The arrival of so many clean, well-built weapons precluded the need for a hired staff to keep them in service. Hodgdon took the opportunity of the new muskets' arrival to disband the armory. He replaced it with a system of contracts for the repair of weapons on an as-needed basis. Most of the men he contracted with were former employees of the armory.[58] These men knew the material resources of the DCGMS and used them. Likewise, rather than force his weapons contractors to search out their own resources, Hodgdon provided them not only with iron, steel, coal, and charcoal, but also with musket components that remained in the government's store after the armory's dissolution.

Hodgdon learned the value of private gunsmiths from an agreement made for the sake of expediency. As noted in chapter 3, French gunsmith Pierre Penet proposed to Congress in January 1779 that under contract with government support, he could manufacture one hundred thousand muskets in the United States. He intended to import gunsmiths and build a substantial gun factory in Philadelphia. Congress willingly supported the plan, but Penet was unable to get travel documents for any gunsmith to leave France. Undaunted, Penet was able to recruit only a private gunsmith, J. Couloux. Together the gunsmiths approached Hodgdon and offered to build a smaller factory and repair guns for Congress at a nominal price. In exchange they wanted access to the resources of the DCGMS. Hodgdon believed he had little to lose. He provided Penet and Couloux with $170 worth of damaged bayonets, gunstocks, ramrods, gun barrels, gunlocks, and gun mountings. Hodgdon also provided iron, steel, and coal. Penet and Couloux charged Hodgdon $747 to produce 110 reconstructed muskets, at a cost of $6.79 apiece. The market rate for such repairs was about $8. Hodgdon benefited not only from the cost but also from the fact that he had delivered materials to the French gunsmiths in June and had the guns in July. He received fifty-six more in September, sixty in October, and sixty-one in January 1781.[59] Hodgdon realized that since he could provide the materials, the only cost to him was labor. This was a useful situation to be in when the department was forced to cut costs. Though the Philadelphia armory was productive, it had high overhead costs. The hired men demanded the same rations as enlisted men, and they were paid whether or not there was work to be done. There were also the costs and time involved in managing the armory, overseeing Joseph Perkins, who directed the armory, and coordinating the flow of resources among all those individuals. Private contractors simplified the production process, so it was a relatively smooth transition from government to private labor when Hodgdon closed the armory.

Hodgdon employed twenty-one gunsmiths in addition to the Frenchmen from summer 1781 until the end of the war. The majority of the gunsmiths received material support from the DCGMS in order to accomplish their work, and those who did not receive support never did more than incidental repair work for the department. The fourteen private contractors who received some type of material support repaired over five thousand muskets from August 1781 to December 1783. To accomplish this, the government provided them with 390 pounds of steel, 2,900 pounds of iron, and 124 bushels of coal. The gunsmiths who did not receive support repaired just over eight hundred muskets.[60] Material support from the government was critical to the development of private military stores activities.

No gunsmith used government support to better advantage than Joseph Perkins. Perkins served for three years as superintendent of the Philadelphia armory. After he was released from service, he received government support to develop a private gunsmith operation. He repaired 726 muskets for the government by early 1782, when he was approached by Hodgdon to oversee a contract to clean the department's muskets for storage. From 1782 to 1784, Perkins and his staff cleaned eleven thousand Continental muskets at a cost of $3,000. With the government's investment of material, men like Perkins were able to develop manufacturing operations critical to the DCGMS. More importantly, by providing material, the department could secure the services of the best-qualified craftsmen.[61] In this way the government was assured the quality production of military stores.

Though there has been only brief mention thus far of the distribution of anthracite coal by the DCGMS to its contractors, the department made a significant investment of time and money into securing this fuel source. The government went to great lengths to mine and ship anthracite to its contractors, operations that saved those contractors time and money. The government's distribution of coal reveals how far the DCGMS was willing to go to support private manufacturing for the war effort.

Coal was not used in the war to the complete exclusion of charcoal, but several factors made coal more useful to the revolutionary movement. First, charcoal was too brittle to transport. If charcoal was moved roughly, suddenly jostled, or squeezed too tightly, it began to crumble. Once the charcoal was made, it had to be shoveled into a wagon. Too much time on a rutted and rocky colonial road was known to shake charcoal to dust. The charcoal then had to be shoveled again into a hearth, coal cart, or basket for delivery to a hearth, furnace, or coal storage house. Each step in this delivery process degraded the charcoal a bit. Haulers, who were responsible for charcoal once it was in their wagon, would usually not take charcoal more than twenty miles. Charcoal transport required finesse, care, and time. Anthracite, or stone coal, on the other hand, was a hardy fuel. It could be transported without fear of disintegration. Even if a hammer was taken to it, very little was lost to dust. It could also be stored for extended periods, whereas exposed charcoal would disintegrate.[62] Fuel was needed quickly, and charcoal was simply not easy to transport, making it an unreliable fuel in towns and cities with few nearby timber reserves. Philadelphia, which was the largest arsenal and the hub of private military stores manufacturing, was too distant from sources of charcoal for it to be a reliable fuel for urban military stores contractors.

A second factor that limited the usefulness of charcoal to the war effort was that it took time and money to make because its production was a skilled craft. Charcoal took literally months to make properly. Wood had to be cut and stacked in order for it to dry. Once dry wood was ready, it took about a month to convert it into charcoal. When the charcoal was ready, the coals had to cool for almost two more weeks before they could be loaded into a hauler's wagon. Colliers normally only made charcoal from May to October, when winds were calmer, in order to avoid a flare-up of flames in the production process, which could turn coals to ash. One cord of wood could produce thirty-five to forty-five bushels of charcoal. An average set of colliers could make nine hundred to one thousand eight hundred bushels of charcoal per burn. This equaled two thousand seven hundred to five thousand four hundred bushels per season. An energy equivalent amount of stone coal could be mined year-round. Enlisted soldiers could mine coal in open pits without any special skills. The distance of coal mines from the seat of war made the relative price of the two fuels similar, so if one could be procured more quickly than another, it was the better resource. This made it an attractive fuel even at the Carlisle Arsenal, which had charcoal supplies in close proximity.[63]

The final factor that precluded the use of charcoal in some cases was that it was the fuel of choice for the nation's ironmasters, whose furnaces consumed prodigious quantities of it. A typical iron furnace used eight hundred bushels of charcoal a day, or about three hundred thousand bushels a year, if kept continually in blast. This required colliers to cut down 365 acres of forest per year for each furnace in operation. Such large amounts of charcoal limited its widespread availability on the open market, especially at a distance from furnaces. Most charcoal was supplied by colliers working on an ironmonger's staff.[64] This limited the number of self-employed colliers for the government to hire. Charcoal quickly became a scarce commodity, especially in Philadelphia.

The cost and scarcity of charcoal was a problem not only for the DCGMS but for its private craftsmen as well. Philadelphia's distance from the frontier forests made it unlikely that large amounts of charcoal would survive a trip to the city, and military stores officials did not want to waste money purchasing a risky product. Since the government did not have the funds to consistently pay manufacturers or purchase charcoal, it took it upon itself to supply those manufacturers with coal using the resources it had available: labor and transport.

The chief drawback of stone coal was its location. The main seam of coal available to Continental manufacturing complexes was in Pennsylvania's Wyoming Valley. Daniel Joy, prior to becoming superintendent of ordnance, told Congress, "I know that coal can be obtained in the Wyoming Valley near the Shawnee burying ground."[65] Several isolated outcroppings in the Delaware Valley were known as well, but nothing of any real worth.[66] In western Pennsylvania, anthracite coal was also available in the hills surrounding Fort Pitt. The government arsenals had to draw their coal from at least one hundred miles away. Distance, however, was not an insurmountable obstacle.

What blocked American access to the coal in northeastern Pennsylvania was the Indians who lived on or near the land and who considered that land sacred. Joy's comments take this to be common knowledge. Though the Delaware Indians had been pushed out of the Wyoming Valley after the French and Indian War, they had not given up hope of returning there. When civil war broke out in the British Empire, the Mohawks took the British side and assisted their Delaware brothers in reclaiming the valley. Thus the region became a battleground culminating in the 1778 Wyoming Valley Massacre in which Mohawks, Loyalists, and British troops killed 231 militia near modern Wilkes-Barre. John Sullivan's 1779 campaign did force Indians out of the region for a short period, but they remained at least a marginal threat to the area until the end of the war.[67] Sargent believed that attempts to retrieve coal in the region "will be attended with a great deal of difficulty and some danger from the Indians."[68] The movement of coal from Fort Pitt was inhibited by the sheer difficulty of moving it such a long distance over difficult terrain.

Coal was secured primarily through the use of government miners. At least twice, armed artificers made expeditions to the north, mined the coal, rented boats, and floated the mineral down to Harris's Ferry (Harrisburg) from where it was moved by wagon to the arsenals. In June 1778, Lukens assured Flower "that the Coal, etc shall be sent for."[69] In November 1780, Sargent reported to Flower, "We are getting off a party for coal to the Wyoming by order of the Board[;] have laid the best plan we can contrive."[70] It is likely that Flower, too, sent artificers up the Delaware or Schuylkill River to mine coal and bring it back to Philadelphia in a fashion similar to the Carlisle men. Government operations were not limited to mining missions by artificers. In late 1778 or early 1779, a garrison of three to five miners was established in the Wyoming Valley. An inventory of the post in May 1779 indicates it was under the command of either Carlisle specifically or the DCGMS more generally. Based on the fact that Lukens had sent an expedition to the Wyoming Valley in late 1780, the mining garrison there was probably closed earlier that year.[71] From 1781 through the end of the war, there seems to have been enough coal on hand for the department's uses, and private contractors met any additional needs.

Private miners delivering coal to government depots was a secondary way the mineral was secured for the arsenals. A great deal of coal had been gathered at Head of Elk, Maryland, in 1778, independent of government activity. It could have arrived there by either being floated down the Susquehanna River or sailed up the Chesapeake from Virginia's mines.[72] Lukens wrote to the quartermaster at Head of Elk, requesting some of the coal that was reported to have arrived there. "Nothing must prevent the coal from coming it must be had at all events or cannon cannot be made," Lukens wrote.[73] As will be mentioned later in this chapter, there are no records of how much coal was used at Carlisle, but Lukens's comments regarding the coal at Head of Elk reveal that the post was dependent on the mineral. Military stores bookkeeper Cornelius Sweers, too, attempted to purchase some earlier in the year at Allentown. Hodgdon's departmental account book recorded in May 1780 the payment of $2,703 to William Bennett for securing and delivering one hundred bushels of coal. Small amounts of anthracite coal were also brought back occasionally from Fort Pitt on army supply wagons returning from delivering stores to that frontier post. In this case, wagoners hired by the government to move supplies to the west returned with coal as a way of supplementing their army wages. An undated wagoner's proposal presented to Sargent promised to bring back two tons of coal in every wagon sent with supplies to Fort Pitt.[74] What became of the project is unknown.

Anthracite coal was used in all aspects of the arsenal program and provided to private contractors. Carlisle's artificers used it in the foundry and the smiths shop. It was used in the Philadelphia armory and ordnance yard. It was also used by the file cutters and sent to the Main Army for use by the brigade armorers and field commissary department. The Quartermaster Department requisitioned supplies of coal from Flower's department. From March 1780 to October 1783, Hodgdon recorded that the department used or sold over two thousand bushels of anthracite coal. By the end of the war, Hodgdon was delivering excess coal to arms-repair contractors and Philadelphia blacksmiths not only for the government work they were doing but also for their own private manufacturing work. Roughly half of the stone coal procured by the DCGMS in Philadelphia was delivered to private manufacturers. From March 1780 until the end of the war, Hodgdon delivered 179 bushels of coal to men like James Pearson, whose mill made steel wire for the department, and John Thompson, who made ramrods and bayonets in addition to steel.

Hodgdon began selling coal in August 1781 as a way of raising money for his departmental bills and paying for production work. Ultimately, he sold 873 bushels of the mineral to sixteen gunsmiths and blacksmiths around Philadelphia.[75] The DCGMS was committed to the material support of the nation's private military stores manufacturers.

The government's investment in private enterprise extended from money and material to transport as well. The problems of army transport were well known to Americans. The army advertised everywhere for wagoners, teams, and wagons, and quartermasters approached farmers for assistance along every line of march and near every encampment.[76] Owners of horses or wagons realized the risks involved. Continental currency was virtually worthless, and the rough service in the army was expected to damage most any materiel used. The private transport of goods for the army, let alone as a business enterprise, was also a precarious activity. Any travel around New York could lead to seizure by the British army. At various times throughout the war, transporting goods around Philadelphia, Boston, the Hudson Valley, or the whole of South Carolina could risk confiscation of the load by armed detachments of soldiers or militias. Wagons and horses were also difficult to procure for private use during the war because of their impressments by the British and American armies, especially later in the war.[77]

The Continental Army and its commissaries never found it an easy process to move the hundreds of tons of food, clothing, and materiel needed annually by the soldiers. The DCGMS eased the problem partially by manufacturing at least two hundred ammunition wagons at the arsenals. These wagons carried stores to the army and then remained with it to provide transport. Wagons required horses, and wagoners to direct them. The acquisition of these transport elements fell to the Quartermaster Department throughout the war. Horses were expensive to obtain but usually available.[78] "Providing enough wagoners [on the other hand] was a critical problem," noted historian Erna Risch.[79] At the time, private wagoners were paid either by distance or by percentage of cargo. Congress, however, was only willing to pay them a flat laborer salary, which was rejected by most dependable wagoners, who viewed themselves as skilled teamsters. The army was thus moved by an inconsistent corps of wagoners willing to take meager wages in the hope that the difference in their actual pay and their expected pay could be equalized through the theft of stores. According to Risch's reading of George Washington's general orders, wagoners were notorious for poorly caring for horses, transporting camp followers, destroying farmland, and straggling behind the army.[80] The army's transportation abilities were made worse by inflation. The Quartermaster Department found it nearly impossible to hire men or rent teams because the money the department used was worthless. Soldiers, inexperienced in the skills of driving a

This 1789 drawing of a covered ammunition wagon reveals what the apparatus diagramed on page 103 looked like in action. Here a team of oxen and a horse are led by a Continental Army conductor, who was responsible for the crates and barrels loaded inside the wagon. The open design of the wagon made it a multi-purpose transport vehicle able to move artillery, large artillery accouterments, ammunition, and boxes of smaller stores. (*New York Public Library*)

horse team and controlling a wagon, were forced into duty as wagoners. The whole system was not reformed until late 1780, when Timothy Pickering was named quartermaster general and initiated several cost-saving reforms similar to Hodgdon's. Yet despite the Quartermaster Department's many problems, the DCGMS was not only able to move materiel but was also able to provide transport to private manufacturers.

The DCGMS possessed a number of transport advantages. First, the Board of War so valued military stores that it ordered the Quartermaster Department to spare no expense in moving those stores and assisting the DCGMS in any way necessary. Second, the DCGMS made its own wagons and could use them however it saw fit once teams had been procured. Third, the department hired its own corps of conductors to oversee the movement of stores from the arsenals to camp. Finally, the department's extensive private contracts and arsenal capacity generated storehouses of materials that could be used to coerce the Quartermaster Department into action when its resources were especially scarce. Military stores personnel learned to trade their supplies for quartermaster service. With these foundations, military stores officials could secure transport not only for departmental needs but for contractors' needs as well.

The Board of War issued orders that the Quartermaster Department should do all in its power to assist the DCGMS and refrain from inhibiting its work. On June 11, 1778, John Davis, regional quartermaster in Carlisle, was issued orders to "furnish on Flower's order, or his representative, horses with saddles and bridles for the use of the public works as they shall need them for public work." He was "not to interfere with the work of the commissary of military stores."[81] Davis took this to mean that he was obligated to provide the arsenal with whatever assistance was needed. From that point on, he regularly forwarded horses, wagons, and carts to Samuel Sargent and Charles Lukens for the movement of wood, boards, charcoal, and iron. Hodgdon's correspondence suggests that Philadelphia's quartermasters were also issued orders to assist the DCGMS. Hodgdon regularly followed up on communications when he did not receive the result he desired. From the time he took over the department in March 1780 until January 1781, he had six interactions with quartermasters in Philadelphia and Trenton, New Jersey. In April, he requested teams to move stores from Trenton, which was apparently accomplished because there is no further reference to it. Over the next several months, he requested transport for nearly eighteen tons of Andover iron. Hodgdon's communication with Mark Thompson, the man to whom the iron was sent, clearly indicates that the iron was transported. Finally, in December, Hodgdon requested that the Philadelphia quartermaster send teams to bring Thompson's steel to the city.[82] Just two weeks later, he wrote the quartermaster, saying, "Thank you for sending some of the pig metal and stores by boat to this city."[83] The DCGMS was able to procure transport at times when the army was unable to move its own stores. The value of weapons to the army was clearly understood by the Board of War and Congress. Orders alone, however, were not always enough to mobilize quartermasters to assist the department. Occasionally, Hodgdon had to grease the wheels of transport with favors for his fellow administrators. Deputy Quartermaster General Samuel Miles wrote Hodgdon in late 1780, asking to borrow steel because he had no cash with which to purchase it on the open market.[84] In response, Hodgdon wrote to the local Philadelphia quartermaster to bring the finished steel down to the city from Thompson's forge. Less than a month after his original request, Miles again asked for anthracite for his own artificers because they were "entirely out" of the fuel.[85] Once again, Hodgdon complied in order to build a useful working relationship with the Quartermaster Department.[86] Congressional impetus as well as interagency assistance allowed the DCGMS access to relatively reliable transport services whenever the need arose.

Flower and Hodgdon hired conductors to manage the movement of stores in an effort to overcome the difficulties of obtaining hired wagoners. Conductors were given two chief responsibilities. First, they were managers of transport, commissioned with the movement of stores within the department as well as oversight of the quartermaster's movement of stores for the department. Second, conductors were hired to be custodians of the valuable stores being moved between the arsenals and the armies. In essence, the conductors were representatives of Flower and Hodgdon in the field, with all the authority to dispose of the stores as they saw fit. Hodgdon sent Archibald Shaw to conduct a supply of stores to Horatio Gates's Southern Army in 1780. Shaw was to "get on board the schooner transporting the cartridges and see them . . . on to Halifax [North Carolina]. Apply to the local deputy quartermaster for teams to transport."[87] He was to get assistance from the staff of the military stores commissary in Virginia, Samuel French. If aid was not available, the conductor was authorized to see to the transport of stores all the way to the Southern Army. When Shaw returned, he managed a delivery of muskets and accouterments to the Main Army in New Jersey. In each case, Hodgdon had secured transport from the Quartermaster Department, but management of that transport was delegated to a military stores official. The conductors carried specie with them to purchase service, and Hodgdon credited expenses to their account. In the same way that Hodgdon built a relationship with quartermaster officials, so, too, he developed the loyalty of his conductors. Such oversight prevented much of the abuse that plagued the Quartermaster Department in general.[88] In some cases it also freed quartermasters from the responsibility of finding teams for the DCGMS; conductors would hire their own teams.

Flower employed fifteen conductors by 1779, with regularly assigned delivery routes and responsibilities. Seven of these men moved stores between Carlisle, Philadelphia, and the armies. Eight men operated between Boston, Springfield, and the armies. Flower's 1779 departmental report claims that as many as six of the men employed as conductors in Massachusetts were superfluous to the needs of the department. All eight were dismissed the following year, and the seven conductors from Pennsylvania served the department until the end of the war. The conductors were willing to remain in the service of the department because Hodgdon advanced them their pay in specie, which amounted to $45 per month when a laboratory laborer was making about $30 per month depending on the exchange rate of paper for specie money.[89] Military stores conductors were treated like skilled rather than as unskilled labor.

The final advantage that the DCGMS had in the way of transport was the fact that departmental artificers made the wagons used in transport. The construction of wagons and carts saved quartermasters the trouble and expense of renting them, which allowed more to be spent on horse teams and wagoners. Carlisle artificers made at least one hundred ammunition wagons for the use of their own department, the Quartermaster Department, and the army. Springfield artificers made at least forty wagons and one hundred ammunition carts.[90] There are no clear records for the production of these items at Philadelphia, but artificers there undoubtedly added to the numbers. An example of the importance of arsenal production in this area can be seen in a letter from Hodgdon to Luke Bliss, commissary at Springfield:

"When last at Springfield I observed several waggons . . . almost finished these are much wanting in the army you will immediately after the receipt of this endeavor to have them finished completely and ready for delivery when applied for. Application will probably be made by the quartermaster general. Without further advice you will provide them."[91] The army relied on the transportation manufactured by the DCGMS.

Hodgdon and his commissaries were able to pass their access to transportation on to those who were willing to contract with the DCGMS. Part of Hodgdon's agreement with ironmonger Mark Thompson was that the government would deliver iron to his forge and remove the steel he made from that iron. The same agreement was also extended to George Ross and Thomas Potts.[92] Hodgdon was able to get the Quartermaster Department's cooperation because that department needed steel as much as did the DCGMS. Hodgdon also gained the department's assistance because he provided his conductors as transport managers. Military stores clerk James Boyer wrote quartermaster Samuel Miles, "when the transportation is ready [to move the iron at Trenton] . . . I shall send a person to see that it is moved safely."[93] Hodgdon was able to secure contracts with these ironmongers because he not only provided them with the materials they needed, but with transport for their finished product as well.

Hodgdon provided transportation on other contracts as well. Just two months after taking over command of the department, he promised Maryland's Hughes brothers that he would see to the removal of shot, shell, and ordnance from their furnace as soon as the items were complete. Hodgdon sensed the government's debt catching up with his department when he wrote, "As transportation will soon become difficult, I request you make every effort to finish soon so that your ordnance can be forwarded to this city."[94] When Hodgdon contracted with Joseph Perkins for the cleaning of eleven thousand government muskets in 1781, he agreed as part of the contract to deliver and pick up all the muskets at government expense.[95] Combined with the material support discussed earlier, Perkins was freed from two major aspects of a craftsman's operations: securing raw materials and transporting finished goods to market. In 1780, Hodgdon saw to the delivery of artillery ammunition from Elizabeth Furnace to Philadelphia, again removing the responsibility of transport from a government contractor. The quartermaster at Carlisle also directed teams to secure iron from Elizabeth Furnace in 1781, for the use of the Carlisle Arsenal. In fact, Carlisle's location so far from the Main Army provided numerous needs for government transport of private goods.

Lukens and Sargent regularly used their own men or conductors to move goods from contractors and worked with the quartermaster for his assistance in such operations. Lukens contracted with numerous mills, forges, and furnaces in the vicinity of Carlisle to supply the arsenal. Quartermaster wagons and teams were used to bring saw wood up from a mill built on Flower's land. The regional quartermaster also provided wagons to bring flour to the post from two local gristmills. Before Hodgdon got involved with the Hughes brothers, Lukens used the Quartermaster Department to move ordnance and ammunition from their furnace to the army's Hudson River encampment. The Carlisle and Johnston Forges were saved the expense of transporting iron to Carlisle Arsenal by the dispatch of wagons from the arsenal to those sites. Finally, wagons and teams were sent by Lukens to Maryann Furnace to move shot and shells produced there to Philadelphia.[96] These are only a sample of the various transport operations that the Carlisle Arsenal and its regional quartermaster provided to government contractors. Such support saved contractors money, making government contracts more attractive to private manufacturers.

Lack of money was a major reason the government was willing to provide alternate means of support to government contractors. But it was not the only reason, nor the most important reason. Providing raw materials and transportation allowed the government an element of control over the private manufacture of military stores. In mid-1780, Hodgdon made a contract with James Johnson of Baltimore for artillery ammunition. In October 1780, the ammunition began arriving in Philadelphia before Daniel Joy could get to Maryland to inspect it. Hodgdon wrote Johnson, "I am sorry to find any of the shells removed before they were proved as this may subject you to an additional expence should they finally prove faulty."[97] Hodgdon had contracted to provide transport for Johnson's production because this allowed him to control the processes of review and storage. If Hodgdon were in charge of removing the ammunition, he could send a representative to inspect it before delivery and order the product to be remade if necessary. Furthermore, by providing and removing iron from Thompson, Ross, and Potts, Hodgdon could renegotiate contracts and end partnerships if (as occurred) a producer failed to meet the parameters of a contract.

THE GOVERNMENT PROVIDED CONTRACTORS WITH CASH ADVANCES, RAW materials, and transportation to secure the services of skilled craftsmen as well as to control their production to some degree. Such economic activities were not a part of Congress's original plan to oversee and mobilize the nation's production of military stores. Investment developed over time as a necessity and a means of control. It was difficult for manufacturers to mobilize for military stores production. Raw materials were difficult to obtain, and cash was scarce. Congress learned from its earliest contracts that private producers did not have the resources they needed to support the war effort. Money and material were distributed by the Board of War prior to the creation of the DCGMS. Flower and

Hodgdon, however, turned acts of convenience into a policy of support. The commissary generals used cash to help manufacturers buy material and hire workers. They protected the department's credit by paying forward on contracts. The department procured raw materials for producers and moved those materials between manufacturers and government magazines. Nowhere is the government's desire to promote private production seen in sharper focus than in its efforts to secure coal to fuel manufacturing operations. The DCGMS sent its own men to mine the coal and transport it back to government arsenals. Military stores conductors guided coal and other materials to manufacturers and returned to government magazines with the produce of those contractors. All of these activities saved time and money for producers and allowed them to develop their production activities. The DCGMS was a visible hand of guidance in the Revolutionary War market of military stores.

8

"The American Foundery"

MILITARY STORES ACTIVITIES
AFTER THE REVOLUTION

J OSEPH PERKINS READ THE LETTER HE HAD JUST BEEN HANDED. HE knew Samuel Hodgdon's handwriting, and he had been expecting the missive for some time. There was nothing formal about the note; the initial few lines had been crossed out and rewritten, and the date, July 31, 1798, had been quickly scribbled across the top. Corrections and ink stains pocked the paper, indicating Hodgdon's desperation to get the information to his friend quickly so Perkins could be about his business.

The familiarity and excitement of the letter reveals the relationship shared by the two men. They had been through a great deal together since first meeting in 1779. Though Benjamin Flower had recruited Perkins to manage the armory at the Philadelphia Arsenal, Hodgdon had become his commander when Flower took ill. Perkins efficiently and effectively managed the armory for four years, becoming one of Hodgdon's most valuable assistants. Budgetary constraints led to the armory's closure and Perkins's dismissal from service, but Hodgdon immediately contracted with his premier gunsmith to manufacture and repair weapons as a private manufacturer. Perkins was only too happy to continue his relationship with Hodgdon and used government contracts as the foundation on which he built a gun manufactory to serve the Philadelphia market. Throughout the 1780s and '90s, Hodgdon continued to direct contracts to Perkins's gun shop. Perkins and Hodgdon had developed military manufacturing during the war, and in the postwar years they used their experience to cultivate private manufacturing.

The military stores department had been designed for war, but Hodgdon and Perkins both saw how it could function in peace as well. Hodgdon needed military manufacturing to keep weapons ready for future conflicts, while artisans like Perkins used government spending to support their work and grow their businesses. As in war, so in peace, the military stores department mobilized American manufacturing. Now, after nearly twenty years of promoting American innovation together, Hodgdon and Perkins were joining forces for the creation of a manufactory that would have far-reaching effects on American industrialization. The letter in Perkins's hands said, "With the approbation of the President; I appoint you Superintendent of the Armoury about to be established at Harper's Ferry."[1] Perkins immediately set off into the Virginia wilderness with several other government appointees to construct mills, shops, barracks, canals, and warehouses. Perkins reported to Hodgdon in December 1798 that his men had three forges in operation making weapons and had begun digging a canal to provide waterpower to the site.[2] And so the seeds laid by the DCGMS germinated into a new program of government sponsorship of manufacturing and innovation. The DCGMS was no more by 1798, but it had survived the war and served through the 1780s and '90s to become a foundation for the Federalist program that gave birth to the Harpers Ferry and Springfield Armories. In so doing, the department completed the translation of European ideas of manufacturing into the future of American industrialization.

It was clear to Congress in 1782 that the DCGMS had reached the end of its days. There was simply no need for the department, its production, or its purchasing. Budget-conscious and war-weary legislators were eager to put the army to rest and with it the expenses of its arms and equipment. The war was visibly winding down. The British army had not moved from its bases for months and showed no signs of offensive activity. Word had reached Congress in the wake of Yorktown that the British government wanted to work out a peace treaty. Several months later, the news was that congressional peace commissioners in Paris were nearing a deal. Congress believed it could begin demobilizing its army and shuttering its military operations. If the army itself was unnecessary, the infrastructure built to arm those troops was even more superfluous. This viewpoint was reinforced by the arrival of immense supplies of military stores from France and the capture of masses of materiel from surrendering British armies. Tens of thousands of new weapons and accouterments arrived from France between 1781 and 1783. And large supplies of ammunition, artillery, muskets, and camp equipage were taken from the British at Yorktown or abandoned by them when they evacuated Charleston and Savannah in late 1782, and New York City in late 1783.[3] Continental magazines were full to overflowing with stores. The success of contracting operations in 1780 and 1781 reinforced the idea that arsenals were unnecessary. Contractors had helped save the government money in the waning years of the war and were seen as a viable alternative to government manufacturing. Add to this the corruption issues that had arisen at Springfield and the location of Carlisle far out near the frontier, and Congress seemed to have legitimate reasons to close down the military manufacturing complex. As early as 1779, congressmen had noted, "When our sea ports shall be perfectly secure we confess a post so far removed as Carlisle will not be of much importance."[4] Peace was coming, the ports were open, and American provisions were no longer needed. As far as Congress was concerned, peace meant that the DCGMS could be demobilized and its workers discharged. The future of the department seemed hopeless, until a memo appeared in Congress from Secretary at War Benjamin Lincoln. That document breathed new life into the department and gave it a mission that translated its wartime operations into peacetime activities.

Lincoln was in a position to influence congressional policy through his appointment as the nation's first secretary at war. In the wake of final ratification of the Articles of Confederation in 1781, the national government sought to organize itself along more European lines. Congress's various committees were eliminated and their powers given over to individual ministers who exercised authority on behalf of the confederation. Thus, the Treasury Board's responsibilities were assumed by a superintendent of finance, the Foreign Affairs Committee's role was given to a secretary of foreign affairs, and the Board of War was replaced by the secretary at war. The secretary's responsibilities did not extend to making policy and commanding the army. Instead, the secretary was charged with managing the day-to-day operations of the army and with gathering information for Congress to make decisions about military policy. Lincoln also made the position a type of administrative assistant to the commanding general, supporting his operations rather than directing them. Luckily, he had a great deal of military experience that made him an ideal candidate for the post of war secretary.

Lincoln rose to the rank of major general during his service with the Continental Army, commanding militia for most of his career. He participated in the battles at Saratoga and Yorktown, admirably serving in the role of deputy commander for his superiors. Unfortunately, Lincoln went unsupported in his own independent command and was forced to surrender the American Southern Army at Charleston in 1780. While Lincoln was, in general, a mediocre commander, he nevertheless displayed an undaunted willingness to press on and face challenges. He had a quick mind and a strong character.[5] These traits served him well when he battled the political forces of Congress on behalf of the military manufacturing.

Lincoln believed that the DCGMS was critical to American independence, and his memo to Congress on the issue pulled no punches. "It would be idle for a people to talk of Independence," he wrote, "who were indebted for the means of their existence to any nation on earth." Such dependence on the fruits of another nation was a "circumstance too humiliating to be submitted to by any people desiring freedom." The war had proven that an independent nation needed to be able to manufacture the weapons of its own defense. The problem the war revealed was that Americans lacked the manufacturing experience necessary to mobilize for war production. Americans had grown too reliant on Europe prior to the war. "By the best accounts . . . labour expended on the principal articles of export from the Continent before the War—those articles cost us more labour than would have been expended had we manufactured all the articles necessary for our defence, from the raw materials in our possession." The war had forced Americans to do for themselves, and Americans had proven that domestic manufacturing could rise to the necessities of war when encouraged to do so. The lesson to be learned, said Lincoln, was that the nation should not wait until a war arises before promoting the activities that will be necessary to support the army in that war. "[W]ar," he wrote, "is not the [only] reason to establish Manufactures which are . . . perfected by time and long experience— Therefore this business should not be deferred until the necessities of such a situation declare its propriety."[6]

By the time Congress decided to mobilize domestic manufacturing to fight the War for Independence, the war was two years old. Lincoln believed that the United States could not afford that kind of delay in its next war. The government had to take the lead in American manufacturing in order to keep the nation on a footing to defend itself. While Congress believed it could rely on European imports, the truth was far different. Hodgdon reported in 1783 to the superintendent of finance, Robert Morris, "I have examined the arms lately arrived from France and find them in a ruinous situation and unless they are immediately put into the hands of the workmen to extract the ball, clean and repair them, they will be entirely lost to the states."[7] He believed that over ten thousand of the eighteen thousand arms that had arrived from France in the preceding two years needed attention. The munitions taken from the British were in no better shape. Having faced long service in the south or the Hudson Valley, a great number of the guns were in need of repair.[8] Hodgdon was also concerned about the storage facilities available to him. Most of the military structures used at the Philadelphia Arsenal were rented, and to save money Congress ordered stores packed as tightly as possible, without regard to the safety of the stores.[9] A lighting strike at Philadelphia nearly destroyed the munitions stored there because they were in wooden warehouses unsuited for military storage. Lincoln, with

Hodgdon's support, made a compelling case that the military stores program was not as unnecessary as Congress thought.

Lincoln knew that though the military stores program was designed for a nation at war, it could be useful for a nation at peace. Government manufacturing would serve the added benefit of mobilizing national manufacturing in general to the betterment of the whole nation. Lincoln called for a system of public inspection over private production as well as a system of material and cash investment. Lincoln had seen during the war that such a process was beneficial to the government and private industry, and he believed it should be continued. He said as much to Congress. "Manufactures should be erected under the immediate inspection of the public— and such bounties be given as would be sufficient inducement for individuals to attempt their establishement and perfection."[10] As critical as these operations

Benjamin Lincoln (1733– 1810) served as the nation's first secretary at war from 1781 to 1783, during which time he promoted military manufacturing as a basis for developing production innovation in the United States. (*National Portrait Gallery*)

were, wrote Lincoln, the happy truth was that the confederation was already engaged in those operations. All Congress had to do was approve the continuation of the military stores program and Lincoln would see to it that the government continued to mobilize American manufacturing on a foundation necessary to ensure national independence. Lincoln, however, had more in mind than just the status quo.

Just as the wartime arsenals had been built to react to the needs of the Continental Army, Lincoln believed that well-placed and productive arsenals would allow the nation to meet future threats. He noted with "satisfaction . . . that we have a large quantity of powder on hand," but, he observed, "there is not a magazine in any of the United States suitable to receive it, and it is now lodged in different wooden buildings in the most exposed situations."[11] Besides being insecurely stored it was also too dispersed to be cared for by government personnel. The powder, Lincoln wrote, "cannot be conveniently shifted, or have that care taken of it necessary to preserve it from rain." He therefore recommended that Congress immediately erect "four brick Magazines sufficient each to containe two thousand barrels of powder. That their be one at Springfield in the State of Massachusetts, One at West Point, One at Reading in the State of Pennsylvania, and one at New London in Bedford County in the State of Virginia. A fifth will be requisite as soon as it may be erected with safety near the boundary of North and South Carolina far up the country."[12]

Each of the magazines would be located along major transportation networks to support resistance against foreign invasion or frontier violence. "These Magazines," wrote Lincoln, "will at all times be necessary, and . . . their use will not terminate with the present war"[13] He believed that five separate arsenals should be constructed to serve specific geographical regions and that "Manufactories for military stores should be erected at the same places—and the laboratory business should, thou in small degrees, be carried on in all its various branches."[14] In addition, all arsenals as he envisioned them would also possess teaching facilities where troops recruited from local states could be trained in military science. "[A]ll arrangements," he told Congress, "should be such that [a] number of men might take the field upon the shortest notice completely equipped." To accomplish this, he suggested "the propriety of depositing at these Magazines in equal proportions all the military stores belonging to the United States."[15] Lincoln not only wanted Congress to approve the continuation of the military stores program but its enlargement so its impact was felt nationwide.

Lincoln's 1783 "memo regarding arsenals and academies" gave peacetime meaning to the wartime military stores program. This meaning translated into two separate operations: the development of regional arsenals to maintain the nation's defensive capabilities and government promotion of a national manufacturing infrastructure.[16] During the war, public and private production were needed to keep an army in the field; in peacetime such operations were necessary to keep the army ready for future conflicts. Just as government involvement in manufacturing during the war was necessary for the army, so in peacetime was government promotion of manufacturing necessary for the nation as a whole. War had shown the nation what domestic manufacturing could accomplish, and now in peacetime the DCGMS should, according to Lincoln, assist the nation in developing economic and diplomatic strength. The military stores infrastructure could serve numerous purposes, which made it relevant despite its costs. This last point was the most critical battle Lincoln would fight, for once he had proven to Congress the necessity of continuing its military stores program, he would then have to convince legislators to pay for it. He argued that Congress would have to make a choice between relaxing budgetary restraints and endangering national security: "This is one of those expences which cannot be dispensed with. . . . [I]t is essential that we should establish and maintain proper Magazines and Arsenals . . . To preserve our Freedom and Independence."[17]

Congress debated Lincoln's proposal and in October 1783 approved it. A committee was created to examine the fiscal situation of the war department and to recommend how to proceed. That committee asked for and received reports from the superintendent of finance and the secretary at war. The superintendent was hesitant to fund anything, but the secretary believed that the sale of superfluous stores would allow for commencement of the plan he had proposed. Although an alternative to a national military stores program was one funded and managed by the states, Congress had learned that "a provision by the United States of the forces necessary to be kept up will be made upon a more systematic and oeconomical plan than a provision by the states separately." Congress therefore authorized Lincoln "to establish founderies, manufactories of arms, powder &c. by means of which the labor of a part of the troops . . . will furnish the United States with those essential articles on easy terms, and contribute to their own support." Soldiers were to be set to work at "Arsenals and Magazines . . . in different parts of the United States," as proposed by Lincoln. Government artificers were to manufacture and maintain "complete equipment of twenty [to] thirty thousand men, for the field or for a siege calculated on a three years' supply."[18] On the matter of supporting domestic manufacturing, Congress resolved by default to allow the secretary at war to coordinate necessary activity through the commissary general of military stores and the superintendents of the arsenals. Lincoln successfully recommitted Congress to the support of operations necessary to keep the nation on a proper defensive posture. Budgetary constraints, however, kept the postwar military stores program from developing as extensively as Lincoln envisioned.

Lincoln began reforming the military manufacturing program even before he got congressional approval to do so. Soon after taking office, he implemented three operations in the DCGMS. First, he began building new magazines for the storage of military stores. Second, he initiated the construction of a national ordnance foundry. Finally, he centralized the contracting processes for arms and ordnance. Lincoln, as both a general and a friend of Knox's and Washington's, realized the need for new magazines for the nation's military stores. In 1782, Lincoln still had access to the stone-and-brick buildings at Carlisle and the brick construction of Carpenter's Hall in Philadelphia. However, Springfield's original magazine was built in a marsh, so dampness damaged the powder and other materiel stored there. During the war the army had also developed a headquarters and camp around West Point, New York, where numerous military stores were kept in temporary wooden buildings. Lincoln's first initiative as secretary, therefore, was the construction of new magazines at Springfield and West Point. He sent orders to John Bryant, superintendent of the Springfield Arsenal, and Knox to prepare the necessary materials and draw up plans for the construction of new brick magazines at Springfield and West Point.

Bryant immediately gathered timber, contracted for making bricks and mortar, and hired workers to supplement his laboratory staff. He asked

"Continental Magazine at Springfield, Erected 1782." Springfield Arsenal commander John Bryant and his men built a new stone magazine at the post in 1782 because various earlier magazines were inadequate, wooden, and poorly located on wet ground. This structure was located to the far east of the arsenal and can be seen on the bottom right of the map on page 103. It was torn down in 1842, but its front door mantle was preserved as an informal monument at Springfield Armory until the late nineteenth century, when it was lost. (*Genesis of the US Armory*)

the town council for the use of land south of town on a hill overlooking Springfield. It agreed, and he set his enlisted and hired men to work building a new brick magazine for powder and ammunition. Bryant finished the new Springfield magazine in September, by which point Knox was still corresponding with Lincoln about how best to accomplish the construction of a magazine at West Point. Lincoln begged Knox to put men to work, but Knox dragged his feet. He sought out the most modern French magazine design and sought Lincoln's approval. By the time Knox felt comfortable with the project, the war was over.[19] Lincoln informed Knox in July 1783 that "little can be done . . . to construct arsenals" because peace has arrived and the government was preparing to furlough most of the troops, who could have been used as construction labor.[20] By the end of the summer, Lincoln put some of the men left in the service to work building the new magazine. Lincoln was annoyed with the delay, but he did not realize the poor state of the DCGMS until budgetary constraints revealed it.

After initiating the construction of new magazines, Lincoln took a tour of the magazine at Philadelphia and then an extended inspection visit to the Carlisle Arsenal. He appreciated the large buildings and production facilities that he saw at Carlisle and intended to keep them operating. Likewise, he continued to support Hodgdon's operations in Philadelphia. Lincoln's only real budgetary concession was to release superfluous officers. Luke Bliss was relieved of duty as regional commissary at Springfield and his duties given to arsenal superintendent Bryant. Samuel

Sargent was also dismissed, and Carlisle was turned over to a caretaker who maintained the stores there. Most artificers there had already been transferred to Philadelphia, and those who remained were dismissed. At this point all the other regional commissaries were also dismissed, and the superintendent of arms and ordnance positions eliminated. Lincoln used some of the money he saved to order the construction of a new magazine at the temporary arsenal established in Virginia. Lincoln was preparing to make Springfield and Philadelphia the government's manufacturing centers, and West Point, Carlisle, and Westham, Virginia, into depots.[21]

Lincoln then reassigned departmental personnel in order to save money. James Byers was a major asset to the DCGMS. Byers had been hired in 1777 to manage an ordnance furnace for Congress in Philadelphia. Rather than cast ordnance, however, the air furnace that Byers managed in Southwark cast musket components and musket balls. Byers had nevertheless been promised a large salary that had never been paid. By 1783, the government owed him nearly $3,500. With the war seemingly over in 1782, Byers approached Lincoln for his pay and release from service. Both men faced an awkward situation. Because of his meager budget, Lincoln could not pay Byers the full amount of his back pay, but neither did he want to lose Byers's services. Byers knew he could make more money in the private sector, but he believed that if he quit government service he might never get paid. To resolve the situation, Lincoln offered Byers a deal. He asked him to contract for the construction and operation of an ordnance foundry for the confederation. For his services, Byers would be paid $2 per day. In exchange for this renegotiated contract, Lincoln promised to pay Byers immediately in cash half of the money owed him by the government. Faced with the opportunity to put his skills to use and secure money from the cash-strapped Congress, Byers took the deal.[22]

In late 1782, Lincoln sent Byers to Springfield to coordinate construction of the foundry with operations at the arsenal. Byers rented property near the post and hired an assistant to help him cast. He then engaged Bryant's artificers to construct an air furnace and a boring mill for him. Byers provided the design specifications, paid the men on his account, and directed the construction. Early in 1783, he could report success to Lincoln: "I have now six 5 1/2 inc howitz cast, and shall have as many more in a short time—The furnace works extreemly well." After hearing of Byers's initial success, Hodgdon forwarded him "the arms of america and a paper expressing the bigness [he thought] proper to be cast on the heavy ordnance to afford room for the engraving."[23] Hodgdon promised to spare no expense to support Byers's work and said he would pay on sight any receipts Byers issued. About a year passed before Byers's boring mill was complete.

At Springfield, Lincoln demonstrated what could be accomplished by the DCGMS. In the aftermath of war, reasoned Lincoln, the government could invest its resources in making the country partially self-sufficient in the area of ordnance. The government would now be able to oversee the quality production of its own artillery and use the foundry as a model for private contractors. Hodgdon, who reflected Lincoln's excitement, wrote, "The American Foundery shall in some future day, be as celebrated as that of Charon or any other European whatever."[24] Hodgdon was referring to Britain's Carron Works, which supported the work of James Watt and was one of the biggest iron firms in the world at the time. Hodgdon believed that operations at Springfield had the potential to become an American version of the Carron Works. He, like others in the eighteenth century, spelled Carron phonetically.

Lincoln decided in 1782 to centralize the contract production of ordnance ammunition in the hands of John Faesch. Until 1781, Hodgdon made ammunition contracts with twelve furnace owners. It seems that once Lincoln had evaluated the operations of the war department and settled in as secretary, he decided that only one major contractor was necessary. This made economic sense because it limited the need for cash advances, transport, and inspections. Relying on one contractor also allowed centralized oversight of Faesch's activities by the government. Faesch also offered advantages of his own. First, the ironmonger had a strong relationship with Knox, who was in turn a close friend of Lincoln's. Second, Faesch had access to three furnaces that he either owned, partially owned, or rented. It did not hurt that Faesch's operations were all within a short distance of the Main Army's camp in the Hudson Highlands.[25]

Thus, by the end of his first year in office, Lincoln had done much to make the DCGMS more effective. It could rely on its own foundry for ordnance, get sufficient ammunition from a single major contractor, and was in the process of constructing suitable storage facilities for its many stores. Lincoln was moving the DCGMS toward the form that Congress had intended, a centralized agency that could oversee the production of military stores that met government specifications. It was at this point that congressional finances conspired to undermine Lincoln's activities and drove him to frustration.

The Confederation Congress was broke. Despite securing huge loans from France, Spain, and the Netherlands, the United States had far too many debts, far too many expenditures, and far too little income. The confederation, like the Continental government before it, had no power to tax and relied on the states for contributions to the national Treasury. The result was that Congress had no secure, regular source of income. What exasperated Lincoln was that Congress approved cutting his budget even as it gave him the go-ahead to expand his programs. Robert

Morris, the superintendent of finance, was given virtually unchecked power to determine which bills to pay, which budgets to fund, and which paychecks to ignore. Lincoln was incredulous: money was granted by Congress for arsenal repair and construction, but Morris refused to release it. Morris claimed that the arsenals were not important enough to the nation to warrant further expenditures. To many congressmen, Morris's reasoning made sense; not all congressmen agreed with supporting Lincoln. Congress had already complained that the corruption and incompetence at Springfield had made its operations a drain on the budget, and the exigencies of war had been the only reason to keep it operational.[26]

Lincoln's reform measures were not enough to satisfy Congress, which wanted less cost as well as more efficiency. Congress began limiting DCGMS expenditures and eliminating expenses without consulting the secretary at war. Congress ordered Hodgdon to close Carlisle and move its stores to Philadelphia. It also ordered him to pack the government's stores in Philadelphia tightly and give up as many rented buildings as possible.[27] Morris refused to issue Lincoln funds to pay for the construction of new magazines in Virginia and West Point, writing, "The reasons you assign for advancing money to build a magazine are very forcible & similar reasons will doubtless apply for building the other Magazines particularly that which is projected at West Point. . . . I cannot but feel the sincerest wish to comply with [your request] but the situation of the treasury will by no means permit the attempt."[28] Nor would Morris pay the men whom Hodgdon had contracted to repair the French muskets.

Lincoln, however, did not accept the superintendent's decisions and sought to secure the funding he was promised by Congress. He had asked Morris for cash to pay for construction supplies and transportation, as he believed he could get enlisted men to build a magazine in Virginia.[29] Unfortunately, not only did Morris refuse, but he issued Lincoln suggestions regarding the management of his department. He told Lincoln to consider revising his plans for Virginia and West Point "instead of adding to our debts while as at present the prospect of paying them seems hourly to diminish and the resources we have relied on are fast drying up." He suggested "the propriety of selling all those Stores which would be lost from the want of proper covering, as by that means something may be raised towards absolving present engagements."[30]

There is no record of Lincoln's response, but based on Morris's next letter, it must have been full of exasperation and disbelief. Morris wrote Lincoln, "Your Excellency will easily conceive the Situation to which I am driven. . . . It is certainly of Importance that Arsenals should be erected . . . , [b]ut the Reasons against advancing Money are uncontrovertible." Morris continued "that many of the Stores may be wasted and destroyed from the want of—Magazines . . . [b]ut such Loss must be added to the Mass of Injuries . . . America has already sustained, by not complying with the Requisitions of Congress. It is a Loss, which in its Consequences must fall upon the States themselves; who are the immediate authors of it."[31] To Lincoln it appeared that Morris was not refusing because he did not have the money but rather to make a point against the states that refused to pay their annual contributions to the congressional Treasury. The same day that Lincoln received Morris's second letter, Lincoln met with the president of Congress and laid the matter and the letters before Congress.[32]

Congress did not seem to understand the source of Lincoln's frustration. Lincoln was flabbergasted by the fact that Congress and the superintendent of finance were running his department without him. He believed that he was unable to exercise control over his own budget because of what he saw as Morris's intransigence. Lincoln also felt slighted by the fact that Congress was eliminating elements of his department without consulting him. Though Lincoln was able to keep Congress from eliminating the military stores program by giving it a peacetime purpose, he was forced to compromise on the extent of the program. Congress agreed to allow him to reorganize his department as he saw fit, but only within the budgetary constraints of the cash-strapped government. Aggravated and worn out, Lincoln doubted he could carry out the work Congress had entrusted to him.[33] After two years of politicking, in addition to six years as an active military officer, he was exhausted. At the end of 1783, he resigned as secretary at war. It took almost two years for Congress to convince Henry Knox to take Lincoln's place. The artillery commander foresaw ending up in the same situation as his friend and put off accepting the post until Morris resigned. Thus, from 1783 until 1785, when Morris did finally leave his post, the senior official in the war department was Samuel Hodgdon. He was left with the task of continuing Lincoln's plan without the money or authority to accomplish the job properly. Even after Knox took over as secretary, though, Hodgdon continued to exercise a great deal of autonomy in directing the DCGMS.

STRUCTURE OF MILITARY STORES MANAGEMENT, 1784–1794

Hodgdon's first move was to take a thorough accounting of all military stores. That took about four months and required the work of numerous individuals. Hodgdon could easily count the stores in his own possession, but his budget was too small to allow him to travel to the various locations where stores had been deposited. He asked quartermasters and commissaries throughout the nation to list their stores. He also wrote to contractors asking for accounts of stores not yet delivered to a government magazine. Reports came in from Head of Elk, Charleston, and Providence, Rhode Island, as well as Carlisle, West Point, Virginia, and Springfield. He found that the war had led to the distribution of items randomly throughout the country. Large numbers of ordnance and ammunition were at Head of Elk, yet carriages and accouterments for them were at Philadelphia and Carlisle. There were musket cartridges at West Point, but most muskets were in Philadelphia. And most of the artificer tools in the department were in Philadelphia, though the government's artificers were at work in Springfield and West Point. Large amounts of shot and shells were still deposited at Mount Hope, Salisbury, Durham, and Hughes Furnaces. Hodgdon reported to Congress that the nation's military stores were being kept at a minimum of twelve locations in eight states.[34]

The variety of locations was not as much a problem as the lack of care and security with which the stores were deposited. Those at Head of Elk were left in the open on a shipping wharf.[35] Hodgdon told Congress, "Those [stores] in Virginia . . . are scatterd into several Towns, are in but indifferent order and are exceedingly exposed, nor can they be collected or better secured untill buildings are erected for their reception, which I humbly recommend being immediately done."[36] The powder, ammunition, and few muskets at West Point were also stored in the open or in temporary wooden shacks, while ordnance stores still with the ironmasters were not being secured at all. These, Hodgdon wrote, were "subject to embezzlement" by anyone who might want to cart them off.[37] Once he had accounted for the government's stores, Hodgdon made his second task the implementation of Lincoln's plan for the care of those stores. Hodgdon intended to complete the magazines begun by Lincoln and deposit the nation's military stores proportionally at five arsenals throughout the country. Before he could care for the stores, Hodgdon had to deal with the limitations of his budget.

The government's military stores budget during the latter 1780s and early 1790s was not a significant government expenditure. Most of the national budget went to pay salaries, debt, and interest, leaving little for other expenditures. As late as 1787, Congress was in debt for up to $67 million on unpaid loan certificates and $10 million in foreign loans.[38] The confederation was unable to pay its bills let alone pay down its debt because it had no taxing power and relied on payments from the states. The states were notorious for their failure to financially support the government. The confederation's finances were so tight that the Treasury Board wrote Knox "the fact is there are not sufficient sums in the treasury to defray the salaries of the public officers whose services are indispensibly necessary for the support of the mere form of the civil government."[39] The total war department budget from 1784 through 1787 was just over $789,000 out of a total national budget of roughly $8 million.[40] Military stores expenditures amounted to just 12 percent of the war department's expenditures and a mere 1 percent of the national budget. From 1784 to 1787, Hodgdon spent only $96,950 of the government's money. The majority of this outlay occurred in 1784, when $78,419 was expended to initiate Lincoln's plan. Thus, Hodgdon spent only $18,000 of the government's money over the following three years. In 1786, Hodgdon budgeted $24,000 but was given only one-third that sum.[41] Despite these fiscal restraints, Hodgdon was able to accomplish a great deal. He applied the same financial finesse to the postwar DCGMS that he did to the wartime department, assisted by the vast amount of stores he had at his disposal.

Hodgdon reasoned that an easy way to supplement his department's budget was to sell stores not needed by the department. Lincoln had approached Congress earlier with the idea of selling superfluous stores. Many congressmen received the idea with disdain, reasoning that the government had in most cases paid a premium for its military stores and that it was absurd to sell them for the depreciated values resulting from the arrival of peace. Congress could not accept that its once-valuable weapons and accouterments be auctioned off at a lower price, and it rejected Lincoln's idea.[42] Hodgdon used the military stores data he collected to convince Congress to change its mind. Stores were located at such a variety of places that the costs of moving them were higher than they were worth. Hodgdon's prime example was the ordnance at Head of Elk. Much of it was damaged British artillery. It would cost more to repair the cannons than it would to cast them new. They were more valuable as scrap metal. Hodgdon told Congress, "It should be carefully remembered that many of the Stores, are in their nature perishable, and . . . proper attention will always be necessary to prevent great loss to the States."[43] He went on to explain the propriety and necessity of selling stores:

> In all governments, where Magazines are established one fifth part [of powder] is sold off every Year, whereby the whole is chang'd for new every five Years; The age of that we have on hand cannot be ascertained on which account I should suppose it better to dispose of one half immediately . . . the money to be appropriated for as occasion may require. Fixed Ammunition, may not be depended on more than one Year and numerous other species might be mention'd with their consequences.[44]

Some of the stores, wrote Hodgdon, were going to perish; selling them now allowed for the purchase of fresh stores and the care of those that could be preserved. Hodgdon's report argued that the department had both far more stores than it could care for, and more stores than the army could use at its reduced, peacetime, size. In late 1784, Congress agreed to let Hodgdon sell those stores he judged unnecessary.

The sale of stores added a significant amount of money to Hodgdon's budget. As mentioned earlier, the government gave him $96,950 to spend from 1784 to 1787. But the commissary's accounts indicate that he spent just under $177,000. The difference between these figures indicates that the sale of stores provided Hodgdon's department with over $80,000 in the form of paper and specie currency. Hodgdon's ability to make money was such a boon to the war department that Hodgdon disbursed about $10,000 to Knox to cover expenses in other sectors of the department. Sales were accomplished in a variety of ways. Hodgdon's account book indicates he ordered a large public auction at Carlisle, two at Springfield, and one in Virginia. Carlisle's auction, conducted by the storekeeper there in 1786, raised $3,152. Nathaniel Irish held an auction as part of the process of closing the Virginia Arsenal in 1784 and raised $2,748 to defray his costs.[45] There are no complete records for what was sold at Springfield, but at least $1,255 was raised at that post.[46] Aside from major auctions, Hodgdon sold stores regularly at Philadelphia to merchants and craftsmen who desired them. Bryant at Springfield did the same.[47] Hodgdon's account book reveals that the DCGMS advertised not only the sale of items but also the availability of raw materials that might be of interest to the public.[48] The extent of these sales is unclear because Hodgdon did not record them in his account book, though he did mention such sales in his correspondence.[49] He also directed his storekeepers to sell the powder and condemned ordnance they possessed. It is unclear how many of these items were sold, because while it was reported to Hodgdon that it had been done, the correspondence does not indicate the money raised. Head of Elk was a significant source of income because it was close enough to major urban centers like Lancaster, York, Carlisle, and Baltimore to sell powder, and near enough to major furnaces to sell ordnance as scrap. The final way Hodgdon disposed of stores was by selling them back to their producers. He raised most of the money earned from the sale of stores in this fashion.[50] His records on this topic are vague because in some cases he credited the stores as payment back to an ironmonger's account while at other times, as with Faesch, he received money for them.[51] Estimates can be made to show that Hodgdon sold about $30,000 worth of shot and shells back to the ironmasters who had made them. He supported the department by selling stores, crediting accounts with stores sold, and paying interest on debts with the cash he had on hand. In this way he was able to put the department's financial house in order and get to work organizing the stores and implementing Lincoln's plan.

Despite Hodgdon's ability to raise money, his budget was less than a quarter of what it had been during the war, a financial limitation that forced him to make difficult choices. Lincoln had desired the establishment of five arsenals, but this was simply not feasible for Hodgdon.[52] The commissary general decided to invest in the Springfield Arsenal because it already had a manufactory, new magazine, and workshops.

West Point would continue in operation because it had a large supply of stores that made movement expensive. The Philadelphia Arsenal would remain in place because of the significant numbers of stores there, the proximity of trained craftsmen, and the fact that Hodgdon lived there. Hodgdon decided to cut the department's losses in Virginia and South Carolina. There were government stores in those states, but they were small. Hodgdon closed the Virginia Arsenal, which had been temporary to begin with, and deposited all the government's stores at the Virginia State Magazine in Richmond.[53] He paid for this by giving the state access to the stores for its own use. Hodgdon then asked South Carolina's government to care for government stores at its magazine in Charleston. The state did this in exchange for access to the stores.[54] Thus, from 1785 through 1794, the DCGMS centered its repair work, production, and storage facilities at three sites: Philadelphia, West Point, and Springfield.

Philadelphia was, in the 1780s, as it was during the war, the hub of contract operations for the DCGMS. In 1784, Hodgdon closed the laboratories, the ordnance yard, and all the government craft shops.[55] He forwarded sixty-three pieces of ordnance to West Point along with all the shot and shells, which were "neatly piled in the shot stores."[56] Unfit stores were burned; their iron segments were carefully packaged and stored for later use. Workshops in Philadelphia not suitable for storage were given up, and more useful sites were rented. Stores were moved to a rented magazine at Henry Lisle's Wharf.[57] Having vacated Carpenter's Hall, Hodgdon most likely had his office on the waterfront near the wharf. After 1784, there were no enlisted men or hired artificers at Philadelphia. Instead, the arsenal's staff was Hodgdon, a clerk, and a messenger. Hodgdon cared for the stores under his direction and contracted out the repair work necessary to maintain them.[58] He was able to report in 1784 that the stores in "Philadelphia . . . under my own immediate care . . . are secured and at present in good order."[59]

Two important repair contracts were carried out by Hodgdon in Philadelphia. The first, with Joseph Perkins, was a carryover from the waning years of the war. Perkins, former armory superintendent, had been contracted to clean and repair eleven thousand French muskets that arrived in Philadelphia in 1783. This contract was not finished until the end of 1784 because Morris refused to pay Perkins for the work he performed. Nevertheless, Hodgdon finished the contract, and by the end of 1784 had stored the newly cleaned weapons.[60] Repair contracts were put on hold in Philadelphia during the mid-1780s because troops stationed at West Point provided less-expensive labor. In 1788, however, Hodgdon signed a new repair contract with John Thompson. For eight shillings each, Thompson agreed to clean and repair one thousand muskets at a rate of 150 a month for seven months.[61] These thousand muskets joined several hundred other new ones Hodgdon purchased to replace older stores sold at auction.[62] Though it was not as important to the postwar military stores program as it was during the war, the Philadelphia Arsenal still provided valuable service by taking advantage of craftsmen like Perkins who called the city their home. Recall that in this period, Hodgdon was also investing in Stacy Potts's attempts at steel innovation and Pierre Penet's work developing large-scale weapons production. Operations in Philadelphia were expensive, however, and Hodgdon relied more and more on enlisted artificers at Springfield and guards stationed at the army's West Point fortress.

While West Point did not develop into the large-scale magazine Lincoln had hoped for, it did become a significant munitions facility for the confederation. West Point was an important confederation depot for two reasons. As the army's base of operations in the Hudson Highlands during the war, it held a special place in Henry Knox's heart. Second, it was a strategic location that guarded the Hudson River.[63] Neither of these reasons, however, made West Point a logical choice to act as a depot in peacetime. West Point had strategic value during the war, but with New York City in American hands, the Hudson could be better protected farther south. With the end of hostilities, it was unlikely that an invasion would be forthcoming up the Hudson. Nevertheless, Knox decided to station a small company of fifty men at the post.[64] There were legitimate reasons for the post to be used as a depot and arsenal, reasons that made it a more useful site than Philadelphia. West Point was a government installation, which saved money on rent. The post was located along the Hudson River, which offered transportation to the coast and the frontier via the Mohawk River.

Major John Doughty of the artillery took command of West Point in mid-1784. He directed a company of fifty-eight men who guarded and maintained the stores at the post.[65] Soon after his arrival, Doughty took stock of his command and reported to the war department. West Point comprised "a number of aged work shops for armourers with some tools & Barracks to quarter them in," Doughty wrote. "The powder & stores [were] tolerably well stored except for the arms," which needed a better magazine. Without protection from the weather, weapons used in the war were beginning to rust, and those shipped from France were beginning to fall out of their rotting shipping crates.[66] The powder, too, was a problem, because while it was properly stored at the moment, Doughty knew it would need to be turned, dried, and repackaged every two years to remain useful. Thus, Doughty was faced with buildings that needed upkeep, a majority of the arms at the post that needed care, and powder and ammunition that needed proper packaging.

He accomplished a great deal during his first year of command. His initial achievement was the completion of the magazine Lincoln had authorized two years previously but Knox had failed to erect. It was completed

at a cost of $1,046 and "the Labour of the Garrison." Doughty report-
ed "it [was] a good Building . . . [and] will hold about five thousand
stand of Arms."[67] Yet it was not large enough for the nearly twenty-five
thousand weapons at the post. Nevertheless, Doughty sought permission
at the end of 1784 to put his men to work repairing arms and West
Point's decaying buildings. Though the magazine could not hold all of
the arms, Doughty wanted to preserve some of them and then repair
buildings to store the others. Hodgdon, however, directed instead the
preservation of the powder. He procured two thousand empty barrels
and their component parts early in 1785 and directed Doughty to have
his men dry the powder at West Point.[68] By September the "powder
[was] dried and repacked in good Casks, and it is well deposited," Knox
reported to Congress. Once the men were at work on that task, however, Hodgdon procured money to hire armorers to work with Doughty's
men, allowing Doughty to accomplish the task he had wished to begin
with, the repair of arms. Knox reported that a "party of fourteen armorers has been imployed during the Summer in repairing and cleaning of
Arms."[69] But the number of arms in need of repair or cleaning was just
too great for the department's budget. Knox reported to Congress after
inspecting the post that it would take sixty men nine months to service
all the weapons at West Point. Such a project was unrealistic with the
resources available. Over the next three years, Doughty's men repaired
over "five thousand arms," though there were "about ten thousand of
the others . . . worth repairing." It was a seemingly never-ending task, but
"necessary work [continued] going on at that post on a small scale."[70]
The department simply did not have enough cash to expand operations
at West Point, despite the fact that by 1787, Knox wrote, "The stores at
West Point are daily diminishing in value."[71] The real problem with West
Point was that it was not an arsenal in the sense that it was not designed
as a repair-and-production center. Knox reported to Congress in 1788,
"To employ the number of workmen requisite to effect the business [at
West Point] in one year would be too expensive for the public
finances."[72] Costs were so high primarily because the buildings were
inadequate, having been built for the field commissary, who was charged
with arms repair on only a small scale. West Point was also too far from
significant sources of raw materials and contract labor. The post was useful during the confederation period, but its expense proved it was not a
wise manufacturing center for the long term. Washington's secretary of
war, Knox, moved West Point's arsenal operations to Springfield in 1794.

Springfield was the most extensive of the confederation's military
stores operations. Eleven enlisted artillerymen were employed at the post
to turn over the stores and care for them. Post superintendent Bryant also
hired several laborers to work in the post's craft shops in the repair and
production of stores. And the ordnance foundry produced howitzers and

mortars. The arsenal was very close to the ideal post envisioned by Lincoln. Though the manufacture of weapons was not accomplished there, the facilities for such operations existed. The Springfield Arsenal contained not only shops for armorers, carpenters, blacksmiths, and harness makers, but a newly built powder magazine as well. It also possessed the nation's first functional brass ordnance foundry complete with coal house and boring mill.[73] Springfield was a storage and manufacturing arsenal with the capacity to mobilize the manufacturing base of the surrounding region to support the nation's army.

Hodgdon outlined Springfield's postwar agenda in orders sent to Bryant in April 1784. "The Powder in the Magazine, must be immediately overhaul'd," was Hodgdon's first directive. Next, "The new Muskets must be oiled (cleaned)." Then Bryant was to see to the repair of the arsenal's buildings to ensure that all stores could be housed properly and securely. He was then to "make the collection of the Stores in Connecticut," and in all of the work keep "monthly Returns." Bryant was authorized to sell as many damaged and useless stores as possible in order to fund his operations. Hodgdon hoped the stores would bring their "intrinsic" value, but left the details of execution of all his directives to Bryant's discretion. Bryant was given command of all troops stationed by the war department at Springfield and the liberty of engaging any hired men he saw fit.[74] Bryant's first operation at the arsenal was the sale of stores to raise money. He held a public auction in September 1784 and continued to sell stores occasionally from that point on to pay for activities at the post.[75]

Bryant focused the effort of the artillerymen at Springfield toward the accomplishment of two projects: the continual care and turnover of gunpowder and the making and remaking of cartridges. Ammunition maintenance was a complicated process in the eighteenth century, when paper cartridges were the primary ammunition on the battlefield. Musket cartridges could spoil if they were kept in storage too long. The paper and powder could both either get damp and mold or dry out and crumble. Gunpowder, too, naturally separated into its component parts in extended storage. The confederation had hundreds of thousands of musket cartridges when the war ended. To preserve the powder, Springfield artillerymen unrolled the cartridges and repackaged all the component parts. Bullets were put into ammunition boxes, powder into casks, and paper and twine into bundles. At the same time, the artillerymen remade cartridges out of fresh powder. Seven years after the war ended, Springfield was storing only 74,799 musket cartridges. Cannon cartridges were likewise disassembled and stored as components, which preserved the powder and the flannel, of which most of them were made. The artillerymen then took casks of powder out of the magazine, dumped them into vats, remixed the powder, and repackaged it.[76] Hired artificers working at the post supported these operations through the production of new ammunition boxes and powder kegs. Knox reported to Congress in 1786 that over the past year, "The powder amounting to upwards of thirteen hundred barrels of excellent quality have been shifted, dried, and repacked," by the men at Springfield.[77] In addition to packing the powder, Bryant hired a local powder maker to prove the powder and inspect it before putting it into storage. Bryant's records show that he accomplished the turnover of the powder that Hodgdon requested by selling old powder at auction and purchasing new powder. He also replaced powder by gathering stores from throughout New England into the magazine at Springfield.[78]

While Hodgdon went about the task of centralizing the storage of supplies elsewhere, he commissioned Bryant with the task of gathering the dispersed stores closest to Springfield. In mid-1784, William Whiting, the owner of Salisbury Furnace, wrote Hodgdon about the fact that there was a great deal of shot and shells at the furnace belonging to the government.[79] Hodgdon was keen on removing the stores because Whiting was a creditor to the government and was not willing to pay for the ammunition being kept by the government at his furnace. Hodgdon notified Bryant and Knox "of the insecure situation of a large quantity of shot and shells at Salisbury in Connecticut, amounting to about two hundred tons."[80] It took Bryant about a year to raise the funds necessary to hire teams to move the stores. This was accomplished in late 1785. At this point, the post artillerymen were employed to weigh, inspect, and stack the ammunition, a project that took about two months.[81] Unfortunately, Knox hoped that Bryant would be able to next move the government stores being kept in the Rhode Island state magazine, but he simply did not have the cash to accomplish this. Nevertheless, the transportation, inspection, and care of two hundred tons of ammunition was a significant accomplishment for the cash-strapped department.

In the third project, Bryant directed hired and enlisted men to repair and store muskets that had arrived from France in 1783 and 1784. Beginning in 1785, Bryant had his enlisted men disassemble and clean the muskets at the arsenal. Damaged muskets found among the inventory were sent to the armory to be repaired by contract gunsmiths. The whole process took just over a year. Knox reported to Congress in 1786 that at Springfield "during the course of the last and present year the new arms and bayonets about seven thousand in number have been taken to pieces, cleaned and put in perfect condition for use."[82] Once Bryant had put the arsenal's stores in order, he moved on to the last of Hodgdon's assignments, the care of the post itself.

In addition to the stores work done at Springfield, artificers also rehabilitated the post's structures. Bryant purchased boards in 1785 for his men to reclapboard the arsenal buildings. Foundations were repaired, and a new doorway was added to the magazine. The men's barracks were also repaired. The armed uprising of Massachusetts farmers known as Shays's Rebellion was a threat against the arsenal that also caused Bryant to engage in some major additions to the post. Bryant, with the help of the Massachusetts militia, built several blockhouses to defend the arsenal.[83] In the aftermath of the rebellion, Bryant designed a stone wall to surround the arsenal. He purchased lime, clay, and stone from local merchants, and in 1787 his men began building the enclosure. About a year and a half later, a three-foot wall running the length of the post's perimeter was completed.[84] By 1789, Bryant and his men had put Springfield's stores and buildings into proper order.

Once they had finished Hodgdon's major assignments, Bryant's men were put into a routine of stores maintenance and furnace support. Knox reported to Congress in 1788 that the laboratory work at Springfield was following a regular schedule: "The powder at Springfield . . . has been annually . . . aired, cleaned, proved, well packed, and also turned frequently."[85] Bryant hired five men to build and repair carriages for the ordnance that Byers was casting at the foundry. Wheelwrights were hired to make carriage wheels and carpenters to make the cheeks and tails of a cannon carriage. Blacksmiths were hired to make all the iron hardware and the carriage wheels. Once the various components were completed, they were assembled by artillerymen at the post. This was done because, Bryant noted, neither carpenters nor blacksmiths wished to contract to make an entire carriage until they had practiced making one.[86] Thus, several Springfield craftsmen supplied the component parts for ordnance carriages to arsenal workers who assembled the completed product. Once the carriages were finished, they were used to mount the various howitzers and cannons delivered from Byers.

Byers was successful at constructing the nation's first ordnance foundry. Perhaps 99 percent of all ordnance cast by Americans during the war was made of iron, though brass was considered the more modern casting material. Prior to his work for the DCGMS, Byers was successful at casting brass ordnance. Lincoln wanted a brass foundry because Britain's Woolwich Arsenal had one. Byers, therefore, built an air furnace that cast exclusively brass ordnance. By early 1783, Byers had completed six 5.5-inch howitzers and was preparing to cast several three-pound cannon. In early 1784, Byers reported to Hodgdon that he had cast an additional ten eight-inch howitzers. He noted, too, that he had completed construction of a boring mill and had bored out and finished both his most recent castings as well as those from the previous year. Production records for the foundry do not reappear until 1790, when Bryant recorded that Springfield had two 8-inch howitzers and nine 5.5-inch howitzers, apparently made at the foundry. Three years later, Byers delivered two cannons to Springfield, most likely three-pounders, and received in return a mortar and four four-pound cannons to recast into howitzers. Six months later, Byers delivered to Springfield twenty-eight 5.5-inch howitzers and twenty three-pound cannons.[87] Throughout the late 1780s, Bryant's men were manufacturing cannon carriages, revealing that they were receiving ordnance from Byers's furnace. Knox reported generally that, "The brass cannon and Mortars are, and will remain fit for immediate service," though it is unclear if he was referring to Springfield's production or artillery in general.[88] Byers cast no fewer than sixty pieces of ordnance in his ten years of service to the government. This did not match the production activity of the Woolwich Arsenal, which produced eighty-two pieces of ordnance a year from 1775 to 1782.[89] Byers's production, however, was a sign of the government's desire to promote weapons manufacturing.

Though it faced several challenges, the confederation's military stores program did meet the needs of the small postwar army. The confederation's armed forces in December 1784 numbered only 436 men. The majority of these troops were stationed on the frontier at Fort Pitt in western Pennsylvania and Fort Schuyler in western New York. Fifty-three men were stationed at West Point and eleven at Springfield.[90] Despite their small size, the frontier forces were charged by Congress with protecting settlers moving west along the Ohio and Mohawk rivers and establishing American hegemony over the lands beyond the Appalachian Mountains that had been given to the United States in the Treaty of Paris. Congress also pressured Knox to take "posts on the Lakes Erie and Ontario . . . occupied by the troops of his Britannick Majesty."[91] Congress hoped to support Knox in this endeavor with more troops, but it never did. Knox, however, used the materiel available to him in the DCGMS to augment the magazines at Fort Pitt and Fort Schuyler. This allowed the commanders at those posts to take aggressive measures against Native Americans who threatened white settlers in the Ohio and Mohawk valleys.

The DCGMS supported frontier activities in two ways. In 1783 and 1784, Hodgdon forwarded a large number of artificer tools, raw materials, and traveling forges to Fort Pitt. A commissary of military stores with the army (descended from the field commissary position) used the resources Hodgdon sent to establish a small repair facility at Fort Pitt. He was thus able to engage troops and local craftsmen to assist him in the care and repair of weapons and accouterments on the frontier. Josiah Harmar, commander at Fort Pitt, was freed from sending his damaged stores back to Philadelphia or Springfield for repair. The second support offered the frontier posts by the DCGMS was the resupply of stores. Hodgdon engaged in two operations. He scraped together funds to move stores, including cannons and powder, from Albany to Fort Schuyler in 1785.[92] The New York post was defended by only one hundred men, who were continually called on to defend outlying settlements. The arrival of more stores, especially cannons, allowed fewer men to care for the post and more men to be sent on patrols. In 1786, Hodgdon moved three tons of lead and three tons of powder from Carlisle to Fort Pitt.[93] The reinforcement of the frontier posts allowed Harmar to dispatch troops down the Ohio River into the Northwest Territory in 1788. At Marietta, Ohio, he established Fort Harmar to defend settlers who had purchased land from the confederation. The DCGMS continued to accomplish the tasks assigned it in the 1780s as it had done during the war. The department was also able to maintain the quality of the stores used by the military. It continued to inspect stores repaired or produced by contractors. All of these tasks were limited by the government's fiscal problems, but the department was not stagnant.

Despite all the obvious activity within the DCGMS, Henry Knox was still convinced that the program designed by Congress was not as good as it could have been had it been initiated exactly as he designed it. Recall that Knox was not pleased that he did not have oversight of military manufacturing from the inception of the program in 1776. He carried this resentment with him for nearly twenty years. He took several opportunities during the war to attack the efficacy of the DCGMS, even circumventing the department on occasion. Then, when he came to manage the department in the postwar period, Knox looked for opportunities to attack the DCGMS and gain approval for its overhaul. It is unclear why he did not simply use his authority to reform the department, but two events in the 1780s gave weight to his calls for change. The first incident was the threat to the Springfield Arsenal by Shays's Rebellion; the second was the establishment of the constitutional government. Knox reported to Congress in early 1787 that between one thousand five hundred and two thousand disaffected farmers "attempted to prevent the execution of the law in their country" by seizing the stores at Springfield with which to arm themselves.[94] These farmers, identified by the state as Daniel Shays's rebels, though he was not their leader, wanted to close the state's courts to prevent foreclosures on their farms. In response to the threat, Knox called on Bryant to secure the stores and the governor of Massachusetts to call out the militia and defend the post. Governor James Bowdoin raised an army of militia to subdue the rebels, and he asked Knox for the use of the stores at Springfield.[95] Bryant reported that from the arsenal the state army "mounted three four pounders and one 5.1/2 in. Howitzer under direction of Captain Stephens who was in the corps of Artillery in the War. Some hundred of new french arms have been delivered out, and powder & musket cartridges from the magazines."[96] Equipped with confederation arms, the state militia was able to suppress the rebels and restore order. In the aftermath of the rebellion, several congressmen questioned Knox about the feasibility of maintaining operations at Springfield.[97] This gave Knox the opportunity he had been waiting for to propose reform of the military stores system.

Knox's report to Congress on Springfield, presented in March 1787, digressed into a number of topics relating to the arsenal system and the government's management thereof. He began by explaining the benefits of Springfield specifically. Though rebels threatened it, wrote Knox, it had been defended admirably and was now under the protection of militia. He went on to say that not only would it cost an astronomical amount of money to move the operations at the Springfield Arsenal, but the government would also be giving up a generous ninety-nine-year lease on the property. Not to mention, Knox wrote, the government did not have the money to move the stores or establish a new site to receive them. The real problem, wrote Knox, was that the government was not active enough in the care and control of its own property: "[Y]our Secretary is decidedly of the opinion that no Arsenal or Magazine of the United States, can be deemed perfectly secure, unless guarded by a military force bound to obey the orders of Congress. He therefore is utterly at a loss to point out any place, where the stores will be more secure than at Springfield." And Knox reiterated that he "cannot report in favor of removing them a measure, [because] the expenses . . . would be great and immediate, the consequences at least equivocal, if not politically injurious."[98] The heart of the matter for Knox was not Springfield specifically, but Congress's inability to pay for troops to guard its own arsenals or put the arsenals on what Knox believed was a proper footing.

The remainder of Knox's report on Springfield was an examination of necessary reforms in the DCGMS. He began his proposal with an innocuous statement that held great meaning: "Your Secretary has had under his consideration for a long period, a system for the establishment of permanent national Magazines, & Arsenals, throughout the United States." Knox's implication was that the arsenal activities carried on during and after the war were only temporary measures. He was telling Congress that its emergent arsenals needed to be replaced by professional and specifically designed production facilities. Knox's statement reveals that even ten years after the founding of the DCGMS, he did not understand what had been accomplished during the war. He believed Congress had failed, never creating a proper arsenal program because it did not follow his ideas to the letter. He proposed that there be four "principal national deposits" at Springfield, somewhere in Pennsylvania or Maryland, Richmond, and Camden in South Carolina. He noted the importance of transportation and defense in the selection of each site. Within each arsenal he "proposed that the number of one hundred thousand arms, shall be deposited in the respective arsenals [along with] a team of battering artillery and every kind of Stores necessary thereto, field artillery and every necessary equipment for a army of every species of troops."

Knox's recommendations illuminate his underlying frustration. Congress was not doing, and had never done, enough to support the army. He had called for the production of nearly one hundred thousand muskets during the war because he was of the opinion that a replacement musket should be available for every soldier in the field. Knox apparently was not happy with the idea of repair. Repair facilities were not needed, according to Knox, production facilities were: "The Arms Ordnance & Stores deficient, should be manufactured . . . within the United States."[99]

Knox seems to have been ignorant of the manufacturing operations going on in his own department, or how they had evolved from wartime activities. Springfield was producing cannons and carriages throughout the 1780s. There was no need to manufacture tens of thousands of weapons, because there were tens of thousands already in repair or in need of repair. Congress had initiated arms manufacturing during the war but saw no reason for it to continue because of the huge stock of weapons on hand. As late as 1787, when Knox presented his report, he and Congress still had divergent ideas of what constituted adequate stores for the army. What finally bothered Knox, and many other Americans, was that Congress's activities were limited by its own financial weakness. It could not collect taxes, and the states rarely contributed enough to the confederation Treasury.[100] The reason Knox had "not brought [his ideas] forward [before is] because the state of the public treasury has been such as to preclude any expences, but those which are essential to immediate existence."[101] Knox believed that Congress was ignoring future emergencies because it was incapable of doing more than living from day to day.

The various operations of the confederation arsenals were irrelevant to Knox because he believed that Congress did not know what it was doing and that it was not spending enough money to do anything properly. Knox's 1787 comments match very nearly his comments of 1778, which claimed that no one knew more about the proper management of the military stores program than he:

> The Resolutions which the honorable Congress were pleased to pass the 11th of last february, investing the Commissary of Military Stores with the sole charge of all preparations of Ordnance and Military Stores for the field, deprived me as Head of the Ordnance Department of any direction of the department except in a certain degree in the field. During the . . . past campaign I have repeatedly on an emergency found myself at a loss to know where to send for Stores—If I am to continue at the Head of the Ordnance Department I humbly request that I may be invested with the power incidental to the office. That all Artificers, Directors of Laboratories,

Commissaries, Conductors, Clerks, etc. in the department may be put immediately under my direction and myself accountable.[102]

Knox had never given up his belief that Congress had not organized the military stores program correctly and did not offer it proper oversight. But the Confederation Congress was, in Knox's opinion, not interested in nor capable of reforming the military stores program it had created in 1777. It ignored Knox's report, not raising it for discussion until October 2, 1788, a year and a half after it was submitted. Congress had other problems, and the military stores program worked as well as it should for the army's immediate needs. It did not implement Knox's ideas, but political changes were taking shape that would provide fertile ground for Knox to implement his long-held ideas of the proper organization of military stores.

The confederation government was collapsing by 1787. Congress could barely raise a quorum with which to conduct business. The government's Treasury was empty, and Congress could neither pay its bills nor support Knox's efforts to take control of the frontier away from the British. Debts were piling up, government salaries were unpaid, and Congress could not even keep its own arsenal at Springfield secure. Americans who believed the nation needed a stronger central government called for a change, which led to a convention in Philadelphia to reform the confederation. The result was the Constitution of 1787. By 1788, enough support had been secured from the states to implement the new frame of government, and in early 1789, George Washington took office as the first president of the constitutional government. One of his first actions was to secure the creation of a new Department of War and appoint Knox to the command of it. Knox brought his confederation department, its administrators, and all the old government's stores with him into the new government.[103] Washington had always been a supporter of Knox's ideas, and their political relationship at the top of a new, more-centralized government allowed Knox the opportunity to implement his ideas.

Knox was not immediately able to reform his department in the manner he chose. The same problems that haunted the old government haunted the new one: debts and income. The constitutional government inherited the confederation's debts. And though the new government had the ability to levy taxes, it would take time to collect those taxes and create a stable stream of income. Such activities were the government's first priority. Taxes were levied, tax collectors were assigned, and a treasury department was created to organize the government's finances. Finally, a national bank was created to jump-start the nation's financial sector and strengthen the government's fiscal policies.[104] Not until 1791, when these other issues had been dealt with, did Washington broach the issue of military stores. In his second State of the Union address, Washington told Congress that though "the urgency of other affairs has hitherto post-poned any definitive resolution, [the] importance [of] the militia—the post-office and post-roads—the mint—weights and measures—[and] a provision for the sale of the vacant lands of the United States [are] object[s] of primary importance." All those issues bore heavily on the nation's defense and economic development. But so did another issue, he went on to say: "[W]hether viewed in reference to the national security, to the satisfaction of the community, or to the preservation of order . . . the establishment of competent magazines and arsenals . . . naturally present themselves to consideration. The safety of the United States, under Divine Protection, ought to rest on the basis of systematic and solid arrangements [in this matter]."[105]

The respectability of the government and the maintenance of order and security depended, according to Washington, on the establishment of a system of arsenals to support the army and properly care for its military stores. Washington may have been quoting Lincoln on this issue, but that is impossible to know. With matters like debt repayment and taxation to deal with, Congress did not take the time to authorize reforms of the military stores program. Knox was left with the direction of the system he had inherited from the confederation. He was not, however, interested in managing the system; he wanted to change it.

By the 1790s, Knox still had not departed from his idea that the continental arsenals were not a proper system. His recommendations to Washington regarding arsenals stated "the importance . . . necessity and propriety of establishing a system of national defense." Establishing "magazines and arsenals and furnishing them with all necessary apparatus" was a critical component of keeping the nation secure.[106] Knox was repeating what Lincoln had said a decade before. Knox's opposition to the system in existence kept him from seeing what it was and what it had accomplished and investing any additional funds into it as secretary of war under Washington. Instead, he allowed the DCGMS to languish until it could be replaced completely by his own system. The arsenals were left to continue as they had been since 1783, though by 1793, the government had enough money to support Knox with a respectable budget. Knox did not request more for the DCGMS in 1793 than the roughly $23,000 it was already spending annually.[107] Rather than request funding to expand the system he had, Knox chose instead to continue his calls for change. He convinced Washington, and Washington in turn convinced Congress, of the "imperfections in the scheme" and the need to create a new system. Congress's failure to act quickly on the part of a new program led Washington to make it a significant segment of his third State of the Union address. The nation would be unable to present itself to the world and pursue its policies effectively, said Washington, without "placing ourselves in a condition of complete defence, and of exacting from them the fulfillment of their duties towards us."[108] Such "complete defence" was being undermined by the fact that a great number of military stores were being neglected, and the nation, seemingly, had no public or private manufacturing capable of arming its troops. Of course, the opposite was true. Thus, when it came time to reform the military stores system, Washington and Knox actually maintained a great deal of the earlier program and used it as a foundation for their system.

Congress moved quickly after Washington's second request for increased attention to the nation's arsenals and magazines. It did so because the army had suffered several recent defeats at the hands of Native Americans in the Ohio Valley.[109] The House of Representatives created a committee to investigate what the nation needed and what the president specifically wanted in terms of military stores. On March 12, 1794, the committee presented a report to the full House regarding the subject. One day later, the report was made into a bill "for erecting arsenals and magazines" and ordered to lie until a final vote on March 17.[110] On March 17, the House approved $81,865 in spending "for the erecting and repairing of Arsenals and Magazines" and "for the establishment of as many as four national armories [giving] the president wide discretionary powers in executing the order."[111] The bill was passed by the Senate and signed by the president in April.[112] Washington immediately got to work reforming the system. The position of commissary general of military stores was retitled intendant of military stores under the secretary of war. Military manufacturing was taken away from the intendant's responsibilities and made into an independent command under the secretary. Finally, the treasury department was given more responsibility than confederation treasurers had ever had over military stores purchasing.

The cosmetic changes initiated relative to military stores suggested a greater change in arsenal activity than actually occurred. Adjustments chiefly occurred in terms of military stores procurement, but nothing that substantially altered the system. The intendant of military stores retained a great deal of the commissary general's functions. He was in charge of determining, with the help of the war secretary, what weapons and stores were needed by the army. He was also charged with caring for stores that had been procured, and thus the arsenals remained within his command. The intendant did not, however, either procure stores or oversee their production at the armories. The armories were each made into a separate command under the secretary of war, while the actual act of procurement was delegated to the treasury department, which had also taken on the task of purchasing quartermaster stores and provisions for the army. The intendant would draw up a list of what stores were needed, and the treasury department would purchase them. It was then up to the intendant to dispatch inspectors to examine contracted stores and see to their delivery to local depots and arsenals.[113] This was not dissimilar to Continental purchasing operations. Allowing Treasury officials to make the purchases did somewhat complicate the procurement system, and within a decade this element of the system changed and the war department handled all elements of procurement. The only real difference between the old system and the new was that the military stores officer in the war department no longer had charge over the government's production of military stores. What Knox's plan did was remove the armories as subfunctions of the government arsenals and place them on equal footing with those arsenals. The armories were answerable directly to the secretary of war, while the arsenals were answerable to the intendant of military stores. Eventually, the military stores department was subdivided into production components (ordnance, logistics, etc.), with each answerable to the war secretary, but in the short term there was direct continuity from the DCGMS into the federal program.[114] What was most interesting about the federal program was that it made Knox, as secretary of war, the center of all military stores activities, just as he had wanted to be since 1776.

STRUCTURE OF MILITARY STORES MANAGEMENT, 1794–1811

In the new system, the federal government established two national armories, which were intended to become its musket and pistol factories. One armory was constructed at Springfield and the other at Harpers Ferry (after a brief stay at New London, Virginia). At Springfield, weapons manufacturing was separated from other arsenal activities, but the arsenals facilities were given to the armory. Military stores personnel had to find new housing and storage for their operations. Throughout its existence, the Springfield Armory retained a physical layout based on the Springfield Arsenal's original construction. There was a great deal of expansion at Springfield in the nineteenth and twentieth centuries, but the oldest section of the post consisted of manufacturing buildings and warehouses built around a central open square, today known as Armory Square. New buildings were put up next to the eighteenth-century structures, and then as the old arsenal buildings were torn down, new ones were built in their place.[115] An 1817 description of the armory by a visitor reconstructs it this way:

> At the Armory, on the hill, "there is one brick building, 204 by 32 feet, two stories high. . . . One brick building, 60 by 32 feet, two stories high. . . . One building, 100 by 40 feet, two stories high, also of brick . . . ; one brick shop, . . . seventeen dwelling houses. One Pay-Office; Ordnance Yard; Magazine; Block House; and Lumber Yard. The aforesaid buildings are arranged northern the great state road leading to Boston, bordering on a large flat square piece of ground,

fenced and set out with trees, around which is a road about 60 feet wide, leading to the several dwelling houses, occupied by the officers and workmen, the whole assuming a handsome and regular appearance."[116]

Of the buildings mentioned by the visitor, the one-hundred-by-forty-foot structure, the magazine, the block house, the ordnance yard, and the lumber yard were all remnants of the Springfield Arsenal. The magazine was the last remaining structure of the Continental establishment, torn down in 1842. The continuity of the post was assisted by the stone wall built by John Bryant and his men, which encircled most of the armory until well into the nineteenth century. Before the Civil War, the post expanded west with the construction of the New Arsenal Building, which was outside the wall, as can be seen in contemporary drawings. After the 1860s, the post expanded beyond the wall to the north and east, and it was mostly removed, though end sections of the wall remained extant until nearly the end of the century. Military manufacturing under the federal government was built on the physical foundations of the Continental government's Springfield Arsenal.[117]

Washington relied on several key people from the old system, revealing just how little the 1794 system changed what had preceded it. Samuel Hodgdon was the first intendant of military stores, and he served in that position for almost a decade. Using his fourteen years of experience in procurement, Hodgdon developed the policies and procedures used by the government to contract and inspect the private production of weapons. John Bryant, superintendent of the Springfield Arsenal, was kept on as deputy commissary of military stores at the site and charged with purchasing and contracting supplies for workers in the Springfield Armory as well as managing the storage of accouterments. Also remaining at Springfield was brass founder James Byers. While Byers's ordnance furnace was shut down, he was kept on as a foundry man making components for muskets and accouterments as needed by the department until his retirement in 1798. Bryant and Byers shared their experience with the new directors of activities at Springfield and surely had an impact on operations. When Harpers Ferry was finally put into operation, its first superintendent was Joseph Perkins. After serving as superintendent of the Philadelphia armory during the revolution, Perkins worked privately for the military stores department until the early 1790s. In 1794, he was appointed superintendent of the federal armory at New London, Virginia, which was a temporary activity until Harpers Ferry could be surveyed and laid out. Perkins recruited three men to work with him at his new post who had served with him at Philadelphia: William Clark, William Gardiner, and Samuel Bedford. It is likely that Gardiner went with Perkins to Harpers Ferry in 1798, as did newly hired men from

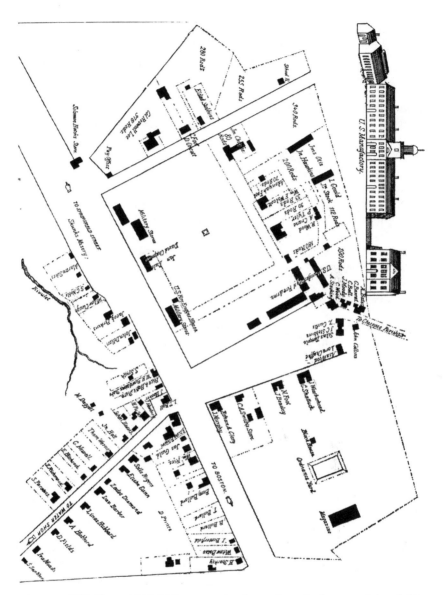

"Armory Hill About 1810." The magazine located on the bottom right of this map is the structure pictured on page 180. It and the ordnance yard made up the east side of the arsenal's square layout. Further original military stores buildings can be seen just to the left of the map's center along what was the southern edge of the arsenal's layout. Other workshops were located on the opposite, or northern, side of the square, but these had been torn down and replaced by 1810. Most of the other structures on the map, were added after the revolution. (*Records of the Springfield Armory. Research and Engineering Division. Box 020, Folder 02, Neg 6570-SA*)

New London who had been trained by the former gunsmiths of the Philadelphia armory. In many interpersonal ways, the experience of military manufacturing from revolutionary Philadelphia became the foundation for production at Harpers Ferry. Perkins served as superintendent until his death in 1806, and not only designed and built the original armory but initiated its first production runs.[118] Several significant and influential human elements of the 1794 military stores program were carried over from the older Continental program.

The final element of continuity from the Continental military stores system to the federal system was in the area of mobilizing private manufacturers. In 1798, the United States came to the brink of war with France in what was known as the Quasi War. Even with its armories, the US Army was not prepared materially for a large-scale conflict. To supplement government production, therefore, the war department embarked on a massive contract process that offered bounties (cash advances) to those manufacturers willing to promise to produce a set number of weapons for the federal government. Manufacturers were committed to producing according to a federal musket pattern, and the muskets had to be produced within a set period of time, which varied according to each contract. Generally, the time limits were one to three years. Hodgdon distributed pattern muskets to the contractors and was charged with examining all finished products. History has remembered the 1798 musket contract as the first instance in which the national government mobilized domestic production through bounties and with the use of a standard pattern, which was a significant step toward interchangeable parts manufacturing similar to what Jean-Baptiste Gribeauval had accomplished. The aura of this historical mythology was enhanced by the fact that Eli Whitney was one of the government's biggest 1798 contractors and one who promised to accomplish interchangeable-parts manufacturing and introduce it to the United States through the contract process. Whitney, of course, is famous as the inventor of a successful cotton gin, and his name became synonymous with manufacturing.

What really struck historians, however, was that a large number of 1798 contractors were not gunsmiths but blacksmiths, tinsmiths, or file makers. The government gave them money with the idea that they would invest in their operations to make them gun manufactories. The government was consciously trying to mobilize national manufacturing with the goal of building domestic weapons-producing capacity. But this was not a new idea. Hodgdon had accomplished this twenty years previously during the war, and Lincoln had called for the government to continue this process. Hodgdon had advanced money to gunsmiths, blacksmiths, furnace men, carpenters, and clothiers with the idea that they use that money to invest in their production capacity or retool to produce for the

Continental government. Hodgdon had very specific, successful experience in contracting, and this came to bear in the 1798 contract operations. The difference in 1798 was that the issuance of the cash was done by the treasury department, which did not always heed Hodgdon's or the war department's calls for greater oversight of contract operations. Hodgdon and his assistants could only evaluate weapons and either accept or reject them.[119] It was up to Treasury officials to continue funding manufacturers or cut them off. Not until after the War of 1812 did the Army gain greater oversight of its own budget. But the concept of using government resources to promote private contract production of weapons was a direct lesson from the DCGMS.

THE WASHINGTON ADMINISTRATION'S ARMS PROGRAM HAS GENERALLY been acknowledged as the beginning of government involvement in American manufacturing. This, however, belies the value of the foundations laid by the DCGMS. The military stores program initiated during the revolution did not die with the revolution. The DCGMS was not as extensive in the confederation period as it was during the war, but the Confederation Congress invested as much money as it could in the care, repair, and acquisition of stores for the support of its army. And these activities kept the nation prepared for war. From 1784 to 1788, as many as twenty-four thousand muskets were repaired, cleaned, and stored.[120] Ammunition was turned and repackaged for proper storage, and stores disparately placed at the conclusion of the war were gathered and placed in proper storage. The confederation military stores system saw the construction of the nation's first brass ordnance foundry and the construction of new magazines at Springfield and West Point. Congress was not able to fully implement the military stores program that Lincoln designed, but it did as much as it could. Production and repair facilities were kept operational at Springfield, West Point, and Philadelphia, though money was not available for construction of two southern arsenals. When Washington put together a new military stores plan, he and Knox used the system that was already in place. They built the Springfield Armory on top of the Springfield Arsenal and used the arsenal's buildings. They used personnel from the Philadelphia Arsenal to develop the Harpers Ferry Armory. And they used a contract-production system to mobilize domestic manufacturing just as the DCGMS had done. The 1776 military stores program seemed destined for dissolution at the end of the revolution. Challenges faced the department from two directions: purpose and funding. If Lincoln had not become an outspoken advocate for military manufacturing, the DCGMS might never have developed a long-term mission. If Hodgdon had not used the same financial finesse in the postwar period that he did during the war, the DCGMS would have collapsed. With the department's collapse, the infrastructure of private manufacturing that existed in the United States would not have been available to support the nation. The 1776 military stores policy impacted government procurement policy over twenty years, from the beginnings of independence through to the founding of a constitutional armory program, and then indirectly for a much longer period.

Conclusion

O N NOVEMBER 26, 1777, NATHANIEL IRISH COMPOSED A REPORT for Benjamin Flower. He provided a detailed outline of the work done by his men at the Carlisle Arsenal over the course of the previous eight months. He began by listing the ammunition and supplies that had been produced as well as the numbers and types of tools that had been made. Irish identified almost every one of the buildings that had been constructed, giving their dimensions and framework. He discussed the logs that had been cut, the mill that had been built miles from the post, and even the blacksmith shop repaired and put into use by his men within the town of Carlisle. Lastly, Irish mentioned the construction of a "magazine of stone and brick 32x70 covered with boards and near ready for powder."[1] The structure, seemingly an afterthought, is the only structure built by the DCGMS to survive to the present.

Nestled within Carlisle Barracks US Army Garrison, the "Hessian Powder Magazine," as it is known, sits on a well-manicured side road.[2] It is surrounded by homes arranged in a suburban setting, just down the street from the Army War College. Despite the bucolic atmosphere, the low, grey stone walls of the magazine give it a brooding appearance. The building's aspect has not changed much in the 250 years since it was built. In 1777, the magazine stood at the end of the lane leading into the arsenal and was the first thing a visitor to the post would see. Its dark appearance contrasted sharply with the bright red and yellow of the brick and wooden workshops behind it. Most of the other structures

Hessian powder magazine at Carlisle Barracks, US Army Garrison. This structure can be located on the map on page 101 directly under the word "United." It was used as a powder magazine and store house until the twentieth century. (*Author*)

were two stories, dwarfing the magazine and making it seem gloomy. It was not meant to be an inviting building. Individuals could only enter the magazine through one of two doors, or rather small tunnels, built into the four-and-a-half-foot-thick walls. The interior walls were brick and covered with plaster, which helped to lighten the confining feel of the building's heavy construction. Six brick interior dividing walls created seven spaces for storing various types of ammunition: loose musket and cannon powder, as well as fixed musket cartridges and artillery shot. To provide air flow for the magazine, vents were built through the walls around foundation pillars that gave the building additional stability and security in case of explosion. The magazine was an innovative adaptation of John Muller's work that survived the revolution, Confederate arsonists, service with the Quartermaster Department, and use as an Indian school.[3] It stands today as a lone testimony to the short- and long-term impact Continental operations had on American history.

The DCGMS provided its most significant impact by equipping the Continental Army with the weapons it needed to fight and win the War for Independence. It did this by mobilizing American manufacturers and craftsmen to large-scale production using innovative ideas, workspace organization, and labor methods. The result was the successful introduction of the Industrial Revolution to America through the revelation that large-scale manufacturing and industrial organizations could be productive in the domestic economy. Over the long term, the DCGMS influenced the role of the federal government in guiding national manufacturing. It also continued to encourage American producers to push the boundaries of manufacturing innovation and develop more effective large-scale operations.

The DCGMS was a fluid organization that expanded, contracted, and diversified its operations during the war. In early 1780, the department had a staff of more than four hundred administrators and laborers working at three national arsenals and several storage depots. Under the commissary general, deputies procured stores and directed their shipment. Within the arsenals were craftsmen of every type manufacturing weapons, accouterments, and ammunition. The department employed superintendents of arms and ordnance to oversee contractors' operations and assist with production. In addition to government activities, the department engaged in the production of more than 130 craft facilities, ironworks, forges, and mills. Through these varied activities, the department achieved large-scale production of weapons and accouterments. Arsenal armorers and private gunsmiths manufactured or repaired over sixty-two thousand muskets and a comparable number of ramrods and bayonets. Public and private craftsmen made thousands of cartridge boxes, priming wires, artillery tubes, fuses, and bayonet scabbards. Government artisans manufactured over two hundred artillery carriages and two hundred ammunition wagons that were supplemented by the private production of over 150 pieces of artillery and 785 tons of shot and shells. Additionally, Continental laboratory workers fixed thirty-five thousand artillery shot and eleven million musket cartridges. Throughout every element of production, the DCGMS produced its own tools and shared them with private manufacturers and other government departments.[4]

While it is difficult to determine if government operations were effective in meeting the needs of the Continental Army, a correlation can be drawn between government production of military stores and their availability on the battlefield. Military commanders produced dozens of widely varying estimates throughout the war regarding the amount of stores necessary for the war effort, leaving no clear comprehension of the Continental Army's military stores needs. It is telling, however, that following the government's mobilization efforts, army inventories consistently revealed reserves of weapons, accouterments, and ammunition. And from that point on, George Washington's army was never in want of arms. Reflecting on his service in the Continental Army, Joseph Plumb Martin wrote that "Uncle Sam was always careful to supply us with . . . arms and equipment."[5] It was only because of government action that weapons were available to arm General Horatio Gates's army when it faced off against John Burgoyne at Saratoga in 1777. The following year, the department armed General John Sullivan's operation against the Iroquois and allowed Washington's army to take the field at Monmouth Courthouse. The DCGMS provided enough support that Americans tried, unsuccessfully, to beat back the British invasion of Savannah, and Washington considered an attack against British-held New York City.

Moreover, the department equipped the Southern Army not once but three times in 1780, after each of its major defeats. There were then enough stores produced to support Washington's army at Yorktown in 1781. Ultimately, when the war ended, vast amounts of stores were left unused in government depots. The production and impact achieved by the DCGMS was only possible because innovative methods had been used to overcome significant wartime dislocations and economic challenges.

The nation was struck with several tribulations that the DCGMS strove to overcome. First, the colonies were not prepared for war. As the Continental Congress called up troops, it relied on the colonies to supply those troops with weapons, accouterments, and ammunition. Colonial governments complained that they could not gather enough weapons to arm their men because there were simply not enough weapons on hand in the colonies. Stores were taken from the British army, from British fortifications, and from citizens, both Loyalist and patriot. State governments tried to purchase weapons from gunsmiths and invested in their operations as a means of encouragement. Governments looked overseas for weapons, but trade could not be accomplished at the level needed by a nation at war. And worse, many imported stores were of poor quality.

No typical sources of production or acquisition were sufficient, which was the second problem the DCGMS faced. On their own, American craftsmen could not meet the needs of the Continental Army. Several states established public manufacturing operations, but these were expensive and slow to mobilize because they relied on traditional craft operations.

Such activities served only to reveal a third problem, this one faced by craftsmen themselves. The war destroyed established means of supply and transport. The British Royal Navy intercepted trade bound for the Americas and often stopped even intercoastal trade. The British army destroyed infrastructure, and the army's presence in various places kept craftsmen from their suppliers and markets. In response, the US government embarked on a program to mobilize and innovate the nation's manufacturing sector.

Government arsenals were the heart of the military stores program. Artificers employed at Philadelphia, Carlisle, and Springfield manufactured and repaired numerous stores for the army. Management and coordination of production processes made large-scale production of supplies possible. The government employed management processes developed in Europe. American administrators borrowed production systems from European arsenals and other large-scale manufacturing operations, and they adapted them to their own wartime needs. Such systems like the protofactory allowed for the rapid production of numerous simple items like a cartridge, while centralized manufacturing promoted the rapid production and repair of more complex items like a gunlock.

Congress and its military stores administrators knew that arsenals alone could not supply all of the army's needs. Private manufacturing had to be mobilized. Quantity and quality could be directly controlled at government arsenals by government administrators, but a system of control also had to be developed over private production. That system was an assortment of inspectors who oversaw contracts at various levels. Deputy military stores commissaries and arsenal managers reviewed the purchases they made from private contractors. The government also employed superintendents of arms and ordnance to inspect the production of those items at private gunsmith shops and iron furnaces. In most cases, craftsmen had never produced military stores, and government inspectors not only reviewed products but also assisted in the production process. Inspectors drew up plans and product specifications; they trained craftsmen in the organizational techniques they would need to produce on a large scale. Throughout the war, the inspection system not only directed private production but identified areas where public resources were necessary to jump-start operations. The DCGMS responded to artisans' economic struggles by providing cash, materials, and transport.

The Continental government and its administrators learned how to innovate production through the idea exchange that was at the heart of the eighteenth century Atlantic economy. Written evidence of the ideas of the Industrial Revolution abounded in America before the war. The Woolwich Arsenal was often a topic of discussion in colonial newspapers, and books by professor John Muller of the arsenal's artillery academy were available in lending libraries. In addition, bookstores provided numerous volumes on military arts. During the war, Frenchmen arrived in the United States to help the nation win its freedom, and they brought knowledge of industrial developments. Peter Penet and Lewis Garanger taught Americans how to centralize and promote manufacturing. Americans had also experimented with large-scale production methods prior to the war, but aside from iron plantations, these attempts had been unsuccessful. The United Company had never been able to rely solely on factory production, while centralized pottery mills and glassworks had only survived for short periods of time. Ironworks had shown a remarkable ability to grow to meet the needs of the local American economy, but their development had been gradual and was not widespread by the time of the revolution. Together, these various elements of thought and example were a significant base of knowledge for Americans to draw from when organizing wartime manufacturing.

The war did not bring an end to Congress's military stores program, but it did remove a great deal of the meaning behind the program's existence. Benjamin Lincoln took it upon himself to give a postwar purpose to the program and instructed Congress on the peacetime value of government manufacturing and government encouragement of private manufacturing. Lincoln told Congress in 1783 that the government's arsenals and contracting operations were necessary to keep the nation prepared for war. The revolution proved the capacity of American manufacturing if it was properly supported. Congress needed to continue to take an active role in promoting domestic manufacturing to make the nation not only economically self-sufficient but capable of defending itself as well. As secretary at war, Lincoln tried to implement these ideas and convinced Congress to support them, but he was frustrated by Congress's financial and administrative limitations. After Lincoln's resignation, Samuel Hodgdon took on the task of continuing the military stores program. Stores were gathered and repaired. A national ordnance foundry was created, and contractors were retained to assist the department. Budget limitations kept the department small during the confederation period, but it was active, laying the foundation for the development of larger government manufacturing operations under the constitutional government. As president, Washington reformed the military stores program, but the resulting system continued to coordinate the public and private manufacture of weapons for the army.

The most important legacy of the DCGMS was a culture of innovation that Hodgdon brought with him from the old system into the new one created by Washington. Hodgdon served as director of the military stores program for almost twenty years, and while he did not implement many of the operations within the department, he came to know them better than perhaps anyone else. It was Henry Knox, Benjamin Flower, Joseph Boehm, Joseph Perkins, Daniel Joy, David Mason, and others who created government production systems using wage labor, managed labor, and centralized manufacturing. These men led the building of integrated production facilities and oversaw the initial mobilization of the arsenals.

When Hodgdon took over the system in 1779, he had to get his head around the complex organization the DCGMS had become. He learned how impactful the government was in promoting manufacturing and how it influenced private producers to greater efforts. Hodgdon used the system he inherited to encourage iron makers to continue and increase their production. He sought knowledge from men like Perkins and Penet. Until the end of the war, Hodgdon was intimately connected with each element of departmental operations and involved in every production contract through either initiation or review. Hodgdon was, therefore, well prepared to manage the system that Lincoln initiated after the revolution. He contracted with his wartime associates and invested in the innovative ideas of Thomas Potts. Many of the businesses in which Hodgdon invested were still in operation well after the war. Ebenezer Cowell, John Faesch, Richard Backhouse, Thomas Lawrence, Jacob Baldwin, and numerous ironmasters survived the war and thrived afterward because of the investment of the DCGMS. Hodgdon took all this experience to the position of intendant of military stores under Washington. The collective knowledge of the DCGMS flowed through Hodgdon into the armory system created by the president and Knox, his secretary of war.

The armory program rested heavily on a foundation built by the DCGMS. In 1794, Congress initiated the construction of two facilities for the production of weapons for the army. Springfield was chosen as the site of the first armory because of government operations already occurring there. John Bryant, superintendent of the arsenal, continued in that position but had the armory removed from his command. His post became the supply-and-storage facility serving the armory's needs. James Byers, brass founder at the arsenal, was repurposed from making ordnance to casting musket components as he had done during the war. The second armory site was at Harpers Ferry, and the man chosen to get it up and running was Joseph Perkins. Perkins had been director of the Philadelphia armory during the war but had gone into private production in the 1780s. Hodgdon recruited him back into government service, and Perkins brought several Philadelphia armory associates with him when he headed south to Virginia. After a burst of initial involvement, the personnel from the DCGMS involved in the armory program faded away. But their ideas did not, and Springfield and Harpers Ferry became seats of innovation in the early republic. It was at Springfield that Thomas Blanchard developed a machine lathe that virtually removed human involvement in the making of gunstocks. The federal establishment in this period also adopted Gribeauval's system of gauges and worked to streamline production activities. One result of this adoption was that John Hall first demonstrated machine-made interchangeable-parts production at Harpers Ferry. More important than the innovations themselves was the fact that the armory staffs shared their developments with each other as well as with private manufacturers. It was no coincidence that the Connecticut River valley (home to the Springfield Armory) became a hotbed of machine-tool and arms manufacturing. It was these operations, like Samuel Colt's armory, that translated government innovations into private-sector usage. These developments, while several decades after the revolution, rested on the ideas championed by the DCGMS, that the government should support manufacturing and improvements in manufacturing.

"To preserve our Freedom and Independence" wrote Benjamin Lincoln in 1783, "we should . . . maintain proper Magazines and Arsenals [and] Manufactories for military stores . . . erected under the immediate inspection of the public." Moreover, wrote the secretary at war to Congress, "such bounties [should] be given as would be sufficient inducement for individuals to attempt [manufacturing] establishement and perfection." Lincoln had learned from the revolution what Benjamin

Flower had understood from the beginning. The United States had to produce its own weapons and mobilize its own resources in order to fight the British Empire. But Lincoln had also absorbed a more important lesson from the war that Flower had not lived long enough to learn. The nation, he wrote, "should not [defer] this business . . . until the necessities of such a situation [shall again] declare its propriety."[6] Having secured liberty through manufacturing, wrote Lincoln, the United States could only maintain that independence by continuing to promote manufacturing.

Notes

ABBREVIATIONS

CBC   Carlisle Barracks Collection

CBOB   *Carlisle Barracks Orderly Book*

JCC   *Journals of the Continental Congress*

LSH   Letters sent by Commissary General of Military Stores and Assistant Quartermaster Samuel Hodgdon, . . . July 19, 1778 to May 24, 1784

MCS   Minutes of the Council of Safety

MEC   Minutes of the Executive Council

PAFS   *Pennsylvania Archives, First Series*

PASS   *Pennsylvania Archives, Second Series*

PCC   *Papers of the Continental Congress*

PGW   *Papers of George Washington*

PHK   *Papers of Henry Knox*

PWH   *Papers of William Heath*

RMS   Records of Military Stores Received and Delivered at Philadelphia, March 1780 to September 1784

INTRODUCTION

1 *Journal of the Provincial Congress of New York*, vol. 2, 286, 304, 313, quoted in Hugh Jameson, "Equipment for the Militia of the Middle States, 1775–1781," *Journal of the American Military Institute* 3, no. 1 (Spring 1939): 33; William Heath to George Washington, June 30, 1777, Springfield Papers, Massachusetts Historical Society Collection, 7th ser., vol. 4, 113, cited in Harry Andrew Wright, comp., *The Genesis of the United States Armory at Springfield, Massachusetts: Being Excerpts from Contemporary Documents* (Springfield: U.S. Army Military History Research Collection, 1919), hereafter *Genesis of the US Armory*. The term *accouterments* refers to a host of items that were part of an army's operation, including cartridge boxes, canteens, axes, haversacks, bayonets, bayonet sheaths, knives, and similar items. Accouterments of war were usually grouped with weapons in the term *military stores*, which identified a broad assortment of weapons, cannons, accouterments, tools, and items that made an army a fighting force. They differ from quartermaster stores in that quartermaster stores made army life livable. Quartermasters provided food, clothing, housing, and transport. Military stores personnel provided weapons, ammunition,

ordnance, and the supplies that assisted in their use. Military stores either killed people or made it possible for another store to kill people.

2 Letter of an Officer of Burgoyne's Captured Army, November 15, 1777, *Letters of Brunswick and Hessian Officers* (Albany, NY: 1891), cited in Wright, *Genesis of the US Armory.*

3 Robert Middlekauff, *The Glorious Cause: The American Revolution, 1763–1789* (New York: Oxford University Press, 1982), 378–384; George Washington to Philip Schuyler, July 12, 1777, 10:261–262, and Ezekiel Cheever to George Washington, March 15, 1777, 14:187, in John C. Fitzpatrick, ed., *The Writings of George Washington from the Original Manuscript Sources, 1745–1799* (Washington, DC: Government Printing Office, 1931–44); Samuel Chase Motion Regarding Springfield Arsenal, October 4, 1777, r42, i36, v1, p13, in *Papers of the Continental Congress* (Washington, DC: Government Printing Office, 1948), microfilm, hereafter PCC.

4 Fred Anderson, *Crucible of War: The Seven Years' War and the Fate of Empire in British North America, 1754–1766* (New York: Alfred A. Knopf, 2000), 560–562. The British army removed most stores from America because it continued to use them in other parts of the empire, to support troops sent to Canada, Appalachia, the West Indies, and India. Royal garrisons in the thirteen colonies had supplies to support the troops stationed there, but few others. At sites like Fort Ticonderoga, where large amounts of stores were left, those stores were old and of marginal quality.

5 Military stores department records indicate that 88,556 muskets arrived from France either directly or through the West Indies during the course of the war. Of those weapons, 46 percent, or just under forty-one thousand, arrived prior to 1780. Sixty-five percent of the forty-one thousand that arrived prior to 1780 (twenty-seven thousand) required repair work, and about seven thousand went into the hands of provincial government purchasers. Thus, out of the possible store of French weapons in 1777, only about seven thousand were immediately available to the Continental Army. The majority of weapons received from the French arrived after June 1781, and were not available for use against the British in the southern campaigns. From June 1781 until the end of the war, 47,586 muskets were delivered from the king's own arsenals. These weapons, delivered when the Americans no longer needed them, were mostly all new. The author has calculated these figures and others referenced below from the PCC and the "Records of Military Stores Received and Delivered at Philadelphia, March 1780 to September 1784," *Numbered Record Books Concerning Military Operations and Service, Pay and Settlement of Accounts and Supplies in the War Department Collection of Revolutionary War Records,* microfilm (Washington, DC: Government Printing Office, 1973), M853, rolls 37, 38, vols. 94, 122, 132, and 133, hereafter RMS.

6 *Journal of the Provincial Congress of New York,* vol. 2, 286, 304, 313, quoted in Jameson, "Equipment for the Militia" 33; Don Higginbotham, *The War of American Independence: Military Attitudes, Policies, and Practice, 1763–1789* (Boston: Northeastern University Press, 1983), 308.

7 For full examination of wartime economic dislocations see Richard Buel Jr., *In Irons: Britain's Naval Supremacy and the American Revolutionary Economy* (New Haven: Yale University Press, 1998).

8 PCC, Commissary of Military Stores Return of Ordnance and Stores, March 18, 1784, r155, i143, 211–241.

9 The National Archives has compiled these records on microfilm as *Numbered Record Books Concerning Military Operations and Service, Pay and Settlement of Accounts and Supplies in the War Department Collection of Revolutionary War Records* (Washington, DC: Government Printing Office, 1973), microfilm, M853.

10 Buel, *In Irons*, 58–59; Walter Millis, *Arms and Men: A Study of American Military History*, paperback (New York: Mentor, 1956), 33.

11 Erna Risch, *Supplying Washington's Army* (Washington, DC: Center of Military History, 1986), 338. Risch's statement implies that the guns delivered by *Amphitrite* were fit for service.

12 Neil Longley York, *Mechanical Metamorphosis: Technological Change in Revolutionary America* (Westport, CT: Greenwood, 1985), 76–77.

13 Ibid., 79. York wrote on page 73 of *Mechanical Metamorphosis*, "If not for the tremendous volume of foreign aid brought to the colonies in American-built merchantmen and coasters throughout the war, and from 1775 to 1777 in particular, the patriot war effort might have foundered." He went on to give American gunsmiths credit for their work, stating, "With . . . an expanded domestic industry after 1777, and official French aid in 1778, the most glaring [weapons] deficiencies were eradicated." But, he wrote, "Munitions imported from Europe and the West Indies were vital to the American war effort. The patriots were simply not prepared for war and could not fend for themselves. They were fortunate that Europeans willingly bailed them out." (79–80). York's comments suggest that while Americans strove to produce sufficient numbers of weapons, their army would have been unable to take the field without European support. This was not the case.

14 Ibid., 80.

15 Lucille Horgan, *Forged in War: The Continental Congress and the Origin of Military Supply and Acquisition Policy* (Westport, CT: Greenwood, 2003), 152.

16 David Lewis Salay, "Arming for War: The Production of War Material in Pennsylvania for the American Armies during the Revolution" (PhD diss., University of Delaware, 1977), 14.

17 Ibid., 18.

18 Benjamin Flower to Johnston Smith, November 11, 1777, in Charles Lukens, et al., *Carlisle Barracks Orderly Book, 1777–1780* (Pittsburgh: Microfilm Corporation of Pennsylvania, 1980), microfilm, 1–3, hereafter *CBOB*.

19 Michael Stephenson, *Patriot Battles: How the War of Independence Was Fought* (New York: HarperCollins, 2007), 122–126, 131, 140–143; Don Nardo, *Weapons of War* (San Diego: Lucent Books, 2003), 16–30.

20 RMS; Nardo, *Weapons of War*, 23.

21 Harold L. Peterson, *Round Shot and Rammers: An Introduction to Muzzle-loading Land Artillery in the United States* (New York: Bonanza Books, 1969), 41.

22 Ibid., 41, 42, 48.

23 Melvin H. Jackson and Carel de Beer, *Eighteenth Century Gunfounding: The Verbruggens at the Royal Brass Foundry, a Chapter in the History of Technology* (Washington, DC: Smithsonian Institution Press, 1974), 60.

24 Peterson, *Round Shot*, 24–30; S. James Gooding, *An Introduction to British Artillery in North America*, 6th printing (Alexandria Bay, NY: Museum Restoration Service, 1988, originally published 1965), 38–41.

25 Peterson, *Round Shot*, 13–62.

26 The effective range of an aimed musket shot was roughly fifty yards. Beyond that distance, musket-ball trajectories varied widely, making it useless for troops to aim at their enemy. Troops were never instructed to aim at a specific target because by the time opposing forces were close enough for aiming to matter, they were instructed to fix bayonets and charge for hand-to-hand combat.
27 Nardo, *Weapons of War*, 47–62.

CHAPTER 1: "THE PEOPLE . . . CANNOT HELP THEMSELVES"

1 John Gallagher, *The Battle of Brooklyn 1776* (New York: Sarpedon, 1995), 115, 119; Christopher Ward, *The War of the Revolution*, 2 vols (New York: Macmillan, 1952), 1:223.
2 PCC, George Washington to the President of Congress, October 4, 1776, r167, i152, v3, p103.
3 Gallagher, *Battle of Brooklyn*, 264–266, 274.
4 George Washington to John Hancock, November 14, 1776, *The Papers of George Washington, Revolutionary War Series*, Philander D. Chase, ed. (Charlottesville: University Press of Virginia, 1985–1991), 7:155, hereafter *PGW*.
5 Ibid., George Washington to John Hancock, December 31, 1776, 7:495.
6 June 6, 1775, and November 28, 1776, *Journals of the Continental Congress*, "A Century of Lawmaking for a New Nation, U.S. Congressional Documents and Debates, 1774–1873," Law Library of Congress, accessed January 8, 2002, https://memory.loc.gov/ammem/amlaw/lwjc.html, hereafter *JCC*. Retreating Continental and militia troops abandoned arms and accouterments that had been damaged in battle. Continental quartermaster Thomas Mifflin was able to secure some five hundred thousand musket cartridges to resupply the army but no weapons or accouterments. Pennsylvania's military stores commissary, Robert Towers, emptied his magazine for the Continental Army but could provide no more than one hundred thousand cartridges, one hundred rounds of shot, and seven six-pound cannon. New Jersey had nothing available to support its own militia let alone Washington's army. *PGW*, Thomas Mifflin to George Washington, November 26, 1776, 7:219–220; September 18, 1776, October 4, 1776, and January 22, 1777, Minutes of the Council of Safety, *Pennsylvania Archives, Colonial Records*, 16 vols., ed. Samuel Hazard (Philadelphia: Joseph Severns, 1852–), vols 10–11, hereafter MCS; PCC, Samuel Griffin to Richard Peters, September 8, 1776, r95, i78, v10, p33.
7 Richard M. Ketchum, *The Winter Soldiers: The Battles for Trenton and Princeton* (New York: Henry Holt, 1973), 359.
8 "Robert Auchmuty to the Earl of Huntingdon, January 8, 1777," *The American Revolution: Writings from the War of Independence*, ed. John Rhodehamel (New York: Library Classics, 2001), 233.
9 See E. Wayne Carp, *To Starve the Army at Pleasure: Continental Army Administration and American Political Culture, 1775–1783*, (Chapel Hill: University of North Carolina Press, 1984), xi, 14–15.
10 JCC, May 27, 1775.
11 JCC, June 10 and July 16, 1775.
12 JCC, June 3 and November 4, 1775; Edmund Cody Burnett, *The Continental Congress: A Definitive History of the Continental Congress from Its Inception in 1774 to March 1789* (New York: W.W. Norton, 1964, first published in 1941), 82.

13 Anderson, *Crucible of War*, 11–32; Howard H. Peckham, *The Colonial Wars, 1689–1762* (Chicago: University of Chicago Press, 1964), ch. 1; Woody Holton, *Forced Founders: Indians, Debtors, Slaves & the Making of the American Revolution in Virginia* (Chapel Hill: University of North Carolina Press, 1999), 33–38; Ian Barnes, *The Historical Atlas of the American Revolution* (New York: Routledge, 2000), 14; *Colonial Williamsburg Official Guidebook & Map*, 6th ed. (Williamsburg, VA: Colonial Williamsburg Foundation, 1970), 34–36; Marjoleine Kars, *Breaking Loose Together: The Regulator Rebellion in Pre-Revolutionary North Carolina* (Chapel Hill: University of North Carolina Press, 2002), 13–17.

14 Robert A. Gross, *The Minutemen and Their World* (New York: Hill and Wang, 1976), 68–69.

15 Letter of Nathaniel Shaw Jr. to Eliphalet Dyer, December 14, 1774, *Naval Documents of the American Revolution*, 11 vols., ed. William Bell Clark (Washington. DC: Government Printing Office, 1964–1981), 1:178, cited in James Mulholland, *A History of Metals in Colonial America* (Tuscaloosa: University of Alabama Press, 1981), 120–122; Charles Hoadly, et al., comp., *The Public Records of the State of Connecticut, 1776–1784* (Hartford: 1894–), 15:17–18, 90–91, 199, 187–290, cited in York, *Mechanical Metamorphosis*, 65; Louis F. Middlebrook, *Maritime Connecticut during the American Revolution* (Salem, MA: Essex Institute, 1925), 14–15; Samuel Green Arnold, *History of the State of Rhode Island, 1700–1790*, 2 vols. (New York: D. Appelton, 1860), 2:343; Report of the Committee appointed to proportion the Powder, &c., to the several Towns, April 22, 1775, *Records of the Colony of Rhode Island and Providence Plantations in New England*, ed. John Russell Bartlett (Providence: A. Crawford Greene, 1862), 309; Richard Francis Upton, *Revolutionary New Hampshire* (Hanover, CT: Dartmouth College Publications, 1936), 22–23; Townsend Scudder, *Concord: American Town* (Boston: Little, Brown, 1947), 80–81; PCC, Benjamin Church to Maurice Cane, n.d., 1775, r166, i152, v1, p193, Return of Artillery at Ticonderoga and Crown Point, July 7, 1775, r189, i170, v1, p25.

16 Joseph Tiedemann, *Reluctant Revolutionaries: New York City and the Road to Independence, 1763–1776* (Ithaca, NY: Cornell University Press, 1997), 233; Higginbotham, *War of American Independence*, 50; York, *Mechanical Metamorphosis*, 65, 99; Buel, *In Irons*, 84–85; Middlebrook, *Maritime Connecticut*, 11–12.

17 Horgan, *Forged in War*, 6.

18 JCC, April 9, 1777.

19 MCS, September 7, 1775. The Pennsylvania Council of Safety was created by the colonial assembly in 1775 to replace the governor and exercise executive power within the province. After independence in 1776, it was re-formed as the Committee of Safety, but for continuity the organization will be referred to as the Council of Safety. Pennsylvania did not have an organized militia. The provincial government, so long dominated by Quakers, never saw a need for one. Consequently, Pennsylvanians organized themselves into local associations. Known as Associators, they purchased arms and ammunition for themselves and voluntarily trained for combat. Patriots made use of these men as a police force against Tories in the early days of the revolution and purchased arms for recruits.

20 MCS, October 14, 1775.

21 Order of Committee Respecting Fire Arms, December 30, 1775, 4:692, *Pennsylvania Archives, First Series*, 12 vols., ed. Samuel Hazard (Philadelphia: Joseph Severns, 1852–), hereafter *PAFS*.

22 *PCC*, George Washington to President of Congress, July 21, 1775, r166, i152, v1, p35, August 4–5, 1775, r166, i152, v1, p51; Middlekauff, *Glorious Cause*, 291–292.

23 *PCC*, Richard Gridley Inventory of Ordnance Stores Necessary for an Army of 20,000 Men, October 20, 1775, r186, i169, v1, p103, W. James Return of Ordnance, November 3, 1775, r179, i161, p452, Thomas Cooper's Return of Ordnance Stores on the Vessels Captured Near Montreal, November 20, 1775, r172, i153, v1, p114, Return of Artillery at Ticonderoga and Crown Point, July 7, 1775, r189, i170, v1, p25, Anthony Wayne to John Hanson, April 26, 1776, r179, i161, p194, Philip Schuyler to John Hancock, September 19, 1775, r172, i153, v1, p109. Wayne and Schuyler were capable of exaggeration. Wayne could have been trying to make a point to get results from Congress. Schuyler may have been angry at not receiving command of the Canadian expedition and therefore did not want to support it. *JCC*, February 20, 1776. Washington's first chief of artillery, Samuel Gridley, estimated that the Main Army would need at least seventy-six cannons to face the enemy. The Northern Army would need a similar number. There were, however, strategic sites throughout America that needed defending by artillery. Americans seized artillery early in the war, but much of it was already used before the Continental Army even existed. A congressional committee formed in February 1776 to review the army's artillery situation found that despite the numbers of ordnance confiscated, an additional 372 pieces of ordnance were required. Risch, *Supplying Washington's Army*, 350; Battalion Returns, Winter–Spring 1776, 10:1–253, *Pennsylvania Archives, Second Series*, 19 vols., ed. John B. Linn and William Henry Egle (Harrisburg, PA: Benjamin Singerly, 1874), hereafter *PASS*; MCS, September 11, 1775, October 20, 1775, October 23, 1775, November 8, 1775. Congress agreed to purchase weapons for the remainder of the Pennsylvania troops raised, but this did not correct the problem of procurement.

24 *PASS*, Committee of Safety's Recommendations to Manufacture Pikes, August 26, 1775, 1:587–88.

25 *PCC*, George Washington to John Hancock, April 22, 1776, r166, i152, v1, p603.

26 MCS, September 29, 1775. John J. McCusker, *Money and Exchange in Europe and America, 1600–1775: A Handbook* (Chapel Hill: University of North Carolina Press, 1978), 7n9; John J. McCusker, "How Much Is That in Real Money? A Historical Price Index for Use as a Deflator of Money Values in the Economy of the United States," *Proceedings of the American Antiquarian Society* 3, pt. 2 (October 1991): 319. According to McCusker's calculations, one British pound was equal to $4.44 in 1775. *Dollar* was the term for a Spanish piece of eight, which was the coin on which the American government based its Continental currency. Likewise, state-issued currencies were related to the Spanish dollar because they tied their value to Continental currency. All monetary units in this book will either be expressed in, or can be correlated to, dollars at the conversion amount $4.44:1 pound. When figures are cited from DCGMS or other government sources, they reflect inflation generally starting from a basis of the value expressed here. The $90,132 as expressed by the state was £20,300. Buel, *In Irons*, 37. Buel noted that when Parliament decided to start seizing ships

entering or leaving American ports after March 1, 1776, it was merely formaliz-ing a situation that had existed since the war began. August 13, 1778, 11:551, Minutes of the Executive Council, *Pennsylvania Archives, Colonial Records*, hereafter MEC; *PAFS,* Robert Morris to Council, December 23, 1778, 7:125. The Executive Council replaced the Council of Safety in early 1777. *JCC,* September 18, September 25, December 20, and December 26, 1775; *Pennsylvania Gazette,* August 7, 1776; PCC, Robert Morris to John Hancock, December 21, 1776, r150, i137, v4, p21. The Secret Committee was titled as such because all congressional minutes were public. Congress did not want its arms acquisition efforts to be on record, so while all Secret Committee reports were mentioned in the records, its specific activities were not recorded.

27 PCC, Report of Henry Gardner, October 5, 1775, r79, i65, v1, p67; *The Journals of Each Provincial Congress of Massachusetts in 1774 and 1775 and of the Committee of Safety* (Boston: Dutton and Wentworth, 1838), 30, cited in Mulholland, *History of Metals,* 121. Using McCusker's conversion rate, $7,259.40 is equal to £1,635, and $88,800 is equal to £20,000, which is how the values were expressed in the original documents. McCusker, *Money and Exchange,* 7n9; McCusker, "How Much Is That," 319.

28 PCC, Henry Gardner statement on actions of Massachusetts in war, October 5, 1775, r79, i65, v1, p67, Massachusetts Council to John Hancock, March 20, 1777, r79, i65, v1, p191, Maryland General Assembly resolve regarding state militia, April 7, 1777, r84, i70, p189. MCS, September 29, 1775. The number of arms purchased by the state government was found by adding individual pur-chases reported in the minutes of the following council dates: September 11, October 20, 23, November 8, 17, 29, and December 23, 1775. The figure as expressed by the state for purchase expenditures was £40,825. By the end of September 1775, the council estimated it had spent and would spend by the end of the year over $386,280 to purchase arms, ordnance, and other military sup-plies. McCusker, *Money and Exchange,* 7n9; McCusker, "How Much Is That," 319, for currency conversion rates.

29 PCC, New York Committee of Safety to John Hancock, September 23, 1775, r81, i67, v1, p75.

30 PCC, Virginia Council of State to John Hancock, July 27, 1776, r85, i71, v1, p37. The Council of State was an advisory body that assisted the governor in managing the state government. The council's findings were supported by events in South Carolina, where the Provincial Assembly offered $4,440 for the con-struction of an iron furnace in the state to support munitions manufacturing. The bounty was never claimed. Peter Force, ed., *American Archives,* 9 vols. (Washington, DC: M. St. Clair-Clarke and Peter Force, 1837–1853), 4:71–73, cited in York, *Mechanical Metamorphosis,* 67.

31 JCC, February 12, 1776, and March 21, 1776; PCC, John Hancock to Trenton Committee, January 25, 1776, r23, i12A, v1, p46, Trenton Committee of Safety to John Hancock, January 30, 1776, r82, i68, p59. MCS, February 27, 1776, April 27, 1776, May 20, 1776, June 17, 1776, July 15, 1776.

32 York, *Mechanical Metamorphosis,* 65; PCC, William Heath to George Washington, April 21, 1777, r167, i152, v4, p151, George Washington to the President of Congress, July 7, 1777, r167, i152, v4, p327.

33 John J. McCusker and Russell R. Menard, *The Economy of British America, 1607–1789, with Supplementary Bibliography* (Chapel Hill: University of North Carolina Press, 1991, originally published 1985), 309–330; Carl Bridenbaugh,

The Colonial Craftsman (New York: Dover Publications, 1990, originally published 1950), 129; Edwin Tunis, *Colonial Craftsmen and the Beginnings of American Industry* (Baltimore: Johns Hopkins University Press, 1965), 14; Joel Ferree to Benjamin Poultney, August 7, 1775, *PASS*, cited in Carlton O. Wittlinger, "The Small Arms Industry of Lancaster County, 1710–1840," *Pennsylvania Magazine of History and Biography* 24 (April 1957): 127. Wittlinger noted that Joel Ferree of Lancaster County could, with his assistants, manufacture three muskets per week, or one per person per day, if a master and two assistants worked together.

34 Arcadi Gluckman and L.D. Satterlee, *American Gun Makers* (Harrisburg, PA: Stackpole, 1953). Gluckman and Satterlee's book is a listing of all gunsmiths they could find reference to in available sources from 1700 to 1860. Their sources for the revolutionary period included published archives of state governments during the war. The term *gunsmiths* refers to both musket and rifle makers. Gluckman and Satterlee point out that gunsmiths were hired in the colonial period to arm militiamen. Rifle makers, on the other hand, provided weapons for the consumer market on the frontier. Both types of gunsmiths were skilled in the production of gunlocks, which were the most complex part of a firearm. Many rifle makers, however, continued to find a market for their products on the frontier during the war and chose to produce for consumers rather than for government contracts.

35 *PAFS*, Commissioners, &c. of Bedford, to Committee of Safety, February 9, 1775, 4:712.

36 Though craftsmen produced 806 weapons for the province, this does not represent all production. The provincial government of Virginia tried to purchase weapons in Pennsylvania, though the outcome of this attempt is unclear. Private individuals and associators also purchased weapons during the war. Thus, Pennsylvania craftsmen may have produced more than 806 weapons, but it would be speculation to say how many. MCS, July 6, 1775, July 31, 1776. *PAFS*, An Account of Cannon Cast at Reading and Warwick Furnaces, 1776, 5:36; *PASS*, Return of Cannon and Stores at Fort Island, February 22, 1777, 3:132.

37 *PCC*, Jonathan Trumbull to George Washington, July 17–19, 1776, r166, i152, v2, p293.

38 *PCC*, Philip Schuyler to John Hancock, January 25, 1777, r172, i153, v1, p138.

39 Adam Ward Rome, *Connecticut's Cannon: The Salisbury Furnace in the American Revolution* (Hartford, CT: American Revolution Bicentennial Commission of Connecticut, 1977), 15. Without factoring for inflation, the $78,792.24 spent on Salisbury Furnace equaled approximately £17,000. McCusker, *Money and Exchange*, 7n9; John J. McCusker, "How Much Is That," 319, for currency conversion rates. Hoadly, et al., *Connecticut Public Records*, i, 132, 172, 179, 236, 258, 399, 403, 467, 518–519, cited in Rome, *Connecticut's Cannon*, 11, 13.

40 *PCC*, Samuel French to the Board of War, August 28, 1779, r95, i78, v9, p283, Board of War to John Jay, September 6, 1779, r157, i147, v2, p469; Gluckman and Satterlee, *American Gun Makers*, 167.

41 MCS, February 26, 1776, March 6, 1776, April 2, 1776, July 4, 1776, July 15, 1776, July 27, 1776, August 5, 1776, August 15, 1776, August 24, 1776, September 14, 1776, September 23, 1776, October 30, 1776, November 11, 1776, December 3, 1776, December 5, 1776, December 9, 1776, December 21, 1776, January 15, 1777, January 20, 1777, January 27, 1777, February 22,

1777, March 4, 1777, March 5, 1777;. MEC, August 13, 1777, September 1, 1777, November 7, 1777, December 1, 1777, December 23, 1777, June 27, 1778, August 3, 1778, October 9, 1778, October 27, 1778, December 11, 1778; *PASS*, Benjamin Rittenhouse to the Committee of Safety, February 16, 1776, 1:614, Minutes of the Board of War, April 8, 1777, 1:27; *PAFS*, Committee of Safety to Benjamin Rittenhouse, February 9, 1776, 4:712, William Lane to Council, June 25, 1780, 8:360, Memorial of Gun Stockers in the State Factory, October 30, 1777, 5:733, Council to President of Congress, October 10, 1778, 7:12; *Pennsylvania Gazette,* April 17, 1776 and February 12, 1777. The Council of Safety spent $102,120 to build, rebuild, and operate the provincial gun factory over the course of its thirty-month life. Based on a contemporary description of a gun factory, it would have cost about $11,322 to construct initially, using numbers from Arthur Bining's extensive research. The factory was rebuilt twice, setting fixed costs at around $33,966. Thus only two-thirds of the money the council expended on the factory paid for weapons. According to DeHaven and the Council of Safety, it cost $22.20 to make a musket in 1776, when the factory started operations, and rose to $44.40 in 1778, when the factory closed. At an average cost of $32.41 per musket, it can be estimated that the factory workers manufactured 2,046 weapons. The council had also paid about $33,966 for buildings, transport, and tools. Divided by 2,046 weapons, fixed costs added to variable costs places the price for each musket at roughly $47.51. Market prices for a musket varied from $19.54 in 1776 to just over $26.64 in 1778. The costs of a gun factory are provided in Arthur Cecil Bining, *The Rise of American Economic Life,* 3rd ed. (New York: Charles Scribner's Sons, 1955), 96. According to Bining, "At the end of the colonial period, an iron plantation, including the land, blast furnace, forges, houses, gristmill, sawmill, and all equipment cost from £7,000 to £12,000 [$31,080 to $53,280 using McCusker, *Money and Exchange,* 7n9; John J. McCusker, "How Much Is That," 319, for currency conversions rates]. Plantations having only forges and the other equipment, but no blast furnace, were valued at £5,000 to £7,000 [$22,200 to $31,080]. The smaller ironworks usually located in towns or boroughs, varied in cost. A slitting mill could be built for £1,200 [$5,328], a steel furnace for £700 [$3,108], a plating mill for £300 [$1,332], a blacksmith shop for £150 [$666], and a nailery for about the same figure, all exclusive of land. An air furnace was worth about £200 [$888]."

42 Risch, *Supplying Washington's Army,* 349; PCC, George Washington to President of Congress, January 15, 1776, r166, i152, v1, p415.

43 *PGW,* George Washington to Philip Schuyler, October 22, 1776, 7:14.

44 PCC, George Washington to John Hancock, May 3, 1776, r166, i152, v2, p1.

45 Risch, *Supplying Washington's Army,* 350.

46 Gallagher, *Battle of Brooklyn,* 54; PCC, John Hancock to Trenton Committee, January 25, 1776, r23, i12A, v1, p46.

47 Gallagher, *Battle of Brooklyn,* 56.

48 Risch, *Supplying Washington's Army,* 347–348.

49 Gallagher, *Battle of Brooklyn,* 54.

50 Stephenson, *Patriot Battles,* 120.

51 General Orders, January 21, 1776, *The Writings of George Washington,* 39 vols., ed. John C. Fitzpatrick (Washington, DC: Government Printing Office, 1932–1945), 4:264, cited in Risch, *Supplying Washington's Army,* 350.

52 General Orders, July 12, 1777, *Writings of George Washington,* 8:387–389:

PGW, General Orders, July 14, 1777, 8:405–406; George Washington to Ezekiel Cheever, November 10, 1776, 7:130; Burnett, *Continental Congress*, 230; *PCC*, Committee at Camp Report Regarding Artillery, September 27, 1776, r30, i21, p29, Robert Harrison to Board of War, October 22, 1776, r186, i169, v2, p314, Congress Plan for an Artillery Yard, November 28, 1776, r30, i21, p3; *JCC*, December 21, 1776.

CHAPTER TWO: "LABORATORIES . . . ORDNANCE. . . ARTIFICERS [AND] AMMUNITION"

1 Samuel Hodgdon to Joseph Eayers, May 2, 1780, "Letters sent by Commissary General of Military Stores and Assistant Quartermaster Samuel Hodgdon, . . . July 19, 1778 to May 24, 1784," *Numbered Record Books*, microfilm, record group 853, roll 33, vols. 92 and 110, hereafter LSH.
2 LSH, Samuel Hodgdon to Samuel Sargent, May 2, 1780.
3 LSH, Samuel Hodgdon to Board of War, May 4, 1780.
4 LSH, Samuel Hodgdon to George Ingells, CMS Lancaster, May 6, 1780.
5 Thomas Lonergan, *Henry Knox: George Washington's Confidant, General of Artillery, and America's First Secretary of War* (Rockport, ME: Picton, 2003), 9–18.
6 *PCC*, Henry Knox plan for the establishment of an artillery corps, undated, r167, i152, v3, p381.
7 *PCC*, Committee at Camp Report Regarding Artillery, September 27, 1776, r30, i21, p29.
8 *PCC*, Congressional Plan for an Artillery Yard, November 28, 1776, r30, i21, p39.
9 Ibid.; *JCC*, December 27, 1776. The words *laboratory* and *elaboratory* were used interchangeably in the eighteenth century to refer to a site for preparing gunpowder and ammunition.
10 *PCC*, James Wilson to Robert Morris, December 28, 1776, r104, i78, p339, John Hancock to Massachusetts Council, December 28, 1776, r23, i12A, v2, p91; *PGW*, John Hancock to George Washington, December 27, 1776, 7:461–462.
11 *JCC*, November 19, 1776, and February 11, 1778. It took over a year to reform the board and then another year to establish its place in command of the army and its departments.
12 The flying camp was a reserve force of Pennsylvania and New Jersey militia recruited into the Continental Army in spring 1776. It was kept in readiness for an emergency as a rapid-reaction force.
13 *PCC*, Congressional Plan for an Artillery Yard, November 28, 1776, r30, i21, p39, Robert Harrison to Board of War, October 22, 1776, r186, i169, v2, p314.
14 *PCC*, Henry Knox to George Washington, June 15, 1778, r168, i152, v6, p205, George Washington to Henry Laurens, August 3–4, 1778, r168, i152, v6, p199.
15 *PCC*, Benjamin Flower Deposition Regarding Commissary Department, August 19, r76, i62, p639; McCusker, *Money and Exchange*, 7n9; John J. McCusker, "How Much Is That," 319. Using McCusker's conversion rate, $2,000 would be £450, though it was originally expressed as dollars.
16 *PCC*, George Washington to Committee at Philadelphia, January 7, 1777, r167, i152, v3, p441.
17 *PCC*, Committee at Philadelphia to John Hancock, January 7, 1777, r150,

i137, v4, p77. Rather than employ Byers directly and assume the rental contract that Pennsylvania had with the owner of the state-run furnace in Southwark, Congress directed the Pennsylvania Council of Safety to pay Byers's salary and continue renting the furnace. Congress then deducted the value of the salary and the furnace rent from Pennsylvania's existing debt with the national Treasury. The council, however, refused to pay for a new furnace after the British tore down the original one during their occupation of Philadelphia. In 1778, Congress was forced to take over management of the furnace directly, making Byers's salary a budget item within the military stores department.

18 *PCC*, Benjamin Flower Deposition Regarding Commissary Department, August 19, 1778, r76, i62, p639.

19 *PCC*, George Washington to John Hancock, January 17, 1777, r167, i152, v3, p469; in *Genesis of the US Armory*, Henry Knox to James Bowdoin, April 6, 1777.

20 *PGW*, Washington's Orders to Henry Knox, January 16, 1777, 8:85–86.

21 *PCC*, George Washington to President of Congress, February 14, 1777, r167, i152, v3, p525.

22 *JCC*, April 14, 1777.

23 *Genesis of the US Armory*, Payroll List by Ebenezer Hancock, Deputy Paymaster General, July 23, 1777; Ezekiel Cheever to William Heath, May 6, 1777, 4:124A, and David Mason to William Heath, May 6, 1777, 4:124, in *Papers of William Heath* (Boston: Massachusetts Historical Society Collections, 1905), microfilm, hereafter *PWH*; *PGW*, George Washington to William Heath, August 12, 1777, 10:591–592.

24 *PWH*, Ezekiel Cheever to William Heath, July 31, 1778, 10:158, Ezekiel Cheever to William Heath, July 13, 1777, 5:151; *Genesis of the US Armory*, Return of Artificers of the United States of America Stationed at Springfield Under the Direction of Lieut. Colo. David Mason of the Artillery, for the Month of May 1777, July 23, 1777; *PGW*, George Washington to Philip Schuyler, July 12, 1777, 10:261–262, William Heath to George Washington, July 30, 1777, 10:460–461, George Washington to William Heath, August 12, 1777, 10:591–592. Congress's directives and Washington's orders made no reference to Schuyler's army. In practice, Springfield supplied the Northern Army with a great deal of stores, but most supplies sent north were first sent to the Main Army. This was done so Washington could maintain oversight of activities in the Northern Army.

25 *PCC*, Joseph Nourse to Committee at Philadelphia, January 23, 1777, r157, i147, v1, p37.

26 *PGW*, Board of War to George Washington, August 5, 1777, 10:510, and 10:498n; *CBOB*, Board of War to Thomas Butler, October 29, 1777, 17, Board of War to Thomas Butler, November 11, 1777, 17–18, James Armstrong to Benjamin Flower, November 30, 1777, 40, Benjamin Flower to Board of War, December 1777, 44.

27 *CBOB*, Board of War to Thomas Butler, October 29, 1777, 17, Board of War to Thomas Butler, November 11, 1777, 17–18, Benjamin Flower to Board of War, December 1777, 41–43, Board of War to Benjamin Flower, December 3, 1777, 41–44. *PGW*, editor's note, 10:498n.

28 *CBOB*, Board of War to Benjamin Flower, November 3, 1777, 44.

29 *PGW*, editor's note, 10:498n; *CBOB*, Instructions for William Henry, April 21, 1778, 90–92; *PCC*, John Hall to Congress, 1782, r54, i42, v3, p435.

30 *PCC*, George Washington to Board of War, August 5, 1777, 10:510, General Orders, August 12, 1777, 10:590–591. LSH, Samuel Hodgdon to Benjamin Flower, August 17, 1778, Samuel Hodgdon to Henry Knox, September 9, 1779.
31 *PCC*, Board of War with James Byers, February 21, 1778, r48, i41, v1, p329, Daniel Brodhead to John Jay, October 9, 1779, r91, i78, v3, p355; *CBOB*, Board of War to John Davis, June 11, 1778, 28.
32 *JCC*, February 11, 1778.
33 *PCC*, Henry Knox to George Washington, June 15, 1778, r168, i152, v6, p205.
34 *PGW*, George Washington to Committee at Camp, March 1, 1778, 14:4.
35 *PGW*, George Washington to Henry Laurens, August 3, 1778, 16:236–40; LSH, Samuel Hodgdon to Benjamin Flower, August 17, 1778; *PCC*, Benjamin Flower Deposition Regarding the Commissary Department, August 19, 1778, r76, i62, p639.
36 *JCC*, February 18, 1779; *PCC*, Henry Knox to James Duane, February 5, 1779, r187, i169, v5, p191, George Washington to Horatio Gates, June 13, 1779, r172, i153, v1, p159; LSH, Samuel Hodgdon to Board of War, September 25, 1779; Henry Knox to Samuel Hodgdon, September 11, 1779, 20676, and Asa Copeland Receipt for Stores Delivered to Maryland April 24, 1780, in *Miscellaneous Numbered Records in the War Department Collection of Revolutionary War Records, 1775–1790s* (Washington, DC: Government Printing Office, 1972), microfilm, 30587.
37 *PCC*, Return of the Commissary of Military Stores department by Benjamin Flower, December 1, 1779, r46, i39, v2, p409.
38 Ibid.; *Miscellaneous Numbered Records*, Nathaniel Irish to Samuel Hodgdon, November 3, 1780, 20631, Nathaniel Irish to Samuel Hodgdon, November 10, 1780, 20632. *Strategic* and *operational* are modern terms that would not have been used in the eighteenth century. They are used here to clarify the command systems in the military stores department.
39 *PCC*, Certification of Benjamin Flower, August 7, 1778, r95, i78, v9, p179, Benjamin Flower Deposition Regarding the Commissary Department, August 19, 1778, r76, i62, p639, Board of War report re Samuel Hodgdon, February 11, 1780, r159, i147, v4, p129, Robert Crothers to Congress, June 15, 1780, r53, i42, v2, p76, Benjamin Flower to General John Sullivan, May 26, 1779, r95, i78, v9, p429; Benjamin Flower to James Pearson, December 20, 1779, Benjamin Flower to James Pearson, January 5, 1780, Benjamin Flower to James Pearson, January 6, 1780, Verlenden Family Collection, 1703–1863, Historical Society of Pennsylvania, Philadelphia; *Miscellaneous Numbered Records*, Memorial of Samuel Hodgdon, July 24, 1785, 30482, Report to the Treasury Board, June 21, 1788, 30607; *CBOB*, Cornelius Sweers to Nathaniel Irish, January 29, 1778, 29, Charles Lukens to Cornelius Sweers, June 15, 1778, 54–55; *Pennsylvania Gazette,* May 2, 1781. Flower was upset over his pay because he discovered that Samuel Hodgdon was being paid a higher salary as assistant commissary general than Flower was making as commissary general. This had occurred because of an oversight in which Congress adjusted for inflation all pay rates in the department except Flower's. This seems to have been done because Flower had received a raise just prior to the inflationary adjustment.
40 *Genesis of the US Armory*, Payroll List by Ebenezer Hancock, Deputy Paymaster General, July 23, 1777, and Lieut. Colo. David Mason of the Artillery, for the Month of May 1777, July 23, 1777; *PGW*, George Washington to William Heath, August 12, 1777, 10:591–92; *PWH*, David Mason to William

Heath, May 6, 1777, 4:124, Ezekiel Cheever to William Heath, May 6, 1777, 4:124A, Account of Court Martial at Springfield, December 17, 1777, 7:106, Ezekiel Cheever to William Heath, July 31, 1778, 10:158.

41 PCC, John Collins to Samuel Hodgdon, May 20, 1780, r159, i147, v4, p449, Benjamin Chapman to Samuel Hodgdon, June 10, 1780, r159, i147, v4, p449; *Genesis of the US Armory*, Payroll Report, July 23, 1777, and Examination of Witnesses under Oath, November 27, 1778; PWH, David Mason to William Heath, enclosing a copy of the court martial transcript, December 8, 1777, 7:83. LSH, Samuel Hodgdon to Joseph Eayers, May 2, 1780.

42 PCC, John Lamb to the Board of War, February 21, 1780, r159, i147, v4, p450.

43 JCC, July 26, 1780.

44 PCC, John Lamb to the Board of War, February 21, 1780, r159, i147, v4, p450.

45 Carp, *To Starve the Army*, 68, 104; Value of 1000 Continentals Depreciated, March 18, 1780, William Henry Papers, Historical Society of Pennsylvania, Philadelphia; Buel, *In Irons*, 145; *Miscellaneous Numbered Records*, Account of Ege and Gwynn for shot and shell, November 16, 1781, 20438. Buel wrote that initially the new emission failed as a currency, which is true, but commissary accounts with ironmasters like George Ege and William Gwynn reveal that within a year of the new emission, it had recovered some of its value and had stabilized. The currency had, according to Hodgdon, depreciated, but it recovered from a low of 10 to 1 versus a specie dollar to 4 to 1, and by the end of 1781 to a high of 2.5 to 1, where it remained until the end of the war. *JCC*, August 12 and November 25, 1780.

46 LSH, Samuel Hodgdon to David Mason, Joseph Eayers, Nathan Chapman, and Ezekiel Cheever, September 6, 1780, Samuel Hodgdon to David Mason, September 6, 1780, Samuel Hodgdon to John Bryant, September 7, 1780, Samuel Hodgdon to Board of War, November 27, 1780, Memorial of Benjamin Flower to the Board of War, May 17, 1780, Circular Letter to Commanders, December 8, 1780, Samuel Hodgdon to Jonathan Gostelowe, December 11, 1780, Samuel Hodgdon to Board of War, December 21, 1780, Samuel Hodgdon to Lt. Henry Stroop, December 22, 1780; PCC, Return of the Commissary of Military Stores department by Benjamin Flower, n.d., 1779, r46, i39, v2, p409, Samuel Hodgdon to the Board of War, October 19, 1780, r159, i147, v4, p621, Samuel Huntington to General Washington, November 25, 1780, r24, i15, p166, Board of War Report Regarding Artificers, March 23, 1781, r160, i147, v6, p335; JCC, August 30, 1780.

47 LSH, Benjamin Flower to Board of War, March 28, 1780, Samuel Hodgdon to Board of War, October 23, 1780; PCC, Estimate of Ammunition needed for 30 Days Firing, June 27, 1780, r22, i11, p256; JCC, April 8, 1780. Congress exchanged old dollars for new ones at a rate of 40 to 1. Hodgdon exchanged paper and specie dollars at varied rates, from 10 to 1 in early 1781, to 4 to 1 by the end of the year, to 2.5 to 1 by early 1782. Hodgdon exchanged £1 for $2.66 in specie from 1781 until the 1790s. This was an increase in the value of the dollar from its inception in 1775, which was discussed in the chapter 1 note about currency equivalences. Using Hodgdon's figures, $1.3 million equals roughly £130,000; $5.1 million equals roughly £486,000; and $4.2 million equals roughly £400,000. Hodgdon was able to write down his debts because of deflation in the currency conversion rates.

48 LSH, Samuel Hodgdon to William Thorne, March 22, 1780.

49 LSH, Samuel Hodgdon to Board of War, June 1, 1780; *JCC*, March 27, 1780. This warrant reflects the inflationary situation of the nation in early to mid-1780. Hodgdon was left by Congress to deal with the fact that because of inflation, the $1 million warrant Congress granted him was worth roughly $250,000 in specie. Unfortunately, few Americans were buying loan certificates to support the war effort, and, therefore, the loan office could not give Hodgdon the money he needed.

50 LSH, Samuel Hodgdon to Board of War, August 7, 1780.

51 *PCC*, Board of War to President of Congress, August 18, 1780, r161, i148, v1, p172.

52 Ibid.

53 *PCC*, Samuel Hodgdon to Samuel Huntington, December 21, 1779, r96, i78, v11, p483.

54 *PCC*, Robert Morris to Samuel Huntington, June 20, 1781, r148, i137, v1, p65; *JCC*, October 14, 1780; LSH, Samuel Hodgdon to Secretary of War, November 20, 1782. Using Hodgdon's conversion figures, this amounts to £1 million.

55 *PCC*, Board of War Report on Ironmasters, October 14, 1780, r159, i147, v4, p597, Board of War Report on Ironmasters, December 20, 1780, r159, i147, v4, p749, Board of War Estimate on Ammunition Contracted, 1780, r160, i147, v6, p152, Pennsylvania Ironmasters to Congress, February 23, 1781, r57, i43, p219, Hodgdon to Superintendent of Finance, January 3, 1784, r150, i137, v3, p407; LSH, Samuel Hodgdon to William Thorne, March 22, 1780, Samuel Hodgdon to the Board of War, April 10, 1781, Samuel Hodgdon to Colonel Mitchell, Deputy Quartermaster General, May 12, 1780, Samuel Hodgdon to Colonel Weiss, Deputy Quartermaster General, July 12, 1781, Samuel Hodgdon to Board of War, September 8, 1780, Samuel Hodgdon to the Superintendent of Finance, June 22, 1782, and October 9, 1782. Hodgdon reported he could get cartridge boxes made for bills due at sixty days, with other manufacturers willing to extend the government three months' credit. On April 10, 1781, he wrote, "I have money left over from the last allotment to pay the taxes, but the money was appropriated to different needs. With your approval though, I can pay forward on rents and another important business, the repair of muskets." JCC, July 25, 1780; RMS.

56 LSH, Samuel Hodgdon to Jonathan Gostelowe, May 12, 1780, Samuel Hodgdon to Jonathan Gostelowe, June 9, 1780, Samuel Hodgdon to the Board of War, June 17, 1780, Samuel Hodgdon to Joseph Perkins, June 17, 1780, Samuel Hodgdon to Henry Knox, June 24, 1780, Samuel Hodgdon to the Board of War, July 18, 1780, Samuel Hodgdon to the Board of War, February 17, 1781, Samuel Hodgdon to the Board of War, February 20, 1781, Samuel Hodgdon to the Board of War, May 31, 1781, Samuel Hodgdon to Henry Knox, June 9, 1781. On February 17, 1781, Hodgdon listed the arms and accouterments received from the Pennsylvania Line and the estimated costs of repair. On May 31, 1781, he related the process of turning over weapons, "The muskets . . . have frequently been culled for repair and are in very bad condition, most of them wanting stocking yet they are capable of being made good muskets." For a further repair estimate, see *PCC*: Return of Muskets in Philadelphia and Estimate of Repair Costs, June 4, 1781, r160, i147, v5, p283. Hodgdon wrote Knox about the situation, "We have sent so many supplies, especially cartridges to the south that our magazines here are nearly exhausted." RMS, June–September, 1781.

57 *PCC*, Board of War Report regarding cartridges, January 6, 1781, r160, i147, v6, p47, Board of War Report regarding artificers, March 28, 1781, r160, i147, v6, p351, Henry Knox Return of Ordnance and Military Stores Captured at Yorktown and Gloucester, October 1781, r171, i152, v10, p335, List of Commissary of Military Stores for 1782, undated 1782, r163, i149, v2, p395, Secretary at War estimate of pay for Officers for 1783, undated 1782, ibid., r156, i144, p20; LSH, Samuel Hodgdon to Samuel Sargent, June 30, 1781, Samuel Hodgdon to the Board of War, July 9, 1781, Samuel Hodgdon to the Board of War, August 11, 1781, Samuel Hodgdon to Samuel Sargent, August 13, 1781, Samuel Hodgdon to Samuel Sargent, August 16, 1782, Samuel Hodgdon to John Hall, May 20, 1782; *Miscellaneous Numbered Records*, Board of War to Samuel Hodgdon, November 14, 1781, 20602. Fatigue duties refer to any physical work other than training or battle. Such duties included trench digging, wood splitting, fort building, barracks construction, and general camp maintenance.
58 *PCC*, Benjamin Lincoln to President of Congress, November 26, 1781, r162, i149, v1, p1; *JCC*, February 7, 1781.
59 *PCC*, Benjamin Lincoln memo regarding arsenals and academies, March 5, 1783, r45, i38, p285.

CHAPTER THREE: "ON THE SAME PLAN AS . . . WOOLWICH"

1 "Journal of David Mason," Bryant-Mason-Smith Family Papers, 1767–1861 (Massachusetts Historical Society, Boston); John Muller, *A Treatise of Artillery*, reprint (Bloomfield, Ontario: Museum Restoration Service, 1977, originally published 1757).
2 Maxine Berg, *The Age of Manufactures 1700–1820: Industry, Innovation and Work in Britain*, 2nd ed. (London: Routledge, 1994), 75.
3 Ken Alder, *Engineering the Revolution: Arms and Enlightenment in France, 1763–1815* (Princeton, NJ: Princeton University Press, 1997), 5.
4 Berg, *Age of Manufactures*, 144.
5 Alder, *Engineering the Revolution*, 163–220.
6 Berg, *Age of Manufactures*, 262.
7 Ibid., 74.
8 Oliver Frederick Gillilan Hogg, *The Royal Arsenal: Its Background, Origin, and Subsequent History* (London: Oxford University Press, 1963), 274.
9 Ibid., 252, 393–451.
10 Ibid., 393–451, including map opposite 451.
11 Further understanding of how British military manufacturing influenced private manufacturing can be seen in Clive Trebilcock, "'Spin-Off' in British Economic History: Armaments and Industry, 1760–1914," *Economic History Review*, new ser., vol. 22, no. 3 (December 1969): 474–490.
12 "A Biography of Roger Sherman (1721–1793)," American History: From Revolution to Reconstruction and Beyond, accessed September 4, 2015, http://www.let.rug.nl/usa/biographies/roger-sherman/;."Lewis, Francis (1713–1803)," Biographical Directory of the United States Congress, 1774–Present, accessed September 4, 2015, http://bioguide.congress.gov/scripts/biodisplay.pl?index=L000282. For background on the workings of Congress during the period of the creation of the military stores department, see Burnett, *Continental Congress*,103–104, 146–169, 230–247.
13 William R. Bagnall, *The Textile Industries of the United States* (New York: Augustus M. Kelley, 1971, originally published 1893), 70.

14 Ibid., 63.
15 Benjamin Rush, "Speech to the United Company of Philadelphia for Promoting American Manufactures (1775)," in *The Philosophy of Manufactures: Early Debates over Industrialization in the United States*, ed. Michael Brewster Folsom and Steven D. Lubar (Cambridge: MIT Press, 1982), 5–6.
16 Benjamin Marshall to John Scott, December 14, 1765, *Pennsylvania Magazine of History and Biography* 20 (1896): 211, quoted in Whitefield Bell Jr. "Some Aspects of the Social History of Pennsylvania, 1760–1790," *Pennsylvania Magazine of History and Biography* 62 (July 1938): 287.
17 Gary B. Nash, *The Urban Crucible: The Northern Seaports and the Origins of the American Revolution*, abridged ed. (Cambridge: Harvard University Press, 1986, originally published 1979), 216; *Pennsylvania Gazette*, September 20, 1775.
18 Bagnall, *Textile Industries*, 63.
19 Ibid.; Nash, *Urban Crucible*, 119–120, 216; York, *Mechanical Metamorphosis*, 22–23; Mac Whatley, "Southern Quakers and Industry," notes by Mac Whatley for a speech to the Friends Historical Society, Guilford College, November 8, 2001, titled "Friends of Industry: Quakers and the Industrial Revolution in the South," accessed September 9, 2015, http://sites.google.com/site/macwhat/southernquakersandindustry.
20 Bridenbaugh, *Colonial Craftsman*, 62–63.
21 Ibid., 62; Bining, *Rise of American Economic Life*, 98.
22 Edna Handwork, "First in Iron: Berks County's Iron Industry, 1716 to 1815," *Historical Review of Berks County* (Fall 1960): 123.
23 Robert B. Gordon, *American Iron, 1607–1900* (Baltimore: Johns Hopkins University Press, 1996), 60.
24 Ibid. The cost of iron operations made it cost effective to work with other iron manufacturers or operate separate facilities within a larger complex. Consequently, furnace owners enclosed their stacks with workshops, built forges and workshops, and hired farmers to grow food to provide sustenance to the workers. According to Bining, "At the end of the colonial period, an iron plantation, including the land, blast furnace, forges, houses, gristmill, sawmill, and all equipment cost from £7,000 to £12,000 [$31,080 to $53,280 at John J. McCusker's conversion rate]. Plantations having only forges and the other equipment, but no blast furnace, were valued at £5,000 to £7,000 [$22,200 to $31,080]. The smaller ironworks, usually located in towns or boroughs, varied in cost. A slitting mill could be built for £1,200 [$5,328], a steel furnace for £700 [$3,108], a plating mill for £300 [$1,332], a blacksmith shop for £150 [$666], and a nailery for about the same figure, all exclusive of land. An air furnace was worth about £200 [$888]." Bining, *Rise of American Economic Life*, 96; McCusker, *Money and Exchange*, 7n9; McCusker, "How Much Is That," 319.
25 Keach Johnson, "The Genesis of the Baltimore Ironworks," *Journal of Southern History* 19, no. 2 (May 1953): 175.
26 Berkshire Furnace figures here and afterward compiled by the author from *Berkshire Furnace Journal, 1774–1778*, Forge and Furnace Collection, Historical Society of Pennsylvania, Philadelphia, and *Berkshire Furnace Journal, 1778–1780*, Forge and Furnace Collection, Historical Society of Pennsylvania, Philadelphia.
27 Mulholland, *History of Metals*, 116; Arthur Cecil Bining, *British Regulation of the Colonial Iron Industry* (Philadelphia: University of Pennsylvania Press, 1933), 26.

28 Bining, *British Regulation,* 30.

29 Carlton O. Wittlinger, "Industry Comes to the Frontier," *Pennsylvania Magazine* 43 (1930): 156; Stephen H. Cutcliffe and Karen Z. Huetter, "Perfection in the Mechanical Arts: The Development of Moravian Industrial Technology in Bethlehem, Pennsylvania, 1741–1814," in *Backcountry Crucibles: The Lehigh Valley from Settlement to Steel,* ed. Jean R. Soderlund and Catherine S. Parzynski (Bethlehem, PA: Lehigh University Press, 2008), 161–184. Cutcliffe and Huetter place a caveat on mechanical development in Bethlehem, arguing that though the town "developed . . . a concentration of crafts and trades . . . at such a relatively early date . . . that growth subsequently stagnated." Ibid., 162.

30 Wittlinger, "Industry Comes to the Frontier," 157; Bridenbaugh, *Colonial Craftsman,* 117–119.

31 Bining, *Rise of American Economic Life,* 98–99; York, *Mechanical Metamorphosis,* 15, 21; Bridenbaugh, *Colonial Craftsman,* 58, 62–63. The rise of glassmaking in southern New Jersey was part of Philadelphia's regional market. Caspar Wistar built a glass factory that eventually comprised two furnaces and several finishing buildings. However, he only employed as many as five skilled glassblowers, showing that while Americans were building larger structures, they were achieving greater output by the use of more-skilled workers.

32 *Pennsylvania Gazette,* August 10, 1758, August 24, 1758, January 25, 1758, February 1, 1758, June 28, 1759, March 20, 1760, September 4, 1760, April 17, 1766, and August 30, 1775.

33 Nathan L. Swayze, *The Rappahannock Forge* (N.p: American Society of Arms Collectors, 1976), 3.

34 *PCC,* Lewis Garanger to Congress, 1783, r95, i78, v10, p439; Harold Coffin Syrett, ed., *The Papers of Alexander Hamilton: May 1, 1802–October 23, 1804* (New York: Columbia University Press, 1979), n366.

35 *PCC,* Lewis Garanger to Congress, 1783, r95, i78, v10, p439.

36 *PCC,* Pierre Penet to Congress October 7, 1781, r100, i78, v18, p465; Brian N. Morton and Donald C. Spinelli, *Beaumarchais and the American Revolution* (Lanham, MD: Lexington Books, 2003), 45.

37 *JCC,* January 2, 1779.

38 James Gilreath, "American Book Distribution" *Proceedings of the American Antiquarian Society* 95, pt. 2 (October 1985): 502.

39 Joseph Towne Wheeler, "Booksellers and Circulating Libraries in Colonial Maryland," *Maryland Historical Magazine* 34, no. 2 (June 1939): 117–126.

40 Tim Hughes, "Newspaper Circulation in the 1700's," *History's Newsstand Blog,* July 27, 2009, Timothy Hughes Rare & Early Newspapers, accessed September 17, 2015, http://blog.rarenewspapers.com/?p=1782.

41 *PCC,* Committee at Camp Report regarding artillery, September 27, 1776, r30, i21, p29.

42 *Pennsylvania Gazette,* August 27, 1741, and September 17, 1741.

43 Ibid., June 10, 1762. This was a way of calculating overtime pay. The concept of overtime did not exist in the modern sense at the time, so laborers were paid for an extra day's wages based on a certain level of extra work at the arsenal. Since the work week was six days, these workers were paid for working an extra half-day for each day of the week.

44 Ibid., March 20, 1766.

45 Ibid., October 1, 1767.

46 Ibid., December 1, 1773.

47 John Muller, *A Treatise Containing the Practical Part of Fortification* (London: A. Millar, 1755), 222.
48 Ibid., 281, 227.
49 Ibid., v, vi (italics added).
50 Muller, *Treatise of Artillery*, iii.
51 Muller, *Treatise of Artillery*, vi.
52 Shipping Manifest, March 10, 1774, 48:63, *Papers of Henry Knox*, 55 reels (Boston: Massachusetts Historical Society, 1960), microfilm, hereafter *PHK*.
53 Charles Henry Hart, "Some Notes Concerning John Norman, Engraver (Died June 8, 1817, Age 69)," reprinted from *Proceedings of the Massachusetts Historical Society*, October 1904 (Cambridge: John Wilson and Son, 1904).
54 PCC, John Norman list of subscribers for Muller's *Treatise of Artillery*, 1777, r51, i41, v7, p11.
55 Ibid.
56 *CBOB*, Cornelius Sweers to Charles Lukens, January 12, 1778, 49–51; *Pennsylvania Gazette*, February 7, 1778.
57 Craftsmen were enlisted on terms little better than those offered to men enlisting as privates in the army. Congress believed craftsmen would enlist as a way of providing patriotic service without having to fight on the battlefield.

CHAPTER FOUR: THE "REGIMENT OF ARTILLERY ARTIFICERS" . . . AND "HIRED MEN"

1 No documentation is available to state explicitly where all of these operations were located. RMS; *Miscellaneous Numbered Records*, 20483, 20499, 20502–20504, 20524; Mapping West Philadelphia, "Landowners in October 1777," accessed multiple dates, http://www.archives.upenn.edu/WestPhila1777 /map.php.
2 *PCC*, Benjamin Flower return of officers in the Commissary of Military Stores, r46, i39, v3, p375, George Baker list of laborers employed in the Philadelphia arsenal, r46, i39, v3, p379.
3 For use of local tanneries, see LSH, Samuel Hodgdon to Jonathan Gostelowe, May 13, 1780.
4 Generally speaking, the processes for creating musket cartridges and fixed cannon ammunition were the same, differing only in the size of the finished product. There was one important difference, however. Musket cartridges held ball and powder within a wrapping of paper. Fixed cannon ammunition contained a bag of powder separate from the cannon shot, both set on top of a wooden plate that served as a base. The pieces were then held together by two perpendicular iron straps wrapped around them, the powder encased between the plate and the shot. Because of the extra blacksmith work involved, the straps were often left off, and ammunition was sent to the army separately as cannon cartridges and loose balls. As mentioned in the introduction, fixed shot would be saved for emergency situations. Workers making artillery ammunition performed a number of tasks. They folded paper or cloth into cartridges, fixed ammunition with straps, filled fuses, and filled shells. All these operations occurred for different size ammunition and had to be done separately so as not to confuse items for one type of gun with another.
5 Hogg, *Royal Arsenal*, 105; Jenny West, *Gunpowder, Government and War in the Mid-Eighteenth Century* (Suffolk, UK: Boydell Press, 1991), 87–97,

108–113. West's research found that most of Britain's cartridge and arms production was done on contract with private manufacturers. The armories were used for repairs and the production of emergency stocks of ammunition. West, 87. *PCC*, Henry Knox return of ordnance and military stores captured at Yorktown and Gloucester, October 1781, r171, i152, v10, p335. The patriots collected enough cartridges to suggest that each British soldier was armed with thirty rounds. But the patriots also collected enough powder and lead for making thirty more rounds per man. West's research also revealed that the British government found it cheaper for soldiers to make ammunition than it was for contractors to do so. Thus, while some ammunition was made by British manufacturers and the government, such production was not relied on by the army. West, 87–97.

6 *PGW*, Nathanael Greene to George Washington, October 27, 1776, 7:38, Nathanael Greene to George Washington, October 29, 1776, 7:46, Thomas Mifflin to George Washington, November 26, 1776, 7:219–220, Benjamin Flower to Benjamin Harrison, August 29, 1777, 11:88, Horatio Gates to George Washington, April 29, 1778, 14:627; *PAFS,* George Bryan to Board of War, June 5, 1779. The extent of camp laboratory work was unclear, though it can be approximated at about one and a half million cartridges. *PCC*, Benjamin Flower deposition regarding commissary department, August 19, 1778, M247, r76, i62, p639. The Lebanon laboratory produced for the army through the first six months of 1778, making seven hundred fifty thousand cartridges for the army. *PCC*, Return of Sundry Military and Ordnance Stores, July 31, 1778, M247, r157, i147, v2, p199.

7 RMS; *Miscellaneous Numbered Records*, Ordnance Accounts: Male and Female Employees, 1779–1780 in the Laboratory at Philadelphia, 20452; *PCC*, Return of the Commissary of Military Stores Department, December 1, 1779, M247, r46, i39, v2, p409; C. Keith Wilbur, *The Revolutionary Soldier, 1775–1783* (Old Saybrook, CT: Globe Pequot Press, 1993, first published 1969), 22.

8 *PAFS*, Plan of a Powder Magazine, 1776, March 2, 1776, 4:715–716; LSH, Samuel Hodgdon to Colonel Hughes, August 6, 1782; *CBOB*, Memorial of the Work Done by Carpenters at Carlisle, November 26, 1777, 31–33; Hogg, *Royal Arsenal*, map opposite 451. Exact amounts of these materials present at a worktable at any one time cannot be made clear from the records available.

9 Wilbur, *Revolutionary Soldier,* 22; *Miscellaneous Numbered Records*, Ordnance Accounts: Male and Female Employees, 1779–1780 in the Laboratory at Philadelphia, 20452.

10 Ibid.; RMS.

11 *PCC*, Nathanael Greene to Benjamin Lincoln, April 26, 1782, r162, i149, v1, p383.

12 *PCC*, George Washington to President of Congress, November 1–3, 1777, 168, i152, v5, p161. *Miscellaneous Numbered Records*, An Account of Sundries Received from Flower for Use of the Lab at Fifth Street, October 1780, 20447; RMS; Nardo, *Weapons of War*, 18–20; Wilbur, *Revolutionary Soldier,* 20, 54; *PGW*, George Washington to Ezekiel Cheever, July 13, 1777, 10:267.

13 Four separate accountings of cartridge production exist for the months from August 1778 to July 1780. These include RMS and *Miscellaneous Numbered Records*, Ordnance Accounts: Male and Female Employees, 1779–1780 in the Laboratory at Philadelphia, 20452; Account of Musket Cartridges Made at the

Lab at Fifth Street, 20496, Powder Account Book, 20447. After July 1780, the only record of production at the factory is available from RMS. The number of workers at the laboratory was stable from February to November, so shifts in production were not a result of changes in workforce.

14 LSH, Hodgdon to Board of War, April 4, 1781. The laboratory, and in fact all departmental operations, remained productive through this time even though Hodgdon constantly complained to the Board of War that he had no credit, no money, and no prospect of supplying the army. Rather than really being out of supplies, money, and options, Hodgdon seems to have complained for more money as a preparatory measure for future operations. The board did not give him money unless he needed it, so Hodgdon constantly complained that he needed it, despite the fact that production records show the department was meeting the requests made of it. See LSH, Hodgdon to Board of War, October 8, 1781, for a complaint made by Hodgdon at a time when cartridge and musket production was actually up.

15 LSH, Hodgdon to Secretary at War, July 8, 1782.

16 RMS.

17 *Miscellaneous Numbered Records*: Ordnance Accounts: Male and Female Employees, 1779–1780 in the Laboratory at Philadelphia, 20452.

18 *CBOB*, Board of War to Benjamin Flower, July 6, 1779, 136–141.

19 LSH, Samuel Hodgdon to Chamber, Conductor of Military Stores, July 3, 1780, Samuel Hodgdon to Board of War, January 7, 1781. The dollar amounts used are Hodgdon's and reflect the impact of depreciation on American currency as the war progressed.

20 H. Heaton, *The Yorkshire Woollen and Worsted Industry*, 2nd ed. (Oxford: Oxford University Press, 1965), 269, quoted in Berg, *Age of Manufactures*, 190.

21 RMS; LSH, Samuel Hodgdon to Board of War, January 7, 1781. Hodgdon reported costs at the cartridge factory to Congress using British currency. He calculated laboratory costs when the depreciation of American currency had already reached its high point and Congress was attempting to control it. In 1780, Congress revalued the paper dollar by issuing a new emission dollar to replace all the old dollars it had printed. It exchanged old dollars for new ones at a rate of 40 to 1. This revalue and the government's budgetary austerity helped stabilize the paper dollar against its specie equivalent. Unfortunately, Hodgdon never exchanged money in his records directly from pounds to specie dollars. His records exchanged pounds for paper dollars, and paper dollars for specie dollars, seemingly because exchange rates were still very fluid. I have averaged Hodgdon's conversion rates. Hodgdon exchanged paper and specie dollars, at varied rates from 10 to 1 in early 1781, to 4 to 1 by the end of the year, to 2.5 to 1 by early 1782. Hodgdon exchanged £1 for $2.66 in specie by the end of 1781. I have chosen to convert cartridge-factory expenses at an average of 4 to 1. In the case of the cartridge factory, then, £310,000 in expenses became $842,600 in specie and $3,370,400 in new emission paper.

22 There were at least ten hired blacksmiths and twelve hired carpenters in the yard in June 1780, aside from all other enlisted artificers and hired craftsmen. A return of rations in the department shows that the number of men varied through November 1780 but averaged out at seventeen. LSH, Samuel Hodgdon to Daniel Joy, June 9, 1780. *Miscellaneous Numbered Records*: Return of Rations Drawn, November 28, 1780, 30561. PCC, Return of the Commissary of Military Stores, December 1779, r46, i39, v2, p409.

23 RMS; Benjamin Flower to James Pearson, February 9, 1780, Verlenden Family Collection, 1703–1863, Historical Society of Pennsylvania, Philadelphia. Jordan investigated stores left on the roads around Philadelphia, which was a function normally done by Joy. See LSH, Samuel Hodgdon to the Board of War, July 15, 1780. For an example of shared leadership of the yard, see LSH, Samuel Hodgdon to John Jordan, August 8, 1780.
24 RMS.
25 RMS; Gooding, *Introduction to British Artillery*, 5–7; Albert Manucy, *Artillery through the Ages: A Short Illustrated History of Cannon, Emphasizing Types Used in America* (Washington, DC: Division of Publication, National Park Service, 1985, originally published, 1949), 31–60.
26 RMS.
27 Ibid.; Manucy, *Artillery through the Ages*, 23–27.
28 *Miscellaneous Numbered Records*, Valentine Hoffman to Samuel Hodgdon, April 13, 1780, 30600; RMS; Muller, *Treatise of Artillery*, 138–140. Proof of the efficacy of the artificer's tool production can be seen in the fact that Hodgdon's correspondence never mentioned that the artificers lacked proper tools with which to work, and near the end of the war, Hodgdon began selling some of the department's tools. Tool returns that do exist provide inconclusive production figures because tools were repaired, remade, and shipped to the front on a regular basis, according to the department's account book. These activities are evident based on the item transfers between offices as recorded in the RMS.
29 *PCC*, Return of the Commissary of Military Stores Department, December 1, 1779, M247, r46, i39, v2, p409; RMS, December 14, 1780; *Miscellaneous Numbered Records*; 35421.
30 *PCC*, Return of the Commissary of Military Stores Department, December 1, 1779, M247, r46, i39, v2, p409.
31 *PAFS*, Plan for Carrying on a Gun Factory, June 4, 1776, 4:767–768.
32 RMS.
33 LSH, Samuel Hodgdon to Board of War, June 17, 1780. Armorers, with artificer assistance, produced a significant number of spare items for the Continental Army. Armorers and blacksmiths combined their efforts to produce 16,217 ramrods from March 1780 to December 1781. This was a surplus of 981 over the ramrods needed for the muskets produced in the same period. Armorers and blacksmiths made 1,870 extra gun barrels and repaired 1,221 more. Turners in the arsenal combined to make 4,358 surplus stocks, while lock makers in the armory repaired 1,381 locks and manufactured 4,800 more. Bayonets were the only item the armory failed to produce in numbers equal to its output of muskets. Armorers and blacksmiths made or repaired only 12,178 bayonets, which was 3,000 less than the number of muskets produced from March 1780 through August 1781. This shortfall was covered by the production of private bayonet makers in Philadelphia.

CHAPTER FIVE: "ARTIFICERS WHO PREFER LIBERTY TO SLAVERY"

1 *CBOB*, Cornelius Sweers to Charles Lukens, January 12, 1778, 49–51.
2 *CBOB*, Benjamin Flower to Nathaniel Irish, April 8, 1777, 21–22. After Flower met with Congress in winter 1777, he left Philadelphia with master carpenter Nathaniel Irish to scout Carlisle for a proper location to build a government manufacturing facility. Congress had debated numerous locations for the site. It considered Lancaster and York, choosing Carlisle because several old

British barracks were still standing near the city. Unfortunately, the British barracks, built for the French and Indian War, were dilapidated, and the Le Tort Creek, which flowed past the buildings, was small and needed damming to be made useful. Flower and Irish chose a site one-half mile outside of Carlisle to build the arsenal, on a flood plain of the LeTort Creek where a dam could be built to provide water power.

3 *CBOB*, Benjamin Flower to Nathaniel Irish, March 6, 1777, 23–24.

4 *CBOB*, Benjamin Flower to Nathaniel Irish, April 8, 1777, 21–22.

5 *CBOB*, James Glen to Benjamin Flower, December 1777, 27, Memorial of Carpenters at Carlisle, November 26, 1777, 31–33, Charles Lukens, et al., to Benjamin Flower, October 31, 1777, 37, Thomas Wylie to Benjamin Flower, November 28, 1777, 33–34, Thomas Wylie to Benjamin Flower, November 28, 1777, 33–34; Muller, *Treatise Containing the Practical Part of Fortification*, 227.

6 *Pennsylvania Gazette*, February 7, 1778.

7 *CBOB*, Charles Lukens to Cornelius Sweers, January 20, 1778, 52, Cornelius Sweers to Charles Lukens, January 12, 1778, 49–51; *PCC*, Benjamin Flower Deposition Regarding the Commissary Department, August 19, 1778, r76, i62, p639, Return of the Commissary of Military Stores Department, December 1779, r46, i39, v2, p409.

8 *CBOB*, James Glen to Benjamin Flower, December 1777, 27, Memorial of Carpenters at Carlisle, November 26, 1777, 31–33; Carlisle Barracks, 1828, Drawn at request of Colonel Wm. Linnard, August 1828, Carlisle Barracks Collection, Military History Research Collection, Military History Institute, Carlisle, PA, Box 1, Miscellaneous Papers, hereafter CBC. While the map used to describe the early Carlisle Arsenal is from a later period, many factors prove it is a close representation of the layout of the arsenal in the revolution. First, the lengths of the buildings relative to one another match the configuration of the buildings described by Flower. There are specific references on the map to a magazine and armory, which in 1828 were not needed on the post. Finally, there are two dams on the LeTort Creek, one that is connected to an existing mill and one that is unconnected to any structure. This implies that there was a facility that made use of the dam and mill race, and I believe that facility was the arsenal forge, which is the only building not seen on the map that was referenced by Flower.

9 *PASS*, 10:1–253, Pennsylvania Line, Independent Company of Artillery, 1777–1780, 11:246–251; *Miscellaneous Numbered Records*, Report of the State of the Department, May 24, 1780, 20718.

10 *PCC*, Return of the Commissary of Military Stores, December 1779, r46, i39, v2, p409.

11 *CBOB*, Cornelius Sweers to Nathaniel Irish, January 29, 1778, 54–55.

12 Ibid.

13 Numbers compiled by the author from sources throughout *CBOB* and RMS; *CBOB*, Cornelius Sweers to Charles Lukens, January 12, 1778, 49–51, Memorial of the Work Done by Carpenters at Carlisle, November 26, 1777, 31–33, Board of War to Charles Lukens, March 6, 1778, 73.

14 *Miscellaneous Numbered Records*, Ordnance Returns, 1778, 35421; RMS, Mulholland, *History of Metals*, 131; *CBOB*, Charles Lukens to Isaac Coren, March 31, 1778, 79.

15 *CBOB*, Charles Lukens to Jonathan Gostelowe, June 15, 1778, 108, Board of War to Charles Lukens, March 6, 1778, 73, Charles Lukens to Board of War,

March 15, 1778, 74–-75, Board of War to Charles Lukens, March 6, 1778, 73.
16 *CBOB*, Charles Lukens to Board of War, March 15, 1778, 74–75, Samuel
Sargent to Benjamin Flower, November 7, 1777, 24–26, Cornelius Sweers to
Charles Lukens, January 12, 1778, 49–51, Board of War to Charles Lukens,
February 25, 1778, 71, Board of War to Charles Lukens, February 28, 1778, 70,
Board of War to Commissary of Military Stores at Carlisle, March 18, 1778, 82,
Charles Lukens to Board of War, May 16, 1779, 129, Charles Lukens to Board
of War, June 14, 1779, 130; RMS.
17 *PWH*, Ezekiel Cheever to William Heath, May 6, 1777.
18 *Genesis of the US Armory*, Return of the Artificers of the United States of
America Stationed at Springfield under the Direction of Lieut. Colo. David
Mason of the Artillery for the Month of May 1777.
19 *PCC*, George Washington to President of Congress, May 3, 1777, r167, i152,
v4, p147, William Heath to George Washington, April 26, 1777; *Genesis of the
US Armory*, William Heath to George Washington, April 9, 1777, William Heath
to George Washington, June 12, 1777, George Washington to William Heath,
May 2, 1777, George Washington to William Heath, May 10, 1777, William
Heath to Jonathan Trumbull, May 13, 1777, William Heath to George
Washington, April 26, 1777, William Heath to George Washington, May 19,
1777, Ebenezer Hancock Pay Roster of Men at Springfield, July 23, 1777,
William Heath to George Washington, April 26, 1777, George Washington to
William Heath, May 10, 1777; *PWH*, Ezekiel Cheever to William Heath, July 13,
1777, 5:151.
20 *PHK*, Plan of Construction for Carriage for Cannon, March 1, 1777, 3:128.
21 *Genesis of the US Armory*, Massachusetts Council to Colonel Thomas Dawes,
July 17, 1777, William Heath to George Washington, July 23, 1777, Bill
Rendered to the Massachusetts Council by Dawes for Services in Consideration
with the Proposed Works at Springfield, February 26, 1778. The council expected that pursuant to Congress's resolves, it would be reimbursed for its expenditures.
22 Ibid., William Heath to George Washington, July 23, 1777.
23 Ibid., Resolution of the Springfield Town Council, August 5, 1777, Resolution
of the Springfield Town Council, August 9, 1777; *PCC*, Thomas Stebbins to
Thomas Dawes, August 11, 1777, r79, i65, v1, 285, Thomas Dawes to
Massachusetts Council, August 15, 1777, r79, i65, v1, p273.
24 Ibid., From a Letter of an Officer of Burgoyne's captured army, November 15,
1777.
25 None of the documents in the *PWH*, *PHK*, or *Genesis of the US Armory*
reveal any continual oversight of the Springfield Arsenal by any senior
Continental officer.
26 *PWH*, David Mason to William Heath, April 19, 1779, 12:117. In this letter,
Mason seeks approval to give rations to Captain Thomas Bolter's men because
he has no right to do so because they are not part of his command.
27 *PWH*, Ezekiel Cheever to William Heath, August 26, 1777, 6:53, David
Mason to William Heath, September 28, 1777, 6:94.
28 *PWH*, Ezekiel Cheever to William Heath, May 1, 1779, 12:131.
29 *Genesis of the US Armory*, Minutes of Committee of MA Council to Answer
a Petition to the Selectmen of Springfield and West Springfield, November 25–27,
1778.
30 Ibid.

31 Ibid.
32 CBC, Recruiting Instructions for Nathaniel Chapman, May 1, 1778, Box 11, Miscellaneous Papers.
33 LSH, Samuel Hodgdon to Joseph Eayers, May 2, 1780.
34 *PCC*, Horatio Gates to George Washington, July 18, 1779, r172, i153, v1, p154.
35 Ibid.
36 Ibid., John Lamb to Board of War, February 21, 1780, r159, i147, v4, p450.
37 LSH, Samuel Hodgdon to Joseph Eayers, May 2, 1780, Samuel Hodgdon to the Board of War, July 10, 1780; *JCC*, July 26, 1780; *PCC*, John Collins to Samuel Hodgdon, March 24, 1780, r159, i147, v4, p449, Joseph Eayers to Samuel Hodgdon, May 20, 1780, r159, i147, v4, p449, Henry Knox to Samuel Hardy, June 13, 1784, r184, i167, p431; *Genesis of the US Armory*, Minutes of Committee of MA Council . . . , November 25–27, 1778.
38 These figures were compiled by the author from *PWH* and *Genesis of the US Armory*.

CHAPTER SIX: "DEVISE WAYS AND MEANS FOR PROCURING [CANNON]"

1 Today that cannon is in the possession of the historical society of Washington County, Maryland. "18WA288 Antietam Furnace c. 1761–1790," Diagnostic Artifacts in Maryland, Jefferson Patterson Park and Museum, accessed September 4, 2015, http://www.jefpat.org/diagnostic/SmallFinds/Site%20 Summaries/18WA288AntietamFurnaceSiteSummary.htm; "Jonathan Hager House, Circa 1740," HMdb.org The Historical Marker Database, accessed May 2, 2016, http://www.hmdb.org/Marker.asp?Marker=1157.
2 *JCC*, January 15, 1776.
3 This figure is based on John J. McCusker's conversion rate of $4.44:£1. The actual figure was £2,000. McCusker, *Money and Exchange*, 7n9; McCusker, "How Much Is That," 319.
4 *Miscellaneous Numbered Records*, Board of War Account with Daniel Joy, May 7, 1778, 20464.
5 Ibid.; *JCC*, February 23, 1776.
6 MCS, December 6, 1775; *Miscellaneous Numbered Records*, Board of War Account with Daniel Joy, May 7, 1778, 20464; *Berkshire Furnace Journal 1774–1778*; *Berkshire Furnace Journal 1778–1780*; PHK, Profile of Howitzer Shell, 1781, 55:162. Benjamin Flower only ever worked on one major ordnance contract, with John Patton of Berkshire Furnace in Berks County, Pennsylvania. In this case, he delivered all his specifications verbally.
7 *Miscellaneous Numbered Records*, Board of War Account with Daniel Joy, May 7, 1778, 20464.
8 Brass was generally considered a better material for cannons because it was lighter and easier to cast than iron. Brass took less time to burn, and more cannons could be cast per ton of brass than iron. Some military minds argued, though, that iron was better than brass because it was stronger and less liable to bursting after prolonged use. The following quote from Albert Manucy, while discussing bronze, applies equally to brass. Bronze was a mixture of copper and tin, while brass is a mixture of copper and zinc. The similarity in the metals was such that the words were occasionally used interchangeably in the eighteenth century. "In the 1700's cast-iron became the principal artillery afloat and ashore, yet

cast bronze was superior in withstanding the stresses of firing. Because of its toughness, less metal was needed in a bronze gun than in a cast-iron one, so in spite of the fact that bronze is about 20 percent heavier than iron, the bronze piece was usually the lighter of the two." Manucy, *Artillery Through the Ages*, 46. As military bureaucrats argued over the respective benefits of brass versus iron, cannons ended up being made of both. The British military, for instance, authorized both iron and brass cannon because artillery officers preferred to use different types of cannons in different situations. Ultimately, politics, rather than the respective merits of the metals, were the deciding factor in which metal was used. Both brass and iron were replaced by steel ordnance in the nineteenth century, when casting with that material became technologically and economically viable. Manucy, *Artillery through the Ages*, 41–61; Jackson and de Beer, *Eighteenth Century Gunfounding*, 35–66; Gordon, *American Iron*, 220–231.

9 Jackson and de Beer, *Eighteenth Century Gunfounding*, 126–139.

10 Gordon, *American Iron*, 4, 7–18; Gerald G. Eggert, *The Iron Industry in Pennsylvania*, Pennsylvania Historical Studies No. 25 (Harrisburg, PA: Huggins Printing, for the Pennsylvania Historical Association, 1994), 1–21. Knowing when to tap a furnace and how to charge it was how furnace men made their reputations, and their large incomes.

11 JCC, May 14, 1776; *Miscellaneous Numbered Records*, Board of War Account with Daniel Joy, May 7, 1778, 20464.

12 JCC, May 14, 1776, July 22, 1776; *Miscellaneous Numbered Records*, Board of War Account with Daniel Joy, May 7, 1778, 20464; PCC, Daniel Joy to Committee at Philadelphia, January 21, 1777, r97, i78, v13, p35. Though Joy never specifically discusses a boring mill, his comments show an intimate knowledge of Pennsylvania's iron furnaces and the potential for casting cannons. He was also able to bore out cannons he was sent to inspect throughout 1776 and 1777, though the furnaces he inspected did not have boring mills.

13 Peterson, *Round Shot*, 24–30, 63–67; Manucy, *Artillery through the Ages*, 65–67. Canister and grapeshot can be placed in the category of solid shot, as they were each essentially boxes of many small individual solid shots.

14 Ibid.

15 PCC, William Heath to George Washington, April 21, 1777, r167, i152, v4, p151, Samuel French to the Board of War, August 28, 1779, r95, i78, v9, p283, Return of the Commissary of Military Stores, December 1, 1779, r46, i39, v2, p409. French's lack of influence is proved more by the lack of material relating to his assignment than to the depth of material. RMS; PWH, Nathaniel Barber to William Heath, May 6, 1777, 4:125, Nathaniel Barber to William Heath, August 1, 1777, 6:11.

16 *Berkshire Furnace Journal, 1778–1780*, No records are available documenting how many of these passed inspection, though the furnace's journal does not record that any shot or shells were returned by Flower. This is significant because the furnace manager kept meticulous records, even making a distinction between which items were delivered to Flower and which were picked up by him. If any of the furnace's products had failed proof, they would have been returned for recasting and such an occurrence would almost surely have been recorded in the furnace journal.

17 Charles S. Boyer, *Early Forges and Furnaces in New Jersey* (Philadelphia: University of Pennsylvania Press, 1931), 26–33.

18 JCC, January 15, 1778; *Pennsylvania Gazette*, December 7, 1785.

19 *PCC*, Thomas Mayberry and James Morgan to Congress, March 17, 1780, r55, i42, v5, p179.

20 *Cornwall Furnace Journal, 1776–1782*, November 12, 1777, Forge and Furnace Collection, Historical Society of Pennsylvania, Philadelphia; *CBOB*, Charles Lukens to Samuel Hughes, May 18, 1779, 128. CBC, Samuel Sargent to John Davis, June 7, 1779, 10:13274:29, Samuel Sargent to John Davis, July 16, 1779, 10:13274:48, Samuel Sargent to John Davis, July 23, 1779, 10:13274:52, Samuel Sargent to Samuel Postlewaite, August 21, 1779, 10:13274:62, Samuel Sargent to Samuel Postlewaite, September 20, 1779, 10:13274:66, Charles Lukens to John Davis, September 29, 1779, 10:13274:68; *PCC*, Benjamin Flower Deposition Regarding Commissary Department, August 19, 1778, r76, i62, p639.

21 CBC, Samuel Miles to John Davis, October 4, 1781, 7:13267:1128, Samuel Sargent to John Davis, July 3, 1779, 10:13274:42, Charles Lukens to John Davis, July 28, 1779, 10, Misc. Papers: 2.9, Grier to John Davis, October 5, 1781, 7:13267:1130, Victoria Lyles, "Forges and Furnaces of York County," *Papers of the Historical Society of York County*, 11:13277.1:9, Charles Lukens to John Davis, June 11, 1779, 10:13274:33; *Miscellaneous Numbered Records*, Account of Ege and Gwynn for Shot and Shell at Maryann Furnace, November 16, 1781, 20438; LSH, Samuel Hodgdon to Colonel Mitchell, Deputy Quartermaster General, April 18, 1780.

22 CBC, Certificate from Gibson, Captain of Artificers, March 31, 1781, 10:13276:202, Certificate from Gibson, Captain of Artificers, April 24, 1781, 10:13276:203, James Gibson to Samuel Sargent, May 16, 1780, 10:13275:140, Biggs to Postlewaite, August 8, 1780, 10:13276:151; *Cornwall Furnace Journal, 1776–1782*, March 22, 1780.

23 The author has calculated these figures and others referenced below from RMS and "Ledgers of Accounts with Officers, Other Persons and States, 1778 to 1792," *Numbered Record Books*, microfilm, M853, r36, v100 and 144, hereafter "Ledgers of Accounts," *Numbered Record Books*.

24 LSH, Samuel Hodgdon to Jonathan Gostelowe, May 12, 1780.

25 *PCC*, Return of the Commissary of Military Stores, December 1, 1779, r46, i39, v2, p409.

26 *PWH*, Ezekiel Cheever to William Heath, July 19, 1777, 5:163, Ezekiel Cheever to William Heath, August 17, 1777, 6:41, Return of Militia, September 25, 1777, 6:91, Ezekiel Cheever to William Heath, September 3, 1778, 11:89.

27 *PGW*, William Heath to George Washington, June 7, 1777, 9:634-635, Board of War to Washington, October 24, 1777, 11:598.

28 *PCC*, Joseph Nourse to Committee at Philadelphia, January 23, 1777, r157, i147, v1, p37.

29 Ibid.

30 Ibid.

31 *PCC*, Joseph Nourse to Committee at Philadelphia, January 25, 1777, r157, i147, v1, p45.

32 Ibid.; *PCC*, John Hall to Congress, 1782, r54, i42, v3, p435.

33 *PGW*, editor's note, 10:499n; *PCC*, Benjamin Flower Deposition Regarding Commissary Department, August 19, 1778, r76, i62, p639, John Hall to Congress, 1782, r54, i42, v3, p435; *CBOB*, Thomas Butler to Charles Lukens, December 15, 1777, 46-47.

34 *PCC*, John Hall to Congress, 1782, r54, i42, v3, p435; *CBOB*, Jonathan

Gostelowe to Charles Lukens, January 24, 1778, 57, Instructions for William Henry, April 21, 1778, 90–92; MEC, November 6, 1777, December 5, 1777.

35 MEC, May 18, 1778; CBC, John Davis to John Barchuly, September 6, 1778, 3:13254:172, Samuel Sargent to John Davis, April 19, 1779, 10:13274:27, Samuel Sargent to John Davis, August 24, 1779, 10:13274:63, William Henry to unknown, November 10, 1779, 11:13277:31.

36 PCC, Joseph Perkins to Congress, February 27, 1781, r51, i41, v8, p142.

37 RMS.

38 RMS; LSH, Samuel Hodgdon to Jonathan Gostelowe, December 11, 1780; *Miscellaneous Numbered Records,* Receipt of Work Done on Muskets: Couloux, Penet and Company, 1780, 20473.

39 PCC, John Hall to Congress, 1782, r54, i42, v3, p435.

40 RMS; LSH, Samuel Hodgdon to James Pearson, June 6, 1781.

41 *Miscellaneous Numbered Records,* Various Accounts with the Commissary of Military Stores, 1784, 20466. Springfield was located at such a distance from government inspectors in Pennsylvania that a separate system had to be established there. The primary responsibility for reviewing repair and manufacturing work at the Springfield Arsenal fell to David Mason and Ezekiel Cheever. When these men were replaced in late 1780, Luke Bliss, the new commissary of military stores in the area, was given responsibility to inspect all work at the arsenal. All work done by the government's artificers or contracted out was deposited in the post magazine before being sent to the army. Bliss made regular inspections of the magazine, producing detailed reports of all the items in storage. These reports were forwarded to Hodgdon, who kept a record of what was being done at Springfield and the materiel available there for use. These records he provided to Knox, who used them for requesting stores from the post. Even after many reforms, Springfield remained closer to the army than it did to the operations of the military stores department. LSH, Samuel Hodgdon to the Board of War, September 25, 1779, Samuel Hodgdon to John Bryant, September 7, 1780, Samuel Hodgdon to the Board of War, October 8, 1781.

42 LSH, Samuel Hodgdon to John Hall, May 20, 1782.

43 JCC, February 18, 1779.

44 JCC, May 3, 1779. The Board of War most likely bypassed Flower's authority in this matter because of his illness and because the contract may have been made by Lukens. CBC, John Davis to Board of War, June 30, 1779, 3:13257:454, Richard Peters to John Davis, August, 25, 1779, 10:13274:64. LSH, Samuel Hodgdon to Daniel Hughes, October 7, 1780.

45 *Miscellaneous Numbered Records,* Return of Shells at Berkshire Furnace, March 20, 1780, 30589, Return of Shells at Oley Furnace, March 21, 1780, 30579.

46 *Miscellaneous Numbered Records,* Return of Shells at Warwick and Elizabeth Furnace, March 15, 1780, 30588. Potts requested that a government representative attend his forges to review the work they had done. According to Hodgdon's account book, he had the shells delivered to Philadelphia.

47 *Miscellaneous Numbered Records,* Certification by Daniel Joy, June 2, 1784, 30625.

48 Ibid.; LSH, Samuel Hodgdon to James Johnson and Company, October 10, 1780.

49 *Miscellaneous Numbered Records,* Certification by Daniel Joy, June 2, 1784, 30625.

50 Ibid.

51 LSH, Samuel Hodgdon to Daniel Joy, January 12, 1781.

52 Ibid.; *Miscellaneous Numbered Records*, Daniel Joy's Invoice of Shot and Shell Cast by Several Furnaces, June 14, 1781, 20700, Invoice of Batsto Furnace by Daniel Joy, May 10, 1781, 20699. Ten-inch shells weighed between seventy-five and eighty-one pounds each, while eight-inch shells weighed forty-two pounds each. The Durham Furnace made useful but less-consistent shells of seventy pounds for a ten-inch and thirty-nine pounds for an eight-inch shell.

53 LSH, Samuel Hodgdon to the Director of Hibernia Furnace, August 31, 1778.

54 LSH, Samuel Hodgdon to John Jacob Faesch, August 6, 1779, Samuel Hodgdon to John Jacob Faesch, January 1, 1780; *Miscellaneous Numbered Records*, Account of John Faesch, undated, 20432. Faesch was paid over £179 to keep his furnace in blast in 1778 and £126,378 to keep it in blast in 1779 and 1780. The large increase was due to the inflation in Continental currency that occurred in that time.

55 *PCC*, Board of War Report Regarding Ordnance, July 22, 1780, r159, i147, v4, p456. JCC: July 25, 1780. This amount was highly inflationary, having not been revalued from old emission into new emission, something Congress was in the process of accomplishing in mid-1780. In 1780, Congress revalued the paper dollar by issuing a new emission dollar to replace all the old dollars it had printed. It exchanged old dollars for new ones at a rate of 40:1. This revalue and the government's budgetary austerity helped stabilize the paper dollar against its specie equivalent. Unfortunately, Hodgdon never exchanged money in his records directly from pounds to specie dollars. His records exchanged pounds for paper dollars, and paper dollars for specie dollars, seemingly because exchange rates were still very fluid. The author has averaged Hodgdon's conversion rates. Hodgdon exchanged paper and specie dollars at varied rates, from 10:1 in early 1781 to 4:1 by the end of the year to 2.5:1 by early 1782. Hodgdon exchanged £1 for $2.66 in specie by the end of 1781. Thus, this amount equals no more than $100,000 in new emission, $10,000 in specie, or £3,759, using Hodgdon's conversion figures.

56 *Miscellaneous Numbered Records*, Account of John Faesch, undated, 20432; *PCC*, John Faesch Note on His Furnace to Henry Knox, July 7, 1780, r22, i11, p257. Using Hodgdon's conversion figures, Faesch was requesting roughly $53,000 in specie or $530,000 in new emission paper.

57 *Miscellaneous Numbered Records*, Return of the Shells, Carcasses, and One Pound Shot at Hibernia Furnace, December 23, 1780, 30622, Account of John Jacob Faesch, undated, 20463; *PHK*, Bomb Shells Proved at Pompton by Captain Lieutenant John Callender, July 22, 1780, 5:70.

58 LSH, Samuel Hodgdon to James Boyer, October 25, 1780.

59 *Miscellaneous Numbered Records*, Elijah Austin and Company to James Boyer, November 24, 1780, 20640. Boyer reported to Hodgdon that 196 eight-inch shells and 100 twenty-four pound shot had been manufactured at the Stafford Furnace.

60 *Miscellaneous Numbered Records*, John Jacob Faesch's Account of Shot and Shell with the United States, November 7, 1782, 20435, Receipt of John Jacob Faesch, August 1, 1784, 30628; LSH, Samuel Hodgdon to John Faesch, May 7, 1782, Samuel Hodgdon to the Superintendent of Finance, November 19, 1782.

61 LSH, Samuel Hodgdon to John Lamb, July 9, 1782, Samuel Hodgdon to Captain Stevens, July 9, 1782.

62 *Miscellaneous Numbered Records*, John Jacob Faesch's Account of Shot and Shell with the United States, November 7, 1782, 20435, Account of Shot and Shell Cast, November 7, 1782, 20436, William Stevens, Captain of the Second Artillery, to Benjamin Lincoln, November 7, 1782, 20557.
63 *PHK*, Shells Cast at Salisbury Furnace, July 27, 1782, 9:55; Rome, *Connecticut's Cannon*, 8–16. *Miscellaneous Numbered Records*, Account of Shot and Shell Cast, November 7, 1782, 20436.

CHAPTER SEVEN: "WE MANUFACTURED ALL THE ARTICLES NECESSARY FOR OUR DEFENCE"

1 Darwin Stapleton, "General Daniel Roberdeau and the Lead Mine Expedition," *Pennsylvania History* 38 (October 1971): 361–371.
2 *PCC*, Daniel Roberdeau to John Jay, June 30, 1779, r101, i78, v19, p285.
3 John A. Myers, "Daniel Roberdeau," Pennsylvania Center for the Book, fall 2009, accessed September 10, 2015, http://pabook.libraries.psu.edu/palitmap/bios/Roberdeau_Daniel.html.
4 Thomas Doerflinger, *A Vigorous Spirit of Enterprise: Merchants and Economic Development in Revolutionary Philadelphia* (Chapel Hill: University of North Carolina Press, 1986), 199.
5 Ibid., 204.
6 Ibid., 200.
7 RMS; "Ledgers of Accounts," *Numbered Record Books*.
8 "Ledgers of Accounts," *Numbered Record Books*. Cast iron came directly out of a furnace and was usually cast in pigs. Bar iron was cast iron refined in a forge. Nail rod iron was bar iron that was further refined and made into long strips from which to cut nails. Steel was a specially refined iron with certain trace amounts of impurities.
9 Ibid.; *Miscellaneous Numbered Records*, Account of Luke Bliss, June 29, 1782, 20428; *CBOB*, Memorial of Work Done by Carpenters, November 26, 1777, 31–33, Thomas Wylie to Benjamin Flower, November 28, 1777, 33–34; CBC, An uncompleted Paper by the Christian P. Humrich, Esq. Read before the Hamilton Library Association, Carlisle, Pa., February 19th, 1907, by His Daughter-in-law, Mrs. Charles F. Humrich, 11: miscellaneous loose papers.
10 "Ledgers of Accounts," *Numbered Record Books*.
11 RMS, "Ledgers of Accounts," *Numbered Record Books*.
12 Ibid.; *Miscellaneous Numbered Records*, Commissary of Military Stores Account of Money Advanced, November 30, 1783, 20421. The figure of $832,000 is the total of all spending recorded for those years by Hodgdon in his ledgers and is recorded in new emission dollars. Hodgdon listed some of his expenditures in British pounds, others in old emission dollars, and most in new emission dollars. The author converted all figures into new emission dollars, using a conversion rate Hodgdon expressed in his ledgers of $2.66:£1 and $2.50 old emission to $1 new emission. All monetary figures that follow are expressed either as Hodgdon expressed them or as Hodgdon would have converted them.
13 "Ledgers of Accounts," *Numbered Record Books*, 9.
14 Ibid., 51.
15 Ibid., 46.
16 Ibid., 17.
17 Ibid., 46, 73.
18 Ibid., 47, 48, 53, 55, 61, 74.

19 Eggert, *Iron Industry*, 10–11. It was a complex process to keep a furnace in blast, leading furnace owners to gather as much fuel and ore as the furnace would use for an extended period of operation.

20 Buel, *In Irons*, 127–133, 191–206; LSH, Samuel Hodgdon to the Board of War, October 8, 1781; PCC, Board of War to the President of Congress, September 4, 1780, r161, i148, v1, p187.

21 Joseph E. Walker, *Hopewell Village: The Dynamics of a Nineteenth Century Iron-Making Community* (Philadelphia: University of Pennsylvania Press, 1966), 27–29; JCC, August 22, 1776, April 8, 1778, May 8, 1778, October 14, 1780. The monetary figures expressed here are based on Hodgdon's figure of $2.66:£1, and those given by Walker. PCC, Mark Bird to Congress, September 14, 1783, r73, i59, v3, p215, Report of Congress Committee on Mark Bird, September 19, 1783, r26, i19, v1, p363; *Berkshire Furnace Journal, 1774–1778*; *Berkshire Furnace Journal, 1778–1780*; "Ledgers of Accounts," *Numbered Record Books*, 27, 44.

22 "Ledgers of Accounts," *Numbered Record Books*; *Miscellaneous Numbered Records*, Commissary of Military Stores Account of Money Advanced, November 30, 1783, 20421, Certification by Daniel Joy, June 2, 1784, 30625; Gordon, *American Iron*, 7–89; Eggert, *Iron Industry*, 5–14; Boyer, *Early Forges*, 96–99, 136–139; Thomas Doerflinger, "Hibernia Furnace during the Revolution," *New Jersey History* 90 (Summer 1972): 113–114; PCC, John Faesch note on his furnace, July 7, 1780, r22, i11, p257.

23 "Ledgers of Accounts," *Numbered Record Books*, 14, 28, 88; LSH, Samuel Hodgdon to John Jacob Faesch, January 1, 1780.

24 LSH, Samuel Hodgdon to John Jacob Faesch, January 1, 1780.

25 Doerflinger, "Hibernia Furnace," 114.

26 LSH, Samuel Hodgdon to the Board of War, October 8, 1781.

27 "Ledgers of Accounts," *Numbered Record Books*.

28 RMS.

29 "Ledgers of Accounts," *Numbered Record Books*.

30 "Ledgers of Accounts," *Numbered Record Books*, 5. Homes converted the iron to steel and then made bayonets from the steel.

31 Ibid.; RMS.

32 "Ledgers of Accounts," *Numbered Record Books*.

33 Ibid. This figure was arrived at by comparing the amount of resources used by other bayonet makers against Eckfeldt's usage.

34 "Ledgers of Accounts," *Numbered Record Books*, 15.

35 Ibid., 51.

36 JCC, January 15, 1778; Boyer, *Early Forges*, 26–33; Gordon, *American Iron*, 60.

37 PCC, Thomas Mayberry and James Morgan to Congress, March 17, 1780, r55, i42, v5, p179; "Ledgers of Accounts," *Numbered Record Books*.

38 Gordon, *American Iron*, 173–74.

39 LSH, Samuel Hodgdon to Thomas Wylie, May 30, 1780.

40 LSH, Samuel Hodgdon to Mark Thompson, May 5, 1780, Samuel Hodgdon to Mark Thompson, February 3, 1781, Samuel Hodgdon to Colonel Jacob Weiss, February 3, 1781, Samuel Hodgdon to Colonel Jacob Weiss, May 24, 1782, Samuel Hodgdon to Mark Thompson, July 12, 1781; "Ledgers of Accounts," *Numbered Record Books*, 6.

41 RMS.

42 Gordon, *American Iron*, 61.

43 *PCC*, Benjamin Flower to Samuel Huntington, December 10, 1779, r95, i78, v9, p299.

44 *PCC*, Board of Treasury Report Regarding Benjamin Flower and William Palfrey, March 25, 1780, r147, i136, v4, p153; RMS. The monetary sum expressed here represents a high amount of inflation. In March 1780, Congress resolved to exchange all of its old emission dollars for new emission dollars at a rate of 40:1. Therefore, just weeks after Congress granted Potts $260,205, it would legally be depreciated to a balance of $6,505.

45 *Miscellaneous Numbered Records*, Estate of Colonel Thomas Potts with the United States, 20461. The monetary figure here is expressed in new emission dollars based on Hodgdon's exchange rate. Potts noted his desire for payment for steel at £4,500 per ton. Both figures reveal the depths to which inflation had driven the American economy. Steel could be had in 1775 for £30 ($133) to £40 ($177) per ton; these exchanges using John J. McCusker's rate of $4.44:£1. McCusker, *Money and Exchange,*7n9; McCusker, "How Much Is That," 319; "Ledgers of Accounts," *Numbered Record Books*, 6.

46 LSH, Receipt of Thomas Potts, September 21, 1780.

47 LSH, Samuel Hodgdon to Thomas Potts and Downing, March 22, 1782.

48 LSH, Samuel Hodgdon to Thomas Potts and Downing, April 9, 1782.

49 LSH, Samuel Hodgdon to Colonel Weiss, Deputy Quartermaster General, May 24, 1782.

50 Ibid.; *Miscellaneous Numbered Records*, Estate of Colonel Thomas Potts with the United States, 20461. Steel valued at $47,000 per ton in 1780 was worth $285 per ton in 1788.

51 LSH, Samuel Hodgdon to Thomas Potts and Downing, April 9, 1782.

52 *PCC*, William Houston to Elias Boudinot, May 3, 1783, r39, i32, p479.

53 *PCC*, Stacy Potts to Elias Boudinot, June 28, 1783, r39, i32, p483–501.

54 *PCC*, William Houston to Elias Boudinot, May 3, 1783, r39, i32, p479.

55 *PCC*, Report of Congressional Committee on Manufacturing, August 19, 1783, r28, i19, v5, p211.

56 *Miscellaneous Numbered Records*, Commissioners of the Board of Treasury Conversion Chart, undated, 30612, Memorial of Investigators Regarding Potts Iron, May 15, 1788, 30611.

57 *Miscellaneous Numbered Records*, Memorial of Investigators Regarding Potts Iron, May 15, 1788, 30611.

58 LSH, Samuel Hodgdon to Joseph Perkins, June 17, 1780, Samuel Hodgdon to John Hall, May 20, 1782; *PCC*, Board of War Report Regarding Artificers, October 19, 1780, r159, i147, v4, p617, Return of the Commissary of Military Stores, December 1, 1779, r46, i39, v2, p409; *Miscellaneous Numbered Records*, Invoice of Artillery Stores from France, Taken from the Royal Magazines at Brest and Shipped June 15, 1781, 20703, Various Accounts with the Commissary of Military Stores, undated, 20466; "Ledgers of Accounts," *Numbered Record Books*.

59 *PCC*, Penet to Congress, May 20, 1780, r100, i78, v18, p291; "Ledgers of Accounts," *Numbered Record Books*, 16. Monetary figures here are taken from Hodgdon ledgers and reflect currency conversions.

60 "Ledgers of Accounts," *Numbered Record Books*. Figures compiled by the author from multiple sections within the "Ledgers of Accounts."

61 Ibid.

62 Gordon, *American Iron*, 33–49.

63 Continental soldiers mining coal moved it on barges down the Susquehanna River to Harris's Ferry. At Harris's Ferry it was placed on wagons for transport to Carlisle or Philadelphia.

64 Not until the nineteenth century did anthracite coal replace charcoal as the major fuel source in American furnaces. Ironmongers returned to charcoal after the revolution because wood was more readily available than anthracite. The market and social forces that made anthracite attractive during the war were no longer applicable. However, the road, canal, and rail revolutions of the nineteenth century made the anthracite seams of Pennsylvania and Virginia more accessible to ironmongers. At the same time, overharvesting of wood and the expansion of the iron industry made charcoal more expensive to ironmongers. As a result, anthracite replaced charcoal in the American iron industry. Gordon, *American Iron*, 33–49; Eggert, *Iron Industry*, 2–26. "Because they had such large coal resources, American miners could easily dig as much [anthracite] as customers wanted." Gordon, *American Iron*, 45.

65 PCC, Daniel Joy to the Committee at Philadelphia, January 21, 1777, r97, i78, v13, p35. Joy was unaware of the state's second important seam of coal west of what is today Jim Thorpe, though he did know of some "up the main Branch of the Schuylkill near Mr. Hughes Mill," which was in that vicinity.

66 *Pennsylvania Gazette*, May 12, 1768.

67 Ward, *War of the Revolution*, 2:629–632, 638–654.

68 *Miscellaneous Numbered Records*, Samuel Sargent to Benjamin Flower, November 12, 1780, 30523.

69 *CBOB*, Charles Lukens to Cornelius Sweers, June 15, 1778, 29. Lukens asked Sweers to pass this message on to Flower.

70 *Miscellaneous Numbered Records*, Samuel Sargent to Benjamin Flower, November 12, 1780, 30523.

71 *Miscellaneous Numbered Records*, A Return of Arms, Ammunition, Accoutrements, Entrenching Tools, etc. at Wyoming, May 15, 1779, 35429; *CBOB*, Charles Lukens to Cornelius Sweers, June 15, 1778, 29.

72 LSH, Samuel Hodgdon to Samuel Sargent, December 12, 1780; *CBOB*, Charles Lukens to Henry Hollingsworth, June 16, 1778, 109. Coal was taken from outcroppings and shallow mines in the vicinity of Richmond, Virginia, as early as 1748. By 1763, Samuel Du Val advertised for sale, "any Quantity of good coal, from my Pits, in the Colony [of Virginia]." Likewise Gerrard Ellyson announced in 1765 that he had opened a bank of coal along the James River and had six thousand bushels available for sale. *Pennsylvania Gazette*, March 24, 1763.

73 *CBOB*, Charles Lukens to Hollingsworth, June 16, 1778, 109.

74 *CBOB*, Cornelius Sweers to Charles Lukens, February 1778, 65–70; *Miscellaneous Numbered Records*, Samuel Hodgdon Account for Incidental Expenses in the Commissary of Military Stores Department, September 1780, 20425. Payment to Bennett was made in as £257.10, but has here been converted into dollars for continuity. Hodgdon's conversion figures of $2.66:£1 were used. CBC, Proposal to Carry Coal by Wright, 2:13254:217.

75 *Miscellaneous Numbered Records*, Mr. Perkins Return of Stores for the Armory for One Year, undated, 20688, Samuel Miles, Deputy Quartermaster to Samuel Hodgdon, November 30, 1780, 30577, Receipt of Work Done on Muskets by Couloux, Penet, and Company, 1780, 20473; RMS; *CBOB*, Charles

Lukens to Hollingsworth, June 16, 1778, 109. Hodgdon delivered thirty bushels of coal to Penet's gun works during its period of operation.
76 Continental agents would take whatever horses were available to move goods, whether they were draft horses or not.
77 Carp, *To Starve the Army*, 19–98; Risch, *Supplying Washington's Army*, 90–91.
78 Risch, *Supplying Washington's Army*, 64–96.
79 Ibid., 75.
80 Ibid., 72–73.
81 *CBOB*, Board of War to John Davis, June 11, 1778, 28.
82 LSH, Samuel Hodgdon to Mark Thompson, May 5, 1780, Samuel Hodgdon to Mark Thompson, June 2, 1780, Samuel Hodgdon to Colonel Jacob Weiss, Deputy Quartermaster General, December 29, 1780.
83 LSH, Samuel Hodgdon to Colonel Jacob Weiss, Deputy Quartermaster General, January 10, 1781.
84 *Miscellaneous Numbered Records*, Samuel Miles, Deputy Quartermaster to Samuel Hodgdon, November 6, 1780, 30527; LSH, Samuel Hodgdon to Colonel Jacob Weiss, Deputy Quartermaster General, December 29, 1780.
85 *Miscellaneous Numbered Records*, Samuel Miles, Deputy Quartermaster, to Samuel Hodgdon, November 30, 1780, 30577.
86 RMS.
87 LSH, Samuel Hodgdon to Archibald Shaw, June 22, 1780.
88 Ibid.; LSH, Samuel Hodgdon to Archibald Shaw, September 1, 1780; "Ledgers of Accounts," *Numbered Record Books*, 3, 10, 17, 19, 43, 65, 72, 78, 82, 114, 132. According to Carp, wagoners in the Quartermaster Department often engaged in several nefarious schemes because they were effectively without oversight on their transportation runs. They would sell stores they were transporting; dump the stores and transport private stores or camp followers; or dump the stores they were transporting and transport their own goods. Carp attributed such occurrences to the fact that Congress restrained the Quartermaster Department from paying wagoners a decent salary. Therefore, only the most desperate and unskilled wagoners took assignments with the government and usually did so to be in a position to earn money illegally.
89 "Ledgers of Accounts," *Numbered Record Books*; LSH, Samuel Hodgdon to William Chambers, July 2, 1780.
90 See chapter 5 for production activities and output figures at Springfield.
91 LSH, Samuel Hodgdon to Luke Bliss, April 22, 1782.
92 LSH, Samuel Hodgdon to Jacob Weiss, Deputy Quartermaster General, July 12, 1781 (first letter of the day), Samuel Hodgdon to Jacob Weiss, Deputy Quartermaster General, July 12, 1781 (second letter of the day).
93 LSH, James Boyer to Colonel Samuel Miles, February 2, 1782.
94 LSH, Samuel Hodgdon to Daniel Hughes, October 7, 1780.
95 LSH, Samuel Hodgdon to Joseph Perkins and John Nicholson, December 29, 1783.
96 CBC, Samuel Postlewaite to John Davis, March 12, 1779, 10:13274:22, Charles McClure to John Davis, April 27, 1779, 8:13270:60, William Rippey to unknown, May 12, 1779, 4:13258:448, Samuel Sargent to John Davis, June 7, 1779, 10:13274:29, Samuel Sargent to John Davis, June 10, 1779, 10:13274:32, Samuel Sargent to John Davis, July 3, 1779, 10:13274:42.
97 LSH, Samuel Hodgdon to James Johnson and Company, October 10, 1780.

CHAPTER EIGHT: "THE AMERICAN FOUNDERY"

1 Samuel Hodgdon to Joseph Perkins, July 31, 1798, *Papers of the War Department: 1784–1800*, accessed October 21, 2015, http://wardepartmentpapers.org/document.php?id=27850.

2 Joseph Perkins to Samuel Hodgdon, December 5, 1798, *Papers of the War Department: 1784–1800*.

3 PCC, Henry Knox return of ordnance and military stores captured at Yorktown and Gloucester, October 1781, r171, i152, v10, p335, Sebastian Bauman return of ordnance left by British troops, November 11, 1783, r45, i38, p389.

4 *CBOB*, Board of War to Benjamin Flower, July 6, 1779, 136–141.

5 David B. Mattern, *Benjamin Lincoln and the American Revolution* (Columbia: University of South Carolina Press, 1995), 22–120.

6 PCC, Benjamin Lincoln memo regarding arsenals and academies, March 5, 1783, r45, i38, p285.

7 LSH, Samuel Hodgdon to Superintendent of Finance, December 23, 1783.

8 PCC, Henry Knox return of ordnance and military stores captured at Yorktown and Gloucester, October 1781, r171, i152, v10, p335, Sebastian Bauman return of ordnance left by British troops, November 11, 1783, r45, i38, p389.

9 PCC, Benjamin Lincoln to President of Congress, June 14, 1783, r163, i149, v3, p5.

10 Ibid.

11 Ibid.

12 PCC, Benjamin Lincoln to President of Congress, July 29, 1782, r162, i149, v1, p233; *JCC*, April 26, 1782.

13 PCC, Benjamin Lincoln to President of Congress, July 29, 1782, r162, i149, v1, p233.

14 PCC, Benjamin Lincoln memo regarding arsenals and academies, March 5, 1783, r45, i38, p285. Lincoln saw a role for government-sponsored education as well. The military would need educated and trained officers and artillerymen in the postwar period. Lincoln believed that the superintendent of each government arsenal should oversee the education of junior officers sent to serve with him. He also realized that state militia officers and artillerymen could also receive training at the Confederation's regional arsenals. Individuals trained at the arsenals would not only use their education to serve the military but apply them to the nation's private manufacturing sector as well. According to Lincoln's plan, the military stores program would play a twofold role in the development of the nation's manufacturing capacity. It would invest in production and provide a pool of trained workers.

15 Ibid.

16 Lincoln believed that promoting all types of manufacturing would benefit the nation's defensive capabilities in some way, though he wanted to begin by promoting the iron industry, gun making, and the crafts necessary for the production of accouterments.

17 PCC, Benjamin Lincoln to Superintendent of Finance, July 18, 1783, r45, i38, p285, Benjamin Lincoln memo regarding arsenals and academies, March 5, 1783, r163, i149, v3, p89.

18 *JCC*, October 23, 1783.

19 LSH, Samuel Hodgdon to John Bryant, January 15, 1783; *PHK*, Henry Knox

to Benjamin Lincoln, March 3, 1783, 1:177–178, Benjamin Lincoln to Henry Knox, *June* 14, 1783, 12:155, Benjamin Lincoln to Henry Knox, July 23, 1783, 13:107; *Genesis of the US Armory,* Footnote to *JCC,* April 26, 1782.

20 *PHK,* Benjamin Lincoln to Henry Knox, July 23, 1783, 13:107.

21 *PCC,* Benjamin Lincoln to President of Congress, July 27, 1782, r162, i149, v1, p533; LSH, Samuel Hodgdon to Samuel Sargent, August 16, 1782.

22 *PCC,* James Byers to Benjamin Lincoln, May 20, 1782, r150, i137, v3, p311, Report of Congressional committee regarding James Byers, January 24, 1784, r26, i19, v1, p481. The monetary figure here takes into account depreciation and exchange rates of new emission for old emission. *JCC,* January 30, 1784. Two years later, Congress rejected the deal as harmful to Byers, and years later he was still seeking compensation for his work.

23 James Byers to Lincoln, January 18, 1783, *The Benjamin Lincoln Papers,* 13 reels, ed. Frederick S. Allis (Ann Arbor, MI: University Microfilms, 1993), microfilm.

24 LSH, Samuel Hodgdon to James Byers, January 20, 1783.

25 RMS; "Ledgers of Accounts," *Numbered Record Books.*

26 *PCC,* Committee at Camp report regarding artillery, September 27, 1776, r163, i149, v3, p93, John Lamb to Board of War, February 21, 1780, r159, i147, v4, p450, Robert Morris to Secretary at War, July 18, 1783, r163, i149, v3, p89; LSH, Samuel Hodgdon to Superintendent of Finance, May 5, 1784.

27 LSH, Samuel Hodgdon to Samuel Sargent, May 23, 1782, Samuel Hodgdon to Samuel Sargent, August 16, 1782, Samuel Hodgdon to James Pearson, February 18, 1784; *Miscellaneous Numbered Records,* Worsley Emes to Samuel Hodgdon, June 10, 1784, 30519-20; *PCC,* Benjamin Lincoln to President of Congress, April 11, 1782, r162, i149, v1, p233.

28 *PCC,* Robert Morris to Secretary at War, July 21, 1783, r163, i149, v3, p93.

29 *PCC,* Benjamin Lincoln to Superintendent of Finance, July 18, 1783, r163, i149, v3, p89.

30 *PCC,* Robert Morris to Secretary at War, July 21, 1783, r163, i149, v3, p93.

31 *PCC,* Robert Morris to Secretary at War, July 28, 1783, r149, i137, v2, p689. The Articles of Confederation delineated that armed forces were to exist on the state and national levels. During war and peace, the states were to manage and equip their own armed forces. The situation differed for Congress, which in war could recruit its own army but in peace had to rely on the states to provide troops for service to the Confederation. In either event, troops in congressional service were armed and supplied out of the congressional Treasury, which was funded by the states according to annual requisitions made to them by Congress. In the passage quoted here, Morris was blaming potential military stores losses on the failure of the states to provide money to the Treasury. Generally, in both war and peace, state governments chose to pay for state troops rather than provide money for troops in congressional service. Thus, the Confederation's army suffered from a lack of monetary resources after the war, just as it had during the war.

32 *PCC,* Benjamin Lincoln to President of Congress, July 28, 1783, r163, i149, v3, p95.

33 *Benjamin Lincoln Papers,* Benjamin Lincoln to Joseph Carleton, November 6, 1783.

34 Those states were Massachusetts, Rhode Island, Connecticut, New York, Pennsylvania, Maryland, Virginia, and South Carolina. *JCC,* October 2, 1788; *PCC,* Return of stores by Samuel Hodgdon, February 1, 1784, r155, i143, p190–95.

35 *Miscellaneous Numbered Records*, Donaldson Yeates to Hodgdon, October 19, 1784, 30463.
36 *PCC*, Samuel Hodgdon to President of Congress, March 18, 1784, r155, i143, p240.
37 LSH, Samuel Hodgdon to George Ege, April 3, 1783.
38 Merrill Jensen, *The New Nation: A History of the United States during the Confederation, 1781–1789* (New York: Vintage Books, 1950), 383–384, 390.
39 *PCC*, Board of Treasury to Henry Knox, June 14, 1786, r164, i150, v1, p361.
40 *PCC*, Expenditures of the military departments from 1784–87, 1787, r154, i141, v1, p77; Jensen, *New Nation*, 367.
41 *PCC*, Expenditures of the military departments from 1784–87, 1787, r154, i141, v1, p77.
42 *PCC*, Report of Committee on arsenals to Congress, July 29, 1783, r34, i27, p235.
43 *PCC*, Samuel Hodgdon to President of Congress, March 18, 1784, r155, i143, p240.
44 Ibid.
45 "Ledgers of Accounts," *Numbered Record Books*.
46 Compiled from Captain John Bryant Papers, Bryant-Mason-Smith Family Papers, 1767–1861, Massachusetts Historical Society, Boston.
47 LSH, Samuel Hodgdon to Colonel Donaldson Yeates, September 10, 1782, Samuel Hodgdon to Superintendent of Finance, April 1, 1783.
48 "Ledgers of Accounts," *Numbered Record Books*.
49 LSH, Samuel Hodgdon to Colonel Donaldson Yeates, September 10, 1782, Samuel Hodgdon to Superintendent of Finance, April 1, 1783.
50 LSH, Samuel Hodgdon to the Superintendent of Finance, January 3, 1784. Hodgdon sold shells back to the ironmasters who had produced the shells at $29.26 per ton and shot at $21.28 per ton.
51 "Ledgers of Accounts," *Numbered Record Books*.
52 Ibid. The department's three-year budget from 1780 to 1783 was an estimated $800,000, while from 1784 to 1787 it was $177,000.
53 *PCC*, Report of Committee on arsenals to Congress, July 29, 1783, r34, i27, p235.
54 *PCC*, AA Muller to Henry Knox, February 7, 1788, r165, i150, v3, p149–154.
55 LSH, Samuel Hodgdon to James Pearson, February 18, 1784.
56 *Miscellaneous Numbered Records*, Captain Joy's Return of Ordnance in Philadelphia Ordnance Yard, March 6, 1784, 30491, Samuel Hodgdon to Henry Knox, January 31, 1786, 30511.
57 *Miscellaneous Numbered Records*, Receipt for Rent by Samuel Hodgdon, January 1, 1787, 30536.
58 RMS.
59 *PCC*, Samuel Hodgdon to the President of Congress, March 18, 1784, r155, i143, p240.
60 LSH, Samuel Hodgdon to the Superintendent of Finance, May 5, 1784; RMS.
61 *Miscellaneous Numbered Records*, John Thompson to Samuel Hodgdon, 1788, 30516, Contract Between Thompson and Clark, October 18, 1788, 30517.
62 *PCC*, Samuel Hodgdon to Henry Knox, January 31, 1786, 30511.
63 *PHK*, Henry Knox to Benjamin Lincoln, June 14, 1783, 13:107; *PCC*,

Secretary at War report of military stores at Springfield, March 13, 1787, r165, i151, p243.

64 *PCC*, Henry Knox to Samuel Hardy, June 13, 1784, r184, i167, p431.

65 *PCC*, John Doughty return of the garrison at West Point, September 30, 1784, r74, i60, p95.

66 *PCC*, John Doughty to R.H. Lee, October 31, 1784, r94, i78, v8, p81.

67 Ibid.

68 Ibid.; *Miscellaneous Numbered Records*, William Price to Samuel Hodgdon, February 2, 1785, 30508.

69 *PCC*, Henry Knox to President of Congress, September 30, 1785, r164, i150, v1, p95.

70 *JCC*, October 2, 1788.

71 *PCC*, Henry Knox to Arthur Lee, April 27, 1787, r164, i150, v1, p447.

72 *JCC*, October 2, 1788.

73 Returns of Springfield Arsenal, 1790–1794, Massachusetts Historical Society Collections, Massachusetts Historical Society, Boston.

74 LSH, Samuel Hodgdon to John Bryant, April 26, 1784.

75 Bryant Papers, Receipts, September 29, 1784, John Bryant Return to Samuel Hodgdon, February 1, 1785.

76 *JCC*, October 2, 1788; Returns of Springfield Arsenal, 1790–1794, Massachusetts Historical Society Collections; Bryant Papers, Various Receipts from 1785.

77 *PCC*, Henry Knox to Congress, September 20, 1786, r164, i150, v1, p555.

78 Bryant Papers, John Bryant to Samuel Hodgdon, August 14, 1784, Receipt September 29, 1784, John Bryant Return to Samuel Hodgdon, February 1, 1785, Echsard Stebbins Receipt, November 1, 1786.

79 LSH, Samuel Hodgdon to the President of Congress, May 3, 1784; *JCC*, August 1, 1786.

80 *JCC*, August 1, 1786.

81 Ibid. Knox reported to Congress that the ammunition had "been removed to the arsenal at Springfield." Bryant Papers, Return of Shot and Shell Received of Ralph Pomeroy, March 27, 1786, Receipt of Jupiter Richards, April 15, 1786.

82 *PCC*, Henry Knox to Congress, September 20, 1786, r164, i150, v1, p555.

83 *PCC*, Secretary at War report of military stores at Springfield, March 13, 1787, r165, i151, p243.

84 *PHK*, Dimensions for a Wall, undated, 48:75; Bryant Papers, Account of Bryant with Thomas Bates, March 7, 1789.

85 *JCC*, October 2, 1788.

86 Bryant Papers, Account of the Weight of the 8 Inch Howitzers Cast by Mr. Byers for the United States, undated, Receipt, October 8, 1793, Receipt, December 27, 1793, Receipt, April 9, 1794.

87 Mulholland, *History of Metals*, 130–131; *Benjamin Lincoln Papers,* Joseph Byers to Benjamin Lincoln, January 18, 1783; Bryant Papers, Account of the Weight of the 8 Inch Howitzers Cast by Mr. Byers for the United States, undated. Returns of Springfield Arsenal, 1790–1794, op. cit.

88 *JCC*, October 2, 1788.

89 Returns of Springfield Arsenal, 1790–1794, Massachusetts Historical Society Collections; *Benjamin Lincoln Papers,* Joseph Byers to Benjamin Lincoln, January 18, 1783; Bryant Papers, Account of the Weight of the 8 Inch Howitzers; Jackson and de Beer, *Eighteenth Century Gunfounding*, 64.

90 *PCC*, Return of Troops, December 1784, r100, i78, v17, p151.

91 *JCC*, February 21, 1785.

92 LSH, James Boyer to Samuel Sargent, March 25, 1782; *PCC*, Inventory of ordnance and stores at Fort Nelson, at the falls of Ohio, May 10, 1784, r164, i150, v1, p191, Henry Knox to Samuel Hardy, June 13, 1784, r184, i167, p431.

93 *PCC*, Henry Knox to the Board of Treasury, June 9, 1786, r164, i150, v1, p357, Henry Knox to the Board of Treasury, June 9, 1786, r164, i150, v1, p365.

94 *PCC*, Henry Knox to Governor Bowdoin, September 16, 1786, r164, i150, v1, p551.

95 Leonard Richards, *Shays's Rebellion: The American Revolution's Final Battle* (Philadelphia: University of Pennsylvania Press, 2002), 4–36.

96 *PCC*, John Bryant to unknown, January 23, 1787, r164, i150, v2, p177.

97 *PCC*, Secretary at War report of military stores at Springfield, March 13, 1787, r165, i151, p243.

98 Ibid.

99 Ibid.

100 See Jensen, *New Nation*, 63–76, 386–387.

101 *PCC*, Secretary at War report of military stores at Springfield, March 13, 1787, r165, i151, p243.

102 *PCC*, Henry Knox to General George Washington, December 30, 1778, r57, i43, p137.

103 *PCC*, George Washington, Commission to Knox as Secretary of War, September 12, 1789, r72, i59, v1, p228; "Ledgers of Accounts," *Numbered Record Books.*

104 Stanley Elkins and Eric McKitrick, *The Age of Federalism: The American Republic, 1788–1800* (New York: Oxford University Press, 1993), 92–131.

105 *Pennsylvania Gazette*, November 2, 1791.

106 *PHK*, Minutes for President's Speech, October 24, 1791, 29:161.

107 House of Representatives, *Journal of the House of Representatives of the United States, 1789–1793*, Thursday, December 13, 1792, "A Century of Lawmaking for a New Nation: U.S. Congressional Documents and Debates, 1774–1875," Law Library of Congress, accessed May 6, 2016, http://lcweb2.loc.gov/ammem/amlaw/lawhome.html. The journal for this date contains the budgetary request submitted by Henry Knox for his department.

108 *Pennsylvania Gazette*, December 11, 1793.

109 Elkins and McKitrick, *Age of Federalism*, 150–256.

110 *Pennsylvania Gazette*, March 26, 1794.

111 Merritt Roe Smith, *Harpers Ferry Armory and the New Technology: The Challenge of Change* (Ithaca, NY: Cornell University Press, 1977), 28. The first quote is from US Statutes at Large, 1:352; the second is Smith's.

112 Smith, *Harpers Ferry*, 28.

113 Irvine-Newbold Family Papers, 1766–1955, 232 vols., Historical Society of Pennsylvania, Philadelphia, Oliver Wolcott to Samuel Hodgdon, Instructions for the Intendent of Military Stores, October 2, 1794, vol. 12, 93.

114 Ibid.

115 Smith, *Harpers Ferry*, 36–62; David A. Hounshell, *From the American System to Mass Production, 1800–1932: The Development of Manufacturing Technology in the United States* (Baltimore: Johns Hopkins University Press, 1984), 32–46; *A Description of the United States Armory at Springfield, 1817*, Massachusetts Historical Society Collections, Massachusetts Historical Society,

Boston; Jacob Abbot, "The Armory at Springfield," *Harpers New Monthly Magazine* 5, no. 26 (July 1852):145–147.
116 *Description of the United States Armory,* Massachusetts Historical Society Collections, 1.
117 Ibid.; Abbot, "Armory at Springfield," 145–147; "Guns for the Boys in Blue: Thousands Made at Uncle Sam's Workshop in Springfield," *New York Times,* December 16, 1896. John Albright, *Historical Structure Report, Historical Data and Historical Base Map, Springfield Armory National Historic Site Massachusetts* (Denver: Denver Service Center, Historic Preservation Division, National Park Service, 1978), 1–46.
118 Smith, *Harpers Ferry,* 37–63; *Papers of the War Department,* Henry Knox to John Bryant, 1785, John Davis to Samuel Hodgdon, December 1, 1795, John Bryant to Samuel Hodgdon, January 16, 1795, James McHenry to James Byers, February 23, 1798, John Legg to Samuel Hodgdon, November 6, 1793, Samuel Hodgdon to Joseph Howell, July 3, 1794, Armourers at New London to Samuel Hodgdon, August 8, 1794, Thomas Holt to Samuel Hodgdon, November 13, 1794.
119 Hounshell, *From the American System,* 28–32; Jacob E. Cooke, *Tench Coxe and the Early Republic* (Chapel Hill: University of North Carolina Press, 1978), 413–448.
120 This includes twelve thousand repaired in Philadelphia, seven thousand in Springfield, and five thousand in West Point. "Ledgers of Accounts," *Numbered Record Books.*

CONCLUSION

1 *CBOB,* Memorial of the Work Done by Carpenters at Carlisle, November 26, 1777, 31–33.
2 The powder magazine gets its name from the mistaken impression that it was built by Hessian soldiers captured at the Battle of Trenton. There is no evidence that the prisoners of war constructed that specific building, but they were present in Carlisle at this time and did work at the arsenal. Irish's men built a 20-by-20-foot structure to house them.
3 "Historic Carlisle Barracks," Carlisle Barracks, accessed January 4, 2016, http://carlislebarracks.carlisle.army.mil/history.htm.
4 Numbers compiled by author from RMS; "Ledgers of Accounts," *Numbered Record Books; CBOB;* Wright, *Genesis of the US Armory; PWH;* and *PHK.*
5 Joseph Plumb Martin, *Ordinary Courage: The Revolutionary War Adventures of Joseph Plumb Martin,* 2nd ed., ed. James Kirby Martin (St. James, NY: Brandywine, 1999), 39.
6 *PCC,* Benjamin Lincoln memo re arsenals and academies, March 5, 1783, r45, i38, p285.

Bibliography

PRIMARY SOURCES

Bartlett, John Russell, ed. *Records of the Colony of Rhode Island and Providence Plantations in New England*. Providence: A. Crawford Greene, 1862.

Berkshire Furnace Journal, 1774–1778. Forge and Furnace Collection, Historical Society of Pennsylvania, Philadelphia.

Berkshire Furnace Journal, 1778–1780. Forge and Furnace Collection, Historical Society of Pennsylvania, Philadelphia.

Bryant, John. Captain John Bryant Papers. Bryant-Mason-Smith Family Papers, 1767–1861. Massachusetts Historical Society, Boston.

Carlisle Barracks Collection. Military History Research Collection. Military History Institute, Carlisle, PA.

Continental Congress. *Journals of the Continental Congress*, "A Century of Lawmaking for a New Nation, U.S. Congressional Documents and Debates, 1774–1873." Law Library of Congress. Accessed May 13, 2016. https://memory.loc.gov/ammem/amlaw/lwjc.html.

———. *Papers of the Continental Congress*. Washington, DC: Government Printing Office, 1948. Microfilm.

Cornwall Furnace Journal, 1776–1782. Forge and Furnace Collection, Historical Society of Pennsylvania, Philadelphia.

A Description of the United States Armory at Springfield, 1817. Massachusetts Historical Society Collections, Massachusetts Historical Society, Boston.

Fitzpatrick, John C., ed. *The Writings of George Washington from the Original Manuscript Sources, 1745–1799*. Washington, DC: Government Printing Office, 1931–44.

Hazard, Samuel, ed. *Pennsylvania Archives, Colonial Records*. 16 vols. Philadelphia: Joseph Severns, 1852.

———. *Pennsylvania Archives, First Series*. 12 vols. Philadelphia: Joseph Severns, 1852.

Heath, William. *Papers of William Heath*. Boston: Massachusetts Historical Society Collections, 1905. Microfilm.

Henry, William. William Henry Papers. Historical Society of Pennsylvania, Philadelphia.

House of Representatives. *Journal of the House of Representatives of the United States, 1789–1793*, "A Century of Lawmaking for a New Nation: U.S. Congressional Documents and Debates, 1774–1875." Law Library of Congress. Accessed May 13, 2016, http://lcweb2. loc.gov/ammem/amlaw/lawhome.html.

Irvine-Newbold Family Papers, 1766–1955. 232 vols. Historical Society of Pennsylvania, Philadelphia.

Knox, Henry. *Papers of Henry Knox*. Boston: Massachusetts Historical Society, 1960. Microfilm.

Lincoln, Benjamin. The *Benjamin Lincoln Papers*. Edited by Frederick S. Allis. Ann Arbor, MI: University Microfilms, 1993. Microfilm.

Linn, John B., and William H. Egle, eds. *Pennsylvania Archives, Second Series*. 19 vols. Harrisburg, PA: Benjamin Singerly, 1874.

Lukens, Charles, Benjamin Flower, Tom. Pickering, Nathaniel Irish, Horatio Gates, John Wilson, George Norris, et al. *Carlisle Barracks Orderly Book, 1777–1780*. Pittsburgh: Microfilm Corporation of Pennsylvania, 1980. Microfilm.

Martin, Joseph Plumb. *Ordinary Courage: The Revolutionary War Adventures of Joseph Plumb Martin*. 2nd ed. Edited by James Kirby Martin. St. James, NY: Brandywine, 1999. First printing 1993.

Mason, David. "Journal of David Mason." Bryant-Mason-Smith Family Papers, 1767–1861. Massachusetts Historical Society, Boston.

Miscellaneous Numbered Records in the War Department Collection of Revolutionary War Records, 1775–1790s. Washington, DC: Government Printing Office, 1972. Microfilm.

Muller, John. *A Treatise of Artillery*, 1757. Reprint. Bloomfield, Ontario: Museum Restoration Service, 1977.

———. *A Treatise Containing the Practical Part of Fortification*. London: A. Millar, 1755.

Numbered Record Books Concerning Military Operations and Service, Pay and Settlement of Accounts and Supplies in the War Department Collection of Revolutionary War Records. Washington, DC: Government Printing Office, 1973. Microfilm.

Pennsylvania Gazette, 1728–1800.

Returns of Springfield Arsenal, 1790–1794. Massachusetts Historical Society Collections. Massachusetts Historical Society, Boston.

Rhodehamel, John, ed. *The American Revolution: Writings from the War of Independence*. New York: Library Classics, 2001.

Rush, Benjamin. "Speech to the United Company of Philadelphia for Promoting American Manufactures (1775)." In *The Philosophy of Manufactures: Early Debates over Industrialization in the United States*. Michael Brewster Folsom and Steven D. Lubar, eds. Cambridge: MIT Press, 1982, 3–9.

Syrett, Harold Coffin, ed. *The Papers of Alexander Hamilton: May 1, 1802–October 23, 1804*. New York: Columbia University Press, 1979.

Verlenden Family Collection, 1703–1863. Historical Society of Pennsylvania, Philadelphia.

War Department. *Papers of the War Department: 1784–1800*. Accessed October 21, 2015. http://wardepartmentpapers.org/document.php?id=27850.

Washington, George. *The Papers of George Washington, Revolutionary War Series*. Edited by Philander D. Chase. Charlottesville: University Press of Virginia, 1985–1991.

Wright, Harry Andrew, comp. *The Genesis of the United States Armory at Springfield, Massachusetts: Being Excerpts from Contemporary Documents*. Springfield: US Army Military History Research Collection, 1919.

SECONDARY SOURCES

Ahearn, Bill. *Muskets of the Revolution and the French & Indian Wars*. Lincoln, RI: Andrew Mowbray, 2005.

Albright, John. *Historical Structure Report, Historical Data and Historical Base Map, Springfield Armory National Historic Site Massachusetts*. Denver: Denver Service Center, Historic Preservation Division, National Park Service, 1978.

Alder, Ken. *Engineering the Revolution: Arms and Enlightenment in France, 1763–1815*. Princeton, NJ: Princeton University Press, 1997.

Anderson, Fred. *Crucible of War: The Seven Years' War and the Fate of Empire in British North America, 1754–1766*. New York: Alfred A. Knopf, 2000.

Arnold, Samuel Green. *History of the State of Rhode Island, 1700–1790*. 2 vols. New York: D. Appleton, 1860.

Bagnall, William R. *The Textile Industries of the United States*. New York: Augustus M. Kelley, 1971. Originally published 1893.

Barnes, Ian. *The Historical Atlas of the American Revolution*. New York: Routledge, 2000.

Berg, Maxine. *The Age of Manufactures 1700–1820: Industry, Innovation and Work in Britain*. 2nd ed. London: Routledge, 1994.

Bining, Arthur Cecil. *British Regulation of the Colonial Iron Industry*. Philadelphia: University of Pennsylvania Press, 1933.

———. *The Rise of American Economic Life*. 3rd ed. New York: Charles Scribner's Sons, 1955.

Boyer, Charles S. *Early Forges and Furnaces in New Jersey*. Philadelphia: University of Pennsylvania Press, 1931.

Bridenbaugh, Carl. *The Colonial Craftsman*. New York: Dover Publications, 1990. Originally published 1950.

Buel, Richard, Jr. *In Irons: Britain's Naval Supremacy and the American Revolutionary Economy*. New Haven: Yale University Press, 1998.

Burnett, Edmund Cody. *The Continental Congress: A Definitive History of the Continental Congress from Its Inception in 1774 to March 1789*. New York: W.W. Norton, 1964. First published 1941.

Carp, E. Wayne. *To Starve the Army at Pleasure: Continental Army Administration and American Political Culture, 1775–1783*. Chapel Hill: University of North Carolina Press, 1984.

Colonial Williamsburg Official Guidebook & Map. 6th ed. Williamsburg, VA: Colonial Williamsburg Foundation, 1970.

Cooke, Jacob E. *Tench Coxe and the Early Republic*. Chapel Hill: University of North Carolina Press, 1978.

Doerflinger, Thomas. *A Vigorous Spirit of Enterprise: Merchants and Economic Development in Revolutionary Philadelphia*. Chapel Hill: University of North Carolina Press, 1986.

Eggert, Gerald G. *The Iron Industry in Pennsylvania*. Pennsylvania Historical Studies No. 25. Harrisburg, PA: Huggins Printing, for the Pennsylvania Historical Association, 1994.

Elkins, Stanley, and Eric McKitrick. *The Age of Federalism: The American Republic, 1788–1800*. New York: Oxford University Press, 1993.

Gallagher, John. *The Battle of Brooklyn 1776*. New York: Sarpedon, 1995.

Gluckman, Arcadi, and L. D. Satterlee. *American Gun Makers*. Harrisburg, PA: Stackpole, 1953.

Gooding, S. James. *An Introduction to British Artillery in North America*. Alexandria Bay, NY: Museum Restoration Service, 1988. Originally published 1965.

Gordon, Robert B. *American Iron, 1607–1900*. Baltimore: Johns Hopkins University Press, 1996.

Gross, Robert A. *The Minutemen and Their World*. New York: Hill and Wang, 1976.

Higginbotham, Don. *The War of American Independence: Military Attitudes, Policies, and Practice, 1763–1789*. Boston: Northeastern University Press, 1983.

Hogg, Oliver Frederick Gillilan. *The Royal Arsenal: Its Background, Origin, and Subsequent History*. London: Oxford University Press, 1963.

Holton, Woody. *Forced Founders: Indians, Debtors, Slaves & the Making of the American Revolution in Virginia*. Chapel Hill: University of North Carolina Press, 1999.

Horgan, Lucille E. *Forged in War: The Continental Congress and the Origin of Military Supply and Acquisition Policy*. Westport, CT: Greenwood, 2003.

Hounshell, David A. *From the American System to Mass Production, 1800–1932: The Development of Manufacturing Technology in the United States.* Baltimore: Johns Hopkins University Press, 1984.

Jackson, Melvin H, and Carel de Beer. *Eighteenth Century Gunfounding: The Verbruggens at the Royal Brass Foundary, a Chapter in the History of Technology.* Washington, DC: Smithsonian Institution Press, 1974.

Jensen, Merrill. *The New Nation: A History of the United States during the Confederation, 1781–1789.* New York: Vintage Books, 1950.

Kars, Marjoleine. *Breaking Loose Together: The Regulator Rebellion in Pre-Revolutionary North Carolina.* Chapel Hill: University of North Carolina Press, 2002.

Ketchum, Richard M. *The Winter Soldiers: The Battles for Trenton and Princeton.* New York: Henry Holt, 1973.

Lonergan, Thomas. *Henry Knox: George Washington's Confidant, General of Artillery, and America's First Secretary of War.* Rockport, ME: Picton, 2003.

Manucy, Albert. *Artillery through the Ages: A Short Illustrated History of Cannon, Emphasizing Types Used in America.* Washington, DC: Division of Publications, National Park Service, 1985. Originally published 1949.

Mattern, David B. *Benjamin Lincoln and the American Revolution.* Columbia: University of South Carolina Press, 1995.

McCusker, John J. *Money and Exchange in Europe and America, 1600–1775: A Handbook.* Chapel Hill: University of North Carolina Press, 1978.

McCusker, John J., and Russell R. Menard. *The Economy of British America, 1607–1789, with Supplementary Bibliography.* Chapel Hill: University of North Carolina Press, 1991. Originally published 1985.

Middlebrook, Louis F. *Maritime Connecticut during the American Revolution.* Salem, MA: Essex Institute, 1925.

Middlekauff, Robert. *The Glorious Cause: The American Revolution, 1763–1789.* New York: Oxford University Press, 1982.

Millis, Walter. *Arms and Men: A Study of American Military History.* Paperback. New York: Mentor, 1956.

Morton, Brian N., and Donald C. Spinelli. *Beaumarchais and the American Revolution.* Lanham, MD: Lexington Books, 2003.

Mulholland, James A. *A History of Metals in Colonial America.* Tuscaloosa: University of Alabama Press, 1981.

Nardo, Don. *Weapons of War.* San Diego: Lucent Books, 2003.

Nash, Gary B. *The Urban Crucible: The Northern Seaports and the Origins of the American Revolution.* Abridged ed. Cambridge: Harvard University Press, 1986. Originally published 1979.

Peckham, Howard H. *The Colonial Wars, 1689–1762.* Chicago: University of Chicago Press, 1964.

Peterson, Harold L. *Round Shot and Rammers: An Introduction to Muzzle-loading Land Artillery in the United States.* New York: Bonanza Books, 1969.

Richards, Leonard. *Shays's Rebellion: The American Revolution's Final Battle.* Philadelphia: University of Pennsylvania Press, 2002.

Risch, Erna. *Supplying Washington's Army.* Washington, DC: Center of Military History, 1986.

Rome, Adam Ward. *Connecticut's Cannon: The Salisbury Furnace in the American Revolution.* Hartford, CT: American Revolution Bicentennial Commission of Connecticut, 1977.

Salay, David Lewis. "Arming for War: The Production of War Material [*sic*] in Pennsylvania for the American Armies during the Revolution." PhD diss., University of Delaware, 1977.

Scudder, Townsend. *Concord: American Town.* Boston: Little, Brown, 1947.

Smith, Merritt Roe. *Harpers Ferry Armory and the New Technology: The Challenge of Change.* Ithaca, NY: Cornell University Press, 1977.

Soderlund, Jean R., and Catherine S. Parzynski, eds. *Backcountry Crucibles: The Lehigh Valley from Settlement to Steel.* Bethlehem, PA: Lehigh University Press, 2008.

Stephenson, Michael. *Patriot Battles: How the War of Independence Was Fought.* New York: HarperCollins, 2007.

Swayze, Nathan L. *The Rappahannock Forge.* N.p.: American Society of Arms Collectors, 1976.

Tiedemann, Joseph. *Reluctant Revolutionaries: New York City and the Road to Independence, 1763–1776.* Ithaca, NY: Cornell University Press, 1997.

Tunis, Edwin. *Colonial Craftsmen and the Beginnings of American Industry.* Baltimore: Johns Hopkins University Press, 1965.

Upton, Richard Francis. *Revolutionary New Hampshire.* Hanover, NH: Dartmouth College Publications, 1936.

Walker, Joseph E. *Hopewell Village: The Dynamics of a Nineteenth Century Iron-Making Community.* Philadelphia: University of Pennsylvania Press, 1966.

Ward, Christopher. *The War of the Revolution.* 2 vols. New York: Macmillan, 1952.

West, Jenny. *Gunpowder, Government and War in the Mid-Eighteenth Century.* Suffolk, UK: Boydell Press, 1991.

Wilbur, C. Keith. *The Revolutionary Soldier, 1775–1783.* Old Saybrook, CT: Globe Pequot Press, 1993. First published 1969.

York, Neil Longley. *Mechanical Metamorphosis: Technological Change in Revolutionary America.* Westport, CT: Greenwood, 1985.

ARTICLES

Abbot, Jacob. "The Armory at Springfield," *Harpers New Monthly Magazine* 5, no. 26 (July 1852): 145–161.

Bell, Whitefield, Jr. "Some Aspects of the Social History of Pennsylvania, 1760–1790." *Pennsylvania Magazine of History and Biography* 62 (July 1938): 281–308.

Doerflinger, Thomas. "Hibernia Furnace during the Revolution." *New Jersey History* 90 (Summer 1972): 97–114.

Gilreath, James. "American Book Distribution." *Proceedings of the American Antiquarian Society* 95, pt. 2 (October 1985): 501–583.

"Guns for the Boys in Blue: Thousands Made at Uncle Sam's Workshop in Springfield." *New York Times*, December 16, 1896.

Handwork, Edna. "First in Iron: Berks County's Iron Industry, 1716 to 1815." *Historical Review of Berks County* (Fall 1960): 120–127.

Hart, Charles Henry. "Some Notes Concerning John Norman, Engraver (Died June 8, 1817, Age 69)." Reprinted from *Proceedings of the Massachusetts Historical Society*, October 1904. Cambridge: John Wilson and Son, 1904.

Jameson, Hugh. "Equipment for the Militia of the Middle States, 1775–1781." *Journal of the American Military Institute* 3, no. 1 (Spring 1939): 26–38.

Johnson, Keach. "The Genesis of the Baltimore Ironworks." *Journal of Southern History* 19, no. 2 (May 1953): 157–179.

McCusker, John J. "How Much Is That in Real Money? A Historical Price Index for Use as a Deflator of Money Values in the Economy of the United States." *Proceedings of the American Antiquarian Society* 3, pt. 2 (October 1991): 297–373.

Stapleton, Darwin. "General Daniel Roberdeau and the Lead Mine Expedition." *Pennsylvania History* 38 (October 1971): 361–371.

Trebilcock, Clive. "'Spin-Off' in British Economic History: Armaments and Industry, 1760–1914." *Economic History Review*, new ser., vol. 22, no. 3 (December 1969): 474–490.

Wittlinger, Carlton O. "Industry Comes to the Frontier." *Pennsylvania Magazine* 43 (1930): 153–161.

———. "The Small Arms Industry of Lancaster County, 1710–1840." *Pennsylvania Magazine of History and Biography* 24 (April 1957): 121–136.

Wheeler, Joseph Towne. "Booksellers and Circulating Libraries in Colonial Maryland." *Maryland Historical Magazine* 34, no. 2 (June 1939): 111–206.

ONLINE

"Lewis, Francis (1713–1803)." Biographical Directory of the United States Congress, 1774–Present. Accessed September 4, 2015.

http://bioguide.congress.gov/scripts/biodisplay.pl?index=L000282.

"A Biography of Roger Sherman (1721–1793)." American History: From Revolution to Reconstruction and Beyond. Accessed September 4, 2015. http://www.let.rug.nl/usa/biographies/roger-sherman/.

"Historic Carlisle Barracks," Carlisle Barracks. Accessed January 4, 2016. http://carlislebarracks.carlisle.army.mil/history.htm.

Hughes, Tim. "Newspaper Circulation in the 1700's." *History's Newsstand Blog,* July 27, 2009. Timothy Hughes Rare & Early Newspapers. Accessed September 17, 2015. http://blog.rarenewspapers.com/?p=1782.

"Jonathan Hager House, Circa 1740," HMdb.org. The Historical Marker Database. Accessed May 2, 2016. http://www.hmdb.org/Marker.asp?Marker=1157.

Mapping West Philadelphia. "Landowners in October 1777." Accessed May 13, 2016. http://www.archives.upenn.edu/WestPhila1777/map.php.

Myers, John A. "Daniel Roberdeau." Pennsylvania Center for the Book, fall 2009. Accessed September 10, 2015. http://pabook.libraries.psu.edu/palitmap/bios/Roberdeau_Daniel.html.

Whatley, Mac. "Southern Quakers and Industry." Notes by Mac Whatley for a speech to the Friends Historical Society, Guilford College, November 8, 2001, titled "Friends of Industry: Quakers and the Industrial Revolution in the South." Accessed September 9, 2015. http://sites.google.com/site/macwhat/southernquakersandindustry.

"18WA288 Antietam Furnace c. 1761–1790." Diagnostic Artifacts in Maryland, Jefferson Patterson Park and Museum. Accessed September 4, 2015. http://www.jefpat.org/diagnostic/SmallFinds/Site%20Summaries/18WA288AntietamFurnaceSiteSummary.htm.

Acknowledgments

THROUGHOUT THE PROCESS OF WRITING THIS BOOK, I FOUND MY inspiration, as Ethan Allen said, "in the name of the great Jehovah and the Continental Congress." The former has never let me down and has given me the strength to see this project through to the end. I am forever in His debt. The latter consistently let people down but nevertheless sparked a revolution in America that continues to impact the world. These dynamics of divine guidance and transformation continue to encourage me to study history and have hope for the future.

My sincere thanks go to my colleagues at Northampton Community College in Bethlehem, Pennsylvania, for their help with this book. Mike McGovern was always available with edits and suggestions. He offered his insights on more than one occasion, and I am proud to call him my mentor and friend. Christine Pense is a skilled problem solver and was consistently ready with ideas and optimism. She helped me see light at the end of the tunnel. Patrick Grubbs took time out of his busy schedule to make sure that all my ramblings made sense. I enjoyed our lengthy conversations and hope they continue. Cathie Grozier has kept me on task and is always willing to help. Thanks for never letting anything fall through the cracks.

My thanks extend to my mentors at Lehigh University who started me on this project as a graduate student. John Smith rarely offered answers but was quick to turn my questions into dozens more. He would load me up with queries and send me off to research. John encouraged me to keep digging into the papers of the Continental Congress to see what they would yield. Monica Najar was also unwilling to let me off with easy answers, and I appreciate continuously being challenged to search for the right answer. Steve Cutcliffe always took time to help me reflect on the big questions, which taught me to put things in perspective. The seeds of this project were planted in seminars conducted by Jean Soderlund and Roger Simon. Thank you.

Further gratitude is owed to several historians who have assisted me. Merritt Roe Smith and John McCusker took time to offer their insights and guidance with elements of this project, while Rob Martello was kind enough to extensively edit my work. Michelle McDonald provided valuable feedback as a panel moderator when part of this book was presented at the 2014 annual meeting of the Society of Historians of the Early American Republic. Michelle also served as a mentor through the Landmarks in American History and Culture Workshop sponsored by the National Endowment for the Humanities. She and this program opened up several research opportunities for me in Philadelphia.

I offer my deep appreciation for the assistance I received from several organizations. The staff and resources at the old downtown Philadelphia branch of the National Archives were superb. Everyone was quick with answers, and any material not on-site was ordered. I enjoyed all the time I spent there poring over microfilm. Working with the staff of the Military History Institute was a pleasure, and they were always willing to dig deeper. The libraries of the Massachusetts Historical Society and Historical Society of Pennsylvania were invaluable. Thank you to the editors and staff of Westholme Publishing. I appreciate your willingness to bring this book to fruition, and I hold your creativity and attention to detail in the highest regard.

My final and greatest thanks go to my family, who have walked with me through this whole process. I could not ask for better, or more motivating, parents. Mom, thank you for your commitment to us. Dad, I appreciate all those stories you told, and I wish you were here to read mine. Sam and Henry, I am blessed that you are both here to read this book, and you brighten every day of my life. Robin, none of this was possible without you, and my life is richer because of you. I love you.

Index

Aikman, William, 66
Alder, Ken, 54
Alexander, William, 152
Allen, William, 126
Alsop, John, 58–59
ammunition
    casting process for, 123–124
    Lincoln and, 182
    for muskets, xviii, xx
    production of, 81–83, 84, 85
    sizes of, 83–84
    supplies for, 85–86
ammunition wagon, 103–104
Amphitrite, ix, xvi
Andover Furnace, 126, 155–156
anthracite coal, xiv, 162–163, 164, 165
armory, at Philadelphia Arsenal, 81,
    93–96
armory plan, 18
artillery. *see* cannons/artillery
artillery cartridges, xxi–xxii, xxiv

Backhouse, Richard, 150, 212
Baltimore Furnace, 62
Baldwin, Jacob, 212
Barber, Nathaniel, 125, 129
Batsto Furnace, 136, 145, 150
battle strategy, xxiv–xxv
bayonets, xviii, 1, 133, 134, 154–155
Bedford, Samuel, 202
Bennett, William, 165
Berg, Maxine, 53, 55
Berkshire Furnace, 13, 62, 123, 125–126,
    135, 136, 149
Bird, Mark, 119, 149, 150
blacksmith work, 93, 95
Blanchard, Thomas, 213
Blaney, John, 63–64
Bliss, Luke, 114, 146, 169–170, 180
Board of Ordnance, idea for, 26–27
Board of War
    creation of, 25
    financial difficulties and, 22
    in production hierarchy, x
    replacement of, 48
    responsibilities of, 23
Boehm, Joseph, 82, 83, 88–89, 212
boring/boring mills, 122–123, 128, 193

Bowdoin, James, 195
Boyer, James, 137, 139, 140, 170
Brandywine, Battle of, 38
brass, xx, 37, 44, 49, 56, 76, 91, 193
British Long Land Pattern musket, xviii
British Royal Artillery, 67
Brookfield Arsenal, 27, 30, 33
Brown Bess, xviii
Bryan, Catherine, 87
Bryant, John, 114, 179–180, 187, 190,
    191–193, 195, 202, 213
Bunker Hill, Battle of, 7
Burgoyne, John, 209
Butler, Thomas, 35–36, 104, 130–132
Byers, James, 31, 37, 181, 193–194, 202,
    213

Callender, John, 139
canister, xxi
cannonballs, 104
cannons/artillery
    ammunition for, xx–xxii, xxi–xxii,
        xxiv
    battle strategy and, xxv
    carriages for, 90–91, 92, 103–104
    casting process for, 121–122
    description of, xx–xxi
    diagram of, xxiii
    finishing processes for, 122
    proving process for, 122
    tools for, 91–92
Carlisle Arsenal
    auction at, 187
    Butler fiasco and, 104–105
    choice of location for, 98
    command structure and, xiii, 102–103,
        105–106
    communications with, 106
    construction of, 98–100
    description of, 99, 100–102
    diagram of, 101
    establishment of, 19, 27, 31–32
    Irish's report on, 207
    iron for, 126
    items produced at, 103–104, 105
    Lincoln and, 180
    private iron production and, 127–128
    production process at, 102

recruitment for, 100
repairs sent to, 132
streamlining of DCGMS and, 44, 47
transportation and, 170–171
Carlisle Forge, 171
Carlisle Furnace, 126, 127
Carpenter's Hall, 78, 79–80
Carron Works, 182
cartridge boxes, xviii, 1
cartridges. *see* ammunition
cash advances, 147–149, 150–151, 153, 204–205
cast iron, 155–156
Chapman, Nathan, 74, 89, 113
charcoal, 162–164
Cheever, Ezekiel, 24, 33–35, 42–43, 106–107, 108, 109, 110–112, 125, 146
Clark, William, 202
Clifton, Nathan, 147–148
coal, 164–165. *see also* anthracite coal
Colebrookdale Furnace, 45, 157
Coleman, Robert, 149, 150
colonies
    arming own troops, 4–5, 6–8
    lack of weapons in, 10
    manufacturing programs in, 13–15
Commissary General of Military Stores,
    Department of (DCGMS)
    accomplishments of, 46
    after war, 174–176
    assessment of, 49–50, 208–214
    attempts to centralize, 37–38, 39
    at Carpenter's Hall, 80
    development of, 22–27
    divisions of, x, xi
    financial difficulties of, 21–22
    Flower and, 28, 30–33
    functioning of, 41
    initiation of program under, xi
    inspection system and, 118
    insufficient funding of, 43–45
    Knox and, 33–35
    Lincoln's reforms for, 179, 180–182
    modifications to, 35–37
    priorities of, xv–xvi
    in production hierarchy, x
    redesign of, 49
    reliance on craftsmen and, 145–147
    responsibilities of, xiii–xiv
    streamlining of, 44, 46–47
commissary general position, creation of, 27
confiscation efforts, 3, 6–7, 11
Connecticut Council of Safety, 13
Constitution (1787), 198
constitutional government, establishment of, 198
Continental Air Furnace, 80

Continental Congress, first meeting of, 79
contract specifications, 119–121
Conway, Thomas, 39
Conway Cabal, 39
Coren, Isaac, 31–32, 100
Cornell, Ezekiel, 111
Cornwall Furnace, 119, 121, 127, 128, 136, 151
Cornwallis, Charles, 46
Coudray, Philippe Charles Tronson du, 59, 64–65
Couloux, J., 161
Cowell, Ebenezer, 212
Cribs, Sarah, 87

Davis, John, 167–168
Dawes, Thomas, 108
DeHaven, Peter, 15
design schematics, 120–121
Doerflinger, Thomas, 144, 145
Doughty, John, 189–190
Downing, Samuel, 158, 159
Duportail, Louis Lebègue dePresle, 59, 64–65
Durham Furnace, 135, 136, 150
Durham Iron Works, 45

Eastern Department, 23
Eayers, James, 113
Eckfeldt, Jacob, 154–155
Elderkin, Jedediah, 13
Elizabeth Furnace, 126, 127, 136, 149, 170

facing, 122–123
Faesch, John Jacob, 76, 137–141, 151–153, 182, 187, 212
field artillery carriages, xxiv
Fifth Street Laboratory, 73–74, 80, 81–89
financial difficulties, 43–45
flintlock muskets
    battle strategy and, xxiv–xxv
    description of, xvii–xx
    loading, xviii
    types of, xviii
    see also musket inspection process
Flower, Benjamin
    administrative structure and, 75
    Andover Furnace and, 126, 155
    appointment of, 28
    background of, 28
    Butler and, 35–36, 131–132
    capture of Philadelphia and, 39
    in Carlisle, 31–32, 99, 100
    coal and, 164
    commissaries under, 124–125
    contributions of, 212
    field commissary and, 36–37

Fifth Street Laboratory and, 82
illness of, 21–22, 41
on importance of domestic manufacturing, xvii
inspection system and, 118, 125
ironmongers and, 149–150
Muller and, 72
papers from, xv
Pearson and, 42
piece-rate system and, 87
Potts and, 157–158
priorities of, 30–31
private manufacturers and, 130
responsibilities of, 22–23, 39–40
running of department by, 32
Springfield Arsenal and, 43, 109, 110,
113
structure of department and, 38
transportation and, 168, 169
forges, traveling, 93, 103, 104
Fort Crown Point, 5
Fort Lee, 2, 16
Fort Pitt, 37, 194–195
Fort Schuyler, 194–195
Fort Ticonderoga, 5
Fort Washington, 2, 16
fortification cartridges, xxii, xxiv
fortress cannons, xxiv
France, weapons from, ix–x
Franklin, Benjamin, 59
French, Samuel, 125, 169
French Charleville musket, xviii
Friend, Catherine, 87
frontier activities, 194–195

Garanger, Lewis, 65, 211
Gardiner, William, 202, 204
Gates, Horatio, 21, 39, 113–114, 169,
209
Germantown, Battle of, 38
Gerry, Elbridge, 58
Glover, John, 6
Gostelowe, Jonathan, 30, 32, 47, 72, 115,
125, 128–129, 132–134, 139, 152
Gouil, Martin, 148
grapeshot, xxi
Greene, Nathanael, 46, 83
Gribeauval, Jean-Baptiste, 55, 65, 70–71,
204, 213
Gridley, Richard, 24–25
Grubb, Curtis and Peter, 151
Guilford Courthouse, Battle of, 46
gun carriages, 90–91, 92, 103–104
gunlocks, 93, 95
gunsmiths, Hodgdon and, 161–162

Hall, James, 138–139, 141
Hall, John, 131, 132, 133, 134, 213

Hamilton, Alexander, 76
Hancock, John, 27
Harmar, Josiah, 194–195
Harpers Ferry, 174, 201, 202, 204, 213
Heath, William, x, 34, 107, 108, 109,
111
Heighberger, George, 148, 155
Henry, William, 36, 44, 76, 132–133
Hessian Powder Magazine, 207–208
Hibernia Furnace, 137, 139, 151, 153
Hodgdon, Samuel
advancement of, 42
after war, 182, 184, 212–213
appointment of, 32
armory productivity and, 96
coal and, 166
command of, 115
communications with quartermasters
and, 168
Congress and, 183
contracts and, 139–140, 161, 204–205
Faesch and, 76, 151–153
field commissary and, 37
Fifth Street Laboratory and, 83, 84,
86, 88
financial difficulties and, 21, 44–46
frontier activities and, 194–195
gunsmiths and, 161–162
on imported weapons, 176
inspection system and, 119, 134
inventory of stores by, 184–185
Johnson and, 171
Joy and, 136–137
Knox and, 139
monetary resources and, 153–154,
185–187
organization and, 95
patterns and, 120
Perkins and, 173–174
Potts and, 157–159, 160
raw materials and, 154–155, 156–157
repair contract and, 188–189
responsibilities of, 22–23, 39
selling of stores and, 186–187
spending cuts and, 133, 160
Springfield Armory and, 202
Springfield Arsenal and, 114, 191–192
streamlining of DCGMS and, 44,
46–47, 48
transportation and, 168–170
Hoffman, Valentine, 89–90, 91, 115
Hogg, O. F. G., 83, 129
Holmes, Samuel, 154
Hopewell Furnace, 119, 120, 121, 149
Hopkins, Esek, 6
Hopkins, Stephen, 59
Horgan, Lucille, xvi–xvii
howitzers, xx–xxi, 125

Hughes, Samuel and Daniel, 117–118, 170
Hughes Iron Works, 126, 128, 134–135
Humphreys, Whitehead, 126
Hunter, James, 64

Industrial Revolution
  adoption of ideas from, xiv–xv
  centralized manufacturing and, 53–58, 61–63
  French and, 64–66
  implementation of ideas from, 74–76, 211
  Mason and, 51–52
  print information on, 66–73
  as source for ideas, 57–59
  traditional understanding of, 52–53
  United Company and, 59–61
inflation, 145
inspection system, for private manufacturers, 118–119
inspectors, 75–76
Irish, Nathaniel, 31–32, 41, 74, 98–99, 102–103, 115–116, 187, 207
iron plantations, 62–63
ironmongers, cash advances for, 148–149, 150–151, 153. *see also* Faesch, John Jacob
Isenhoot, Andrew, 155

Johnson, James, 135, 151, 171
Johnston Forge, 171
Jordan, John, 74, 89–90, 91, 102, 115
Joy, Daniel, 64, 89–90, 117–123, 134–137, 139, 151, 164, 212

Keats, William, 148
Knight's Wharf Laboratory, 80, 104
Knox, Henry
  armory plan from, 18, 19–20
  calls for change from, 195–200
  command of, 25
  Congress and, 28, 30, 37–38
  contracts and, 137–139
  contributions of, 212
  design schematics and, 120–121, 125
  development of military stores department and, 22–23, 24–27
  first assignment for, 24–25
  frontier activities and, 194
  Lincoln and, 180
  Muller and, 71–72
  on powder, 192
  responsibilities of, 40
  as secretary of war, 184
  Springfield Arsenal and, 33–35, 106, 107, 109, 110, 193
  supervision by, 118–119
  West Point and, 189–190

ladle, 91
Lamb, John, 43, 114
Lawrence, Thomas, 212
lead shortage, 142–143
leather manufacturing, 63–64
LeTort Creek, 99
Lewis, Francis, 58
Lexington, Battle of, 3
Lincoln, Benjamin, 48–49, 76, 140–141, 175–179, 180–184, 211–212, 213–214
Linnard, Wm., 101
linstock, 91
Lisle, Henry, 80
Long Island, Battle of, 1, 18
Lukens, Charles, 31, 35–36, 44, 100, 104–105, 124–125, 126–128, 132, 143, 146, 164–165, 170–171

machine lathe, 213
magazines, building of, 177–178, 179–180, 189–190, 207–208
manufacturing during revolution
  adopting industrial revolution, 51–77
  breadth of, xiv
  call for national weapons program, 1–20
  in Carlisle and Springfield, 98–116
  department of commissary general, 21–50
  inspection and instruction for private manufacturers, 117–141
  military stores activities after revolution, 173–206
  overview of, ix–xxv
  in Philadelphia, 79–97
  previous writings on, xvi–xvii
  resources for private manufacturers, 142–172
Marshall, Christopher, 59–60
Martin, Joseph Plumb, 209
Marx, Karl, 52–53
Maryann Furnace, 126, 127, 171
Mason, David, 33–35, 42–43, 51–52, 72–73, 106–111, 212
Massachusetts Council of Safety, 108
Massachusetts Spy, 66
Mayberry, Thomas, 126, 155–156
Mechanical Metamorphosis (York), xvi
mechanization, 53
Middle Department, 23
Middle Forge, 153
Miles, Samuel, 168, 170
military store management system
  1784–1794, 184–201
  1794–1811, 201–205
  budget for, 185–186
  structure of, 34, 40, 47, 48
Monmouth Courthouse, 209

Morgan, James, 126
Morris, Robert, 8, 45, 176, 182–184
Mount Etna Furnace, 123
Mount Hope Furnace, 151, 153
Mulberry, 64
Muller, John, 24, 52, 57, 67–73, 99, 208,
  211
musket inspection process, 130–140
muskets. *see* flintlock muskets
Myrletus, Adam, 154

national weapons program, call for
  context for, 1–13, 16–20
  state efforts preceding, 13–16
New York City, battles of, xiii, 3, 209
New York Committee of Safety, 10
newspapers, 66–67
Nicholson, John, 94–95, 101
Noel, Garret, 71
Norman, John, 71, 72
Northern Department, 23

Oley Furnace, 135, 136, 149
ordnance inspection process, 140–141
ordnance yard (Philadelphia), 81, 89–90

patterns, provided by government,
  119–120
Patton, John, 125, 149–150
Pearson, James, 41–42, 134, 165
Penet, Pierre, 65–66, 161, 211
Penet and Couloux, 133, 161
Pennsylvania Council of Safety, 6, 8, 13
Pennsylvania Gazette, 59, 67
Perkins, Joseph, 64, 94–95, 129, 133,
  139, 161–162, 170, 173–174, 188, 202,
  204, 212–213
Perkins, William, 148
Pettit, Charles, 150–151
Philadelphia
  British taking of, 39, 132
  retreat from, 27
Philadelphia Arsenal
  after war, 188–189
  armory at, 81, 93–96
  command structure and, xiii
  creation of, 27
  description of, 80–81
  organization and, 95–96
  parts of, 31
  repair work at, 133
  streamlining of DCGMS and, 44
Pickering, Timothy, 167
piece-rate system, 87
Pine Grove Furnace, 126, 127
Pompton Furnace, 139, 140, 141
Potts, Stacy, 159–160
Potts, Thomas, 157–159, 160, 170, 212

Principio Furnace, 62, 135
private manufacturers
  assistance for, xiv, 117–119, 144
  contract specifications for, 119–121
  contracts with, 145–147
  inspection system and, 125–141, 211
  promotion of in peacetime, 178
  see also individual manufacturers
procurement system, postwar, 200–201
production system, hierarchy of, x
property damage, 145
protofactories, 58, 73
putting-out, 53–54, 58, 61

Quartermaster Department, 166–167,
  169, 170, 171
Quasi War, 204
Querrill, Susanna, 87

rammer, 91
ramrods, xviii
raw materials
  difficulty procuring, xiii, 144–145
  purchases of, 154–155
Risch, Erna, 166
Rittenhouse, Benjamin, 15
Roberdeau, Daniel, 142–143
Rose, William, 154
Ross, George, 156, 170
Rush, Benjamin, 59, 60
Rutter and Potts, 135, 157–159

Salay, David, xvi, xvii
Salisbury Furnace, 13–14, 140–141, 192
Saratoga, Battle of, xi, 14, 39, 44, 209
Sargent, Samuel, 31–32, 100, 102, 116,
  164, 170, 180–181
Savannah, 209
Schuyler, Philip, 6, 7, 14, 37
Secret Committee, 9, 11
secretary of war, creation of position of,
  48. *see also* Knox, Henry; Lincoln,
  Benjamin
Shaw, Archibald, 168–169
Shay's Rebellion, 193, 195–196
Sherman, Roger, 58
siege guns, xxii
Smith, Adam, 52–53
Smith, Richard, 13
Southern Department, 23
Southwark Air Furnace, 145
Southwark China Works, 63
sponge, 91
Springfield Armory, 201–202, 203, 213
Springfield Arsenal
  after war, 188, 190–193
  auction at, 187
  Byers at, 181

command structure and, xiii, 106, 109–112
communications problems at, 106
Congress's response to, 113
construction of buildings for, 107–108
creation of, 33–35
embezzlement at, 112
establishment of, 19
investigation of, 43
Lamb's assessment of, 114
limitations of, 106
magazine construction at, 179–180
nepotism at, 112
oversight of, 42–43
production levels at, 115
reorganization of, 114
repairs sent to, x–xi
Shay's Rebellion and, 195–196
streamlining of DCGMS and, 47
Woolwich as model for, 69
Stafford Furnace, 140
steel, 154, 156–160
Stevens, William, 140
Stiegel, Henry, 61
stone coal, 164, 165
stores inspection process, 125–130
Stroop, Henry, 148
Sullivan, John, 164, 209
superintendent of arms, 130–131, 134
superintendent of artillery, 40
superintendent of ordnance, 130, 134
Sweers, Cornelius, 32, 41, 102–103, 165

Taylor, George, 58
Thomas, Isaiah, 66
Thompson, John, 156–157, 165, 188–189
Thompson, Mark, 168, 170
Towers, Robert, 6–7
transportation, 144–145, 166–171
Treatise Containing the Practical Part of Fortification, A (Muller), 67–69, 71–72, 99
Treatise of Artillery (Muller), 52, 67–68, 70, 71–72
Trumbull, Jonathan, 14
Turner, Joseph, 126

Udree, Daniel, 149, 150
United Company, 59–61, 211

Valley Forge, repaired weapons for, xi
Vauban, Sebastian de, 68

Warwick Furnaces, 13
Washington, George
    call for national weapons program and, 1–4, 7–8, 17–18, 19–20
    Cheever and, 109–110

Congress and, 38–39
development of military stores department and, 22–23, 24–25, 49–50
field commissary and, 36–37
Flower and, 28
inspection system and, 130
Knox and, 30, 37–38
Muller and, 72
New York campaign preparations and, 16–17
as president, 198–200, 212
regional departments and, 23–24
repaired weapons for, xi
seizure of British weapons by, 6
Springfield Arsenal and, 109, 113
Trumbull and, 14
weapons orders from, 21
Washingtonburg Public Works. *see* Carlisle Arsenal
Watkins, Joseph, 30, 32
Watt, James, 182
Wayne, Anthony, 7
weapons
    craft production of, xii–xiii, 3, 9–10, 11–13
    early procurement activities for, 3–7, 19
    from France, ix–x
    importation of, 3, 8–9, 129
    insufficiency of, 10, 210
    lack of consistency among, 17
    overview of, xvii–xxiv
    purchasing from Europe, xii
    repaired, xi
    seized from British, 174
    seizure of British, 5–6
    supporting equipment for, xiv
    see also cannons/artillery; flintlock muskets
Wedgwood, Josiah, 54
West Point, 179, 180, 188, 189–190
Western Department, 23
Whiting, William, 141, 192
Whitney, Eli, 204
Willing and Morris, 9
Wilson, Thomas, 99
Wistar, Caspar, 61
Woolwich Arsenal Artillery Academy, 52, 56–57, 67–70, 74, 76, 81, 107–108, 123, 211
worm, 91
Wylie, Thomas, 74, 100, 102–103, 156
Wyoming Valley Massacre, 164

York, Neil, xvi
Yorktown, 46, 47, 84, 127, 210